MW01227144

A THREAT TO PUBLIC PIETY

A THREAT TO PUBLIC PIETY

Christians, Platonists, and the Great Persecution

Elizabeth DePalma Digeser

CORNELL UNIVERSITY PRESS
Ithaca and London

First published 2012 by Cornell University Press

Printed in the United States of America

Library of Congress Cataloging-in-Publication Data

Digeser, Elizabeth DePalma, 1959–
   A threat to public piety : Christians, Platonists, and the great persecution / Elizabeth DePalma Digeser.
      p. cm.
   Includes bibliographical references and index.
   ISBN 978-0-8014-4181-3 (cloth : alk. paper)
   1. Persecution—History—Early church, ca. 30–600.
   2. Church history—Primitive and early church, ca. 30–600.
   3. Christianity—Philosophy—History.   4. Platonists.
   5. Violence—Philosophy.   6. Philosophy and religion.
   7. Violence—Religious aspects.   I. Title.
   BR1604.23.D54   2012
   272'.1—dc23   2011037723

Cornell University Press strives to use environmentally responsible suppliers and materials to the fullest extent possible in the publishing of its books. Such materials include vegetable-based, low-VOC inks and acid-free papers that are recycled, totally chlorine-free, or partly composed of nonwood fibers. For further information, visit our website at www.cornellpress.cornell.edu.

Cloth printing   10 9 8 7 6 5 4 3 2 1

For Paige

❧ Contents

 PREFACE

What is the relationship between philosophical or religious thought and violence? In attempting to understand religious violence, sociologists and other social scientists often assume that material conditions and economic interests are the real motivations for violence directed against particular religious groups. If ideas make a difference at all, we see them as rationalizations, justifications, or explanations for violence, not as motive forces in themselves.[1] This book turns the conventional wisdom on its head, for it argues that ideas about correct ritual and metaphysical doctrine inspired people to bring about Rome's last and longest effort forcibly to repress Christianity. And it involves philosophers and theologians as the primary source of these ideas, even though they themselves never called for forcible repression of their doctrinal opponents—as far as the surviving evidence indicates.

This project arose out of my earlier exploration of the involvement of the ancient Christian scholar and theologian Lactantius in defending Christianity against the criticisms that had undergirded Diocletian's "Great Persecution." In *The Making of a Christian Empire: Lactantius and Rome,* I was primarily interested in excavating the evidence for an exchange of ideas between the African theologian and defender of religious toleration and the first Christian emperor, Constantine, who drew upon those ideas in fashioning his religious policy after the persecution ended. In the process of telling that story, however, I began increasingly to wonder who were the people—beyond the imperial court—advancing the arguments to which Lactantius responded in a number of sophisticated works across the last years of his life. The search to discover those voices and make clear their motivations has occupied me across the past decade and more.

---

1. See, for example, Bernard Lewis, *The Crisis of Islam: Holy War and Unholy Terror* (New York: Random House, 2004); Mark Juergensmeyer, *Terror and the Mind of God: The Global Rise of Religious Violence* (Berkeley: University of California Press, 2003); and John McGarry and Brendan O'Leary, *A Time for Peace: Explaining Northern Ireland* (Oxford: Blackwell, 1995).

Looking back toward the inception of this project, I see clearly how indebted I am to others, both for the time and resources to pursue this inquiry and for the guidance and counsel that helped to shape the final project. In this regard, I thank the American Council of Learned Societies, whose Junior Fellowship (1999–2000) allowed me a full year to unravel and translate the tangle of fragments that is the legacy of the Neoplatonist philosopher Porphyry. The Interdisciplinary Humanities Center at the University of California, Santa Barbara, has, throughout my academic career, been an invaluable resource, and their naming me their Resident Fellow for that same year helped me draw deeply on the resources and community of scholars in Santa Barbara. During my next four years at McGill University, I benefited greatly from university research grants and travel grants, which culminated in the award of a Social Sciences and Humanities Research Council of Canada Standard Research Grant in 2003. This funding was the single most important grant I received. Not only did it allow me the funds to gather all the resources I needed; it also facilitated a wide variety of opportunitites for me to present my work for constructive critique. Finally, the award of a UCSB Faculty Senate Annual Research grant in 2005, soon after I returned to Santa Barbara, provided the funds that allowed me to finish my research. Perhaps even more important than funds, however, the support and encouragement of colleagues—from McGill and UCSB to the UC Late Antiquity group— helped me see this project through to the end.

I am indebted to an entire chorus of colleagues, students, and friends for research assistance, critique, and encouragement. Whatever errors remain in this book are my own, but many of the finer points emerged through conversations with Gillian Clark, Paige Digeser, Hal Drake, Olivier Dufault, Susanna Elm, Eric Fournier, Aaron Johnson, Dayna Kalleres, Ariane Magny, Heidi Marx-Wolf, Mike Proulx, Claudia Rapp, Michele Salzman, Lindsey Scholl, and Jeremy Schott. This project also benefited from the indefatigable assistance of Janet Fuchs Jackson, Andy Kauth, Nadine Korte, Ada Kuskowska, and Alison Turtledove. I owe a special debt of gratitude to my late friend and colleague Tom Sizgorich, whose driving and insistent pursuit of truth and excellence will always be an inspiration.

Finally, I am grateful to the many editors and conference organizers (especially Shifting Frontiers and the North American Patristics Association) who helped me hone and polish some of the arguments in the book. The inspiration for chapter 2, "Origen as a Student of Ammonius," appears in "Origen on the *Limes*: Rhetoric and the Polarization of Identity in the Late Third Century," in *The Rhetoric of Power in Late Antiquity: Religion and Politics in Byzantium, Europe, and the Early Islamic World* (London: I. B. Tauris, 2010), which

I edited with R. M. Frakes and Justin Stephens. Parts of chapter 3, "Plotinus, Porphyry, and Philosophy in the Public Realm," appeared as "Religion, Law, and the Roman Polity: The Era of the Great Persecution," in *Law and Religion in Classical and Christian Rome,* ed. Clifford Ando and Jörg Rüpke (Stuttgart: Franz Steiner Verlag, 2006), 68–84; in "Hellenes, Barbarians, and Christians: Religion and Identity Politics in Diocletian's Rome," in *Romans, Barbarians, and the Transformation of the Roman World,* ed. R. Mathisen and D. Shanzer, Shifting Frontiers in Late Antiquity 6 (Surrey: Ashgate, 2011), 121–31; and as "Christian or Hellene? The Great Persecution and the Problem of Christian Identity," in *Religious Identity in Late Antiquity* (Toronto: Edgar Kent, 2006), 36–57, which I edited with R. M. Frakes. An early version of chapter 4, "Schism in the Ammonian Community: Porphyry v. Iamblichus," was published as "The Power of Religious Rituals: A Philosophical Quarrel on the Eve of the Great Persecution," in *The Power of Religion in Late Antiquity,* ed. A. Cain and N. Lenski, Shifting Frontiers in Late Antiquity 7 (Aldershot, UK: Ashgate, 2009), 81–92. Chapter 5, "Schism in the Ammonian Community: Porphyry v. Methodius of Olympus," had its inspiration in "Methodius and Porphyry," *Studia Patristica* 46 (2010): 21–26. And, finally, a short, early version of the conclusion, "The Ammonian Community and the Great Persecution," appeared as "Lactantius, Eusebius, and Arnobius: Evidence for the Causes of the Great Persecution," *Studia Patristica* 39 (2006): 33–46. Finally, I am deeply grateful for the support, input, and guidance of the people at Cornell University Press, Bernie Kendler, Peter Potter, and Marian Rogers.

Abbreviations

In general, abbreviations of the names of periodicals and classical authors and their works follow *L'Année Philologique;* Blaise and Chirat, *Dictionnaire Latin-Français des Auteurs Chrétiens;* Hornblower and Spawforth, *The Oxford Classical Dictionary;* Lampe, *The Patristic Greek Lexicon;* or Liddell and Scott, *A Greek-English Lexicon.* Abbreviations for authors, works, series, and references that occur frequently in the text and notes are listed below.

ACO	*Acta Conciliorum Oecumenicorum* (Berlin, 1927–84)
ACW	*Ancient Christian Writers*
ANF	A. Roberts and J. Donaldson, eds., *The Ante-Nicene Fathers* (Grand Rapids, MI, 1965–70)
ANRW	H. Temporini and W. Haase, eds., *Aufstieg und Niedergang der römischen Welt: Geschichte und Kultur Roms im Spiegel der neueren Forschung* (Berlin/New York, 1972–)
Arn.	Arnobius, *Disputationes adversus nationes*
Aug. *Civ.*	Augustine, *De civitate Dei*
Aug. *Iul.*	Augustine, *Contra Iulianum*
Aug. *Serm.*	Augustine, *Sermones*
CAG	*Commentaria in Aristotelem Graeca*
CSEL	*Corpus Scriptorum Ecclesiasticorum Latinorum*
Eun. *VS*	Eunapius, *Vita sophistarum*
Eus. *Chron.*	Eusebius of Caesarea, *Chronicon*
Eus. *DE*	Eusebius of Caesarea, *Demonstratio evangelica*
Eus. *HE*	Eusebius of Caesarea, *Historia ecclesiastica*
Eus. *PE*	Eusebius of Caesarea, *Preparatio evangelica*
Eus. *VC*	Eusebius of Caesarea, *Vita Constantini*
FrGrTh	H. Erbse, ed., *Fragmente der griechischen Theosophien* (Hamburg, 1941)
GCS	*Die griechischen-christlichen Schriftsteller*

Hieron. *Adv. Pelag.*	Jerome, *Adversus Pelagianos dialogi*
Hieron. *Chron.*	Jerome, *Chronicon Eusebii a Graeco Latine redditum et continuatum*
Hieron. *C. Ruf.*	Jerome, *Adversus Rufinum*
Hieron. *Dan.*	Jerome, *Explanatio in Danielem*
Hieron. *Ep.*	Jerome, *Epistulae*
Hieron. *Ioel.*	Jerome, *Commentariorum in Ioelem liber*
Hieron. *Matt.*	Jerome, *Commentariorum in Matthaeum libri iv*
Hieron. *Quaest. in Gen.*	Jerome, *Quaestionum Hebraicarum liber in Genesim*
Hieron. *Vir. ill.*	Jerome, *De viris illustribus*
Iambl. *DM*	Iamblichus, *De mysteriis*
Iambl. *VPyth.*	Iamblichus, *De vita pythagorica*
Lact. *Inst.*	Lactantius, *Divinarum institutionum libri vii*
Lact. *Mort.*	Lactantius, *De mortibus persecutorum*
LThK	W. Kasper, ed., *Lexikon für Theologie und Kirche* (Freiburg, 1993)
Meth. *Cib.*	Methodius of Olympus, *De cibis*
Meth. *Res.*	Methodius of Olympus, *De resurrectione mortuorum*
Meth. *Symp.*	Methodius of Olympus, *Symposium*
Mos. et rom. leg. coll.	*Mosaicarum et Romanarum legum collatio*
NPNF	Philip Schaff and Henry Wace, eds., *A Select Library of Nicene and Post-Nicene Fathers of the Christian Church* (Grand Rapids, MI 1974–78)
NRSV	New Revised Standard Version of the Bible
Or. *Cant.*	Origen, *Commentarius in Canticum canticorum*
Or. *Cels.*	Origen, *Contra Celsum*
Or. *Comm. in Rom.*	Origen, *Commentarii in Epistulum ad Romanos*
Or. *Ep.*	Origen, *Epistulae*
Or. *Fr. in Lam.*	Origen, *Fragmenta in Lamentationes*
Or. *Jo.*	Origen, *Commentarii in Joannem*
Or. *PA*	Origen, *Peri archōn (De principiis)*
Or. *Philoc.*	Origen, *Philocalia*
Or. *Ps.*	Origen, *Fragmenta in Psalmos*
PG	J.-P. Migne, ed., *Patrologia graeca* (Turnhout, 1857–66)
Phot. *Bibl.*	Photius, *Bibliotheca*
Phot. *Interrog. decem*	Photius, *Interrogationes decem* (PG 104)
PL	J.-P. Migne, ed., *Patrologia latina* (Turnhout, 1857–66)
Plot. *Enn.*	Plotinus, *Enneades*
Porph. *Abst.*	Porphyry, *De abstinentia*
Porph. *Agal.*	Porphyry, *Peri agalmatōn*

Porph. *Antr.*	Porphyry, *De antro nympharum*
Porph. *Chr.*	Porphyry, *Adversus Christianos*
Porph. *Comm. Tim.*	Porphyry, *Eis ton Timaion hupomnēmata*
Porph. *Marc.*	Porphyry, *Ad Marcellam*
Porph. *Phil. or.*	Porphyry, *Peri tēs ek logiōn philosophias*
Porph. *Plot.*	Porphyry, *Vita Plotini*
Porph. *Regr.*	Porphyry, *De regressu animae*
Porph. *Sent.*	Porphyry, *Sententiae ad intelligibilia ducentes*
Porph. *VP*	Porphyry, *Vita Pythagorae*
SC	*Sources Chrétiennes*
SHA	Scriptores Historiae Augustae

A THREAT TO PUBLIC PIETY

Introduction
From Permeable Circles to Hardened Boundaries

In 299 CE a priest, striving to read the auspices before the emperor Diocletian's Antioch court, claimed that the animal's entrails bore no signs of any kind. For centuries, Roman leadership, to discern a venture's promise, depended on haruspicy, the Etruscan art of divining from marks on sacrificial organs. Desperate for a diagnosis, Diocletian (284–305) and Galerius, his junior eastern colleague, consulted a local oracle of Apollo.[1] The god's spokesman blamed the failed ritual on Christian courtiers who had crossed themselves during the proceedings, an act that, all acknowledged, warded off the beings who inscribed portents on the animal's liver. In response, Diocletian commanded flogging for courtiers confessing Christianity and dismissed Christians from the eastern army.

Neither Diocletian nor his two western colleagues, Maximian and Constantius, sought further to disturb the peace. But Galerius, convinced that Christian practice jeopardized the efficacy of Roman ritual, lobbied for repression. Before 302, Diocletian had outlawed Manichaeans, people claiming to be true Christians and whose origins in Persia, Rome's archenemy, made easy targets.[2]

---

1. Elizabeth DePalma Digeser, "An Oracle of Apollo at Daphne and the Great Persecution," *CPh* 99 (2004): 57–77.

2. *Mos. et rom. leg. coll.* 15.3. For 302 as the date, see Timothy D. Barnes, *The New Empire of Diocletian and Constantine* (Cambridge, MA: Harvard University Press, 1982), 55 n. 41; and S. Corcoran,

The following winter in Nicomedia, two court-sponsored speakers critiqued Christian texts, teachings, and traditions, while Diocletian, pressured by Galerius, solicited advice from military officers and administrators. Finally, the senior emperor requested counsel from Apollo's oracle at Didyma. When this voice joined the chorus for coercion, Diocletian unleashed the so-called Great Persecution: in February 303, the empire began its last and longest campaign compelling Christians to uphold traditional religious norms (Lact. *Mort.* 10–12).

The episode in Antioch sparking this series of events seemingly conforms to a stereotype of Romans as persecutors and Christians as victims before the emperor Constantine converted to Christianity in 312. Yet the indirect cause of the persecution, the presence of Christian courtiers in Diocletian's entourage, challenges the familiar image. In fact, during the third century, crosscurrents had rippled throughout the Mediterranean world. Local conflicts between Christians and imperial authorities did mar civil peace in the first decade,[3] building to transprovincial persecution by midcentury. But Christians were also intermingling with fellow Romans along the stoas of philosophical schools and, by the century's ebb, even in the basilicas of civil government. For example, before imperial troops in 272 razed the Brucheion quarter, home to Alexandria's famous library and philosophical salons, Christians and Hellenes had learned from one another there for over half a century.[4] There the heterodox philosopher Ammonius Saccas was the fountainhead for countless Hellene and Christian students, including Origen, the great Christian

---

The Empire of the Tetrarchs: Imperial Pronouncements and Government, AD 284–324 (Oxford: Clarendon Press, 1996), 135–36. Others favor an earlier date; e.g., François Decret, "Le manichéisme en Afrique du Nord et ses rapports avec la secte en Orient," *Aram* 16 (2004): 279–83.

3. Early in the third century, Septimius Severus apparently forbade conversion to Judaism and Christianity, an edict enforced in Syria, Africa, and Alexandria (SHA *Sev.* 17.1; Eus. *HE* 6.1.1, 6.2.2; *Pass. Perp.* 7). Resistance to the edict, recounted by Eusebius and the *Passion of Perpetua,* brought capital punishment; hence the label "persecution" (διωγμόν) in Christian sources.

4. Although Gregory Nazianzen (*Or.* 4.5) accused the emperor Julian (361–63) of changing the definition of "Hellene" from designating a language to identifying a religion, members of Platonist philosophical schools used the term to distinguish themselves from Christians and Jews starting in the late third century. See not only the early fourth-century ps.-Julian *Ep.* 76 449b Wright (181 Bidez/Cumont) but also Plot. *Enn.* 2.9.6.7 and Iambl. *DM* 7.5.259; on the date, see T. D. Barnes, "A Correspondent of Iamblichus," *Greek, Roman and Byzantine Studies* 19 (1978): 99–106. Thus the term "Hellene" is better than "pagan," a description deployed only by Christians and which no late Roman philosopher would accept, given its associations with ignorance and rusticity. For reflections on the religious use of the term "Hellene" in the late third and early fourth centuries, see Polymnia Athanassiadi, "The Oecumenism of Iamblichus: Latent Knowledge and Its Awakening," *Journal of Roman Studies* 85 (1995): 249 (as the term applied to Iamblichus); and Anthony Kaldellis, *Hellenism in Byzantium: The Transformations of Greek Identity and the Reception of the Classical Tradition* (Cambridge: Cambridge University Press, 2007), 160–61. For the date of the Brucheion's demise during the emperor Aurelian's pursuit of a usurper (Zos. 1.61), see Christopher Haas, *Alexandria in Late Antiquity* (Baltimore: Johns Hopkins University Press, 1997), 340.

theologian, and Plotinus, the so-called founder of Neoplatonism. Origen, in turn, taught the Hellene Porphyry of Tyre, the self-appointed continuator of Plotinus's teachings. And in Rome at midcentury Plotinus "brought the mind of Ammonius to bear" in conversations with students (Porph. *Plot.* 14), not only Porphyry, but also several Gnostics, some of whom were Christian. Porphyry then revealed these teachings to the Hellene Iamblichus of Chalcis. Like Porphyry, Iamblichus sought out these doctrines after training under a Christian with Alexandrian connections: in this case, Anatolius, the future bishop of Laodicea. Meanwhile, through their connection to Origen, a generation of eastern Christians could also trace their lineage to Ammonius. In Palestinian Caesarea, this chain of succession linked the historian Eusebius and his mentor Pamphilus, who, in Alexandria, had studied with Pierius or "Origen Junior" (Hieron. *Vir. ill.* 76). In southwestern Asia Minor, Methodius of Olympus led another Origenist circle. In the west, Porphyry's teachings were an early influence on the African Christian apologist Arnobius of Sicca and, through him, his student Lactantius,[5] the Christian scholar, called to Diocletian's Nicomedian court as professor of rhetoric just before the outbreak of religious hostilities (Lact. *Inst.* 5.2.2). Since these masters opened their seminars to future administrators and magistrates, this confessional diversity filtered into public life during Diocletian's reign, populating not only the eastern palaces, but also provincial government with Christian officials (Eus. *HE* 8.1.2).

Overlooking this increasingly common culture, most historians, following the stereotype, describe the persecution as inevitable,[6] either culminating a series of general pogroms or satisfying long-standing religious policy goals of Diocletian or Galerius.[7] But clearly the first justification is unreasonable: however much momentum mounted between the emperor Decius's persecution (250) and Valerian's (253–260), this impetus hardly carried across four decades of peace to prompt Diocletian's edicts in 303. Those who draw rationales from imperial policy have more evidence, but their arguments still falter. For example, some see Diocletian as a committed polytheist whose enthusiasm for divination made persecution inevitable during his reign, even though he waited almost twenty years to pursue it.[8] Diocletian did link

5. Michael Bland Simmons, *Arnobius of Sicca: Religious Conflict and Competition in the Age of Diocletian* (New York: Oxford University Press, 1995), 261. For Porphyry's and Arnobius's influence on Lactantius, see the conclusion to this book.

6. P. Keresztes, "The Imperial Roman Government and the Christian Church II: From Gallienus to the Great Persecution," *ANRW* 2.23.1 (1979): 375–86, is an exception.

7. The pogroms represent the "third phase" in G. E. M. de Sainte-Croix, "Why Were the Early Christians Persecuted?" *P&P* 26 (1963): 6–7.

8. E.g., S. Williams, *Diocletian and the Roman Recovery* (London: Routledge, 2000), 69.

the imperial families to the gods Jupiter and Hercules through the titles Jovius and Herculius, and he industriously restored temples, which had fallen into disrepair during a half century of usurpation and invasion (Lact. *Mort.* 8, 52).[9] Nevertheless, casting this emperor as enthusiastic persecutor yields questions not answers, since the Christian courtiers in Antioch answered to him, he had sanctioned enlisting Christian soldiers, and Lactantius, in Nicomedia by invitation, was not the only Christian connected to that court. These difficulties, together with Diocletian's decision, two decades into his reign, to pursue persecution during an era of peace, explain why Lactantius and Eusebius, both of whom wrote contemporary histories, did not cite him as the prime mover. At least until 299, Diocletian's *modus vivendi* with Christian citizens followed a pluralist approach.

Ancient sources, conversely, designate Galerius, Diocletian's junior colleague, as the leader whose animus toward Christians predetermined persecution: both Eusebius and Lactantius identify him as a zealous activist, instigating the purge and continuing it after Diocletian retired in 305.[10] Nevertheless, Galerius's activities before 299 weigh against persecution as his longtime goal. Not only were Christians employed among the imperial staff in Galerius's residence, Thessalonica, as in Nicomedia and Antioch, but he had also enlisted Christian soldiers, since it was his army that Diocletian purged in 299. This very army had just delivered a stunning victory against a belligerent Persia (298),[11] and so these integrated forces had triumphed and rewarded him richly. The junior emperor, then, turned on Christians only after 299, inspired in part by the aborted auspices in Antioch, but also—at least according to Lactantius—by Galerius's mother's outrage against Christians. Hailing from Dacia beyond the Danube, a region relatively unfamiliar with Christianity,[12] the empress was offended when Christians in the imperial household refused to attend banquets serving meat from sacrificed animals (Lact. *Mort.* 11).

To learn why the emperors embraced persecution after Christians and Hellenes had lived, learned, and worked side by side for forty years, we must peer beyond the palace walls to spot the men in the shadows who promoted persecution when the opportunity arose. Priests and prophets comprise one

---

9. Ibid., 59.

10. In addition to Lact. *Mort.* 10f., cited often here, see also Eus. *HE* 8.16.

11. T. D. Barnes, "Imperial Campaigns, A.D. 285–311," *Phoenix* 30 (1976): 185.

12. Although Philostorgius *HE* 2.5 describes some Christian missionaries active in the third century among the Goths who lived north of the Danube, most ancient Christians associated their conversion with the efforts of Bishop Ulfilas in the mid–fourth century. Hagith Sivan, "Ulfila's Own Conversion," *HThR* 89, no. 4 (1996): 378.

group of activists: both the haruspex in Antioch responsible for the failed auspices and the priests of Apollo who in 299 and 303 branded Christians as polluted and impious. Another circle includes the two lecturers in Nicomedia, summoned probably by Galerius during the winter of 302–3. Lactantius names one spokesman: Sossianus Hierocles, a judge and former prefect of Oriens.[13] A growing consensus identifies the second as Porphyry of Tyre.[14] Plotinus's most illustrious student, Porphyry became infamous in this period for applying his erudition to savage Christian texts and doctrines, especially those linked to Origen. The circles of prophets and lecturers intersect. First, the treatise that Porphyry presented in Nicomedia, the *Philosophy from Oracles*,[15] compiled and analyzed oracles from Apolline and other sources; the hostility to Christianity in some of them indicates that Apollo's prophets had attacked the faith well before they incited Diocletian's attacks in 299 and 303. Next, as chapter 4 will argue, it is likely that the prophet at Daphne was familiar with the philosopher's *On Abstinence,* if not the *Philosophy from Oracles* itself. Finally, the tract that Hierocles delivered in Nicomedia, *The Lover of Truth,* used as its chief source Porphyry's arguments against Christian doctrines, although the two speakers may not have visited Nicomedia together or shared the same objective.[16]

Lactantius, Arnobius, Eusebius, and Methodius all wrote in response to Porphyry, and all were Christians who had connections to Ammonius Saccas, either through Origen or through Porphyry himself.[17] Explaining Rome's turn to persecution in 303, then, requires learning why men who drew their views from a common source and had studied together suddenly divided so sharply that one faction pressured the emperors to force the

---

13. Lact. *Inst.* 5.2; *Mort.* 16.

14. Cf. P. F. Beatrice, "*Antistes Philosophiae:* Ein christenfeindlicher Propogandist am Hofe Diokletians nach dem Zeugnis des Laktanz," *Augustinianum* 33 (1993): 1–47; Elizabeth DePalma Digeser, "Lactantius, Porphyry, and the Debate over Religious Toleration," *JRS* 88 (1998): 129–46; Jeremy M. Schott, "Porphyry on Christians and Others: 'Barbarian Wisdom,' Identity Politics, and Anti-Christian Polemics on the Eve of the Great Persecution," *JECS* 13 (2005): 278; Simon Corcoran, "Before Constantine," in *The Cambridge Companion to the Age of Constantine,* ed. Noel Lenski (Cambridge: Cambridge University Press, 2006), 52. T. D. Barnes, "Monotheists All?" *Phoenix* 55 (2001): 158, denies Porphyry's presence in Nicomedia, arguing that Lactantius *Inst.* 5.2 describes a philosopher who was actually—not metaphorically—blind. All the same, not only is Barnes's argument based on the questionable assumption that, if he had been so handicapped, no Christian opponent could have resisted mocking the elderly Porphyry, whom the Christians reviled. His literal reading also fails to see that Lactantius's passage pointing to Porphyry (*Inst.* 5.2) parodies the philosopher Thales in Plato's *Theaetetus* 174a.

15. Digeser, "Religious Toleration," 129–46.

16. Elizabeth DePalma Digeser, "Porphyry, Julian, or Hierokles? The Anonymous Hellene in Makarios Magnēs' *Apocriticus,*" *JThS* 53 (2002): 466–502.

17. See chapter 5 and the conclusion.

other's conformity. This book argues that Iamblichus of Chalcis played a key role in this shift. Before Iamblichus began teaching in the late third century, Christian and Hellene philosophers, theologians and the educated people in their circles, tended to focus on explaining the character of transcendent divinity and how their souls might draw closer to it. In this enterprise, they were more united than divided. For example, Origenists and Plotinians shared the notion that an intelligible hypostasis or *logos* had emanated from a transcendent divinity, and that an ascetic regime drew attention away from the body so that one could focus on the return of the soul.[18] Further, all of Ammonius's heirs held certain hermeneutical principles in common. These dictated that any text to be interpreted must first pass the test of authenticity.[19] They also taught that anomalous passages in an authentic text required figural exegesis, a practice of substituting figurative for literal readings on the assumption that the former pointed toward higher truths. Finally, Origenists shared with Porphyry the attitude that *for them* traditional animal sacrifice was polluting, demon attracting, and harmful, although only the Christian endorsed the sacrificial and salvific character of martyrdom and the Eucharistic meal.[20]

When Iamblichus began teaching, however, first in Daphne and then in Apamea, he shifted the discourse in two important ways.[21] First, he challenged fellow Hellene philosophers to look beyond themselves and to consider how the souls of ordinary people might return to God. Second, he broke fundamentally with Porphyry in claiming that participation in rituals involving matter (animal sacrifice, for example) was necessary for any soul striving to reascend to its divine origin. For Iamblichus, such rituals were the first step along a path that all people, including philosophers, must travel in order for their souls to return to their divine source. Iamblichus used "theurgy," a term he took from the *Chaldaean Oracles* but used in a more universal way,[22] to denote the wide range of rituals and activities that pulled a soul closer to its divine origin.[23] Because participation in these rituals was salvific, the souls of ordinary people—not just those of philosophers—might achieve some sort of union with the divine (even if it had a humbler character). Iamblichus saw at least some Christians as atheists. Nevertheless, his own system—although it cannot be proved—may have drawn its inspiration

---

18. See chapter 3.
19. See chapter 1.
20. See chapter 2.
21. See chapter 4.
22. See chapter 4.
23. Gregory Shaw, "Neoplatonic Theurgy and Dionysius the Areopagite," *JECS* 7 (1999): 580–81.

from the conviction shared by many non-Gnostic Christians that matter, in this case the human body, whether sacrificed on the cross or in the arena, or consumed as Eucharistic bread, was essential in reuniting a soul with its divine source.

Iamblichus's system, probably in the 290s, provoked a vigorous and comprehensive critique from Porphyry, who saw himself as the custodian of the late Plotinus's teachings.[24] Rejecting Iamblichus's teachings as perverting what Plotinus (and hence Ammonius Saccas) had taught, Porphyry fought, not only to reaffirm his leadership of the Plotinian/Ammonian community, but also to show the fundamental error of *any* system—Christian or Hellene—that prescribed one path to God for all. Porphyry trained his response on exegesis: both Iamblichus's analysis of the *Chaldaean Oracles* that undergirded his universal theology and the figural scripture readings on which Origenists based their own totalizing system. In the first case, Porphyry argued that oracular texts, properly read, testified to the limited utility of traditional rites, divination, and Chaldaean theurgy. Although these practices might purify the lower soul, they could not achieve the union with the One for which the higher soul yearned.[25] In the second case, Porphyry denied that Old or New Testament texts gave any credence to the notion that Jesus was divine, let alone the Logos, or Son of God.[26] However pious Jesus might have been, however accomplished as a Jewish wonder-worker, worshipping him was salvific for no one. As an alternative to the Hellene and Christian systems that stipulated one path for the soul's return to its source, Porphyry, although the evidence is very thin, envisioned several routes leading souls toward different celestial spheres. Some of these paths involved rituals manipulating matter and even animal sacrifice; through such acts, Porphyry argued, ordinary people might glimpse higher divine truths. As a result, the souls of people with varying abilities and backgrounds might ascend via different paths to different heavenly levels. Porphyry continued to assert, however, that only philosophical contemplation, asceticism, and virtue could unite a soul to transcendent divinity, to the One. Yet very few could walk this path, along which lay no ritualistic shortcuts. As a result of this campaign prompted by opposition to Iamblichus, Porphyry not only denied the possibility of any universal salvific ritual or philosophical path but also generated arguments and texts that fundamentally challenged Christian doctrines and scripture.[27]

---

24. See chapter 4 and the conclusion.
25. See chapter 4 and the conclusion.
26. See the conclusion.
27. See chapters 4 and 5 and the conclusion.

Porphyry's arguments further splintered the Ammonian community into three parts, Porphyrians, Iamblichaeans, and Origenists. Despite their rift over how best to lead the philosophical life, Porphyrian and Iamblichaean Hellenes agreed that the souls of ordinary people needed traditional rituals. This fundamental concord, together with the arguments against Christian doctrine and practice that Porphyry had developed in writing against universal religious systems, helped fuel the impetus for the Great Persecution. Porphyry probably first sent to Daphne near Antioch, where Iamblichus was teaching, texts targeting Christian and Iamblichaean universalism, treatises known today as the *Philosophy from Oracles, On Images, On the Return of the Soul,* and *Against the Christians.* From there, they could have quickly found their way into the hands of the administrators, priests, and diviners of this capital city. Given the Iamblichaean circle's involvement with divination, oracular priests and prophets even beyond Antioch could also know of these texts, either because they belonged to the school themselves or because its members visited their temples.[28] They would all have agreed—with Porphyry and Iamblichus—that ordinary Christians should be participating in traditional rituals alongside the rest of the empire's peoples.[29] It is no coincidence then that Antioch witnessed the first challenge to Diocletian's pluralism in 299.

Events in Antioch, Nicomedia, and Daphne thus gave people who might have been more fanatical than Porphyry and Iamblichus themselves opportunities to influence religious policy through the oracles they provided for the imperial court. Priests need not have cynically manipulated the outcome of their divinations in order to have seen what they expected to see in a statue's movements, or heard what they expected to hear in the babble of a prophetess. Nevertheless, their input further radicalized attitudes and played on Diocletian's own active engagement with divination (Lact. *Mort.* 10). Similarly, since Sossianus Hierocles was governor (*vicarius*) in Antioch shortly before 303,[30] he could have discovered Porphyry's anti-Christian writings there, becoming motivated by them to call for persecution. Such a chain of events suggests that Sossianus Hierocles chose independently to discuss the contradictions in scripture that Porphyry had raised in writing against

---

28. Although Iamblichus's *De mysteriis* favored Hermetic and Chaldaean wisdom, Apolline oracles had long looked favorably on Platonists, from the oracle identifying Socrates as the "wisest of men" (D. L. 5.18; Pl. *Ap.* 21a6–7) to that ensconcing the soul of Plotinus among those of Minos, Rhadamanthus, Plato, and Pythagoras in the aether (Porph. *Plot.* 22.51–55).

29. Jews had had an exemption from traditional cult observance since Judaea became part of the empire in the first century BCE. Philo *Leg.* 37.

30. T. D. Barnes, "Sossianus Hierocles and the Antecedents of the 'Great Persecution'," *HSPh* 80 (1976): 245.

Origen. Porphyry, for his part, would have been as concerned to establish the leadership of his group and so presented the emperors with his own system, in the form of the *Philosophy from Oracles*. Unlike earlier persecutions, at least until that of Decius, therefore, the Great Persecution was not driven by a "bottom-up" swell of popular opinion against Christian practice, but by a small group of men tied to Iamblichus in various ways.

The controversy between Porphyry and Iamblichus, on the one hand, and between Porphyry and the Origenists, on the other, might also have remained within the ivory tower had it not been for the significant role that the members of this community attributed to its leadership. For this reason, the controversy over whether there was a universal path to salvation was also a quarrel over which subgroup could rightly assert that it retained the legacy of the truest philosophy. From this perspective, the diversity within the Ammonian community had created a push toward the assertion of orthodoxy,[31] a series of actions and reactions with which the broader Christian community—if not these Hellene philosophers—had been familiar since the second century. But the problem of who maintained the legacy of the truest philosophy was keener still, for all of these Ammonians taught that the spiritual guide-cum-high priest of their group had a duty not only to ensure that his immediate *politeia* or community followed divine law, but also—if he had achieved divine union and had the sovereign's attention—to shape the law of the broader commonwealth. This was the responsibility of the self-styled "Hellene," the person imbued with the truest Greek philosophy infused with the truest ancient religious wisdom, whose expertise had brought divine insight and hence the obligation to advise those in power. Thus the argument over who taught the truest philosophy was not just an intramural disagreement among Ammonius's heirs; it became a public controversy and cause, made more acute by the presence of Christian courtiers in Diocletian's inner circle. When he appropriated the time-honored role of Plato's philosopher advising the emperor in Nicomedia just before persecution began, Porphyry not only allowed the conflict that began within his school to assume its most public face, but also attempted to shape laws embracing his own theology to the detriment of his Origenist and Iamblichaean competitors.[32]

Although these tensions and confrontations occurred over 1,700 years ago, only recently have historians had ready to hand the tools to lay bare

---

31. Cf. J. B. Russell, *Dissent and Order in the Middle Ages: The Search for Legitimate Authority* (New York: Twayne, 1992); and id., *A History of Medieval Christianity: Prophecy and Order* (Arlington Heights, IL: Harlan Davidson, 1968).

32. See chapters 3 and 5.

the foundations that supported the Great Persecution. Several persistent problems have deterred such an excavation. Above all, the ancient sources present almost intractable problems. The Hellenes' voices—Porphyry's in particular—are mainly fragmentary, thanks in part to a Constantinian edict requiring Porphyry's writings against Christians to be destroyed (Socr. *HE* 1.9). What survives of these texts are short extracts—fragments—quoted by Christians writing against him, and so historians have utterly depended on hostile Christian accounts for information about the other side. The Christian accounts, in turn, are stridently polemical, a trait that—however understandable, given the circumstances—makes it difficult to reconstruct how the claims of the other side might have carried any weight. In this regard, Andrew Smith's relatively recent *Porphyrii philosophi fragmenta* has been a vital contribution—and impetus—for Porphyrian scholarship.[33] The fragments, in turn, have often not been used in appropriate ways.[34] Exacerbating the problem is that many historians have read the Christian sources without seeing that Christians wrote within a context involving certain philosophical disagreements: Eusebius, for example, directly refers to Porphyry as his chief antagonist (Eus. *PE* 4.6).[35] In other words, scholars studying the Great Persecution have assumed that Christians were responding to Porphyry only insofar as he espoused anti-Christian positions. They have not explored the extent to which these positions might have been situated in a broader philosophical framework that included these Christian authors.[36] For Eusebius, this oversight was particularly egregious, given his connections through Origen to this philosophical community.[37] Historians have also too easily assumed that late third-century authors such as Eusebius and Porphyry gave an objective picture of their intellectual forebears, whether Ammonius or Origen.[38] Yet both Eusebius and Porphyry wrote with clear apologetic and polemical aims, and so their "historical" reflections need to be read with an awareness of this context. In other words, both ancient authors discuss the

---

33. Andrew Smith and David Wasserstein, eds., *Porphyrii philosophi fragmenta,* Bibl. scriptorum Graec. et Roman. Teubneriana (Stuttgart: Teubner, 1993).

34. For a good critique of these inappropriate readings, see Ariane Magny, "Porphyry in Fragments: Eusebius, Jerome, Augustine, and the Problem of Reconstruction" (PhD diss., University of Bristol, UK, 2011).

35. See, also for example, the translation of Lactantius's *Divine Institutes* by A. Bowen and P. Garnsey (Cambridge: Cambridge University Press, 2003).

36. T. D. Barnes, *Constantine and Eusebius* (Cambridge, MA: Harvard University Press, 1981); Simmons, *Arnobius of Sicca,* is an important exception.

37. Even those who deny that Origen the Christian theologian was identical with Origen the Platonist philosopher must accept Porphyry's assertion (ap. Eus. *HE* 6.19) that Origen studied with Ammonius Saccas. See chapter 2.

38. E.g., Joseph W. Trigg, *Origen* (London/New York: Routledge, 1998), 1–5.

earlier third century polemically because they projected their own conflict into the past.

Modern scholarship on Porphyry has presented a second obstacle to understanding the conflicts and circumstances preparing the way for the Great Persecution. For example, assuming the "orientalist" attitudes of his day, the great Belgian historian of philosophy, Joseph Bidez, saw Porphyry as deeply marked by a youth spent in the Phoenician city of Tyre.[39] Thus Porphyry's writings concerned with traditional piety, the *Philosophy from Oracles* and *On Images,* for example, Bidez reflexively assigned, despite their overwhelmingly Greek character, to the period before he encountered Plotinus. Both Bidez and Porphyry viewed the latter's relationship with Plotinus as a transformative experience. However, whereas Porphyry saw himself as having revolutionized his view of the Intelligible, thanks to Plotinus (*Plot.* 18), Bidez saw their association as leading Porphyry to adopt Plotinian "rationalism." Accordingly, Bidez assigned *On the Return of the Soul* to a later period because, even though it condoned Chaldaean theurgy, it asserted the superiority of philosophical contemplation. Once John O'Meara argued that Porphyry's *Philosophy from Oracles* and *On the Return of the Soul* were really the same text,[40] however, most scholars recognized that the two texts were not as different in perspective and intent as Bidez had assumed. Accordingly, although Pierre Hadot rejected O'Meara's claim for identity,[41] nothing in the extant fragments of the *Philosophy from Oracles* prevents Porphyry from having written it rather late in his life.[42] Another problem in Porphyrian scholarship is that most scholars have assumed that Porphyry's treatises had fixed titles. All the same, it is likely that texts that Constantine officially condemned in the 320s circulated under different titles later in the century, especially among Christian readers.[43]

---

39. J. Bidez, *Vie de Porphyre, le philosophe néo-platonicien avec les fragments des traités "Perì agalmatōn"* *et "De regressu animae"* (Ghent: E. van Goethem, 1913; repr., Hildesheim: G. Olms, 1964).

40. J. J. O'Meara, *Porphyry's Philosophy from Oracles in Augustine* (Paris: Etudes augustiniennes, 1959); and id., *Porphyry's Philosophy from Oracles in Eusebius' Praeparatio Evangelica and Augustine's Dialogues of Cassiciacum* (Paris: Etudes augustiniennes, 1969).

41. P. Hadot, "Citations de Porphyre chez Augustin: A propos d'un ouvrage récent," *RE Aug* 6 (1960): 205–44.

42. A. Smith, "Porphyrian Studies since 1913," *ANRW* 2.36.2 (1987): 732–33.

43. One scholar who has an excellent grasp of this problem is Pier Franco Beatrice. See, for example, P. F. Beatrice, "Quosdam Platonicorum libros," *VChr* 43 (1989): 248–81; id., "Le traité de Porphyre contre les chrétiens: L'état de la question," *Kernos* 4 (1991): 119–38; id., "Towards a New Edition of Porphyry's Fragments against the Christians," in *Sophiēs maiētores / Chercheurs de sagesse: Hommage à Jean Pépin,* ed. Marie-Odile Goulet-Cazé, Goulven Madec, and Denis O'Brien (Paris: Institut d'études augustiniennes, 1992), 347–55, esp. 349 n. 16.

The way that historians have approached ancient philosophers and their schools also left obscure the causes of the Great Persecution. The problems attributable to the narrow perspective of historians of philosophy are several. First, historians of philosophy have tended to avoid situating their subjects in a broader historical context,[44] focusing more on the content of late antique philosophical texts read in isolation than with trying to understand them as products or stimuli of broader historical trends. Next, historians of Roman political thought generally concentrate on Cicero, Seneca, and Augustine, giving very little attention to the third century.[45] There are many reasons for this trend, but it led historians to assume that Plotinus and his successors were politically uninvolved, and to ignore the political implications in their teachings. Dominic O'Meara's *Platonopolis: Platonic Political Philosophy in Late Antiquity* has forcefully negated those assumptions.[46] A third problem in the scholarship on late antique philosophy has been the tendency to identify theurgy—a term that Iamblichus used to cover all types of ritual practice—with magic. As a result, scholars such as E. R. Dodds focused more on the "decline" that Iamblichaean philosophy presented to Plotinian "rationalism" than in trying to understand this philosophical trend to ritual on its own terms.[47]

For these reasons, the scholarship on Porphyry in particular and late antique philosophy in general, until very recently, has obscured the reasons why a man like Porphyry could have worked with Diocletian's court in a philosophical capacity or why Christian apologists responding to him might have deployed anything other than stock arguments against polytheism. Moreover, historians have seldom explored these groups, networks, and schisms and their implications for the broader history of the period.[48]

---

44. For example, although it is a very learned and useful book, J. M. Dillon, *The Middle Platonists* (Ithaca, NY: Cornell University Press, 1996), does not consider the Middle Platonists within the broader culture. Fowden and Athanassiadi are notable exceptions. See, for example, G. Fowden, "The Platonist Philosopher and His Circle in Late Antiquity," *Philosophia* 7 (1977): 358–83; and Polymnia Athanassiadi, "Apamea and the *Chaldaean Oracles:* A Holy City and a Holy Book," in *The Philosopher and Society in Late Antiquity: Essays in Honour of Peter Brown,* ed. Andrew Smith (Swansea: Classical Press of Wales, 2005), 117–43.

45. See, e.g., Christopher Rowe et al., eds., *The Cambridge History of Greek and Roman Political Thought* (Cambridge: Cambridge University Press, 2000).

46. Dominic J. O'Meara, *Platonopolis: Platonic Political Philosophy in Late Antiquity* (Oxford: Oxford University Press, 2003).

47. E. R. Dodds, "Theurgy and Its Relationship to Neoplatonism," *JRS* 37 (1947): 55–68; E. R. Dodds, *The Greeks and the Irrational* (Berkeley: University of California Press, 1951), 55, 58.

48. Apart from the groundbreaking work of Fowden, "Platonist Philosopher," 358–83, see id., "Pagan Philosophers in Late Antique Society: With Special Reference to Iamblichus and His Followers" (D. Phil. thesis, Oxford University, 1979), the implications of which, however, Fowden did not pursue further.

For example, although the conflict between Porphyry and Iamblichus has long been acknowledged,[49] no one considered what its broader ramifications might have been for the empire in which they played such prominent roles.

These problems have been compounded by failures of imagination among scholars studying the Christian side. For decades, Lactantius's tirades against Jupiter and Hercules were read as shrill criticisms of polytheistic deities, without seeing that such commentary in 310 might have targeted a tetrarchic system that had identified this god and his hero son as its particular champions.[50] Similarly, references to Plato and Pythagoras in Lactantius and Eusebius are often still read as a commentary on these philosophers as Greeks of the archaic and classical ages and not as referring to the contemporary schools that claimed to preserve these philosophers' teaching in its truest form.[51] Finally, for whatever reason, scholars have been reluctant to pool the evidence of the three chief eyewitnesses to the persecution to see what might be learned by doing so. Arnobius, Lactantius, and Eusebius all had important Plotinian and Ammonian contacts, and, when the three are read together, themes and arguments emerge that point directly to the involvement of the Porphyrian wing of that school with the forces that pushed for the Great Persecution.[52]

Assumptions about what certain doctrinally oriented groups would do has also profoundly shaped the scholarship on this period until very recently. Most historians of theology and philosophy have simply assumed that Platonist philosophers and Christian theologians would not interact with each other's circles, despite clear ancient evidence to the contrary. For example, scholars have posited two Ammonii in order to keep each figure within his assumed philosophical milieu.[53] More recently, however, historians have more

---

49. E.g., Daniela P. Taormina, "Giamblico contro Plotino e Porfirio: Il dibattito sull'arte e sul movimento (apud Simplicio, *In Categorias* 301.20–308.10)," *SyllClass* 8 (1997): 95–112.

50. See Lactantius, *The Divine Institutes,* trans. M. F. McDonald, vol. 49 of *The Fathers of the Church* (Washington, DC: Catholic University Press, 1964); see also the translation by Bowen and Garnsey.

51. E.g., Glenn F. Chesnut, *The First Christian Historians: Eusebius, Socrates, Sozomen, Theodoret, and Evagius* (Paris: Editions Beauchesne, 1977; repr., Macon, GA: Mercer University Press, 1986),

52. Good exceptions are Aaron Johnson, "Identity, Descent, and Polemic: Ethnic Argumentation in Eusebius' 'Praeparatio Evangelica'," *JECS* 12 (2004): 23–56; and J. M. Schott, "Founding Platonopolis: The Platonic 'Politeia' in Eusebius, Porphyry, and Iamblichus," *JECS* 11 (2003): 501–31.

52. Clearly, the connections were there to be made. As early as P. Courcelle, "Les sages de Porphyre et les *viri novi* d'Arnobe," *REL* 31 (1953): 257–71, Arnobius's chief adversary had been identified as Porphyry.

53. See chapter 1. Scholars posited two Origens as well for the same reason. This is a more complicated problem that will be addressed in chapter 2.

seriously weighed the evidence for fluidity between these circles.[54] Thus it is easier to ask what forces and circumstances led away from a certain unity toward schism, fracture, and alienation.

Finally, the difficulty in seeing what led to the Great Persecution has been aggravated by the nature of the disagreements between the philosophers and theologians involved. For example, the forces calling for persecution did not find Origenist Christianity threatening because it was *different*. On the contrary, this circle of Christians threatened these Hellenes because their beliefs were becoming increasingly similar, and they were sharing overlapping circles of teachers and students. When philosophers such as Porphyry and Iamblichus perceived threats to their leadership or the identity of their school as a beacon of truth, they struck back by distinguishing themselves as very different and superior to Christians. In both cases, these men had appropriated ideas that actually made them look very "Christian," whether this was Porphyry's avoidance of animal sacrifice or Iamblichus's sacramental ritualism. Conversely, Christians with links to these Platonist circles were also vulnerable to accusations that their beliefs were "just like" those of the Hellenes.[55] For this reason, Christians often played up the polytheistic elements of their opponents' systems, even though in both cases the philosophers understand the gods as powers of the divine, leading ordinary humans toward the One.

The argument will proceed across six chapters. The narrative starts by exploring what I will call the "Ammonian community" from its formation under the tutelage of Ammonius. It then discusses the events and efforts that involved his heirs on one side or another as momentum built for the Great Persecution. At the same time, several overarching themes thread the chapters together. First, it is clear that all members of the Ammonian community had a common approach to evaluating and interpreting texts, techniques integral to their philosophical speculations. All began from the premise that "true philosophy," the doctrine that set out the pattern for living that would lead to the soul's reascent to its divine source, was discerned through a process of intellectual engagement with a wide variety of texts. These could be excavated in order to recover this true philosophy as it had been divinely revealed to

---

54. See chapters 1 and 2. For a good discussion of the problem as concerns Christians and Jews, see Daniel Boyarin, *Border Lines* (Philadelphia: University of Pennsylvania Press, 2004), introduction.

55. This connection was abundantly clear in the controversy over Origen's teachings that erupted at the cusp of the fourth century. See René Amacker and Éric Junot, "L'art d'entrer en matière dans une littérature de controverse: Les premières pages de l'«Apologie pour Origène» de Pamphile," in *Entrer en matière: Les prologues,* ed. Jean-Daniel Dubois and Bernard Roussel (Paris: Ed. du Cerf, 1998), 37–51; and Rowan Williams, "Damnosa haereditas: Pamphilus' Apology and the Reputation of Origen," in *Logos: Festschrift für Luise Abramowski,* ed. H. C. Brennecke, E. L. Grasmück, and C. Markschies (Berlin: de Gruyter, 1993), 151–69.

august figures in the remote past—whether Pythagoras, Plato, or Moses. All also agreed that certain methods were required to ascertain the authenticity of texts that might convey the desired information. These practices included ascertaining whether a text was authentic, whether it was what it claimed to be.[56] They might also embrace the procedures that would render the best possible edition of a text from extant available copies. Once the authenticity and reliability of a text had been confirmed or produced, all also agreed that certain interpretive strategies, such as figural reading,[57] should be brought to bear in order to find the true philosophy, the true doctrine, in these texts. Figural reading was necessary because these treatises often conveyed the true philosophy or doctrine as *ainigmata* (puzzles) or *aporiae* in the texts. This assumption reveals that all of these philosophers and theologians believed that the knowledge they sought had an occult character that rendered it potentially unsuitable for or at least unavailable to ordinary people. Such reading strategies not only presupposed a certain amount of training in order to recognize potential *aporiae* and *ainigmata* but also required a thorough liberal arts education and a good library so that the *ainigmata* could be properly decoded.[58]

The second thread lacing the chapters together is the role that the material or sensible world might play in the return of the human soul to its divine source. All members of the Ammonian community believed that the sensible world was the image of the intelligible world. This assumption undergirded their use of figural exegesis to decode *ainigmata*. They disagreed, however, about how these images functioned in the return of the soul. For example, Hellene Ammonians agreed that aspects of traditional polytheism, both the ritual acts themselves as well as the artistic rendering of cult images or music, reflected elements of the intelligible world that were somehow beneficial for the souls of ordinary people. Nevertheless, they disagreed about the level of involvement that virtuous, philosophically educated souls should have with these traditional elements. Origenists were no less convinced that traditional rituals reflected intelligible reality. In their case, however, the traditional

---

56. E.g., Porphyry's analysis concluding that the books of Zoroaster were apocryphal (Porph. *Plot.* 16); his determination that the book of Daniel was really a history of the era of Antiochus IV, but still worth reading as a narrative of *those* events (Hieron. *Dan.* pr.); and Porphyry's assessment that the Gospels were not reliable accounts of Jesus' life and teaching because their authors were ignorant and made so many errors (e.g., ap. Hieron. *Ep.* 57.9).

57. I avoid the term "allegorical exegesis," because it connotes a narrative element often lacking in these interpretations. See Blossom Stefaniw, *Mind, Text, and Commentary: Noetic Exegesis in Origen of Alexandria, Didymus the Blind, and Evagrius Ponticus* (Frankfurt: Peter Lang, 2010).

58. Taking Porphyry's *Cave of the Nymphs* as an example: the section on bees (7) required a knowledge of natural philosophy, and the evaluation of the cave necessitated geographical information (9–10).

rituals that did so were Jewish. Hellenes and Christians also disagreed about how these images worked over time. Plotinus (and probably Porphyry), for example, thought that, insofar as images reflected the form of beauty, ordinary souls gazing on them might make their first contact with the intelligible realm (Plot. *Enn.* 1.6.4). Gazing at beautiful images might be the first step in the eternally cyclical process through which a soul, having fully descended, gradually reascended by progressing through the hierarchy of celestial spheres across a series of lifetimes. Origenists saw Christians as having souls like those of Porphyry's philosophers, no longer needing traditional rituals, Jewish in this case, which they saw as mere shadows of their own reality. Origenists differed from Hellenes, however, in that they saw traditional rituals as playing a necessary role, not in eternity, but in time. These Christians believed in evolution, arguing that different practices were necessary for people at different times in human history (at first people needed the law of Moses to govern them and bring them out of "idolatry," but Jesus' incarnation had put human beings under a new, more divine law). Here the similarities with Porphyry are telling. Not only did his *On Abstinence* outline an evolutionary approach to explain his position on sacrifice, but also, like the Origenists, he thought that he belonged to an elite group for whom traditional rituals were no longer necessary: he was able to live by the law of the intelligible as opposed to the law of the sensible realm. For Porphyry, this advance was possible because his soul had improved across several lifetimes; the Origenists were advantaged because their souls had come into the world after Jesus had brought divine law to earth. For these reasons, Porphyry thought that traditional rituals should maintained, whereas Origenists, given their evolutionary view of human history, thought that they should be abolished. The one sacrificial act that Origenists continued to value, however, was human sacrifice, whether it was Jesus' death in atonement for human sin or its recapitulation in the transformation of the Eucharistic bread and the passion of the martyrs. Although such thinking, especially as it involved the Eucharist, was not far removed from Iamblichus's understanding of sacrifice and the return of the soul, it certainly would have been repellent to Porphyry.

The final thread stitching these chapters together is the Ammonian community's belief in the enlightened philosopher's responsibility to his or her immediate circle and to the broader political community. All Ammonians believed that their true philosophy, their true doctrine, was conveyed through the example and teaching of a spiritual guide, whether Hermes, Pythagoras, Plato, and Jesus in the past or Ammonius, Origen, Plotinus, and Iamblichus in their own age. All Ammonian teachers appear to have opened their circles to different types of students, not only those of different religious commitments, but also those with different goals, whether adopting the true philosophy as a way of life or studying with an enlightened teacher as a stage before assuming a public career. As a result people in the Ammonian circle had direct access to Roman government, even at the highest levels. Such contacts allowed the community to shape imperial policy. Its members who had experienced divine union, in fact, believed that they had a responsibility to advise the sovereign. This particular aspect of the Ammonian community's beliefs led *them* toward the Great Persecution: when this circle broke apart, each group worried that its opponents would lead the empire in the wrong direction.

In order to explain the role of Ammonius's heirs in the theology and politics of the late third century, and the growing push toward persecution, chapter 1 begins by establishing the identity of Ammonius Saccas as their founding figure. The temptation in modern scholarship has been to split figures like Ammonius, who traveled in "pagan" and Christian circles, into two purists who never transgressed each other's boundaries. Nevertheless, the evidence is clear that one heterodox Ammonius, and not two Ammonii, a "Christian" and a "pagan," taught philosophy in early third-century Alexandria. Next, the chapter assesses the function that Porphyry's representation of Ammonius served in its late third-century context. In Porphyry's account, Ammonius perfected an approach to philosophy that became definitive of the Plotinian community in Rome, the Origenist communities in Alexandria and Caesarea, and the Iamblichaean community in Syria. Through philosophy, Ammonius sought to lay a path that would best achieve the return of his soul to its divine source. His method for doing so was to derive a "philosophy without conflicts," mining a wide variety of sources with a tool kit of exegetical techniques. The richest sources for Ammonius were the texts of Plato. All the same, he also believed that Plato's teachings had been corrupted by his later followers. This assumption allowed Ammonius to embrace other sources, particularly Aristotle, whose treatises he used to broaden his understanding of what Plato might have taught beyond what he had actually written down. Ammonius, who came from a Christian family, also evaluated Hebrew and Christian sources in building his philosophy without conflicts: two tracts attributed to him evince an interest in Jesus' life and message, both as presented in the Gospels and as compared to Moses' teachings. Ammonius subjected the Gospel accounts to a rigorous point-by-point analysis, perhaps to identify what might be "reliable" information based on consensus across the texts, a technique that he also applied to the works of Plato and Aristotle. From Porphyry's perspective, this type of systematic, careful analysis as a preliminary to textual exegesis became a point of fracture between Ammonius's

Origenist and Iamblichaean descendants. Finally, for Ammonius, a person dedicated to true philosophy must uphold the laws of the community to which he belonged, a value that Porphyry highlighted in describing Ammonius as the ideal philosopher of his age. Porphyry could use this tenet, not only to challenge Origen's openly encouraging Christians to seek martyrdom, but also to question Iamblichaeans, who, at least in his view, violated standard exegetical rules in their desire to establish theurgy, not contemplation, as the guaranteed path to divine union.

After establishing the identity and teachings of one heterodox Ammonius in chapter 1, chapter 2 addresses the question of Origen's identity, before exploring the theologian's appropriation of Ammonius Saccas's teachings. Both Porphyry and Eusebius maintained that the Christian theologian Origen studied with Ammonius, but most twentieth-century historians downplayed the significance of this association. They either argued, wrongly, that Origen studied, not with Ammonius Saccas, but with a Christian bishop of the same name, the phantom figure whom I dispel in chapter 1. Or they argued that the real conveyer of the Ammonian tradition was a certain "Origen the Platonist," distinct from the Christian theologian. From evidence in the theologian's and "Platonist's" texts and curricula vitae, scholars have demonstrated that the "two Origens" should be reintegrated into one historical figure.[59] My interests in showing the connections between the Christian and Hellene Ammonian groups are satisfied, however, by Porphyry's and Eusebius's testimony that Origen the theologian studied with Ammonius Saccas in Alexandria. Chapter 2 then discusses Ammonius's influence on Origen's teaching and thought. Anyone familiar with Origen's writings recognizes him as a biblical exegete, a charismatic teacher, a zealous ascetic, and a theologian deeply indebted to Plato. I argue that he adopted this way of living and teaching from Ammonius and bequeathed it to his own students, creating a line of succession that potentially challenged the Alexandrian teacher's other heirs in crafting a "philosophy without conflicts." For example, Origen's *Hexapla,* his effort to ascertain what Hebrew scripture actually said by comparing a variety of scriptural traditions (both Greek and Hebrew), resembles Ammonius's comparing the Gospel accounts to establish what Jesus actually did. In turn, Origen needed to have utter confidence in the authenticity of his text because he read scripture through a sophisticated figural exegesis, a hermeneutics that hinged on small textual details. These

---

59. E.g., T. Böhm, "Origenes, Theologe und (Neu-)Platoniker? Oder: wem soll man misstrauen, Eusebius oder Porphyrius?" *Adamantius* 8 (2002): 7–23; Mark J. Edwards, *Origen against Plato* (Aldershot, UK: Ashgate, 2002), is a notable exception.

similarities between Origen and Ammonius, however, only heighten the significance of two salient differences between them. First, Ammonius's system was contingent on the conviction that Plato was the primary font of knowledge, establishing him as a "Hellene," although he called himself a Christian. The teachings of Jesus were Origen's foundation, however: he believed they had brought ancient teachings into proper focus and offered new hope for the human soul seeking return to its source. Second, Origen's conviction that Jesus had brought new insight into ancient teachings led him to cultivate a different relationship with the communities to which he belonged than Ammonius might have condoned. In short, believing that divine law conflicted with Roman law, Origen encouraged his students to testify to that contradiction through martyrdom in the so-called Severan persecution.

While chapter 2 explores how Ammonius's legacy evolved along a Christian path, chapter 3 describes how Plotinus brought this way of living and teaching to Rome, where its development introduced a political emphasis to this dynamic philosophical movement. The exegetical practices, charismatic pedagogy, asceticism, and deep commitment to the teachings of Plato so apparent in Plotinus's circle, I argue, derive directly from the eleven years that this philosopher spent as Ammonius's student in Alexandria. For example, the school's attention to "Gnostic" texts shows the use of textual criticism to ascertain the authenticity of a potential source of ancient wisdom (e.g., the writings of Zostrianus; Porph. *Plot.* 16). Second, just as Origen had read Hebrew scripture figurally, Plotinus explained the relationship between the One, Nous, and Soul by applying these techniques to Greek mythology. Third, building on Ammonius's reputation for harmonizing Aristotle with Plato, Plotinus's *Enneads* muscled Aristotle into a fundamentally Platonist system.[60] Nevertheless, differences between Origen and Plotinus on the attributes of the supreme godhead or "Father" may indicate that Plotinus's transcendent One had moved significantly away from Ammonius's teaching. Plotinus is also unique for situating himself in Rome, where he had access to the imperial court and the Senate, counting senators and public officials among his followers and earning the veneration of the emperor Gallienus (260–68) (*Plot.* 7, 12). Although the mystical elements in Plotinus's philosophy once led historians to assume that he and his students were disinterested in the political world and political philosophy, I argue that Plotinus and Porphyry sought out these political connections. Building on Dominic O'Meara's arguments that Neoplatonists, starting with Plotinus, viewed

---

60. Lloyd P. Gerson, *Aristotle and Other Platonists* (Ithaca, NY: Cornell University Press, 2005), 205f.

Plato's *Laws* as providing the inspiration for the philosopher's relationship to power, I argue that Plotinus and Porphyry had concrete political goals: Plotinus wanted to found a community of philosophers in Campania, and Porphyry believed, as a man who had achieved divine union, that he ought to help craft imperial legislation that would emulate divine law.

With Plotinus's death, however, came challenges to Porphyry and the rest of Plotinus's circle, especially after Iamblichus of Chalcis founded his own school near Antioch. Chapter 4 explores the growing rift between Porphyrians and Iamblichaeans, the earliest evidence for which appears in Porphyry's *On Abstinence*. Porphyry wrote this treatise to explain the harmful effects of pollution (especially from eating animal flesh) on the soul of someone striving to live philosophically. Clues in the text suggest that Castricius, to whom the work is dedicated, abandoned Porphyry to pursue the philosophical life with Iamblichus. After establishing what is known about Iamblichus's formation, the rest of the chapter explores the points of contact and disagreement between him and Porphyry. The differences between the two philosophers, I argue, first coalesced when Porphyry wrote his *Letter to Anebo,* a tract that functions as a series of questions about the hierarchy of divine beings, the character of various forms of divination, and the identification of different divine beings from their epiphanies. The chapter next addresses Iamblichus's response to Porphyry and its ramifications. Porphyry's letter was fairly short, but Iamblichus responded in a ten-volume work, *On the Mysteries,* dependent on Plotinus but taking his ideas in new directions. Iamblichus argues, for example, that all those seeking the ascent of their soul must involve themselves with theurgic rituals, thus with rituals involving matter and even blood sacrifice. This system, as Gregory Shaw's *Theurgy and the Soul* has argued, integrated Hermetic, Chaldaean, Pythagorean, and Plotinian wisdom into a universal path along which all souls could return to their source. It violated, however, Porphyry's vision of the norms that Plotinus had established for the Ammonian community. By challenging his interpretation of Hermetic and Chaldaean literature, Porphyry disputed Iamblichus's claim, based on these texts, that most philosophers required material rituals. Porphyry next attacked all Ammonians—Iamblichaeans and Origenists—who wrongly used their school's exegetical tool kit to craft a "philosophy without conflicts," setting philosophers and ordinary people along a common path to the divine. Fragments now attributed to two treatises, *On the Return of the Soul* and the *Philosophy from Oracles* illustrate Porphyry's exegesis of Chaldaean theurgic oracles and his conclusions that such rituals cannot return the soul to its source. In this context, Porphyry's *Life of Plotinus* (ca. 300) is a manifesto for its author's conception of the orthodox philosophical life: it not only argued for the superiority of Plotinus's doctrines but also asserted Porphyry's standing as their only legitimate custodian. The message of this text, together with *On Abstinence* and *On the Return of the Soul,* is that only by living philosophically can a human soul reascend to its source; since very few could lead such a life, however, Porphyry proposed a three-path salvific system that envisioned how different types of souls might advance toward their divine source across several lifetimes.

Porphyry's attack against universalism was not restricted to Iamblichaeans. Chapter 5 explores the ripple effect of Porphyry's arguments within the branch of the Ammonian community represented by Origen's heirs. I focus on the writings of Methodius of Olympus, Porphyry's contemporary and a teacher in the Origenist tradition. Methodius's background is murky, but his strategies of figural reading and his vision of his ascetic community as philosophers ascending from the sensible into the intelligible world place him among those influenced by Origen's exegesis and pedagogy. Moreover, Methodius's *Symposium* sees Christianity as the one path along which the human soul can return to God, and he envisions the purer soul of the ascetic as particularly able to ascend from the sensible into the intelligible realm, even in this lifetime. In Methodius's writings the significance of Porphyry's concerns is easier to see than in the fragmentary remains of the philosopher's own work. As he had done for Iamblichaeanism, Porphyry attacked Origenism by critiquing the exegesis that supported it. For Christians such as Methodius, who based their philosophy without conflicts on a figural reading of Jewish law, Porphyry's political philosophy caught them in a contradiction: their exegesis was appropriate if Jewish law was true and just; but if so, then Christians ought to follow traditional Hebrew sacrificial customs instead of claiming the superiority of a new, Christian law.

The effect of Porphyry's publications in the 290s, written to respond to both Iamblichaeans and Origenists, reverberated far beyond the walls of these scholarly communities. The final chapter, entitled "Conclusion," starts by analyzing Porphyry's fragmentary anti-Christian works and exploring the philosopher's purpose in writing them. Fragments usually attributed to a work entitled *Against the Christians* show how Porphyry's exegesis of Jewish and Christian biblical texts allows him to undermine their utility as prophetic or historical literature respectively. Porphyry concluded that some Jewish texts, such as the book of Daniel, are apocryphal, and so useless as prophetic literature. Since Porphyry found no evidence in either Hebrew scripture or the emerging New Testament canon to corroborate the Christians' claim for the divinity of Jesus, he concluded that he was a fully human being whose worshippers were polluting themselves with blood sacrifices through the Eucharist. Porphyry's *On Abstinence* had argued that polluted people could disrupt divination and civic rituals. His publications, taken together, therefore allowed Hellene readers, especially priests and officials close to Ammonian circles, to conclude that Christians were a danger to the Roman community. Such people, I argue, were active in Antioch when the failed auspices of 299 motivated the court to purge Christians from the eastern army, and to scourge Christian courtiers who refused to sacrifice. This episode marked the start of the emperor Galerius's campaign to turn Diocletian toward a policy of persecution, an effort that culminated in the presentations of Sossianus Hierocles and Porphyry at the imperial court. As a philosopher who had achieved divine union, Porphyry would have seen his visit to Nicomedia as an opportunity to advise the emperors on proper religious practices for all groups within the empire, from ordinary people to those capable of living philosophically.

In the end, an intramural debate between two philosophical circles over the value of sacrificial rituals for philosophically capable people produced the texts and generated the arguments that led indirectly to the Great Persecution. Whether Porphyry started this project with persecution as a goal is impossible to say. Nevertheless, he and the Iamblichaeans shared two fundamental propositions: first, that traditional sacrificial rituals were beneficial for ordinary souls and the general polity; and, second, that a philosopher who had ascended to God outside the cave ought to help the sovereign create legislation that reflected divine law. As Christians began, at the same time, increasingly to serve as magistrates and courtiers in close proximity to traditional sacrificial rituals, those responsible for these rites would have worried about their efficacy and integrity if Christians attending them were polluted. Widespread evidence from the very oracles that Porphyry cited suggests that some priests, some prophets, and their patrons were, in fact, anxious about the steadily increasing prominence of Christian worship. And given the interest in divination that Porphyry shared with Iamblichus, such "concerned citizens" might well have found diviners and public officials willing to advocate their cause. Sometimes, it seems, ideas can motivate religious violence.

❦ CHAPTER 1

Ammonius Saccas and the Philosophy without Conflicts

Ammonius (fl. 232–43), Porphyry averred, "made the greatest advance (ἐπίδοσιν) in philosophy of our time" (ap. Eus. *HE* 6.19.6). Identifying him as the philosophical inspiration for both Origen, the Christian theologian (6.19.6), and the great Platonist Plotinus (Porph. *Plot.* 3.10), Porphyry saw Ammonius as the fountainhead of the true philosophy for his own generation. This view held for over a century: Hierocles of Alexandria (fl. 430) also believed Ammonius had set philosophy back to rights after centuries of error, and he identified Plotinus as one of his most illustrious pupils.[1] Today, the schools of Ammonius's successors, Plotinus and Origen, have markedly different reputations, the former as the place where Neoplatonism coalesced, the latter as the school in which Christian theology steeped deeply in a Platonist spirit. But for Porphyry, writing in the 290s some half a century after Ammonius's death, Origen's failure to follow the way of life exemplified by his mentor meant that these were competing schools. Each had roots in the Ammonian tradition; each claimed a monopoly on truth. Nevertheless, the significance of this competition for religious life at the cusp of the fourth century has not been recognized, because historians, once reluctant to imagine Christians and Hellenes intermingling freely,

---

1. Hierocl. *Prov.* 7 ap. Phot. *Bibl.* cod. 214, 173a18–40. He also listed Origen among Ammonius's worthy successors (see chapter 2).

posited that there were two Ammonii, a Christian instructing Christians and a Hellene training Hellenes. After dispensing with Ammonius's alter ego and sketching the outline of his career, analysis of his hermeneutics, ecumenism, and community commitment illustrates that these values were not only the foundations of his philosophical practice, but also the issues of deepest contention for his heirs.

Porphyry's allusions to the philosopher who made such advances are a good place to start exploring the sage's career, because they led modern historians to imagine the existence of two Ammonii.[2] Porphyry's testimonial to Ammonius occurred in a work identified by Eusebius as the third treatise ($\sigma\acute{v}\gamma\gamma\rho\alpha\mu\mu\alpha$) of those Porphyry "wrote against Christians" ($\tau\widetilde{\omega}\nu$ $\gamma\rho\alpha\varphi\acute{\epsilon}\nu\tau\omega\nu\ldots\kappa\alpha\tau\grave{\alpha}$ $X\rho\iota\sigma\tau\iota\alpha\nu\widetilde{\omega}\nu$).[3] This treatise "against Christians," however, is no longer extant. Rather, Eusebius's own *Historia ecclesiastica (Ecclesiastical History)*, written about a decade later (306), preserves Porphyry's account of Ammonius as a quotation or fragment.[4] The citation appears in Eusebius's defense of Origen (book 6 of the *Ecclesiastical History*), the motivations for which chapter 2 addresses. Eusebius's label for the treatise he quoted may not have matched Porphyry's title. Nevertheless, Eusebius's description explains the treatise's disappearance, since by 325 the Christian emperor Constantine would call for Porphyry's anti-Christian works to be burned (Socr. *HE* 1.9).[5] In the section quoting Porphyry, Eusebius is eager to assert Origen's stature as a Christian teacher and establish his good name. In particular, Eusebius strives to justify Origen's "training ($\mathring{\alpha}\sigma\kappa\eta\sigma\iota\nu$) in philosophy" and "knowledge of the world" ($\tau\grave{\alpha}\ \kappa\sigma\sigma\mu\iota\kappa\grave{\alpha}\ \kappa\alpha\grave{\iota}\ \varphi\iota\lambda\acute{\sigma}\sigma\varphi\alpha$ $\mu\alpha\vartheta\acute{\eta}\mu\alpha\tau\alpha$) (6.18.14). Key to understanding Ammonius and Origen, the passage is worth quoting in full:

> 6.19.1 Among the Hellenes, witnesses of [Origen's] right action regarding these philosophical activities are the philosophers who flourished in his time, in whose treatises we have found frequent mention of the man, sometimes dedicating their *logoi* to him, at other times bringing their own efforts to him as to a teacher or master. (2) Why is it necessary to say these things? Even Porphyry, having settled in our time

---

2. The Athenian philologist Longinus made the first extant references to Ammonius in his treatise *Peri telous* several decades before Porphyry wrote (Porph. *Plot.* 20).

3. All translations are my own unless stated otherwise.

4. R. W. Burgess, "The Dates and Editions of Eusebius' *Chronici canones* and *Historia ecclesiastica*," *JThS* n. s. 48 (1997): 471–504.

5. See the conclusion for a discussion of Porphyry's religious writings and the difficult problem of their dates and titles.

in Sicily, having begun treatises against us, and having tried therein to discredit the Holy Scriptures or set them at variance, mentioned those who interpreted them. Not having been able to bring one trifling complaint as a charge against our doctrines, for lack of arguments, he takes to reproaching and denigrating their exegetes, of whom his target is Origen most of all. (3) Having said that he knew him during his youth, he tries to malign him. But, as it seems, he recommends the man despite himself, making truthful assertions when it was impossible for him to do otherwise, but also representing things falsely where he believed he could escape notice, sometimes denouncing him as a Christian, at other times describing his contribution to philosophical learning. (4) But hear then the things that [Porphyry] says in his own words:

Some, in fact, having been eager to find deliverance from the bad condition of the Jewish writings (but not by distancing themselves from them), turned to exegeses incompatible with and unfit for the things written. Rather than defending their use of what was foreign, these exegeses simply endorsed and praised what was valued by their own communities (οἰκείοις). For having boasted that things declared openly by Moses are enigmas and conjuring them as oracular sayings full of hidden mysteries, they, having bewitched the critical faculty of the soul, bring forward their exegeses.

(5) Presently, after other things, [Porphyry] says:

This kind of logical absurdity is to be derived from a man whom I fell in with (ἐντετύχηκα) while I was still quite young. Very highly esteemed and still popular on account of the treatises he left behind, Origen's renown has been as a student (ἀκροατής) of Ammonius, the man who made the greatest contribution to philosophy in our time. Considering the magnitude of his experience in *logoi,* Origen did gain profit for himself from his teacher; all the same, considering the correctness of his choice of lifestyle (βίου), he conceived for himself the opposite course to Ammonius. (7) For Ammonius, a Christian, was brought up in Christian ways by his parents. But when he attached himself to thinking of philosophy, he turned himself without reserve toward his *politeia* [to live] according to its laws. Origen, conversely, a Hellene, educated in the *logoi* of the Hellenes, drove headlong into shameless foreign (βάρβαρον) activities (τόλμημα). Indeed, applying himself to this, he even offered his skill in *logoi* for sale, living like a Christian and lawlessly in lifestyle, but Hellenizing in his opinions (δόξας) about things as they are (πραγμάτων) and about God, even bringing [opinions] of the Hellenes into foreign myths. (8) For attending always to Plato, he was acquainted with the treatises of Numenius, Cronius, and Apollophanes, as well as Longinus and Moderatus, and even the men held in high regard among the Pythagoreans. But he also used the books of Chairemon the Stoic and Cornutus; having learned from them the method concerning the symbolic interpretation of the mysteries among the Hellenes, he bestowed it upon the Jewish Scriptures.

These things were questioned by Porphyry in the third treatise of his writings against Christians.

Eusebius cites Porphyry verbatim at such length to provide expert testimony for Origen's philosophical proficiency. Yet the bishop does not accept everything that the philosopher says. Eusebius promotes Porphyry's regard for Origen's learning, in fact, while challenging Porphyry's characterization of how Ammonius and Origen lived as Christians. Porphyry tells the truth, Eusebius says, about Origen's training ($\dot{\alpha}\sigma\kappa\dot{\eta}\sigma\varepsilon\omega\varsigma$) and polymathy, but he "plainly lies" in claiming that Origen was originally a Hellene and that Ammonius became a Christian apostate. Eusebius asserts, on the contrary, that Ammonius "kept his divinely inspired ($\dot{\varepsilon}\nu\theta\dot{\varepsilon}ov$) philosophy unmixed and faultless" until his death. As evidence for Ammonius's Christianity, Eusebius refers to "his extant writings," including a treatise "on the harmony ($\sigma\upsilon\mu\varphi\omega\nu\dot{\iota}\alpha\varsigma$) of Moses and Jesus" and "all the other ones" found among those who love beauty ($\varphi\iota\lambda\sigma\kappa\dot{\alpha}\lambda\sigma\iota\varsigma$) (6.19.9–10).

Despite Eusebius's aggressive reshaping of his narrative, Porphyry writes about both Ammonius and Origen with far more authority.[6] Porphyry's testimony that Origen the theologian studied with Ammonius Saccas, the greatest philosopher of his age, should, therefore, be taken seriously. Indeed, Porphyry had firsthand knowledge of Origen the theologian, whom he had met, he says, when he was young. This encounter between Porphyry and the famous Christian exegete occurred around 248–50 in Caesarea or Tyre, and neither Eusebius nor a host of later Christian and Hellene testimonies contested their association.[7] Porphyry does not identify Origen as his teacher,[8]

---

6. G. Fowden, "The Platonist Philosopher and His Circle in Late Antiquity," *Philosophia* 7 (1977): 368; P. F. Beatrice, "Porphyry's Judgment on Origen," in *Origeniana quinta,* ed. Robert J. Daly (Leuven: Peeters, 1992), 352, 361.

7. See chapter 2 for a detailed discussion of Origen's time with Ammonius. Carlo Perelli, "Eusebio e la critica di Porfirio a Origene: L'esegesi cristiana dell'Antico Testamento come metaleptikos tropos," *Annali di Scienzi Religiosi* 3 (1998): 237 n. 16.

8. Andrew Smith and David Wasserstein, eds., *Porphyrii philosophi fragmenta,* Bibl. scriptorum Graec. et Roman. Teubneriana (Stuttgart: Teubner, 1993), 16 n. 12T.

but his description of the theologian's library favors such a conclusion,[9] for the texts Porphyry lists correspond to the curriculum that Origen offered, according to a former student.[10] Thus Origen himself would have told Porphyry that he had once studied with Ammonius. Porphyry would have learned even more about Ammonius through his own mentor, Plotinus, who studied with the Alexandrian for over a decade (Porph. *Plot.* 3.7–19).[11] Porphyry discloses this information in his *vita* of Plotinus, written in 300 (Porph. *Plot.* 23.13). Indeed, of all the extant sources who discuss Ammonius, only Longinus, a scholar with whom Porphyry also studied, can claim more direct knowledge than Porphyry, since he too was Ammonius's student (ap. Porph. *Plot.* 20.35). With regard to both Ammonius and Origen, then, Porphyry is better informed than Eusebius: Porphyry knew Origen directly and knew three other men who had studied with him, but Eusebius knew him only through the documents he left behind or through friends remaining in Caesarea (*HE* 6.2.1),[12] the theologian's home after leaving Alexandria. Even Eusebius's mentor, Pamphilus, studied not with Origen but with a later Alexandrian Origenist, Pierius (Phot. *Bibl.* 118).

Porphyry states plainly and with considerable authority that the Christian theologian Origen was a student of Ammonius, the great philosopher, information with which Eusebius concurs. Hierocles, the fifth-century philosopher, also notes that the esteemed Platonist philosopher Ammonius had a student named Origen,[13] and his contemporary, the church historian and theologian Theodoret of Cyrrhus, identifies "our (τὸν ἡμέτερον) Origen" as a student of Ammonius the philosopher (*Affect.* 6.60). All the same, for most of the twentieth century scholars assumed that the student of Ammonius named Origen who appears in Hellene sources (i.e., Longinus, Porphyry, Hierocles) was a certain "Origen the Platonist" and not the Christian theologian (see chapter 2). Assuming that Christians and Hellenes did not intermingle, scholars also distinguished two Ammonii as teachers of the two Origens. Eduard Zeller is an extreme example, wondering whether the Christian Origen had the two Ammonii as teachers, and whether Ammonius the

---

9. Beatrice, "Porphyry's Judgment," 354.

10. The evidence comes from a speech attributed to Gregory Thaumaturgos, *Pan. Or.* esp. 7–14. See chapter 2.

11. Beatrice, "Porphyry's Judgment," 353–54.

12. Fowden, "Platonist Philosopher," 368. Discussions of Origen's library at Caesarea and Eusebius's use of it include Anthony Grafton and Megan Williams, *Christianity and the Transformation of the Book: Origen, Eusebius, and the Library of Caesarea* (Cambridge, MA: Harvard University Press, 2006); and Andrew J. Carriker, *The Library of Eusebius of Caesarea* (Leiden: Brill, 2003).

13. *Prov.* ap. Phot. *Bibl.* cod. 214, 173a18–40; cod. 251, 461a24–39.

Platonist had the two Origens as students.[14] These violations of Occam's razor derive directly from downplaying the implications of Ammonius's Christian formation and failing to question the assumption that Alexandrian Hellenes and Christians frequented mutually exclusive philosophical circles—even though scholars now see a significant "fluidity of movement" between these communities in the Egyptian capital beginning in the second century.[15] So entrenched are these old assumptions that historians who argue for two Ammonii must argue that both Porphyry and Eusebius were mistaken about the identity of the man so closely connected to their school traditions, with whom they themselves were deeply engaged.

Ammonius's ghost twin was first conjured in the eighteenth century by scholars who took for granted an inherent superiority and exclusivity of Christianity. For example, Johann Fabricius, editor of the *Bibliotheca Graeca,* asserted in 1732 that there must be two Alexandrian philosophers named Ammonius because "a born Christian" would hardly "conver[t] to paganism," as Porphyry seemed to claim, and the "pagan Plotinus would" hardly "spend eleven years" with "a Christian teacher."[16] Zeller revived this theory in the early twentieth century, and H. Dörrie, Richard Goulet, and Mark Edwards embraced it. Dörrie, adopting a Cold War perspective, claimed that "whoever accepts only one Ammonius" allows him "to be a double agen[t]," a person "simultaneously active in a Christian and a non-Christian sense."[17] Despite Porphyry's authority, their own assumptions about Christian behavior led these scholars to believe that the ancient author was mistaken.

Motivated by similar premises, Zeller and Edwards looked to the testimony of Longinus, Porphyry's teacher and Ammonius's student, to tease apart the two Ammonii. Longinus's *On the End,* a treatise written to Plotinus and his student Amelius, is no longer extant, but Porphyry's *Life of Plotinus* quotes from it in order to record the author's esteem for his teacher and his colleague. The passage discussing Ammonius considers the philosopher as an instructor and author:

> When I was a boy there were not a few masters of philosophical argument....Some of them undertook to give posterity the chance of deriving

---

14. Eduard Zeller, *Die nacharistotelische Philosophie,* vol. 3.2, *Die Philosophie der Griechen in ihrer geschichtlichen Entwicklung* (Hildesheim: Georg Olms, 1923; reprint, 1963), 501 n. 1.

15. Frederic M. Schroeder, "Ammonius Saccas," *ANRW* 2.36.1 (1987): 503; G. Fowden, "The Pagan Holy Man in Late Antique Society," *JHS* 102 (1982): 40–48.

16. J. A. Fabricius, *Bibliotheca Graeca,* vol. 4 (Hamburg, 1723), in Schroeder, "Ammonius Saccas," 496.

17. H. Dörrie, "Ammonios Sakkas," *Theologische Realenzyklopädie* 2 (1978): 467; cf. Schroeder, "Ammonius Saccas," 503.

some benefit from them; others thought that all that was required of them was to lead the members of their school to an understanding of what they held.... Of the second [kind] were the Platonists Ammonius and Origen, with whom I studied regularly for a very long time, men who much surpassed their contemporaries in wisdom, and the Successors at Athens, Theodotus and Eubulus. Some of these did write something, for instance Origen, *On the Spirits* (Περὶ τῶν δαιμόνων) and Eubulus, on the *Philebus* and the *Gorgias* and Aristotle's Objections to Plato's *Republic;* but these are not enough to justify us in counting them among those who have written extensively on philosophy; they are occasional works of men whose interest was in teaching, not writing, and who did not make authorship their main concern. Of Stoics in this group there are Herminus and Lysimachus and the two who lived in town, Athenaeus and Musonius, and among Peripatetics Ammonius and Ptolemaeus, both the greatest scholars of their time, especially Ammonius; there has been no one who has come near him in learning: but they did not write any work of professional philosophy, only poems (ποιήματα) and show speeches which I believe to have been preserved without their consent; they would not have wanted to be known in later times by works of this kind when they had neglected to store up their thought in more serious treatises. (ap. Porph. *Plot.* 20.20, 25, 36–58)[18]

According to Zeller and Edwards, because Longinus says that Ammonius, one of the "greatest scholars" of his time, wrote nothing, he cannot be the person who, according to Eusebius (*HE* 6.19.10), wrote several works (ὅσοι ἄλλοι), including a treatise on Moses and Jesus: a Hellene Ammonius wrote nothing, therefore, and a Christian Ammonius wrote the text that Eusebius knows.[19] The argument for two Ammonii requires Eusebius, the only source to portray Ammonius as a "persisting Christian" and as the author of the treatise comparing Moses and Jesus, to have confused Ammonius the philosopher with a Christian author of the same name.[20] Edwards claims further

---

18. Trans. Armstrong.

19. Zeller, *Die nacharistotelische Philosophie,* as cited in Schroeder, "Ammonius Saccas," 496. Mark J. Edwards, "Ammonius, Teacher of Origen," *JEH* 44 (1993): 174–76. See also E. R. Dodds, "Numenius and Ammonius," in *Les sources de Plotin,* Entretiens Hardt (Geneva: Fondation Hardt, 1960), 24–25; W. Theiler, "Ammonios der Lehrer des Origenes," in *Forschungen zum Neoplatonismus,* ed. W. Theiler (Berlin: de Gruyter, 1966), 1; and H. Dörrie, "Ammonios, der Lehrer Plotins," *Hermes* 83 (1955): 439. Schroeder, "Ammonius Saccas," 508, also rejects Plotinus's teacher Ammonius as the author of the tract on Moses and Jesus.

20. R. Goulet, "Porphyre, Ammonius, les deux Origène et les autres," *RHPhR* 57 (1977): 481 incl. n. 27; A. von Harnack, *Geschichte der altchristlichen Literatur* (Leipzig: J. C. Hinrichs, 1904), 2: 81, in Schroeder, "Ammonius Saccas," 507.

that since Porphyry never specifically identified the Christian Origen as a colleague of Plotinus, no evidence connects the Ammonius who taught Origen to the Ammonius who taught Plotinus.[21]

Despite their endurance, none of the arguments for two Ammonii is sound. The problem with Edwards's claim and with arguments assuming that Christians and Hellenes would not intermingle is that Porphyry is extraordinarily unlikely to have been confused about a connection between Origen the theologian, a man he knew, and the identity of the great philosopher who was also the teacher of his mentor, Plotinus.[22] Porphyry's claim that "Origen's renown has been as a student of Ammonius, the man who made the greatest contribution to philosophy in our time" (ap. Eus. *HE* 6.19.5), positively identifies the theologian's teacher as the man whose "mind," he says, Plotinus always "brought... to bear" in his own philosophical discussions (Porph. *Plot.* 14.16–25).[23] Longinus does discuss Ammonius first as a Platonist and then as an Aristotelian, yet no one but Edwards has ever distinguished two Ammonii on that account.[24] Rather, this dual treatment reflects Ammonius's unique proficiency in both Peripatetic and Platonist philosophy, as the man who had first "brought" Plato and Aristotle "under one and the same *nous*,"[25] a point developed below. The Christian Origen is not known for having an Aristotelian perspective,[26] whereas his deep affinities with the Platonist school that Plotinus carried forward (see chapter 2) will be further evidence for his scholarly connection to the Neoplatonist's mentor.

---

21. Edwards, "Ammonius," 174. Edwards draws this implication out of the second text in which Porphyry mentioned Ammonius, his *Life of Plotinus*. This text refers to Origen twice without in any way describing him as a Christian (and so many historians assume that he refers here to "Origen the Platonist"). In the first passage (*Plot.* 3.24–33), Origen and Plotinus—along with their colleague Erennius—agreed not to disclose any of Ammonius's teachings. In the second (14.16–25), dropping in on one of his lectures, Origen embarrassed Plotinus, who was teaching Ammonius's doctrines. As a candidate for the Ammonius who taught the "Christian Origen," Edwards ("Ammonius," 179–80) suggests "Ammonius the Peripatetic," mentioned, he says, by Longinus (ap. Porph. *Plot.* 20.48–49).

22. F. H. Kettler, "War Origenes Schüler des Ammonius Sakkas?" in *Epektasis: Mélanges patristiques offerts au Cardinal Jean Daniélou,* ed. J. Fontaine and C. Kannengiesser (Paris: Beauchesne, 1972), 334; Schroeder, "Ammonius Saccas," 507; E. Elorduy, *Ammonio Sakkas, I: La doctrina de la creación y del mal en Proclo y el Ps. Areopagita* (Oña [Burgos]: Fac. de Teol., 1959), 417; F. H. Kettler, "Origenes, Ammonius Sakkas und Porphyrius," in *Kerygma und Logos: Beiträge zu den geistesgeschichtlichen Beziehungen zwischen Antike und Christentum; Festschrift für Carl Andresen zum 70. Geburtstag,* ed. A. M. Ritter (Göttingen: Vandenhoeck and Ruprecht, 1979), 323.

23. Trans. Armstrong. Kettler, "War Origenes Schüler?" 323. This is one reason why Edwards's "Ammonius the Peripatetic" cannot be the theologian's teacher (see note 21 above).

24. *L'Année Philologique* shows Edwards as the only author who has written on "Ammonius Peripateticus."

25. Hierocl. *Prov.* ap. Phot. *Bibl.* cod. 251, 461a24–39.

26. See David T. Runia, "Festugière Revisited: Aristotle in the Greek Patres," *Vigiliae Christianae* 43, no. 1 (1989): 7, lists and discusses the passages where Origen draws explicitly on Aristotle.

Porphyry's testimony, therefore, rules out the chance that Origen the Christian theologian studied with an Ammonius other than Plotinus's mentor.

Establishing that Origen the Christian theologian studied with the great philosopher Ammonius, however, still does not eliminate the possibility that Eusebius mistakenly attributed the works of a Christian Ammonius to the Alexandrian philosopher, an argument seemingly bolstered by Longinus's categorizing him among philosophers who did not write. In making this claim, Goulet suggested as possible authors of the pamphlet on Moses and Jesus either Ammonius of Thmuis, who sheltered Origen after his exile from Alexandria (ap. Phot. *Interrog. decem* 9), or the Ammonius who wrote the *Evangelical Canons,* a "harmonized account of the four gospels," to which Eusebius refers in his *Letter to Carpianus.*[27] The tenth-century *History of the Patriarchs of Alexandria,* attributed to a Christian author, Severus of Al-Ashmunein (Sāwīrus ibn al-Muqqaffaʻ), distinguishes Ammonius of Thmuis from an Ammonius who rejected Origen's interpretation of scripture:[28]

> So when Origen, whom Demetrius had excommunicated, saw that the Church had rejected him, he went to the Jews, and expounded for them part of the Hebrew books, in a new fashion. . . . He wrote books full of lies and containing no truth. . . . [With Origen was also another "heretic," named Symmachus.] At this time there was a holy and excellent man, who possessed divine wisdom, named Ammonius; and he refuted them both, and exposed their false and unrighteous explanations of the Scriptures, and their lies. After this, Origen went to Caesarea in Palestine, where he had been made priest, and brought books back to Alexandria, in great abundance. But the Father Demetrius would not receive him, and banished him, because he knew what his conduct was. So Origen departed and went to a place called Thmuis in Augustamnica, and invented a plausible story for the bishop, whose name was Ammonius; so he placed Origen in one of the churches. But when Demetrius heard of this, he went himself straightway to Thmuis, and banished Origen,

---

27. Goulet, "Porphyre, Ammonius," 481 incl. n. 27; for an influential argument, see John A. McGuckin, *The Westminster Handbook to Origen* (Louisville: Westminster/John Knox Press, 2004), 5 n. 33. On the *Letter to Carpianus,* see Harold H. Oliver, "The Epistle of Eusebius to Carpianus: Textual Tradition and Translation," *Novum Testamentum* 3 (1959): 138–45; and the translation by Mark DelCogliano, tertullian.org/fathers/eusebius_letter_to_carpianus.htm (accessed 4 December 2008).

28. F. R. Farag, "The Technique of Research of a Tenth-Century Christian Arab Writer: Severus ibn al-Muqaffa," *Le Muséon* 86 (1973): 46–48. On Severus, see Aziz S. Atiya, "Sāwīrus ibn al-Muqaffaʻ," in *The Coptic Encyclopedia* (1991): 2100–102; and Johannes den Heijer, "History of the Patriarchs of Alexandria," in *The Coptic Encyclopedia* (1991): 1238–41.

and removed the bishop Ammonius who had received him, and in his indignation appointed another bishop in his stead.[29]

Identifying Ammonius of Thmuis as the author of texts that Eusebius found in the library of Caesarea, however, creates more problems than it solves, for the bishop of Thmuis is not known to have written anything either. And why assume that the library, founded by Origen and utilized by Eusebius, held this obscure Egyptian's works and not those of the "holy and excellent" Ammonius whom Severus mentions? The latter Ammonius was not only filled with "divine wisdom," but he also knew enough about Christianity to argue against Origen. He is, of course, Ammonius the Alexandrian philosopher, whose written refutations survived for Severus's source to read. Moreover, since Porphyry indicates that Ammonius was a Christian before (if not after) turning to philosophy, nothing prevents him from having authored treatises comparing Moses and Jesus or the Gospels in that period. And since Eusebius's *Ecclesiastical History* was responding to the furor of persecution and the controversy about Origen that Porphyry's writings had helped fuel (see chapters 2 and 6), the historian probably did not carelessly attribute "a tractate written by some other Ammonius to the famous head of the Platonic school."[30]

Yet discounting the possibility that Eusebius wrongly attributed the texts of Ammonius of Thmuis to the Alexandrian philosopher leaves one remaining problem in establishing the number of Ammonii: the apparent contradiction between Longinus's account of Ammonius as a philosopher who did not write and the existence of the Christian tracts in Eusebius's library. Nevertheless, Longinus, his student, actually does not say that Ammonius wrote nothing at all.[31] Rather, in listing philosophers who did not write but "thought that all that was required of them was to lead the members of their school to an understanding of what they held," Longinus includes men who had written a few things, but "not enough to justify us in counting them among those who have written extensively on philosophy."[32] There are, Longinus continues, "occasional works" by these philosophers, "whose interest was in teaching, not writing, and who did not make authorship their main concern." Among their number Longinus even includes Eubulus, who actually wrote three philosophical treatises. Later, Longinus adds that, while "no one has come near" Ammonius "in learning," he and others studying Aristotle

---

29. Trans. B. Evetts, *Patrologia orientalis*, tome 1, fasc. 2, 169–71 (pt 1, ch. 9).

30. H. Langerbeck, "The Philosophy of Ammonius Saccas," *JHS* 77 (1957): 69.

31. Elorduy, *Ammonio Sakkas*, 394; Schroeder, "Ammonius Saccas," 504–5; Langerbeck, "Philosophy of Ammonius Saccas," 74.

32. See chapter 2.

"did not write any work of professional philosophy (τεχνικῶν)," only creative works (ποιήματα) and epideictic speeches (λόγους ἐπιδεικτικούς). Longinus's testimony does not prevent Ammonius the philosopher from having written *anything;* it precludes him from having written very much. And specifically it does not exclude the possibility that he wrote treatises (e.g., on Moses, Jesus, and the Gospels) that were not philosophical in nature.[33] According to J. E. Bruns, Eusebius cites Ammonius's study of Moses and Jesus in his *Demonstratio evangelica* (*Demonstration of the Gospel*) (3.2).[34] Bruns's identification is probably correct, since Eusebius's knowledge of the work suggests its presence in Origen's library, and the passage in question interrupts Eusebius's flow and style. In that case, then, this was not a philosophical treatise, but a point-by-point comparison of activities in which both Moses and Jesus engaged. Longinus would not have found such a text very interesting. Nor would the scholar have cared about the Gospel concordance that Eusebius describes for Carpianus: a text that, alongside the Gospel of Matthew, "placed the corresponding sections of the other gospels." As Edwards concedes, "it would not be strange that such a pagan admirer as Longinus thought" the survival of Ammonius's treatises to be "a matter for regret."[35] That there were "many other" texts, as Eusebius claims, is unlikely. Since Eusebius mentioned these works in order to emphasize Ammonius's commitment to Christianity, he had an interest in overstating the case. Or, more charitably, he may simply have reasoned that there were more texts than the two that he had in hand.[36]

In short, one Ammonius, a philosopher and sometime Christian, instructed the Alexandrian theologian Origen along with Plotinus and Longinus. Beyond this information, very little evidence for Ammonius's career survives. The sources on the philosopher are few: Longinus is the earliest (ap. Porph. *Plot.* 20), writing some time between the 250s and his death in 273.[37] Porphyry's accounts are next, with the treatise dealing with Christianity dating probably from the 290s and the *Life of Plotinus* to 300.[38] Eusebius's account in the *Ecclesiastical History* follows in 306 (6.19.9); he also quotes

---

33. Langerbeck, "Philosophy of Ammonius Saccas," 69.

34. J. E. Bruns, "The Agreement of Moses and Jesus in the *Demonstratio evangelica* of Eusebius," *VChr* 31 (1977): 124–25.

35. Edwards, "Ammonius," 180; E. Elorduy, "Ammonio escriturista," *Estudios Bíblicos* 16 (1957): 187–88.

36. Langerbeck, "Philosophy of Ammonius Saccas," 69.

37. Cf. L. Brisson and M. Patillon, "Longinus Platonicus Philosophus et Philologus," *ANRW* 2.36.7 (1994): 5214–99.

38. See Eus. *HE.* 6.19.6–7; Porph. *Plot.* 3; 7.16–19; 10.1–3; 14.

from the *Harmony of Moses and Jesus* and describes the concordance to the Gospels. No other references to Ammonius survive from the fourth century until Ammianus Marcellinus (22.16) and Nemesius,[39] both writing very late. During the reign of Theodosius II (408–50), Hierocles of Alexandria and Theodoret of Cyrrhus (*Affect.* 6.60) mention Ammonius,[40] but then a century elapses until Priscian of Lydia makes note of him (*Solutiones ad Chosroes* 42.15).[41] Finally, Ammonius appears in the tenth-century *History of the Patriarchs of Alexandria* (1.4) by Severus of Al-Ashmunein.

The portrait that these sources construct is very faint. Neither the date of Ammonius's birth nor when he opened his school is known, although a good estimate is that he was born around 175 at the latest and began teaching around 200.[42] The timeline that Eusebius lays out for Origen, such as it is (*HE* 6.1), suggests that he would have heard Ammonius teach during the first decade of the third century (see chapter 2),[43] probably around 205:[44] both Eusebius and a letter by Origen set this experience early in the theologian's teaching career, and he began teaching during the hostilities against Christians in the tenth year of Septimius Severus's reign, that is, between 202 and 203 (Eus. *HE* 6.2.2, 12).[45] If these calculations are accurate, it implies that the twenty-something Origen studied with the thirty-something Ammonius. The only firm dates for Ammonius's career come from Porphyry. He says that at age twenty-eight Plotinus began studying with Ammonius, and he stayed for eleven years. The careful chronology of the *Life of Plotinus* (3.6f.) fixes this episode between 232 and 243, when Ammonius himself was heading into his late 60s.[46] Plotinus decided to leave Alexandria in 243 to join the Persian campaign of Gordian III perhaps because Ammonius had just died.[47] Before that year, Ammonius taught not only Plotinus, Longinus, and Origen, but also Erennius (*Plot.* 3.24–27),[48] Olympius of Alexandria (10.1–2), and Heraclas, bishop of Alexandria.[49]

---

39. *Nat. hom.* M.69.12–76.11; 118.7–125.7 (Telfer).

40. Hierocl. ap. Phot. *Bibl.* cod. 214, 171b38–172a8, 173a18–40; cod. 251, 461a24–39.

41. Theiler, "Ammonios," 37; Schroeder, "Ammonius Saccas," 513.

42. Theiler, "Ammonios," 1.

43. W. Theiler, "Ammonios und Porphyrios," in *Porphyre: Huit exposés* (Geneva: Fondation Hardt, 1966), 87; Beatrice, "Porphyry's Judgment," 359.

44. Origen says that he joined the philosopher after Heraclas had been with him for five years (ap. Eus. *HE* 6.19.13).

45. Septimius Severus was proclaimed emperor on 9 April 193: *P. Dur.* 54 (*Feriale Duranum*) col. iii, line 3, in T. D. Barnes, "The Chronology of Plotinus' Life," *GRBS* 17 (1976): 67 n. 13.

46. Schroeder, "Ammonius Saccas," 498. For the accuracy of Porphyry's chronology, see Barnes, "Chronology of Plotinus' Life," esp. 69–70.

47. Beatrice, "Porphyry's Judgment," 358–59.

48. Dodds, "Numenius and Ammonius," 29.

49. Origen ap. Eus. *HE* 6.19.12–14.

The most certain teaching that Ammonius shared with his students is the harmony between the writings of Aristotle and Plato.[50] E. R. Dodds treated this tenet as a commonplace, and indeed a variety of earlier ancient philosophers had proclaimed the "ultimate harmony of Academic and Peripatetic thought."[51] Nevertheless, other, more recent historians of philosophy have rightly drawn attention to the centrality of this doctrine for the Platonist school founded by Ammonius. As Lloyd Gerson has emphasized, for the Neoplatonists, Aristotle, as Plato's most able student, "was an extremely valuable component of the bridge across the gap between what Plato said and what Plato meant."[52] This is not to say that the Neoplatonists saw Aristotle as always correct.[53] Rather, since they were concerned with crafting a "purified version of Plato's philosophy" and presupposed rather audaciously that the Athenian philosopher could not be read simply at face value,[54] Aristotle was an invaluable guide in helping them "eliminat[e] false interpretations."[55] Evidence that Ammonius strove "to resolve the conflict between the disciples of Plato and Aristotle, showing that their understanding was in fact in harmony regarding the important and most necessary doctrines," comes from the testimony of the fifth-century Neoplatonist Hierocles, who also says that Plotinus subscribed to the form of Platonism that Ammonius first promoted.[56] Hierocles discusses Ammonius's philosophy in three passages from *On Providence,* preserved and epitomized in the ninth-century *Bibliotheca* by the Byzantine bishop Photius:

Regarding those who set [Plato and Aristotle] in discord [Hierocles] argues that they were most mistaken about the intention of the men and departed from the truth.... And he claims that all those formed a long chorus, until the moment of Ammonius's wisdom shone.... For Ammonius purified the doctrines of these ancient men and dispensed with the superfluous claims sprouting from both sides. He thus declared that the thought of Plato is in accord with that of Aristotle (σύμφωνον... τὴν γνώμην ἀποφῆναι) as regards the essential and most necessary doctrines.[57]

50. Theiler, "Ammonios," 90; Dodds, "Numenius and Ammonius," 26.
51. Lloyd P. Gerson, *Aristotle and Other Platonists* (Ithaca, NY: Cornell University Press, 2005), 1.
52. Ibid., 16.
53. Ibid.
54. Hierocl. ap. Phot. *Bibl.* cod. 214, 173a18–40.
55. Gerson, *Aristotle and Other Platonists,* 9 n. 28.
56. Ibid., 9. See also Edwards, "Ammonius," 177–78; and J.-M. Charrue, "Ammonius et Plotin," *Revue Philosophique de Louvain* 102 (2004): 103.
57. Trans. George Karamanolis, *Plato and Aristotle in Agreement? Platonists on Aristotle from Antiochus to Porphyry* (Oxford: Clarendon Press, 2006), 192–93. Hierocl. *Prov.* ap. Phot. *Bibl.* cod. 214, 171b38–172a8.

In the sixth book, Hierocles takes up all philosophers after Plato until Ammonius of Alexandria, whose most illustrious disciples are Plotinus and Origen, and considers Aristotle to be the most important among them. He takes as being in accord (ὁμοδοξία) with Plato's judgment all philosophers after Plato and up to those just mentioned who made a name for their wisdom. Yet he considers to be unworthy and harmful all those who tried to break the accord between Plato and Aristotle. Although they acknowledged Plato as their teacher, they considerably corrupted (νοθεῦσαι) Plato's works, and the same happened with the writings of Aristotle at the hands of those who claimed to belong to his own school. . . . . The seventh book examines a new subject; it focuses on the school of the above-mentioned Ammonius, Plotinus, Origen, Porphyry and Iamblichus and their successors, who as [Hierocles] says, are of the same divine lineage, and up to Plutarch of Athens. . . . [58]

Many of the disciples of Plato and Aristotle employed their zeal and study to show their teachers to be in conflict with one another (συγκρούειν ἀλλήλους) in their fundamental doctrines, and went so far in their quarrel and daring as to corrupt (νοθεῦσαι) the writings of their teachers in order to show them to be contradicting (μαχομένους) each other even more. This passion was constantly present in philosophical schools until Ammonius of Alexandria, the one taught by God (τοῦ θεοδιδάκτου). He was the first who had a godly zeal for the truth in philosophy and despised the views of the majority, which were a disgrace to philosophy. He apprehended well the views of each of the two philosophers and brought them under one and the same *nous* and transmitted philosophy without conflict (ἀστασίατον) to all of his disciples, and especially to the best of those acquainted with him, Plotinus, Origen and their successors. [59]

Hierocles' testimony is unambiguous: Ammonius was the first, since the successors of Plato and Aristotle, to believe not just that the doctrines of the two classical philosophers agreed in their "essential" points, but also that their writings ought to be edited (and so freed of "corruption") in such a way as to harmonize their apparent conflicts. This teaching was so revolutionary that it resulted in a new school of philosophy (or a restoration of that of the early fourth century BCE, as Hierocles would have preferred), a "divine lineage" that preserved a "philosophy without conflicts." Although Frederic Schroeder

---

58. Hierocl. *Prov.* ap. Phot. *Bibl.* cod. 214.8, 173a18–40.
59. Ibid., cod. 251.3, 461a24–39.

thinks that the three passages in Hierocles have nothing to do with Ammonius, it seems unwise to posit that Ammonius's successors would have had a mistaken idea of their founder's teachings, especially since they all saw careful scholarship and attention to the lines of discipleship as integral to the school's tradition.[60]

The implications of Hierocles' remarks are highly significant for this "restored," harmonized philosophy and those who came to embrace it: in order to have found an accord between Plato and Aristotle, Ammonius must have had (and encouraged) sufficient intellectual independence to stand apart from the received traditions and doctrines of both schools and distinguish for himself what was trustworthy information and what was "corruption." Moreover, he must have subjected to analytical reasoning not only texts written in the Peripatetic and Platonist traditions, but even the writings of Plato and Aristotle themselves. In other words, to the traditional literature he applied and promoted a sophisticated hermeneutical approach, first culling reliable information from the dross surrounding it (which required, in turn, a vast knowledge of the subjects discussed within the texts), and then searching for places of resonance across texts and authors. Finally, Ammonius must have subscribed to two chief principles in seeking to determine what is true in philosophy: first, one ought to start with Plato; second, truth ought to emerge in areas of agreement. Whether or not Ammonius wrote very much, such a hermeneutics must have guided his reading of philosophy and his teaching. Hierocles says as much, in fact, and, as subsequent chapters show, all those working within the Ammonian tradition shared this perspective, no matter how much they disagreed about how to apply it. Ammonius's *Harmony of Moses and Jesus* and his Gospel concordance apply this exegetical spirit, one that seeks truth through harmony. Even Longinus, who does not make Hierocles' list of great Ammonian disciples, worked in this tradition, insofar as we can discern from Eunapius's late fourth-century description of him as "a living library and a walking museum," who had been entrusted with "the function of critic of the ancient writers."[61]

Apart from Ammonius's synthesis of Aristotle and Plato, later authors attribute only two other doctrines to him, just one of which is original. Both concern the problem of the union of material and immaterial. According to the late fourth-century bishop Nemesius of Emesa (*Nat. hom.* 2.12),[62] both

---

60. Schroeder, "Ammonius Saccas," 522, 509–11, following H. R. Schwyzer, *Ammonios Sakkas, der Lehrer Plotins* (Opladen: Rheinisch-Westfälische Akademie der Wissenschaften, 1983), 39–51.

61. Eun. *VS* s.v. "Porphyrios"; trans. Wright.

62. M.69.12–76.11; William Telfer, ed., *Cyril of Jerusalem and Nemesius of Emesa* (Philadelphia: Westminster, 1955), 206.

Ammonius and Numenius of Apamea held the Peripatetic doctrine that the soul is the immaterial bond that checks the material body's flux and motion.[63] Nemesius, in a passage considering how immaterial and material might be joined, is also the source for Ammonius's second and more unique teaching (3.20):[64] "How," Nemesius asks, "can the soul be one with the body it has put on? When a coat is put on, coat and wearer do not thereby become united."[65] Ammonius, he reflects, "solved the problem thus":[66] For intelligibles, it is in their nature (1) "to be capable of union with things adapted to receive them, just as much as if they were things that would perish with them"; and (2) "to remain, nevertheless, unconfused with them while in union, and imperishable, just as though they were merely juxtaposed"; for, he says, "the union of bodies always involves some alteration in them as they enter into union." But "in the case of intelligibles," conversely, "union takes place and yet no change in the results." This paraphrase of Ammonius articulates a "peculiarly Neoplatonic dogma."[67] Although J.-M. Charrue argued that the second part of this doctrine sets the human person as a being apart from the rest of the created cosmos,[68] Ammonius's statement actually sets out a framework for understanding the divinization of matter, in animating a statue, engaging in any form of divination, or conceptualizing a place as sacred. It also establishes how a soul might be in a suitable condition to achieve some sort of union with the One during this lifetime and to return to its source after the death of the body.

Evidence for Ammonius's doctrines extends just this far. Scholars have tried to extrapolate Ammonius's teachings from doctrines that Plotinus taught. These suggestions are plausible but speculative. For example, W. Theiler claimed that Ammonius opposed the Gnostic conception of an evil demiurge, and Denis O'Brien argued that he taught "émanation intégrale," that everything flowed

---

63. Trans. Telfer. Edwards, "Ammonius," 176–77. See Dodds, "Numenius and Ammonius," 25.

64. M.118.7–125.7. A treatise of Porphyry is his likely source. Dodds, "Numenius and Ammonius," 25; Schroeder, "Ammonius Saccas," 522.

65. Contra John M. Rist, "Pseudo-Ammonius and the Soul/Body Problem in Some Platonic Texts of Late Antiquity," *AJPh* 109 (1988): 402–15, who argues that Nemesius took this doctrine from an anonymous Christian invoking Ammonius's authority. This expression is compelling evidence that Porphyry is Nemesius's source (see note 64), for he describes bodies as "tunics of skin" in *Abst.* 1.31.3 and 2.46.1 (trans. Clark), a turn of phrase that may have its roots in Gen. 3:21. For Porphyry's use of this phrase, see Beatrice, "Porphyry's Judgment," 362, 367 n. 92; and id., "Le tuniche di pelle: Antiche letture di Gen. 3:21," in *La tradizione dell'Enkrateia: Motivazioni ontologiche e protologiche,* ed. U. Bianchi (Rome: Ed. dell'Ateneo, 1985), esp. 468–69.

66. Trans. Telfer.

67. Edwards, "Ammonius," 177.

68. Charrue, "Ammonius et Plotin," 81–83.

indirectly from the One with Soul as the final creator.[69] Nor is it certain that Plotinus's doctrine of the One came from Ammonius, so H. R. Schwyzer.[70] Perhaps Ammonius wrote little because he took seriously Plato's seventh letter, so A. H. Armstrong (344c: "Every serious man in dealing with really serious subjects carefully avoids writing"),[71] or his second (314a: "Beware... lest these doctrines be ever divulged to uneducated people").[72] Perhaps the oath of secrecy that Ammonius's disciples Erennius, Origen, and Plotinus swore upon his death was "an obvious form" of Pythagorean religiosity, so Dörrie,[73] although Longinus does not list him as a Pythagorean. Dörrie also thought that Ammonius might have been an early enthusiast for theurgy, given the title of Origen's treatise *On Daemons* and the efforts of the philosopher's student Olympius to put a "star-stroke" ($\dot{\alpha}\sigma\tau\vartheta o\beta o\lambda\tilde{\eta}\sigma\alpha\iota$) on Plotinus (Porph. *Plot.* 10.1–3).[74] As stated, this possibility is unlikely: Ammonius probably did not know the term "theurgy," given its first appearance in the late second-century *Chaldaean Oracles*,[75] and Dodds conflates theurgy with the harmful activity that Porphyry clearly labeled as "magic" ($\mu\alpha\gamma\epsilon\acute{u}\sigma\alpha\varsigma$) in describing Olympius's efforts to curse Plotinus. Nevertheless, Plotinus, for his part, wanted to see his "companion spirit evoked" ($\alpha\dot{u}\tau\tilde{\omega}$ οἰκείου δαίμονος καλουμένου) in an Egyptian ceremony that Iamblichus might later have called theurgic (see chapter 4). Connecting Ammonius to theurgy through Plotinus's interest is also speculative but is at least in keeping with third-century Platonist usage.

Finally, there are the opinions concerning Ammonius's sobriquet Saccas. This appellation first appears in Ammianus 22.16 (*Saccas Ammonius Plotini magister*) as he identifies a few former residents of Alexandria's Brucheion district. Although Dörrie thinks that the name "Saccas" should be excised from Ammianus's text because it precedes "Ammonius," such an action pre-

---

69. Theiler, "Ammonios," 87; Denis O'Brien, "Plotinus and the Secrets of Ammonius," *Hermathena* 157 (1994): 124–30.

70. H. Savon, "Le prêtre Eutrope et la 'vraie circoncision,'" *RHR* 199 (1982): 273–302, in Schwyzer, *Ammonios Sakkas*, 97.

71. A. Hilary Armstrong, "The Hidden and the Open in Hellenic Thought," *Eranos-Jahrbuch* 54 (1985): 95–96, citing Th. A. Szlesák, "Plotin und die geheimen Lehren des Ammonios," in *Esoterik und Exoterik der Philosophie: Beiträge zu Geschichte und Sinn philosophischer Selbstbestimmung; Rudolf W. Meyer zum 60. Geburtstag*, ed. H. Holzhey and W. Ch. Zimmerli (Basel: Schwabe, 1977), 32–69.

72. Trans. Bury (1929; repr., 1966) for both letters.

73. Porph. *Plot.* 3.24–33; Dörrie, "Ammonios, der Lehrer," 447, contra Dodds, "Numenius and Ammonius," 28 (even though Dodds acknowledges the strong parallel with Pythagoras's pupils); T. Böhm, "Origenes, Theologe und (Neu-)Platoniker? oder: wem soll man misstrauen, Eusebius oder Porphyrius?" *Adamantius* 8 (2002): 16; and Charrue, "Ammonius et Plotin," 94 n. 100.

74. Dörrie, "Ammonios, der Lehrer," 442.

75. For the date, see Sarah Iles Johnston, *Hekate Soteira: A Study of Hekate's Roles in the Chaldean Oracles and Related Literature* (Atlanta: Scholars Press, 1990), 2 n. 5.

supposes that we know which order is correct.[76] The second occurrence of the name is in Theodoret's *Graecarum affectionem curatio* 6.60:[77]

> It is under [Commodus] that Ammonius—named Saccas (ὁ ἐπίκλην Σακκᾶς)—having abandoned the sacks in which he carried wheat, embraced the life of philosophy. He had, it's said, our Origen (τὸν ἡμέτερον) as a student, and Plotinus, of whom we're speaking. It's not for the pleasure of idle gossip that I've given this chronological information, but to show that Plotinus had not only studied the doctrine of the Hebrews, like Plato, but also that of the fisherman and of the carpenter, and that he had learned from this source that it is from the Intellect and its Logos that the Universe takes its origin and its dimensions and had been able to find the harmony that suited it.

The first thing to notice is that Theodoret's syntax does not require "Saccas" to follow "Ammonius" either (phrasing that the Suda preserves). Hierocles referred to Ammonius as taught by God (θεοδίδακτος). If he used this term to mean that Ammonius lacked conventional philosophical training, Theodoret might have correctly construed "Sakkas" as "sack carrier" (although it is possible that Theodoret did not know what to make of this epithet either).[78] In any event, "Saccas" or "Sakkas" probably does not refer to a rough form of the philosopher's garb.[79]

Jean Daniélou suggested an alternative approach to Ammonius's unusual name. Puzzling over the name while lecturing on the fourth century, Daniélou suggested that Ammonius Saccas or Saccas Ammonius was a "latinisation or hellenisation of the Sanskrit 'Muni Sakya' or Sakyamuni, which is a well known form of appellation for the Lord Buddha." If so, "Ammonius, whatever his nationality," might have been "a Buddhist monk, who took on for himself one of the many names by which the master was called."[80] Indeed, Buddhism has a tradition of understanding certain sages as incarnations of Sakyamuni.[81] Such claims used to be dismissed out of hand, but scholarship

---

76. Dörrie, "Ammonios, der Lehrer," 467.

77. The Suda s.vv. "Ammonios," "Plotinos," and "Origenēs" all depend on the latter source.

78. Charrue, "Ammonius et Plotin," 72–74.

79. Contra Langerbeck, "Ammonius Saccas," 68; Schroeder, "Ammonius Saccas," 521; and Schwyzer, *Ammonios Sakkas*, 83.

80. Daniélou, in Paulos Mar Gregorios, "Does Geography Condition Philosophy? On Going Beyond the Oriental-Occidental Distinction," in *Neoplatonism and Indian Philosophy*, ed. Paulos Mar Gregorios (Albany: SUNY Press, 2002), 16.

81. Lide Feng and Kevin Stuart, "Folklore concerning Tsong-kha-pa," *Asian Folklore Studies* 51, no. 2 (1992): 220, 223–24, 226, 234.

has been less quick to jettison the potential connections between India, Persia, and the eastern empire, especially in a city such as Alexandria. In this context, Plotinus's desire to join Gordian's Persian-bound troops in order to study philosophy there and in India would indicate an interest in exploring the roots of Ammonius's thought (Porph. *Plot.* 3.13–17).[82] Such a connection is not as far-fetched as it might sound, for within Ammonius's lifetime, Philostratus's *Life of Apollonius of Tyana* imagined that the first-century sage had traveled extensively in India, absorbing much of its wisdom. And Mani was active in Persia, crafting his own synthesis of Buddhism, Judaism, Christianity, and Zoroastrianism (he considered himself the last in a line of prophets from Adam and Buddha, and Zoroaster to Jesus).[83] Moreover, during the period in which Ammonius was teaching, Buddhism itself was developing the "systematic hermeneutical disciplines known as the Mādhyamika and Vijñānavāda" schools.[84] Like Platonism, Buddhism, an older system, had a set of core texts attributed to the master himself, in addition to centuries of texts purporting to interpret or expand the master's teaching. Buddha, too, like Plato's Socrates, "sought to encourage the individual disciple's ability to think for himself."[85] When Ammonius was active, Buddhist scholars to the east were engaged in hermeneutic excavation of this entire textual tradition, an activity that bears a striking resemblance to Ammonius's approach to finding the "true philosophy." In India, "a practitioner's first task" was to "sift through the complexities of Doctrine to discover its inner meaning." "Hermeneutical strategies" were intended to guide "the practitioner's analytical meditations, wherein the first two stages of wisdom" were "cultivated through a refined discipline of philosophical criticism of all false views . . . as to the nature of ultimate reality and the self." Even the ultimate goal of transcendent experience, which was certainly Plotinus's objective, if not that of Ammonius, was understood as "an affirmation of empiricism, a rational acknowledgement" that reality was never "reducible to what we may say about it."[86]

As a great emporium, Alexandria was home to Indian communities, many of whose residents may have been employed in the trade that connected the subcontinent with Rome via the Red Sea. Dio Chrysostom in the second century mentions Indians participating in Alexandria's "spectacles" (*Or.* 32.40). Pantaenus, a Christian teacher in Alexandria during the second cen-

---

82. Charrue, "Ammonius et Plotin," 72–76.
83. M299a R5–6 in Samuel N. C. Lieu, *Manichaeism in the Later Roman Empire and Medieval China* (Tübingen: J. C. B. Mohr, 1992), 18.
84. Robert A. F. Thurman, "Buddhist Hermeneutics," *JAAR* 46, no. 1 (1978): 20.
85. Ibid., 19.
86. Ibid.

tury, allegedly traveled to India (Eus. *HE* 5.10.2),[87] and Clement of Alexandria, a contemporary of Ammonius, knew specifically of Buddhists (*Strom.* 1.15). I am not interested in proving that Ammonius's approach to Greek philosophy was directly informed by Buddhist hermeneutics. I suggest only that a man who sought true philosophy by distilling common teachings of disparate doctrines might have been open to outside influence, especially if, as Theodoret implied, he came from a working-class family that might have interacted with the merchants who had brought these ideas west.

Whether Ammonius came in contact with Buddhist ideas is a question that can be posed but never resolved, given the little we know of his doctrines. Christianity was a more certain unconventional source of knowledge for Ammonius, at least from the perspective of traditional Greek philosophy. Many scholars assume Ammonius abandoned Christianity, however, upon assuming a philosophical life.[88] Such a claim for apostasy derives from the same assumptions that led many to posit two Ammonii: that Christians were a community apart in Alexandria, and that they held views that Eusebius, our first Christian historical source for the period, saw as normative (i.e., they endorsed martyrdom and deferred to the authority of certain bishops regarding scriptural interpretation).[89] Porphyry (ap. Eus. *HE* 6.19.7) asserts unambiguously that Ammonius turned away from being this sort of Christian. He illustrates this behavior by contrasting Ammonius with Origen, suggesting that a Christian *bios* or style of life is lawless, whereas one guided by philosophy sets a person under the laws of his or her *politeia*. Porphyry's statement indicates that Ammonius achieved "conformity" with the Greco-Roman *mores* and civil code of Alexandria,[90] which, in turn, implies, not that he sacrificed,[91] since such an act does not seem to have been called for, but that he probably did not protest Septimius Severus's

---

87. Although Philip Mayerson, "A Confusion of Indias: Asian India and African India in the Byzantine Sources," *JAOS* 113, no. 2 (1993): 171–72, thinks Rufinus's translation of Eusebius is really referring to southern Arabia.

88. R. Cadiou, "La jeunesse d'Origène: Histoire de l'école d'Alexandrie au début du IIIe siècle," *Etudes de Théologie Historique* 17 (1935): 233–34, in Schroeder, "Ammonius Saccas," 504; Goulet, "Porphyre, Ammonius," 473; Charrue, "Ammonius et Plotin," 79; H. Crouzel, "Origène et Plotin, élèves d'Ammonius Saccas," *BLE* 57 (1956): 193–214; M. Hornschuh, "Das Leben des Origenes und die Entstehung der alexandrinischen Schule," *ZKG* 71 (1960): 1–25, 193–214; Dodds, "Numenius and Ammonius," 1–61; Schwyzer, *Ammonios Sakkas.* For Kettler, "War Origenes Schüler?" 324, not only Ammonius, but also his school, might have originally been Christian. Böhm, "Origenes," 16: "Why should Porphyry invent such a history which Ammonius's pupils would likely reject?"

89. Schroeder, "Ammonius Saccas," 503–4; Dörrie, "Ammonios Sakkas," 467.

90. E. Elorduy, "Ammonio Sakkas, la legenda de su apostasia," *Pensamiento* 3 (1947): 17–20, in Schroeder, "Ammonius Saccas," 503.

91. Contra Langerbeck, "Philosophy of Ammonius Saccas," 69.

edict banning conversion to Christianity (SHA *Sev.* 17.1) when enforced either under Laetus (ca. 202/3) or under Aquila (206–11). What Eusebius calls a persecution ($\delta\iota\omega\gamma\mu\acute{o}\nu$) under this emperor was probably the result of Alexandrian authorities' disciplining those who came forward to protest and resist the edict.[92] As a philosopher, however, Ammonius's *politeia* would also have included the community of philosophers, past and present, whose doctrines he had set at the center of his way of life. Ammonius's achieving conformity with the laws of this *politeia* indicates that Aristotelian logic and time-honored exegetical rules, not the traditions of the mainstream Christian community, would have dictated his reading of texts—including Christian scripture. This conclusion derives logically from re-embedding Porphyry's account of Ammonius into his broader discussion of how Origen violated these very axioms. Accordingly, it is likely that Ammonius was a defector from the form of Christianity we usually imagine when thinking about the past.[93] At the same time, his reorientation need not mean that he lost interest in reading and interpreting Christian texts. As the later example of the emperor Julian indicates, putting philosophy at the center of one's life might require a continuing engagement with Christian texts in order to demonstrate for others what was wrong about the system one had earlier espoused and that so many still followed.[94] Certain modern historians have assumed as much, imagining that Ammonius's school might have been originally Christian, but that its student body changed as Ammonius's beliefs did.[95] Perhaps, they suggest, Ammonius did not leave the church so much as it may have abandoned him, through excommunication after Severus's edicts.[96]

The evidence indicates, however, not only that as a philosopher Ammonius retained an active interest in Christian texts and doctrine,[97] but also that he probably continued to identify as a Christian interested in assessing for himself the truth claims of scripture. In a letter preserved by Eusebius (ap. *HE* 6.19.12–14), Origen says that he wanted to learn about "the doctrines of both the heretics and . . . the philosophers." So, like Heraclas (his student who became bishop of Alexandria), Origen studied with "the teacher of philo-

92. François Ploton-Nicollet, "Septime Sévère et le christianisme: Essai d'étude critique des sources," *LittCael* 1 (2005): 183–84.

93. Edwards, "Ammonius," 180.

94. As Edwards, "Ammonius," 175, observed, it is possible that Ammonius was "a renegade from Christianity, but one who retained such an interest in the traditions of the Church that he continued . . . to discuss them with a sympathy that did not imply belief.

95. Kettler, "War Origenes Schüler?" 324; Böhm, "Origenes," 16.

96. Kettler, "War Origenes Schüler?" 324.

97. Kettler, "War Origenes Schüler?" 324, considers the possibility that Ammonius was excommunicated.

sophic subjects (*φιλοσόφων μαθημάτων*)" (12–13), a reference pointing directly at Ammonius.[98] A comparison of Porphyry's description of Origen's classroom techniques and topics with those of Plotinus provides corroborating evidence for this connection: they are nearly identical (see chapters 2 and 3). In showing that Origen wanted to expose himself to information—both heresy and philosophy—outside what he considered to be mainstream Christian sources, his letter not only proves that he was comfortable studying with a heterodox teacher,[99] but also signals that Ammonius was recognizable to him as a Christian after taking up philosophy. Read with Origen's letter, Porphyry's remarks reveal that Ammonius did not completely leave Christianity to live a philosophical life. Rather, philosophy directed him to embrace the norms guiding his philosophical and political communities.

The two texts for which Eusebius gives Ammonius credit, *On the Harmony of Moses and Jesus* and a harmonized account of the four Gospels, bolster an interpretation of the philosopher as a Christian outside of what Origen would have considered the mainstream. If Eusebius quotes Ammonius's treatise on Moses and Jesus in his *Demonstration of the Gospel* (3.2), then the philosopher set out a systematic, nonallegorical comparison of the two figures, assessing whether Jesus was the one who Moses announced would be "a prophet like me" (Deut. 18:15). Jesus was "like" Moses, according to these parallels: he was an equally exalted prophet, miracle worker, and lawgiver, and he was not God. Eusebius shows that he rejects this typology (and hence that he is quoting someone else) when he later claims that Jesus was "the Word of God, not one like Moses or the prophets that was... the worker of miracles" (*DE* 9.13).[100] A different type of truth claim could have been assessed with Ammonius's harmonized account of the four Gospels, namely that they testified accurately and without contradiction to the life and teachings of Jesus. Eusebius does not acknowledge such a function for this text. Nevertheless, saying that "alongside the Gospel according to Matthew," Ammonius "placed the corresponding sections of the other gospels," Eusebius describes just such a tool. This technique "ruin[ed] the sequential order of the other three gospels, as far as a continuous reading of the text was concerned,"[101] Eusebius complains, but it would have had the salutary advantage of highlighting gaps and discrepancies in the four texts—precisely

---

98. Dörrie, "Ammonios, der Lehrer," 468; Fowden, "Platonist Philosopher," 364; Langerbeck, "Philosophy of Ammonius Saccas," 69, contra Schroeder, "Ammonius Saccas," 495, 505–7, 521.

99. Cadiou, "La jeunesse d'Origène," 233–34.

100. Bruns, "Agreement of Moses and Jesus," 123.

101. Trans. M. Cogliano, http://www.tertullian.org/fathers/eusebius_letter_to_carpianus.htm (accessed 16 January 2009).

the initial approach one would take in assessing the historicity and congruity of the Gospel accounts. Such a project dovetails with the analysis of Moses and Jesus: comparing the Gospel texts would allow the author to have the most confidence that Jesus actually did the things about which the accounts agreed. These more certain activities, then, could be evaluated against Moses' predictions. Both treatises together demonstrate Ammonius's interest in engaging with the literal and historical character of scripture, the foundation on which he seems to have assessed its truth claims. This type of exegesis is also compatible with the analyses Ammonius would have had to apply to Platonist and Aristotelian texts.

This evidence for Ammonius as a sophisticated exegete who applied a strong historical and literal sensibility to scripture concurs with the testimony of the tenth-century Coptic monk Severus of Al-Ashmunein.[102] His account of the Alexandrian patriarchy describes Ammonius as "a holy and excellent man, who possessed divine wisdom." According to Severus, Ammonius "refuted" Origen's efforts to interpret "part of the Hebrew books in a new fashion," a likely reference to Origen's sophisticated figural exegesis, which produced "false and unrighteous explanations of the Scriptures."[103] We already know that Origen chose to study with Ammonius to familiarize himself with heterodox and philosophical perspectives. If Ammonius wrote out some of his more literalist arguments in response to Origen, they might easily have become part of Origen's library for Eusebius to find in Caesarea.[104] In engaging with Origen thus, Ammonius would set a precedent followed by Plotinus, who encouraged his students to analyze the authenticity and logical integrity of Gnostic Christian texts. Chapter 3 argues that Plotinus did this because the proponents of such texts challenged the authority and truth claims of his own school. Ammonius may have been prompted by similar motivations.

Ammonius was not the only Christian of his era to deny the divinity of Jesus on the basis of systematic textual criticism. As Mark Edwards notes, Eusebius cites a third-century source to describe a group, active ca. 200,[105]

---

102. Karen Rae Keck, "Severus of al-Ushmunain," *The Ecole Glossary,* www2.evansville.edu/ecoleweb/glossary.html (accessed 18 January 2006).

103. Bruns, "Agreement of Moses and Jesus," 125; Severus of Al-Ashmunein, *History of the Patriarchs of the Coptic Church of Alexandria,* chap. 4. According to Severus, Ammonius also wrote against Symmachus for his denial that Jesus was the son of God. Here, however, it looks as though he has misread Eusebius (cf. *HE* 6.17), his source, since it was Origen who wrote against the biblical translator Symmachus, for precisely those reasons.

104. Langerbeck, "Ammonius Saccas," 68; Bruns, "Agreement of Moses and Jesus," 124.

105. The "Gaius of Rome" whom Photius (*Bibl.* 48) identifies as the author of a work against Artemon's heresy and the author of the *Little Labyrinth.* Similarities between the extant fragments in

that used Aristotelian logic in their textual criticism of scripture (*HE* 5.28).[106] According to the *Ecclesiastical History,* these people, followers of Theodotus the leatherworker (σκυτεύς),[107] taught that Jesus was "a mere man." He was not the Logos, they thought; rather, from his baptism until his death, the Holy Spirit, working through him, performed the miracles attributed to him (Hippol. *Haer.* 7.23–24). Eusebius's source (5.28.14) grumbles that, instead of learning geometry and reading Euclid, Aristotle, Theophrastus, and Galen—whom they especially admired—Theodotus's followers should have spent that time reading scripture. They then applied their erudition to Christian texts (which could potentially include Jewish materials): Eusebius's source complains that they applied "conjunctive" and "disjunctive" syllogisms" to scripture, "setting aside the rule of faith" and applying "the arts of unbelievers" to actually *correct* the texts, a practice he finds very offensive. These scholars worked collaboratively, for Eusebius's source says that their disciples kept track of all of their changes so that they could easily compare their textual analyses. And he is troubled because one author's changes dis-

---

Eusebius and Hippolytus's *Philosophumena* suggest that Hippolytus is actually the author of the *Little Labyrinth* (Photius elsewhere attributes a work written by Hippolytus to "Gaius" [*NPNF* trans. n. 390 to Eus. *HE* 5.28]). The source describes Zephyrinus of Rome, bishop from 199 to 217.

106. Edwards, "Ammonius," 180. Edwards links Ammonius with the followers of Artemon. But a careful reading of what Eusebius's source says and how he is cited indicates that the parallels Edwards rightly sees should be connected with Theodotus and not Artemon. All we know about Artemon through Eusebius is that he denied Jesus' divinity and that Paul of Samosata in some way "revived" his position (Eus. *HE* 5.28.1; 7.30). The letters of the bishops against Paul, Eusebius's source for this claim (*HE* 7.30), spell out some practices that are similar to the Theodotans. For example, Paul "assails in public the expounders of the Word" who are now deceased, claiming that the psalms to Jesus are "modern productions of modern men," and he "is unwilling to acknowledge that the Son of God came down from heaven" (trans. *NPNF*). It is impossible to know, however, whether he also espoused the Aristotelian, systematic approach to textual criticism, which provides the strongest parallel between Ammonius and the Theodotans. The venues of the two groups may also be different. Eusebius's source links the Theodotans to the city of Rome, whereas Artemon is someone known to Paul and the eastern bishops trying his case.

At *HE* 5.28.1 Eusebius identifies this Artemon with the Artemas referenced in the letter to Dionysius of Rome from the bishops assembled at Antioch in condemnation of Paul of Samosata (ap. Eus. *HE* 7.30). Since the letter sarcastically urges Paul to write to Artemas for help, the editors of the *NPNF* translation of Eusebius's *HE* concluded that Artemon/as must still have been alive in 268—although if he were dead, the satire would be even more biting: "We have been compelled to excommunicate [Paul], since he sets himself against God, and refuses to obey; and to appoint in his place another bishop [Domnus]. … We have informed you [i.e., Dionysius of Rome and Maximus of Alexandria] of this that you may write to [Domnus], and may receive letters of communion from him. But let this man [i.e., Paul] write to Artemas [whose "abominable heresy" he has followed]; and let those who think as Artemas does, communicate with him" (*NPNF* trans.).

107. For the Theodoti, see Hippol. *Haer.* 10.23–24; ps.-Tertullian *Haer.* 8.2–3; Epiphanius of Salamis *Haer.* 54.5; Winrich A. Löhr, "Theodotus der Lederarbeiter und Theodotus der Bankier— Ein Beitrag zur römischen Theologiegeschichte des zweiten und dritten Jahrhunderts," *ZNTW* 87, no. 1 (1996): 101–25.

agree with those of another, and one author even changed his approach to the text over time. Some seem to eschew Jewish texts altogether (ap. Eus. *HE* 5.28). The product of such efforts could be amended versions of Christian and Jewish scripture, whether slight or radical, or even a canon of authentic texts. Further evidence for such activity in the early third century appears in the Muratorian fragment, which not only enumerates a canon and identifies apocryphal works but also hints at some running controversies in its need to assert that "although different points are taught us in the several books of the Gospels, there is no difference as regards the faith of believers."[108]

These similarities are significant, if not to identify Ammonius as a Theodotan. First, they show that Ammonius was not completely anomalous, since other third-century Christians, viewed as heterodox by Eusebius's source, had very compatible ideas. Second, the class of people involved with Theodotus, merchants and tradesmen, draws attention to the type of literate, if not elite circles in which the spread of ideas (e.g., Christianity or Buddhism) might easily take place as commodities and services traded hands—groups in which a working-class Ammonius might have circulated.[109] Ammonius's only known venue was Alexandria, however, whereas known Theodotans—Asclepiadotes, Natalius, and Theodotus the banker—moved in the orbit of the bishop of Rome (ap. Eus. *HE* 5.28).[110] All the same, they and Ammonius deployed the very textual practices that we next see Plotinus's school in Rome applying to certain Gnostic texts. It is tempting to think that after returning from the Persian front Plotinus chose Rome for his school because he knew there would be a community of well-trained sympathetic scholars there, but evidence does not permit this claim.

Ammonius's world was very different from that in which Eusebius and Porphyry wrote, but the fluidity between groups that characterized his Alexandria continued unabated through the late third century. If anything, Gallienus's legalization of Christianity after his father's capture in 260 had intensified these cross-cultural exchanges to involve not only people from the literate trading and craftsman classes, but also more traditional elites. The eagerness with which both Porphyry and Eusebius strove to appropriate Ammonius shows that he was in some way key to their identity either as a Hellene or as a Christian. The way in which they did so, however, illustrates

---

108. For the early date of this text, see E. Ferguson, review of *The Muratorian Fragment and the Development of the Canon,* by Geoffrey Mark Hahneman, *JThS* 44 (1993): 691–97; and William Horbury, "The Wisdom of Solomon in the Muratorian Fragment," *JThS* 45, no. 1 (1994): 149–59.

109. See chapter 2.

110. According to Hippol. *Haer.* 7.23–24; 10.19; Epiph. *Haer.* 54; and Eus. *HE* 5.28 Theodotus the leatherworker came from Byzantium and lived in Rome in the time of Eleutherus or Victor.

their awareness of tensions, unknown to Ammonius, that would culminate in the Great Persecution. Porphyry hints at one of these stresses in focusing on Ammonius's dedication to his *politeia,* whether that meant Hellene culture or the Alexandrian and Roman polities. Here was a man, regardless of his Christian notions, who played by the rules as Porphyry understood them. Such a claim sets great stake in a literal and historical exegesis, as well as a willingness to accept the traditions and laws of the community. Despite his Egyptian residence and ecumenism (including an attachment to Jesus' teachings), factors that, in his own day, would have prevented him from being considered ethnically or culturally "Greek," Ammonius, for Porphyry, was a true "Hellene," because he lived a life that put the divine teachings of Plato and the law of his city at its center. Putting to the side for chapter 3 what this new definition of "Hellene" suggests about Porphyry himself, it nevertheless shows that he had expectations for publicly active Christians trained in the Ammonian tradition—expectations that were not being fulfilled as Origen's theology spread and flourished in Palestine and Asia Minor, and as the Roman government increasingly excused Christian administrators who abstained from traditional cult activity. For Eusebius, Ammonius's significance is that, despite his exposure to Hellene culture and thought, he retained his "divinely inspired philosophy unmixed and faultless" until his death. That is, for Eusebius, Greek philosophy had not corrupted Ammonius's true Christianity. This claim suggests that Eusebius and his circle faced, in addition to the challenge posed by Porphyry, opposition from less culturally fluid Christians who saw contact with Greek philosophy as corrupting their faith and theology. The next chapter addresses where this challenge came from and why.

CHAPTER 2

Origen as a Student of Ammonius

A liminal, hybrid figure whose shadow looms over the third and fourth centuries, Origen of Alexandria is key to understanding both the wide-ranging influence of Ammonius's "philosophy without conflicts" and the new pressures that contributed to the Great Persecution two generations later. Scholars have not appreciated Origen's role in this regard for one of two reasons: either they assumed that he studied with an Ammonius other than Plotinus's teacher, an error addressed in chapter 1, or they downplayed the significance of the Christian theologian's education under Ammonius, assuming that a different philosopher, "Origen the Platonist," was the true heir of his mentor's philosophy. I have argued elsewhere that, like the two Ammonii, the two Origens are an artifact of scholarship conjured by misreading the heated exchange between Eusebius of Caesarea and Porphyry of Tyre embedded in the former's *Ecclesiastical History* (6.19).[1]

---

1. See Elizabeth DePalma Digeser, "Origen on the *Limes:* Rhetoric and the Polarization of Identity in the Late Third Century," in *The Rhetoric of Power in Late Antiquity: Religion and Politics in Byzantium, Europe, and the Early Islamic World,* ed. Robert M. Frakes, Elizabeth DePalma Digeser, and Justin Stephens (London: I. B. Tauris, 2010), 197–218. As chapter 1 noted, in *HE* 6.19, Eusebius refers to Porphyry's "third treatise (σύγγραμμα)" against Christians, not just to condemn its criticisms of Origen, but also to use it as evidence for the theologian's eminence as a philosopher (6.18–19; see chapter 1 for the text). In 1659, Henri de Valois, in his commentary on this work, was the first to use this passage to distinguish between a so-called Platonist Origen and a Christian theologian of the same name. F. H. Kettler, "War Origenes Schüler des Ammonius Sakkas?" in *Epektasis: Mélanges*

The contradictory portraits painted by these two antagonists in their efforts to define him led modern historians to conclude wrongly that two Origens flourished in the third century, a Platonist Hellene and a Christian theologian and martyr. I will not advance the claim for their unity here, since sufficient evidence testifies to the depth of the "theologian's" Ammonian heritage and the problems that he posed for the next generation of Christians and Hellenes working within his tradition.

Analysis of Origen's career and writing shows that his early contact with Ammonius influenced his exegetical methodology and goals. In particular, Origen used some of Ammonius's techniques for handling texts to set out his own "theology without conflicts." Applying these techniques and this goal to Hebrew and Christian scripture, while developing the figural exegesis and conception of Jesus as the incarnate divine *logos* that he learned from Clement of Alexandria, Origen not only countered the view of Jesus as a

---

patristiques offerts au cardinal Jean Daniélou, ed. J. Fontaine and C. Kannengiesser (Paris: Beauchesne, 1972), 327. Valois' commentary is preserved in Migne's edition of Eusebius (PL 20). Valois followed Porphyry in granting that Origen Adamantius, as he called the Christian, had been Ammonius's student. But, he continued, "there was at that same time *another* Origen, a fellow student of Plotinus and Erennius," who is discussed by "Porphyry in the *Vita Plotini*, Longinus in *De fine*, Eunapius, and Hierocles in *De providentia*" (Eus. *HE* 6.1–7.1; Porph. *Chr.* ap. Eus. *HE* 6.19; Or. *Ep.* ap. Eus. *HE* 6.19.12–14; Hierocl. *Prov.* ap. Phot. *Bibl.* 214, 251; Porph. *Comm. Tim.* ap. Procl. *Comm. Tim.* 1.63; Long. *De fine* ap. Porph. *Plot.* 20.35; Porph. *Plot.* 3.24–33; 14.21; Eun. *VS* s.v. "Porphurios"). Although Valois did not consider whether any discernable doctrinal differences existed between "their" ideas, his distinction between a pagan and a Christian Origen so readily conformed to the adversarial relationship between "paganism" and Christianity constructed in the exchange between Porphyry and Eusebius that most subsequent historians simply took his assumption for granted, perpetuating the ancient rhetoric without much question. And so the Platonist Origen was born. Accepted by Fabricius fifty years later (J. A. Fabricius, *Bibliotheca Graeca,* vol. 4 [Hamburg, 1723], 97, 160; cf. P. F. Beatrice, "Porphyry's Judgment on Origen," in *Origeniana quinta,* ed. Robert J. Daly [Leuven: Peeters, 1992], 352, 363 n. 6), Valois' arguments gained momentum in the late nineteenth century with Eduard Zeller. Still without comparing Origen's doctrines as presented in the two groups of sources, Zeller asserted that Porphyry—and possibly Eusebius, too—mistakenly conflated the two figures (Eduard Zeller, *Die nacharistotelische Philosophie,* vol. 3.2, *Die Philosophie der Griechen in ihrer geschichtlichen Entwicklung* [Hildesheim: Georg Olms, 1923; repr., 1963], 513–19, incl. 513 n. 3). In 1955, Heinrich Dörrie perpetuated the assumption that Porphyry had confused a Platonist philosopher with the Christian theologian (H. Dörrie, "Ammonios, der Lehrer Plotins," *Hermes* 83 [1955]: 440–41, 468–72; repeated in id., "Ammonios Sakkas," *Theologische Realenzyklopädie* 2 [1978]: 463–71, esp. 465). As chapter 1 shows, these scholars had also distinguished two Ammonii for very similar reasons. Subsequently, most historians of philosophy and theology accepted their arguments for two Origens as well (K. O. Weber, *Origenes der Neuplatoniker* [Munich: Beck, 1962], 15–40, esp. 34; R. Goulet, "Porphyre, Ammonius, les deux Origène et les autres," *RHPhR* 57 [1977]: 471–96, esp. 485–91; A. H. Armstrong, "Plotinus and Christianity," in *Platonism in Late Antiquity,* ed. Stephen Gersh, Charles Kannengiesser, et al. [Notre Dame, IN: University of Notre Dame Press, 1992], 116; A. H. Armstrong, "Plotinus and Christianity: With Special Reference to 119 (33) 9.26–83 and V8 (31) 4.27–36," *Studia Patristica* 20 [1989]: 83; Mark J. Edwards, "Ammonius, Teacher of Origen," *JEH* 44 [1993]: 169–81; John J. O'Meara, in Origen, *Prayer; Exhortation to Martyrdom,* trans.

Moses-like prophet, teacher, and lawgiver that Ammonius and the Theodotans were promoting, but he also set out a controversial hermeneutics that Porphyry would later challenge. Similarities between the ways in which Plotinus and Origen—both students of Ammonius—presented themselves as teachers suggest that the theologian also appropriated his mentor's pedagogical techniques. In Origen's case, his instruction guided gifted students toward philosophy and the exegetical methods he developed to yield a theology without conflicts. Confidence in this theology without conflicts and the divine law that he believed infused it led Origen to encourage other students, however, to testify to its truth by embracing martyrdom, violating the Roman law to which they were obliged as citizens. Porphyry would condemn Origen's guidance of his students on both counts.

A native of Alexandria, Origen was sixteen when his father died a martyr under the emperor Septimius Severus's edict banning conversion to Christianity or Judaism (202/3).[2] Since he was beheaded, Origen's father must have been either a Roman citizen or a *honestior*—a man of some social standing. Although the family lost its property after his conviction,[3] Origen was able to continue his education, thanks to a rich widow's patronage (Eus. *HE* 6.2.13).

John J. O'Meara, Ancient Christian Writers [Westminster, MD: Newman Press, 1954], 7). All the same, a growing number of scholars now realizes that the so-called Platonist Origen is a mirage (e.g., T. Böhm, "Origenes, Theologe und [Neu-] Platoniker? Oder: wem soll man misstrauen, Eusebius oder Porphyrius?" *Adamantius* 8 [2002]:7–23; Beatrice, "Porphyry's Judgment," 351–67; F. H. Kettler, "Origenes, Ammonius Sakkas und Porphyrius," in *Kerygma und Logos: Beiträge zu den geistesgeschichtlichen Beziehungen zwischen Antike und Christentum; Festschrift für Carl Andresen zum 70. Geburtstag*, ed. A. M. Ritter [Göttingen: Vandenhoeck and Ruprecht, 1979], 322–28; R. Cadiou, "La jeunesse d'Origène: Histoire de l'école d'Alexandrie au début du IIIe siècle," *Etudes de Théologie Historique* 17 [1935]: 184f.). The most compelling evidence for their unity is that the doctrines attributed to the Platonist wholly agree with the extant texts of the Christian theologian. Despite Mark Edwards's arguments to the contrary (Edwards, "Ammonius," 169–81; Mark J. Edwards, *Origen against Plato* [Aldershot, UK: Ashgate, 2002], 54–55; id., *Culture and Philosophy in the Age of Plotinus* [London: Duckworth, 2006], 28), Thomas Böhm has demonstrated this accord (see Digeser, "Origen on the *Limes*," 208–10), but even those scholars who have striven hardest to distinguish two Origens have conceded the unity of "their" doctrines (e.g., Weber, *Origenes,* 30; see also Henning Ziebritzki, *Heiliger Geist und Weltseele: Das Problem der dritten Hypostase bei Origenes, Plotin und ihren Vorkaufern* [Tübingen: Mohr, 1994], 37; and H.-J. Vogt, "Origenes," *LThK* 7 [1998]: 1135–36, in Böhm, "Origenes," 7; Zeller, *Die nacharistotelische Philosophie,* 501 n. 1, is an exception, but he never proves that the theologian "does not have the opinions which we find in the Platonists"). It is not a trivial point: are there any two Hellene and Christian authors for whom we can also say that their views are identical? The identity of the two personae is further confirmed by the data regarding "their" lifetimes, venues, and writings (Böhm, "Origenes," 8).

2. Eus. *HE* 6.2.2, 12; SHA *Sev.* 17.1; Kettler, "War Origenes Schüler?" 323; Weber, *Origenes,* 18–19; Böhm, "Origenes," 19. Septimius Severus was proclaimed emperor on 9 April 193 and passed the edict in the tenth year of his reign. Cf. *P. Dur.* 54 (*Feriale Duranum*) col. iii, line 3, in T. D. Barnes, "The Chronology of Plotinus' Life," *GRBS* 17 (1976): 67 n. 13.

3. T. D. Barnes, *Constantine and Eusebius* (Cambridge, MA: Harvard University Press, 1981), 83.

Supporting himself by teaching grammar (6.2.15, 6.3.9), Origen soon began schooling Christian catechumens before their baptism, a position for which Demetrius, the city's bishop, ultimately gave him exclusive responsibility (6.3.1, 3, 8; 6.4.3).[4] In this task, he probably replaced his former teacher, Clement of Alexandria (6.6.1), who had left the city in response to the Severan edicts.[5]

A few years after starting to prepare Christians for baptism, Origen joined Ammonius's circle (see chapter 1), a move confirmed and explained by a letter he wrote, which is preserved by Eusebius (*HE* 6.19.12): "Since I was devoted to lecturing, and the fame of our proficiency was spreading abroad," Origen remarks, "there approached me sometimes heretics, sometimes those involved in the scholarship of the Hellenes (τῶν Ἑλληνικῶν μαθημάτων)—especially those involved in philosophy, and I thought it right to examine both the opinions of the heretics and also the claims that the philosophers make to speak about truth."[6] The letter shows that as a teacher of grammar and catechesis, Origen was attracting two groups of students whose concerns his education with Clement had poorly equipped him to address. Some, who need not all have been Christians, were interested in Greek philosophy (6.18.1–4); others were Christians outside what Origen considered to be the mainstream. One such heterodox auditor was Ambrose, a Gnostic who, as a result of his training with Origen, not only gave "his adhesion to the true doctrine as taught by the church,"[7] according to Eusebius, but also became his teacher's patron, supplying him with scribes and stenographers (6.18.1, 6.23.1).[8] To be a more effective teacher for these students, Origen went to study with Ammonius Saccas, whom he calls the "teacher of philosophy."[9] Although Origen felt a need to defend his study with a heterodox Christian and Hellene philosopher,[10] this decision was not unprecedented within Alexandria's Christian community: indeed, he

---

4. Barnes, *Constantine and Eusebius,* 83, sees Demetrius's involvement as occurring in 211 or later.

5. Joseph W. Trigg, *Origen* (London/New York: Routledge, 1998), 14.

6. Trans. Oulton throughout unless otherwise noted. Here Oulton's translation is slightly modified.

7. Barnes, *Constantine and Eusebius,* 84, places Ambrosius's conversion after 217, but it is impossible to know when the two men first made contact during Origen's residence in Alexandria.

8. Origen also engaged with other Gnostics when he lived in Alexandria. According to Jerome (*C. Ruf.* 2.18–19), the *Dialogue* with the Gnostic Candidus (now lost) preserved Origen's belief in the devil's potential redemption. And the *Commentary on John* aimed at refuting the arguments of Heracleon, a second-century Gnostic. Origen's interest in addressing Gnostic doctrines may have derived, in part, from his patron Ambrose's involvement and encouragement (Eus. *HE* 6.23.1).

9. See chapter 1.

10. Kettler, "Origenes," 324 incl. n. 20.

justifies his studies by citing the examples of Pantaenus, who first organized Alexandria's catechetical training (5.10.1), and Heraclas, his own student and future Alexandrian bishop, who had already spent five years with Ammonius (6.19.13).[11] Ammonius's and Origen's schools together, then, encouraged some Hellenes and some Christians to discuss philosophy with one another regardless of their teacher's religious affiliation. Alexandria's intellectual life in the early third century, therefore, did not foster sharply circumscribed camps of Christians and Hellenes; rather, these groups intermingled relatively freely. Origen was not only open to teaching Hellenes alongside Christians, but he also included women among his students. Eusebius says that Origen castrated himself to prevent people from criticizing him as a young man meeting with women (6.8).[12]

Between autumn 206 and early 211, as prefect of Egypt Subatianus Aquila resumed the policy of Severus's 202/3 edict prosecuting converts to Christianity and Judaism.[13] Preparing any student for baptism violated the spirit if not the letter of the edict, but Origen pushed his students further into what Porphyry would later condemn as lawlessness: Eusebius records the stories of these students, men such as Plutarch, who abandoned traditional cult (ἀπὸ τῶν ἐθνῶν) for Christianity and then embraced martyrdom (*HE* 6.3.1–2). To protect himself, Origen went underground, teaching in a variety of safe houses in the city (6.3.6). Encouraging some of his students to become martyrs while avoiding it himself suggests that he did not embrace the tenet, later articulated by Cyprian,[14] that one ought not seek out such a death. Rather, he may have thought some souls more suited to join with God through the death of a martyr, others more disposed to find God through scholarly exegesis. He may no longer have been welcome in Ammonius's circle, however. Continuing to act within the law (see chapter 1), Ammonius was concerned, not with making Christians, but with training students to understand the philosophy without conflicts derived from a proper reading of Plato and Aristotle.

In 211, Aquila's prefecture and Septimius Severus's reign ended, and Origen resumed a public life. He began traveling frequently and writing prodigiously. Wanting more time for "the examination and translation of the sacred writings" (Eus. *HE* 6.15.1), he gave up teaching literature (i.e., as a *grammateus*), selling his books and assigning the introductory and more ignorant

---

11. See chapter 1.
12. R. P. C. Hanson, "A Note on Origen's Self-Mutilation," *VChr* 20, no. 2 (1966): 81–82.
13. *PIR*[1] S 681; T. D. Barnes, "Origen, Aquila, and Eusebius," *HSPh* 74 (1970): 314.
14. The classic text is Cyp. *De lapsis* (*Ep.* 54.4), which draws on Matt. 10:23.

(ἰδιωτικωτέρων) pupils to Heraclas (6.15, 18, 26). Taking up an ascetic regimen for himself (6.3.8–9),[15] Origen kept the advanced and the "naturally gifted" (εὐθυῶς) students to whom he taught philosophy (6.15, 6.18.2–3), activities discussed in more detail at this chapter's end.

One of the translation projects that Origen began in this period was the *Hexapla,* a tool for textual criticism of Jewish scripture, which, at its greatest extent, arrayed in six parallel columns the Hebrew text, a Greek transliteration, the Greek translation of Aquila (ca. 130 CE), the late second-century Greek translation of Symmachus, the third-century BCE text of the Septuagint, and the late second-century Greek translation of Theodotion. For this monumental endeavor Origen learned Hebrew (Eus. *HE* 6.16.1), an effort that presupposes close contact with rabbis or Jewish translators. Across the years that he worked on this project (at least into the 230s),[16] Origen continued to include texts of other scriptural books as he discovered them (6.16.1), although where and when he found most of them is unknown.[17] This project closely connects Origen with Ammonius's school, which would have engaged in a similar type of research and analysis to evaluate the reliability of copies of works by Plato, Aristotle, and their commentators. Only after aligning different copies of a work in parallel fashion could apparent contradictions between the texts be resolved as a preliminary to sophisticated exegesis. Origen's project is also analogous in form to Ammonius's concordance of the Gospels, to which Eusebius referred in his letter to Carpianus.[18]

Early in his career at Alexandria, Origen wrote *Peri archōn* (*On First Principles*) (Eus. *HE* 6.24.3). If there was a logical system to his work, *Peri archōn* would have been relatively contemporary with the *Hexapla,* for both are exegetical tools.[19] The *Hexapla* helps the biblical scholar establish the most plausible reading of a given scriptural passage, the first step in any exegetical exercise. The second step, as Origen's treatment of the Doctrine of Peter

---

15. He may have castrated himself in this period (6.3.9), if he had not done so before. Contra Barnes, *Constantine and Eusebius,* 83, dating this act precisely is impossible.

16. References in Origen's *Epistle to Julius Africanus* and his *Commentary on Matthew* indicate that he continued working on the *Hexapla* well into the 230s: T. M. Law, "Origen's Parallel Bible: Textual Criticism, Apologetics, or Exegesis?" *JThS* 59, no. 1 (2008): 4.

17. He found one text at Nicopolis; another, discovered in a jar during Caracalla's reign, came from Jericho (Eus. *HE* 6.16.2–3). He obtained Symmachus's translation from a certain Juliana to whom the translator had given the texts (6.17.1). According to Palladius *Lausiac History* 64, Juliana gave these to Origen at her house in Caesarea. See note 83 below.

18. See chapter 1.

19. G. Bardy, *Recherches sur l'histoire du texte et des versions latines du 'De principiis' d'Origène* (Paris: É. Champion, 1923), 7–8, agrees. Pierre Nautin, *Origène: Sa vie et son oeuvre* (Paris: Beauchesne, 1977), 370–71, sets it after the commentaries on the Psalms and on Genesis because he thinks Origen interrupted these exegetical works to defend his heterodox method with *Peri archōn.*

in the preface to *Peri archōn* makes clear (*PA* pr. 8), is to establish the text's authenticity—a process for which Origen provides no surviving guidelines but which deeply concerned him in this early period.[20] In Plotinus's school Ammonius's heirs also followed these steps in assessing the authenticity of various Gnostic texts before engaging with them philosophically (Porph. *Plot.* 16). The third step is to establish the genre of the text and set it in its historical context.[21] Porphyry, for his part, assiduously took genre into account before engaging in exegesis.[22]

After describing these preliminary exegetical steps, *Peri archōn* then provides the tools for interpreting scripture once the contents, authenticity, and genre of its books have been established. The treatise begins by setting out the elements and foundations of Origen's system. Origen claims that the fundamental principles he will discuss had been preserved in "the teaching of the Church," which received them "in orderly succession from the apostles." To make this claim, Origen follows very closely in Ammonius's footsteps, but they lead Origen to opposite ends. Unlike the great second-century Gallic bishop and theologian, Irenaeus (*Adv. haer.* 3.3.1), Origen does not see bishops per se as the guardians of true doctrine. Rather, he claims that his foundational principles differ "in no respect from ecclesiastical and apostolical tradition" (*PA* pr. 2).[23] In this treatment of received tradition, Origen differs from Ammonius, who thought that later commentators on Plato and Aristotle had not conveyed their masters' teaching accurately.[24] Origen and Ammonius are more similar than they appear, however, since both rejected a more skeptical branch of their tradition in claiming that their teaching carried forward the original doctrine of the tradition's founder. Like Ammonius, who rejected Academic skepticism in favor of a more theologically infused Platonism, Origen

---

20. For example, in his commentary on the first twenty-five Psalms, Origen asserted that there were twenty-two canonical books of Hebrew scripture (ap. Eus. *HE* 6.25.1–2), and his *Expositions on the Gospel of John* show him to be similarly concerned with letters attributed to Paul and Peter (6.25.5, 7–14).

21. See, for example, *CSong* pr. 1.1 and *Comm. in Lam.* 1–3.

22. Porph. *Plot.* 16; *Antr.* 1. See chapter 5.

23. All translations are from the *ANF* edition unless otherwise noted. Apart from a few Greek fragments, *Peri archōn* survives only in the late fourth-century Latin translation of Rufinus. It is likely that his translation of Origen's preface brings it a bit closer to the mainstream than the, now lost, original Greek may have, given the controversies that raged over Origen's theology, not only ca. 300 (see chapter 5), but also late in the fourth century. For a discussion of how Rufinus shaped Origen's text, see Franca Ela Consolino, "Le prefazioni di Girolamo e Rufino alle loro traduzioni di Origene," in *Origeniana quinta: Historica, text and method, philosophica, theologica, Origenism and Later Developments,* ed. Robert J. Daly (Leuven: Peeters, 1992), 92–96; and H. Crouzel, "Comparaisons précises entre les fragments du *Peri Archōn* selon la *Philocalie* et la traduction de Rufin," in *Origeniana,* ed. H. Crouzel, G. Lomiento, and J. Ruis-Camps (Bari: Ist. di lett. crist. ant., 1975), 113–21.

24. See chapter 1.

repudiated people who might be termed Christian skeptics in their denial of Jesus' divinity (*PA* pr. 1–2). One of the elementary principles that Origen asserts is the doctrine that Jesus Christ "was generated from the Father before every Creature" and "became a man, was incarnate, while he was God" (pr. 4). And yet while Origen was writing, the Theodotans, the Christians whose approach to texts and exegesis closely resembled Ammonius's own, were vociferously denying Jesus' divine attributes at Rome.[25] In fact, the Theodotans had chosen a certain Natalius to be the city's bishop in opposition to the already instated Zephyrinus (Eus. *HE* 5.28.10). Origen's assertion that he is following the dictates of tradition thus parallels and directly counters the Theodotans' claim that *they* were the repositories of received tradition.[26] There are good reasons for thinking that Origen wrote with an awareness of this group, whose ideas and methods had such affinity with those of Ammonius: Origen's library was Eusebius's chief reference collection for the *Ecclesiatical History*,[27] so Eusebius's material on the skeptical Theodotans likely came from Origen. Later on, he refers to those "hardened in heart" who, "thinking that they are following the language of the prophecies regarding Him," do not accept Jesus as Christ. One example of a close textual analysis of a prophecy that draws this conclusion is, of course, Ammonius's comparison of Moses and Jesus, preserved in Eusebius's *Demonstration of the Gospel*.[28] Origen directly opposes this view by arguing that Jesus was not a mere human being, but the *logos* incarnate (*PA* 1.2.3), a claim that rests on the Gospel of John.

For our purposes, the most important principle that Origen sets out as "clearly delivered in the teaching of the apostles" (*PA* pr. 4) is the seventh, "that the Scriptures were written by the Spirit of God" (pr. 8).[29] While the apostles might not have contested this claim for Hebrew scripture, Origen asserts that they, and the churches of his day that they inspired, understood "the whole law," that is, the New Testament as well as the Old (*PA* 4.1.1–2), to have a fundamentally "spiritual" (as opposed to a literal) meaning. Evidence for the divinity of the scriptures, in Origen's view, is that "the word"

---

25. See chapter 1.

26. According to Eus. *HE* 5.28.3 the Theodotans said that "all who went before and the apostles themselves received and taught what they now say" up until the reign of Victor, Zephyrinus's immediate predecessor.

27. Andrew J. Carriker, *The Library of Eusebius of Caesarea* (Leiden: Brill, 2003), 4, 54.

28. See chapter 1.

29. The other seven elaborate on the following topics: that there is one God; that Jesus Christ was God's offspring incarnate (probably modified by Rufinus); that the Holy Spirit is equal to them in honor and dignity; that the soul is eternal and will animate the resurrected body (another point probably cleaned up by Rufinus); the existence of the devil, his angels, and their opponents; the creation and end of the world; the existence of angels and influences who aid in human salvation.

had become so powerful in such a short time, despite "the small number of teachers." The "result" is thus "beyond any human power" (4.1.2). For these reasons, he considers Jesus' words "as oracular responses" (4.1.2). Origen refers to a number of prophecies from Hebrew scripture that he says Jesus fulfilled (4.1.3), a move that also, in his view, "demonstrate[s] the deity of Christ" (4.1.5) together with the divine authorship of scripture.

Origen also finds evidence for the divine inspiration of scripture in people's having abandoned their native laws and teachings for the law of Moses and Jesus. This is not an argument for the ethnic superiority of Judaism or Christianity; rather, it illustrates the ability of Christ's message to cross cultural and political boundaries:

> Although there have been very many legislators among the Greeks and the barbarians, and teachers who announced opinions which professed to be the truth, we have heard of no legislator [i.e., other than Moses and Jesus] who was able to imbue other nations with a zeal for the reception of his words; and although those who professed to philosophize about truth brought forward a great apparatus of apparent logical demonstration, no one has been able to impress what was deemed by him the truth upon other nations, or even on any number of persons worth mentioning in a single nation.... Whereas all Greece, and the barbarous part of our world, contains innumerable zealots ($\zeta\eta\lambda\omega\tau\acute{\alpha}\varsigma$), who have deserted the laws of their fathers and the established gods for the observance of the laws of Moses and the discipleship of the words of Jesus Christ, even though those who cleave to the law of Moses were hated by the worshippers of images, and those who accepted the words of Jesus Christ were exposed, in addition, to the danger of death. (PA 4.1.1)

Yet Origen claims that "the spiritual nature of the law of Moses" was apparent only "after the advent of Christ." This statement connects the Mosaic and Christian law codes to whose appeal Origen referred at the beginning of this book in his effort to substantiate the divine character of scripture. Accordingly, in Origen's view, only after Jesus taught could people understand "the light" that "was contained in the law of Moses, but which had been concealed by a veil." Once Christ removed the veil, the "blessings" of the Mosaic law, "the shadow of which was contained in the letter," came "forth gradually to the knowledge [of men]" (4.1.6). Given his conviction that Christian law was superior to all others and spread through its obvious divine force, it is not surprising that he would have broken Roman law himself by schooling catechumens between 206 and 211 or that he would have encouraged others to testify openly to this belief through martyrdom.

Origen develops his exegetical principles from his understanding of the divine and layered character of Hebrew law. Having first claimed that the divine authorship of all genuine scripture was an apostolic tenet, while also indicating that this was not an uncontested claim by presenting evidence for it, Origen then provides the next exegetical tool: he sets out the rules for reading these divinely written texts so that "a coherent and organic whole" may be constructed from them (PA pr. 10).[30] Although it is impossible to know whether their exegetical techniques still agree at this more advanced stage, Origen's goal of producing an all-encompassing system is the same as Ammonius's aim to set out a philosophy without conflicts. To justify his exegesis, Origen first asserts that, as everyone knows, scripture includes certain "mystical transactions" (οἰκονομίαι μυστικαί). These are implicit anomalies (e.g., Lot's incest with his daughters, polygamous marriages) or things, such as the Hebrew tabernacle, that he takes as types, symbolically prefiguring something else (PA 4.1.9). Moreover, Origen asserts that everybody knows the prophecies "to be filled with enigmas (αἰνιγμάτων) and dark sayings (σκοτεινῶν λόγων)" (4.1.10). Indeed, he says that even "the exact understanding of the Gospels," not to mention the book of Revelation or the Epistles, requires grace (χάριτος) (4.1.10).

To read such puzzling texts, Origen asserts, you need the "key of knowledge" (τῆς κλειδὸς τῆς γνώσεος) that, according to Jesus, the lawyers (τοῖς νομικοῖς) confiscated (PA 4.1.10; Luke 11:52).[31] That key, for Origen, is contained in Proverb 22:20 (Septuagint version), where "Solomon" claims to reveal the "words of the wise." The biblical text advises: "Copy them for yourself three times over, for counsel and knowledge on the surface of your heart."[32] In Origen's reading, this passage means that

> the individual ought . . . to portray the ideas of Holy Scripture in a three-fold manner upon his own soul; in order that the simple man may be edified by the "flesh,". . . of the Scripture, for so we name the obvious sense; while he who has ascended a certain way [may be edified] by the "soul," as it were. The perfect man . . . [may receive edification] from the spiritual law, which has a shadow of good things to come. (4.1.11)[33]

The first sense "is capable of imparting edification" to everyone, including "simple believers" (4.1.12). The second, the reading "according to the soul"

---

30. Trigg, Origen, 23.

31. For Origen the lawyers are probably those too indebted to the literal meaning of the law.

32. Trans. NETS, http://ccat.sas.upenn.edu/nets/edition/25-proverbs-nets.pdf (accessed 5 February 2009).

33. This use of Proverbs does not occur in Philo or Clement.

($εἰς ψυχήν$), communicates "ineffable mysteries regarding the affairs of men" (by which he means souls in bodies) so that those "capable of instruction" might learn all God's doctrines in "matters which relate to souls" (4.1.14). Finally, the third, "spiritual" ($πνευματική$) sense is present when "one is able to show the heavenly things of which the Jews 'according to the flesh' served as an example and a shadow, and of what future blessings the law contains as a shadow" (4.1.13), a sense for which Origen uses Paul as a precedent.[34] In other words, the divine inspiration of the scriptures in Origen's view legitimizes figural exegesis across all scriptural texts, Jewish and Christian (4.1.16), in order to yield a coherent, consistent theology without contradictions. Not all passages of scripture, however, have all three senses. For example, some passages have no literal sense (4.2.5),[35] a tenet that implies that ordinary people must always rely on someone more spiritually advanced to interpret scripture for them. Moreover, Origen implies that the very exegesis of scripture brings increasing spiritual benefits, but only, of course, for those able to pursue it. For such people, as opposed to the "ignorant" people he once relegated to Heraclas's instruction, theology and not martyrdom might be a better path for the soul to God. Pursuing theology would thus equip the more intellectually able people to serve as teachers of those of more modest intellect.

Although much in the historical and legal narratives is "true,"[36] in Origen's view,[37] "certain stumbling-blocks" or "offences and impossibilities" within the law or the historical account signal not contradictions in scripture, but the presence of deeper meanings (4.1.15).[38] In some cases, for the sake of "those unable to endure the fatigue of" investigation, these higher doctrines lie hidden under an ostensibly historical narrative describing "things of the visible creation" (4.1.14).[39] Not only does this stratagem of the spirit make exegesis more interesting for those capable of it, but also "the multitude" might be "improved" by the literal meaning (4.1.14). Yet "the laws of truth" are found even below the surface of "the written legislation," including the Commandments (4.1.14). The spirit's most important aim is to convey the

---

34. For example, Paul (1 Cor. 10:4) interprets as Christ the rock that followed Moses' people through the desert (Exod. 17:6; Num. 20:7–11).

35. Citation is from the Butterworth trans.

36. A circumstance that does not impede their psychic or spiritual meanings (PA 4.3.4 Butterworth).

37. E.g., Abraham's burial in Hebron; the stories of Isaac, Jacob, and their wives; Jerusalem as the capital of Judea; Solomon's building of the temple in the Old Testament; the Decalogue; and injunctions against anger and swearing in the New Testament (4.1.19).

38. Some examples: the six-day creation, the tree of life, the devil taking Jesus up the mountain (4.1.16).

39. Presumably the historical narratives make exegesis more fun.

"spiritual sense," Origen avers. In these places, "concealing from the multitude the deeper meaning," the spiritual sense is signaled to the alert reader by

> [the account of] some event that did not take place, sometimes what
> could not have happened; sometimes what could, but did not. . . . And
> a similar practice also is to be noticed with regard to the legislation, in
> which is often to be found what is useful in itself, and appropriate to
> the times of the legislation; and sometimes also what does not appear to
> be of utility; and at other times impossibilities are recorded.[40] (4.1.15)

When something in the text so indicates, the deeper meaning can then be "allegorically [i.e., figurally] understood" (συναλληγορουμένοις) (4.1.20).[41] Moreover, he taught, proper exegesis, that is, that in service to a theology without conflicts, requires these deeper meanings to hold together across all scriptural texts, Hebrew and Christian. So, for example, if Jerusalem really refers to the "heavenly city" reserved for the "souls in this world who are called Israel," then "whatever. . . is narrated or predicted of Jerusalem" must apply to "the heavenly Jerusalem" (4.1.22), just as Egypt, Babylon, Tyre, and Sidon in Origen's view really refer to places where there are souls properly seen as "spiritual" Egyptians, Babylonians, Tyrians, and Sidonians, respectively (4.1.22).

Origen asserted that the divine authorship of scripture, Jewish and Christian, was an apostolic teaching preserved by tradition. He then used this claim to justify—even require—an overarching theology without conflicts generated by using figural exegesis to eliminate apparent contradictions across Jewish and Christian scripture. These claims to tradition, continuity, and logical coherence, however, were actually an aggressive argument against the contemporary theology of the Theodotans and the school of Ammonius. For Origen, people like the Theodotans and Ammonius, who denied Jesus' divinity, misunderstood "Scripture according to its spiritual meaning," interpreting it merely according to the "letter" (*PA* 4.1.9). Origen claims that this failure is "the cause" of all the "false opinions" about God (4.1.9). Origen's own text, therefore, shows clearly the absence of consensus, as he was writing, that scripture, especially the New Testament, had a fundamentally spiritual and not a

---

40. As examples of the latter, Origen mentions the punishments for eating vultures (when no one would eat such a bird), killing babies that had not been circumcised on the eighth day, the utility of sacrificing goat stags (4.1.17) in the Hebrew Bible, and in the New Testament striking on the right cheek and plucking out the offending eye (4.1.18).

41. For the Greek text, Origen of Alexandria, *Origenes vier Bücher von dem Prinzipien,* trans. H. Görgemanns and H. Karpp (Darmstadt: Wissenschaftliche Buchgesellschaft, 1976). Again, Origen takes his cue from Paul: he interprets Paul's statement "Behold Israel after the flesh" (1 Cor. 10:18) as signaling that there is an Israel "according to the spirit" (4.1.21); the former are the Jews, the latter are the Christians.

literal meaning. Thus Origen clearly set out his arguments for the scriptures' divine authorship against these opponents, as well as the Gnostics (4.1.8), and he described the "correct" way of interpreting scriptures for them (4.1.9).

In *Peri archōn*, Origen combined the fruits of his education with Clement and Ammonius in a way that made his school a liminal space, fluent in the language of Platonic pedagogy and Alexandrian Christian allegorism. His contact with Clement, his catechetical teacher, exposed Origen both to the concept of figural reading and to the notion that Jesus was the Middle Platonist *logos* incarnate.[42] Further back is the influence of the allegorizing Jewish theologian, Philo, one of the Middle Platonists who had appropriated the Stoic *logos*.[43] Philo provided the bridge across which Christian authors could link Jesus as God's son with the philosophical concept of the *logos* or "word." Neither Philo nor Clement, however, had used Proverbs 22:40, as Origen had, to justify a threefold system of meanings in scripture, and neither had the goal of developing "a coherent and organic whole" from the texts each deemed as conveying "true" doctrine.[44] Origen's ambition to build a system without conflicts, accordingly, derives from Ammonius, along with his careful, systematic approach to textual criticism, including historical and genre analysis.[45] The similarity in goal is as striking as the disparate results, however: Ammonius, who by century's end will come to represent the "Hellene," assumed that it was Greek philosophy that should be wrestled into a system without conflicts; Origen, the "lawless Christian," in Porphyry's view, assumed that it was Christian scripture. Although Porphyry engaged in figural exegesis, he believed that only certain genres were suitable for such readings: he rejected its application to historical texts, and he thought that figural readings could be applied only to laws that were true, not to those, as

---

42. Clem. *Strom.* 5.3; H. A. Wolfson, "Clement of Alexandria and the Generation of the Logos," *ChHist* 20, no. 2 (1951): 72–81. Clement and Origen understood the generation of the *logos* differently, but Clement upheld the basic claim that Jesus was the *logos* incarnate, an idea that, once suggested to Origen, would also have informed his reading of the Gospel of John.

43. Philo *Agr.* 51–52; *Cher.* 35–36; *Her.* 205; *Mig.* 6; *All. leg.* 3.96; *Creat.* 24. Henry Chadwick, *Early Christian Thought and the Classical Tradition: Studies in Justin, Clement, and Origen* (Oxford: Oxford University Press, 1966), 74; David T. Runia, *Philo in Early Christian Literature: A Survey* (Minneapolis: Fortress Press, 1993), 10; Kenneth Schenck, *A Brief Guide to Philo* (Louisville: Westminster/John Knox Press, 2005), 58–60.

44. See Trigg, *Origen,* 23; Albert C. Outler, "The 'Platonism' of Clement of Alexandria," *JR* 20, no. 3 (1940): 240; Róbert Somos, "An Aristotelian Science-Methodological Principle in Origen's *Commentary on John,*" in *Origeniana octava* (Leuven: Peeters, 2003), 550; Philo of Alexandria, *Philo with an English Translation,* trans. F. H. Colson (Cambridge, MA: Harvard University Press, 1929–62), 1: x–xi; Schenck, *Brief Guide to Philo,* 3.

45. Although Trigg, *Origen,* 17, 25, 32–33, 42, 44, 45–46, 58, 73, sees this activity as simply Origen acting as a "grammateus," the links with Ammonius are clear because the students of Plotinus approached texts in precisely the same methodical way. See chapter 3.

Origen thought, that did "not appear to be of utility." Accordingly, by the end of the third century, Porphyry branded Origen as lawless, a description that embraced the later philosopher's disdain for Origen's figural exegesis, his resulting claim for the superiority of Christian law to Roman law, and paths along which he guided his students. Although Porphyry would have supported Origen's notion that only some students had the aptitude for advanced exegesis, he would not have condoned Origen's encouraging his better students to pursue his flawed exegetical techniques, nor his more average students to flout Roman law in the pursuit of martyrdom.

Between 211 and 215, in the midst of his teaching and these writing projects, Origen took a trip to Rome.[46] Although Eusebius says simply that Origen wanted to see the city, this trip occurred during the episcopate of Zephyrinus (d. 217),[47] the period when the followers of Theodotus had appointed Natalius as his episcopal challenger (Eus. *HE* 6.14.10; 5.28). It is impossible to know whether Origen met with this group or if they were the source of the Hebrew scriptures that he was able to procure (6.16.1).[48] Nevertheless, it is significant that their efforts to produce reliable editions of scripture paralleled his own. How Origen paid for the trip is also a mystery. Grammarians and rhetors did collect fees from their students;[49] but it is more likely that a patron paid his way, perhaps his usual patron, Ambrose, or Demetrius, bishop of Alexandria, who had during the same period dispatched him to Arabia at the behest of its governor (6.19.15).[50] Zephyrinus of Rome might have asked for help from the bishop of Alexandria, the empire's second most

---

46. Barnes, *Constantine and Eusebius,* 84, dates this visit to the period when Origen was first teaching in Caesarea, i.e., 215–17, but Eusebius's text suggests that it happened before Caracalla's edict of 215. Barnes, *Constantine and Eusebius,* 328 n. 25, also connects this visit to Origen's discovery of the copy of Hebrew scripture at Nicopolis. He reasons that Origen is likely to have learned about the version found near Jericho in the reign of Caracalla (d. 217) soon after its discovery. Origen refers to it as the "sixth" text when he uses it in his *Commentary on the Psalms* (for the catena in which this appears, see *PG* 80.30). Since the Nicopolan version is the "fifth," he must have found it before the end of Caracalla's reign. But we do not know that the order of discovery dictated Origen's sequence for the *Hexapla*.

47. K. Wegenast, "Zephyrinus, 198–217 Bischof von Rom," *Paulys Realenzyclopädie* 10A, pt. 1 (1972): 226–27. My chronology diverges here from that of Nautin, *Origène,* who ignores the repercussions of Caracalla's edict (see below).

48. Some of the Theodotans dispensed with Hebrew scripture altogether (Eus. *HE* 5.28.19).

49. Raffaella Cribiore, *Gymnastics of the Mind: Greek Education in Hellenistic and Roman Egypt* (Princeton, NJ/Oxford: Princeton University Press, 2001), 59–65.

50. The Roman legate was possibly Furius Iulianus, consul designate, according to R. M. Grant, *Augustus to Constantine: The Thrust of the Christian Movement into the Roman World* (New York: Harper & Row, 1970), 204. Origen made a second and perhaps a third trip to Arabia at some time after 217 in order to participate in the interrogation of Bishop Beryllus of Bostra. According to Eusebius, Beryllus denied that Jesus' divinity was unique and preexistent. Origen also argued there against Elkesiates and people claiming that the soul died and was resurrected along with the body (Eus. *HE* 6.33.1, 37–38). These visits are impossible to date.

influential city, in prevailing over his Theodotan challenger. Learning of these Roman Christians who denied Jesus' divinity might have motivated Demetrius to send Origen on a mission that could familiarize the young scholar with their habits and texts so that he could refute them. Origen, in fact, having studied with Ammonius, was uniquely prepared for such a task. Demetrius and Origen are often portrayed as lifelong enemies, but the bishop's role in sending Origen to Arabia in the same period suggests otherwise: The Alexandrian bishop supported Origen as long as he added to the luster of his see. He opposed Origen only when the scholar acted independently and so interfered with the bishop's more monarchical ambitions.[51] Indeed, Demetrius is the first known bishop of Alexandria to have asserted the authority of his see, not only over the city itself, but also over its environs.[52]

In 215, an imperial edict again disrupted Origen's work in Alexandria. Visiting the city late in the year, the emperor Caracalla was greeted, according to Cassius Dio (78.7), by rioting young men, perhaps protesting his attacks on the city's Aristotelian philosophers.[53] According to Eusebius, "no small warfare broke out in the city" (*HE* 6.19.15).[54] In response, the emperor canceled the city's public spectacles, banned its dining societies, and in effect instituted martial law, denying Alexandria's citizens freedom of movement.[55] Origen's response was to slip out of the city.[56] He may have headed first to Aelia Capitolina (the former Jerusalem), where Alexander, a fellow student of Clement of Alexandria, had just become bishop (6.8.4, 7; 6.14.9).[57] Ultimately, he found his way to Caesarea in Palestine, a city that had had a connection to the Alexandrian see since the late second century and where Alexander had arranged for Origen to teach.[58] These activities earned Origen the ire of Demetrius, who objected to the scholar, who was

---

51. See Joseph W. Trigg, "The Charismatic Intellectual: Origen's Understanding of Religious Leadership," *ChHist* 50, no. 1 (1981): 5–6.

52. Walter Bauer, *Rechtgläubigkeit und Ketzerei im ältesten Christentum* (Tübingen: Mohr/Siebeck, 1934), 53.

53. A fan of Alexander, Caracalla was incensed by the rumor (Plut. *Alex.* 77) that Aristotle had killed the conqueror. See C. M. Mulvany, "Notes on the Legend of Aristotle," *CQ* 20, no. 3/4 (1926): 160.

54. Nautin, *Origène*, 415–16, and Trigg, "Charismatic Intellectual," 6, take Eusebius to mean that warfare broke out between Demetrius and Origen, but there is no support for this in the text. Indeed, Origen's involvement with the philosophical community in Alexandria potentially put him at risk. See M. Hornschuh, "Das Leben des Origenes und die Entstehung der alexandrinischen Schule," *ZKG* 71 (1960): 1–2; and Barnes, *Constantine and Eusebius*, 83–84.

55. Christopher Haas, *Alexandria in Late Antiquity* (Baltimore: Johns Hopkins University Press, 1997), 66 and 386 n. 50, dates Caracalla's abolition of spectacles to 212, citing Dio 78.23.3.

56. An action that does make one wonder about his—or his students'—involvement in the riots.

57. Glanville Downey, "Caesarea and the Christian Church," *BASO, Supplementary Studies* 19 (1975): 26.

58. Ibid.

not ordained, lecturing in front of bishops and called him back to Alexandria (6.19.17). Origen probably returned to the Egyptian capital after Caracalla's death in 217. Origen was a Christian who had lived in Demetrius's see and so was ostensibly under his jurisdiction. The Alexandrian bishop's reaction to the behavior of Alexander and Theoctistus, bishop of Caesarea, however, also suggests that he saw Caesarea as within his see's sphere of influence.[59] Presumably, Origen continued to teach philosophy upon his return; indeed, a young Plotinus may have been one of his students in the late 220s.[60]

What remains of the works that Origen wrote during this second episode of his life in Alexandria shows his desire to overturn the arguments of two different theological groups.[61] One was the Gnostics,[62] and Origen's objection to their theology is both well documented and well studied.[63] A second target audience included people, like Ammonius and the Theodotans, who maintained the literal sense of scriptural texts, asserting that Jesus was no more divine than Moses as a lawgiver, prophet, and miracle worker.[64] These concerns appear in two places. First, Origen's commentary on the Second Psalm uses the hymn, in part, to assert Jesus' identity with the *logos*.[65] The psalm begins by asking: "Why do the nations conspire and the peoples plot in vain?" But it then asserts: "You are my son; today I have begotten you. Ask of me and I will make the nations your heritage, and the ends of the earth

---

59. See Trigg, *Origen,* 15–16, on Demetrius's assertion of episcopal authority.

60. Thdt. *Therap.* 6.60 says that Plotinus was a student of Origen; if so, it would have had to be before he joined Ammonius in 232 (Porph. *Plot.* 3.6f.; 1). At some point, perhaps in this period, Origen also traveled to Nicomedia, together with his patron, Ambrose. We know this from his letter to S. Julius Africanus (1, 15), whom he may have met in Palestine. I've noted this journey here (although Eusebius mentions the exchange in the context of Origen's life in Caesarea), since Africanus's *Chronicle* ended in 221, and so that is the last certain date for his floruit.

61. The dates for some of these texts are conjectural, based on where they fall in Eusebius's narrative, but in the case of the *Commentary on the Gospel of John,* Origen states that he wrote the first five books upon his return to Alexandria (pr. 2.13), although Nautin, *Origène,* 366–67, 410, argues that this return was quite a bit later, in 231. This position clashes with Eusebius's chronology, such as it is.

62. Origen's *Dialogue with Candidus* and his *On Natures,* both now lost, were directed against Gnostics: Hieron. *C. Ruf.* 2.19; Nautin, *Origène,* 370, infers from the title of *De naturis* that it refuted the Gnostic theory that distinguished three natures of souls.

63. E.g., Mark J. Edwards, "Gnostics, Greeks, and Origen: The Interpretation of Interpretation," *JThS* 44 (1993): 70–89; Jean-Daniel Dubois, "Le 'Traité des principes' d'Origène et le 'Traité tripartite' valentinien: Une lecture comparée de leurs prologues," in *Entrer en matière: Les prologues,* ed. Jean-Daniel Dubois and Bernard Roussel (Paris: Ed. du Cerf, 1998), 53–63; Gilles Pelland, "'Ex ipso sponso splendorum decoris accipiens,'" *Gregorianum* 79, no. 1 (1998): 113–27.

64. This was also the position of the Ebionites, a Palestinian sect to which Symmachus belonged; Origen used Symmachus's translation of Jewish scripture throughout the *Hexapla* (Eus. *HE* 6.17.1; see also 3.27.1, 3). Eusebius apparently deduces Symmachus's position from his "opposition to the Gospel according to Matthew."

65. No. 2 in H. I. Bell and T. C. Skeat, eds., *Fragments of an Unknown Gospel and Other Early Christian Papyri* (London: The Trustees of the British Museum, 1935), cited in R. M. Grant, "More Fragments of Origen?" *VChr* 2, no. 4 (1948): 245–46.

your possession" (Ps. 2:1, 7–8 NRSV). Origen's commentary, preserved on papyrus, links the passage with the Gospel of John, which identifies Jesus with the *logos*. In so doing, Origen refers to his commentary on John (6.55, 58–60), written at about the same time.[66] Second, another fragment from the *Commentary on the Psalms,* preserved in the *Philocalia,* a collection of Origen's writings assembled by fourth-century theologians, shows Origen arguing against Christians who thought that the Law—both Jewish and Christian—ought to be followed in its literal sense. These Christians argued that keeping the Law brings material good (peace in cities, health, bountiful crops), but violating it brings evils such as disease. This reading parallels Porphyry's claims, evident in Methodius, that if the law is divinely inspired, then the literal meaning and the figural reading are equally just, the literal meaning pertaining to the material world of sense, the figural meaning pertaining to the intelligible world.[67] Origen, conversely, thinks that such passages ought to be read only figurally, because, he says, even the prophets sometimes ignored the literal sense of the Law (*Phil.* 26.2–4).[68] A fragment of the preface to the *Commentary on the Psalms* shows that this work asserted many of the exegetical principles set out in *Peri archōn,* namely that scripture is full of "riddles, parables" and "dark sayings," that a key (wrongfully kept by the "lawyers") is needed to unlock its meaning, that it is inspired throughout by the Holy Spirit, and that Paul provides precedent in "interpreting spiritual things by means of spiritual things" (1 Cor. 2:13).[69] Origen liberally employs this type of figural reading in another work written at this time, the *Commentary on Lamentations.* This book of scripture chronicles the Chaldaeans' attack on the city of Jerusalem; it is ostensibly a historical text, but Origen interprets the Israelite capital as a representation of the soul.[70]

---

66. Grant, "More Fragments of Origen?" 245–46: "Then the prophet John, seeing him—not the Light but Jesus—coming to him, says, Behold the Lamb of God who takes away the sin of the world. It is clear that he comes to be sacrificed as an innocent lamb. As it is written, My flesh is true food and my blood is true drink. Now Christ our Passover has been sacrificed for us, but the true Light was not sacrificed, for he is the Beginning with God, and God [i.e., the implications of the figure described in the Psalm who is begotten of God]. This is the true Light, a Sun shining above our sun. He is the true Light for those for whom the Logos, being in the form of God, did not think it robbery to be equal to God." Note that understanding Jesus as the *logos* is only one of the concerns of Origen's commentary on John's Gospel (see Or. *Comm. Ioh.* 1.21.126).

67. See chapter 5.

68. *Phil.* 26.4: "Even some of those who profess wisdom according to Christ have fallen into the snare; for they suppose such promises as these to be made by the Creator [demiurge], and that beyond their literal signification the threats have no meaning." Trans. G. Lewis (Edinburgh: T&T Clark, 1911). The scriptural passages in question are Exod. 15:20; Deut. 28:58f., 22:24, 28.1; Lev. 26:16, 26:3f.; and Matt. 4:23, 9:35; and the remarks arise in a commentary on Ps. 4:6 (Septuagint): "Many say, who will show us the good things?"

69. Trans. Trigg.

70. See, e.g., *Comm. Lam.* 10.

Although Origen's writings between 206 and 230 seem to have used the Ammonian goal of a theology without conflicts to undermine the humbler vision of Jesus that Ammonius and others promoted, not all of Origen's works rejected the philosopher's doctrines outright. For example, Origen's *Commentary on Genesis* picks up on the Septuagint's description of the stars as having been established "for signs" (εἰς σημεῖα), a description that he sees as in keeping with Platonic use of that term. Accordingly he reads the text as a criticism of astrology in a way that resonates closely with Plotinus's later critique of certain astrological tenets. The positions are so close that both likely find their source in the classroom of Ammonius.[71] Moreover, evidence in *Peri archōn* and the *Commentary on the Gospel of John* demonstrates that Origen appropriated Ammonius's notion that the first divine principle, or Father, was responsible for the creation of the cosmos, whereas the second principle, the *logos,* was the intermediary through which creation was carried out.[72]

By 231, a year in which he resumed his travels,[73] Origen was a mature theologian with a number of exegetical treatises to his credit, not only the *Hexapla* and *Peri archōn,* but also commentaries on the first twenty-five Psalms, Genesis, Lamentations, and the first five chapters of John's Gospel. In addition, he had written on the resurrection and on natures, compiled a collection of miscellanies, and authored a dialogue against the Gnostic Candidus in which he had asserted the soon-to-be controversial opinion that the devil would ultimately return to God.[74] Eusebius is vague about the reason for Origen's departure from Alexandria. Before journeying to Athens,[75] Origen visited Caesarea in Palestine, where the city's bishop ordained him with the approval of Alexander, bishop of Aelia Capitolina.[76] By 232, probably as part of the same itinerary,[77] he had visited Antioch at the behest of Julia Mammaea, mother of the emperor Alexander Severus, to share his "understanding of divine things"

---

71. Plot. *Enn.* 3.1, 5–6; 2.3; Trigg, *Origen,* 86.

72. Digeser, "Origen on the *Limes,*" 208–10, discusses the evidence for this position. That it was Ammonius's position is deduced from the agreement of "Origen the Platonist" with Longinus and the this Origen's assertion of the position to Plotinus after a visit to Rome.

73. The *terminus post quem* is 231 because Eusebius (*HE* 6.23) fixes these trips during the tenure of Bishop Pontianus of Rome (231–35). Allen Brent, "Was Hippolytus a Schismatic?" *Vigiliae Christianae* 49, no. 3 (1995): 234.

74. Hieron. *C. Ruf.* 2.19.

75. Barnes, *Constantine and Eusebius,* 328 n. 30, thinks, contra Nautin, *Origène,* 411, 435, that Origen was in Athens long enough to finish his *Comm. in Ezek.* and write the first five books of his *Comm. in song.,* but Eusebius sets these activities in Athens after the accession of Gordian (*HE* 6.32.1).

76. Eus. *HE* 6.23.3–4; Phot. *Bibl.* 118.

77. Nautin, *Origène,* 65f., 366f., 410, 427f., thinks that Origen went first to Antioch, then returned to Alexandria, and then ventured out to Palestine and Greece. But he probably went to Antioch later, given the dates for the court's movements (see note 78).

(Eus. *HE* 6.21.3).[78] Origen may have hoped that his audience with the imperial court, together with his ordination, would be a show of support against
rising opposition to his doctrines in Alexandria. In any case, Demetrius's reaction to his ordination was swift and authoritative: with doctrine, behavior, and
the ultimate authority of the Alexandrian see all at stake, he convened a synod.
The synod, in turn, condemned the role that the Palestinian bishops had
played in Origen's ordination, anathematized his self-castration and some of
his doctrines (including the devil's potential redemption),[79] and excommunicated the independent-minded theologian. According to Jerome, the churches
of Palestine, Arabia, Achaea, and Phoenicia rejected the synod's decree.[80] The
first three sees were, not coincidentally, places that had invited Origen to teach
or adjudicate; he would have had to travel through the last see to reach Julia
Mammaea at Antioch. Excommunication by the Alexandrian bishop, however, cut Origen off from the main intellectual center of the empire. By 233,
Demetrius was dead, and Origen was living in Caesarea (6.26.1).[81] Evidence
in Gennadius, Justinian, Photius, and Severus of Al-Ashmunein suggests that
Origen returned to Alexandria to see whether Demetrius's successor, Heraclas,
would continue the order of excommunication.[82] Since Heraclas had once
been his student, Origen might have hoped—in vain—for leniency.[83]

---

78. The imperial court traveled from Rome to Antioch via Illyricum in 231: *BMC, R. Emp.*
6.192, Sev. Alex. 781; Herod. 6.4.3. Barnes, *Constantine and Eusebius,* 328 n. 27, thinks that they may
not have arrived in Syria until 232, but it is impossible to know for sure.

79. In the hands of Eusebius (6.8.4–5; 6.26), Origen's conflict with Demetrius comes across as
a personal spat. But Jerome (although not altogether trustworthy where Origen is concerned, either
vilifying him or lionizing him depending on the period) makes it clear that the bishop excommunicated him (*C. Ruf.* 2.18–19).

80. Hieron. *C. Ruf.* 2.18; O. W. Reinmuth, "A Working List of the Prefects of Egypt, 30 BC
to 299 AD," *BASP* 4 (1967): 106–9, in R. M. Grant, "Early Alexandrian Christianity," *ChHist* 40
(1971): 135. Hieron. *Ep.* 33.4, after listing the sees that defied Alexandria's decree, adds that "the city
of Rome also consents to his condemnation."

81. "In the tenth year of Alexander," whose accession was 13 March 222. Böhm, "Origenes," 20.

82. Gennadius *De viris inl.* 34; Justinian *Letter to Mennas* (*ACO* III 197, 202); Phot. *Interrog. decem*
9 (*PG* 104 1230); [Severus of Al-Ashmunein/Sāwīrus ibn al-Muqaffa], *History of the Patriarchs of the
Coptic Church of Alexandria,* in *Patrologia orientalis,* ed. B. Evetts (Paris: Firmin-Didot et Cie, 1948),
1.9, p. 170; Beatrice, "Porphyry's Judgment," 359, 366 nn. 68–70; Böhm, "Origenes," 20; Nautin,
Origène, 404–5; Trigg, "Charismatic Intellectual," 6. Eusebius does not describe this trip to Alexandria, but he is unlikely to have noted Origen's violating the bishop's sentence by returning to the city,
especially since his excommunication was never revoked.

83. Böhm, "Origenes," 21. One trip that Origen did *not* make in the 230s was to Cappadocia.
Palladius *Lausiac History* 64 says that "there was a certain Juliana, a virgin of Caesarea in Cappadocia, said to be very learned and most faithful. When Origen the writer fled from the uprising of
the pagans she received him, and supported him for two years at her own cost and waited on him.
I found this written in a very old book of verses, in which had been written by Origen's hand: 'I
found this book at the house of Juliana the virgin at Caesarea, when I was hidden by her. She used
to say that she had received it from Symmachus himself, the Jewish interpreter.'" Some historians

Still keen to regain his standing in Alexandria after his unsuccessful appeal to Heraclas,[84] Origen wrote to the emperor Philip (244–49), the empress Marcia Otacilia Severa (d. 248), and Fabianus, the bishop of Rome (Eus. *HE* 6.36.3),[85] hoping perhaps that they could sway the Alexandrian bishop to rescind his ban. Having appealed for help in writing, Origen could have followed up with the Roman court and see in person, which would put him in Rome between 244 and 248/9.[86] He did visit Athens in winter 245/6 (6.32.2),[87] and could then easily have continued westward to Rome.[88] By 250, Origen was home in Caesarea, just as Decius issued his edict compelling all

have assumed that Origen fled to be hidden in Cappadocia during the "persecution of Maximin Thrax," which Eusebius mentions immediately after the death of Severus Alexander (in 235; *HE* 6.28) (see H. Crouzel, "Origène s'est'il retiré en Cappadoce pendant la persécution de Maximin le Thrace?" *BLE* 64 [1963]: 195–203). But the flourish "in Cappadocia" is probably an embellishment by Palladius. A fan of Origen, Palladius had lived in Cappadocia (*Hist. Laus.* 48) and grown up in nearby Galatia. He may have used Origen's experience in his own region, which had its own Caesarea. Indeed, we know from Firmilian's 256 letter to Cyprian that early in the reign of Maximin Thrax there was a local persecution in Cappadocia and Pontus that some earthquakes had triggered, but that people were able to flee (Cyp. *Ep.* 75 [74].10). See G. W. Clarke, "Some Victims of the Persecution of Maximinus Thrax," *Historia* 15, no. 4 (1966): 445–53, for discussion of this persecution. The evidence for the persecution is scant. Apart from Firmilian, Eusebius *HE* 6.28 (Oulton) says that Maximin Thrax, bearing "ill-will toward the house of Alexander, since it consisted for the most part of believers, raised a persecution, ordering the leaders of the Church alone to be put to death, as being responsible for the teaching of the Gospel. Then ... Origen composed his work, *On Martyrdom* [evidence for which he draws from Origen's *Comm. Ioh.* 22, no longer extant], dedicating the treatise to Ambrose and Protectetus, a presbyter of Caesarea, for in the persecution no ordinary distress had befallen them both." Eusebius concludes by referring to them as "confessors" and noting that the attack lasted no longer than the three years of Maximin's reign. The *Chronica minora* 1: 7f. says that the bishop of Rome Pontianus and the priest Hippolytus were deported to Sardinia. Other sources (e.g., SHA *Max.* 9) state that upon his accession Maximin "put all of Alexander's ministers to death in one way or another" and also "held Alexander's friends ... under suspicion." What Origen and Eusebius call a "persecution" affecting Ambrose and Protectetus in Palestine is probably unrelated to the events described by Firmilian in Cappadocia. Instead, Ambrose, Protectetus, Pontianus, and Hippolytus were caught up in the swirl of threatened executions that jeopardized anyone with a connection to the Severan house. Hippolytus had actually dedicated a treatise on the resurrection to Julia Mammaea (some fragments survive in Syriac: Otto Bardenhewer and Thomas J. Shahan, *Patrology: The Lives and Works of the Fathers of the Church* [Berlin/Munich/Strassburg/Vienna: B. Herder, 1908], 215). Pontianus was Hippolytus's presiding bishop, and it is likely that Ambrose, Origen's patron, and perhaps Protectetus as an assistant, had helped make the arrangements that brought Origen to the empress's court only a few years before. Origen probably feared for Ambrose's and Protectetus's safety, given their interaction with the court (and the very muted tone of *On Martyrdom*) and what had happened to Pontianus and Hippolytus. On the less than urgent character of *On Martyrdom,* see Clarke, "Some Victims of the Persecution," 446.

84. Perhaps he prevailed on his friends to do so as well: Eusebius records a visit to Heraclas from Julius Africanus (*HE* 6.31.2).

85. These letters would date between 244 and 248 if they were written as a group. Beatrice, "Porphyry's Judgment," 360. Fabian was bishop from 236–50 (Cyp. *Ep.* 30.5).

86. Beatrice, "Porphyry's Judgment," 359.

87. In Beatrice, "Porphyry's Judgment," 359.

88. Beatrice, "Porphyry's Judgment," 356–57, accepted by Böhm, "Origenes," 21.

Rome's citizens to sacrifice. This persecution may have motivated Origen to write *Against Celsus*.[89] Eusebius says that Origen died in his sixty-ninth year (*HE* 7.1.1), and Photius says that he breathed his last in Tyre (*Bibl.* 118). Thus the earliest possible date of his death is 254—a year into the reign of Gallienus,[90] although the imprecision of Eusebius's chronology allows Origen to have died as late as 256.[91]

During this last period of the theologian's life, Origen came in contact with a young Porphyry, probably teaching him philosophy, at least for a short time.[92] Porphyry, whose interest in philosophy would take him to Longinus and then on to Plotinus, need not have eventually intended to pursue scriptural exegesis to have benefited from Origen's instruction. Origen, Eusebius says, taught his best students philosophy first (*HE* 6.3.8).[93] According to Eusebius, Origen's method was to introduce his students to the schools of various philosophers, "describing their treatises, interpreting and theorizing upon each one" (6.18.3).[94] These texts probably included those of Platonists such as Cronius and Numenius, and Stoics such as Chaeremon, as well as Pythagoreans.[95] This portrait of Origen's teaching is amply confirmed in an oration of praise attributed to Gregory Thaumatourgos, celebrating his teacher as he returned to his home province (*Or.* 1, 4),[96] and in a letter that

---

89. These setbacks would also not have been in Eusebius's interest to report. Beatrice, "Porphyry's Judgment," 361.

90. Gallienus's regnal dates begin with those of his father, Valentinian. Kettler, "War Origenes Schüler?" 323–24; Böhm, "Origenes," 22. The accession of Gallienus and Valerian "cannot fall long after 29 August 253": cf. *ILS* 531 (21 Oct. 253; Gemellae in southern Numidia), in Barnes, "Chronology of Plotinus' Life," 67 n. 15.

91. I have used Septimius Severus's *dies imperii* to reckon these dates, but the problems are the same regardless of the chronological system that Eusebius was using, whether this, the Egyptian regnal, or the Seleucid regnal. For a more extended analysis of the date of Origen's death, see Digeser, "Origen on the *Limes*," 200–201.

92. The encounter could have occurred in Tyre, Porphyry's hometown, but Caesarea is more likely, given the philosopher's knowledge of the titles in Origen's library. Böhm, "Origenes," 16; Kettler, "War Origenes Schüler?" 324.

93. Contra Goulet, "Porphyre, Ammonius," 474. For an earlier version of this discussion, see Elizabeth DePalma Digeser, "Christian or Hellene? The Great Persecution and the Problem of Christian Identity," in *Religious Identity in Late Antiquity*, ed. R. M. Frakes and Elizabeth Digeser (Toronto: Edgar Kent, 2006), 35–57. See also Origen's letter to Gregory, Or. *Cant.* prol. 3; and Joseph W. Trigg, "God's Marvelous *Oikonomia*: Reflections of Origen's Understanding of Divine and Human Pedagogy in the *Address* Ascribed to Gregory Thaumaturgus," *JECS* 9, no. 1 (2001): 28–29 incl. n. 9.

94. My trans.; Eus. *HE* 6.18.3: εἰσῆγέν τε γὰρ ὅσους εὐφυῶς ἔχοντας ἑώρα, καὶ ἐπὶ τὰ φιλόσοφα μαθήματα, γεωμετρίαν, καὶ ἀριθμητικὴν καὶ τἄλλα προπαιδεύματα παραδιδοὺς εἴς τε τὰς αἱρέσεις τὰς παρὰ τοῖς φιλοσόφοις προάγων καὶ τὰ παρὰ τούτοις συγγράμματα διηγούμενος ὑπομνηματιζόμενός τε καὶ θεωρῶν εἰς ἕκαστα...

95. Porph. *Chr.* frag. 39 Harnack ap. Eus. *HE* 6.19.8.

96. Trigg, "God's Marvelous *Oikonomia*," 30; Trigg, *Origen*, 13–14, 36–38; Beatrice, "Porphyry's Judgment," 354, contra Goulet, "Porphyre, Ammonius," 477.

Origen wrote to Gregory that claims that "the philosophy of the Hellenes" is essential as "a course of preparation" for scriptural exegesis.[97]

After having studied with Origen, Porphyry would have felt at home in Plotinus's school, since the two teachers interacted with their students in very similar ways, suggesting some continuity in both schools with their common Ammonian heritage. Origen's authority as a teacher and spiritual guide, like that of Plotinus,[98] derived not only from his erudition and teaching,[99] but also from a personal asceticism that included fasting,[100] depriving himself of sleep,[101] limiting his possessions,[102] and being chaste.[103] Eusebius considers these activities to shape the proper lifestyle of a philosopher,[104] although Origen's self-castration conformed neither to Greco-Roman nor to Christian norms, as Eusebius's embarrassment makes clear.[105]

Like Plotinus also, Origen drew students from the highest echelons of Greco-Roman society. Not only were *honestiores* among Origen's early students (e.g., Heraclides and Hero; Eus. *HE* 6.4.3), but Eusebius also counts many "distinguished" foreign pupils among Origen's later students (e.g., Theodore, Gregory, and Athenodore; 6.30.1). Nor should we forget that both Plotinus and Porphyry could claim him as a teacher, even though their time with him was probably rather brief. The status of Origen's followers is significant for two reasons. First, in the third-century Mediterranean world, a philosophical education was often not an end in itself or pursued with the object of setting up one's own philosophical school. Rather, many students who trained with philosophers subsequently returned to their native cities where they then became influential in civic affairs. Accordingly, students studying under a Christian teacher, even if they did not adopt his faith for themselves, would return to their communities with perhaps a more positive attitude toward Christianity and Christians than their neighbors. Second, Origen had actively encouraged some of his students, both men and women, to embrace martyrdom during the Severan persecution (6.2–5), that is, to break Roman law.[106] He also dedicated an *Exhortation to Martyrdom* to his patron, Ambrose. While such a stance did not deprive him of a powerful imperial

---

97. *Ep.* 2.1.
98. See also chapter 3.
99. Eus. *HE* 6.3.7, 13.
100. Porph. *Plot.* 2, 8; Eus. *HE* 6.3.9, 12.
101. Porph. *Plot.* 7–8; Eus. *HE* 6.3.9.
102. Eus. *HE* 6.3.10–11.
103. Eus. *HE* 6.8.2.
104. *HE* 6.3.2, 7, 9.
105. *HE* 6.8.1–3, 4–5.
106. *HE* 6.2.3, 5–6; 6.3.2, 4–5, 13; 6.4.1–3; 6.5.1, 3–4.

contact in Julia Mammaea (6.21.3), it was vivid and public confirmation that this illustrious philosopher set the tenets of Christian law above Jewish, Roman, and local civic legislation—a revolutionary curriculum for the young elite of the Roman Empire.

Porphyry, then, even before engaging with Origen's exegetical methods and the conclusions he drew from them, had grounds to decry the theologian's lawlessness, especially in contrast to the behavior of Ammonius. In the end, Origen's career shows both a continued tension and a continued engagement with his philosophical education. It is clear that Ammonius, as well as his Platonism, imbues Origen's methodical approach to texts in preparation for exegesis: gathering exemplars, analyzing translations, and determining authenticity—skills that would serve him well in all of his commentaries and other exegetical works. The fluidity of movement between these scholarly communities, together with the mixed ideological character of these philosophical circles, suggests that we need to dispense with the notion that there were discrete Hellene and Christian groups—in Alexandria, Caesarea, or Rome. All the same, there were clearly disagreements between established teachers: Origen, for example, opposed any Christian teacher who might argue against the identity of Jesus as the preexistent *logos.* There were tensions in the concept of proper behavior as well, with Origen sometimes pushing his students to defy the law and become martyrs, contrary to Ammonius's more conservative approach. These conflicts that stretched across the first half of the third century should not, however, be viewed through the polarized lens of the later period. Notable philosophers who led distinguished schools were always in disagreement with one another. For example, Longinus and Plotinus, both students of Ammonius, quarreled over Plotinus's metaphysics (Porph. *Plot.* 19). One might even suggest that such quarrels were how philosophers maintained their "brand" and their following. Philosophers also sometimes ran afoul of the law. At least in the early empire, Stoic philosophers maintained a notorious opposition to the Julio-Claudian regime and sometimes found themselves deported from the capital. In defying laws he believed were unjust, then, Origen had an illustrious predecessor in Seneca. The point is that these intrascholastic Platonist disagreements were not toxic in themselves in the period in which they occurred. Nevertheless, they became fuel for the fire in the heated polemics of the later century—debates that turned dangerous when the imperial government became involved.

✣ CHAPTER 3

Plotinus, Porphyry, and Philosophy in the Public Realm

Porphyry and Hierocles lauded Ammonius as the founder of their philosophical community, but Plotinus brought Ammonius's teaching into wider renown: Plotinus took Ammonius's ideas to Rome and, by teaching them openly there, gave them a heightened prominence and a more political context. For these reasons, Porphyry, Plotinus's student, called him "the philosopher of our times."[1] For Eunapius, the Iamblichaean historian writing toward the end of the fourth century, contemporary philosophy began with Plotinus, not Ammonius. Regardless of Plotinus's status as founder or promoter of the late antique approach to Plato, however, modern knowledge of him is almost entirely dependent on Porphyry, who collected, arranged and published his mentor's separate treatises as *The Enneads,* prefaced by a substantial biography. Because of this entangled relationship, it is useful to consider the careers of both men together, at least for the period up to Plotinus's death. The extent to which Plotinus incorporated Ammonius's teaching into his own classroom will then be addressed: he apparently adopted Ammonius's exegetical practices, his deep commitment to the teachings of Plato, his openness to alternative sources of wisdom, and his willingness to teach to a diverse group of students, while modifying Ammonius's

---

1. *Plot.* 1.1: ὁ καθ᾽ ἡμᾶς γεγονὼς φιλόσοφος.

conception of the first three hypostases. I will also discuss Plotinus's asceticism as a point of contact with Origen, a practice for which we have no evidence with Ammonius. This similarity may indicate that Ammonius was the common source, but it is also possible that Plotinus was influenced by Origen in these respects. Finally, the chapter addresses the political implications of Plotinus's philosophy and Porphyry's elaboration of it. Here I situate Dominic O'Meara's recent analysis of Neoplatonist political philosophy in its specific historical context.

Virtually everything known about Plotinus comes from the biography Porphyry wrote introducing his systematized edition of his mentor's teachings, the *Enneads*. Since Porphyry studied with Plotinus in the 260s,[2] the *Life of Plotinus* is an important, sometimes eyewitness account of the famous philosopher and his school. This association makes the *Life* more valuable than Eusebius's biography of Origen, since neither the bishop nor Pamphilus his patron knew the theologian. Nevertheless, Porphyry's treatise is still a *bios,* a genre that in antiquity, whether in the hands of Plutarch or Suetonius, presented its subject as a moral exemplar for good or for ill. An ancient biography portraying its protagonist as bringing the divine to earth, an increasingly common theme starting in the third century, should thus be read as hagiography, whether the central character is Jesus in the second century or Apollonius of Tyana, Origen, or Plotinus, all subjects of third- and early fourth-century biographers. For Plotinus, Lucien Jerphagnon has argued that Porphyry, "contrasting the irrational figure of the incarnate God against the rational figure of the disembodied man,"[3] sketched his portrait in response to the Gospels' treatment of Jesus. For this reason, Porphyry's account of Plotinus's early life ought to be handled with great care, even though he says that he included stories that the elder philosopher used to tell about his youth (Porph. *Plot.* 3.1–2).

According to Porphyry, Plotinus was born in 204 or 205 and died in 270;[4] Eunapius says that he was Egyptian and from Lyco.[5] In 231/2, "he felt the impulse to study philosophy." He made the rounds of the most famous Alexandrian teachers, possibly including Origen (Thdt. *Affect.* 6.60–61), but

---

2. *Plot.* 4.1; 5.1; 6.1: Porphyry came to Rome just before Gallienus's tenth anniversary, and he left for Sicily at the end of the emperor's fifteenth year.

3. L. Jerphagnon, "Les sous-entendus anti-chrétiens de la *Vita Plotini* ou l'évangile de Plotin selon Porphyre," *Museum Helveticum* 47 (1990): 43.

4. *Plot.* 2.29–32: the year Plotinus died was "the end of the second year of the reign of Claudius, and . . . he was sixty-six years old." For the conversion of Plotinus's regnal dates into Julian dates, see T. D. Barnes, "The Chronology of Plotinus' Life," *GRBS* 17 (1976): 65–70.

5. *VS* s.v. "Plotinos"; i.e., Lycopolis; cf. the Suda. Lycopolis, now Asyut, is about 190 miles up the Nile from Alexandria.

he found none whom he liked (Porph. *Plot.* 3.7–11). "Full of sadness," Porphyry recounts, he "told his trouble to one of his friends," who, "understanding the desire of his soul," sent him to Ammonius, whom Plotinus declared to be "the man I was looking for" (3.13–14). He stayed with Ammonius for the next eleven years, gaining "so complete a training in philosophy that he became eager to make acquaintance with the Persian philosophical discipline and that prevailing among the Indians."[6] In 243, for this reason, Plotinus joined the emperor Gordian's campaign against Persia (3.13–19). It is worth asking whether something about Ammonius's teaching motivated his student to venture east, even though he never reached his intended destination.[7]

After Gordian's death in Mesopotamia (244), Plotinus found his way to Antioch, journeying from there to Rome after Philip's accession that same year. He began meeting with all sorts of students (Porph. *Plot.* 1.14–15), including Amelius Gentilianus of Tuscany, who joined him in 246 (7.1–2; 3.38–43). A former student of Lysimachus,[8] Amelius was also an admirer of the second-century philosopher Numenius.[9] In this period, Porphyry claims, Plotinus kept an agreement he had made with two other Ammonians to avoid disclosing their teacher's doctrines (3.24–28). One of these fellow students was Erennius, otherwise unknown.[10] The other was Origen, usually assumed to be "the

---

6. Porph. *Plot.*3.16: ὡς καὶ τῆς παρὰ τοῖς Πέρσαις ἐπιτηδευομένης πεῖραν λαβεῖν σπεῦσαι καὶ τῆς παρ᾽ Ἰνδοῖς κατορθουμένης.

7. Thomas McEvilley, *The Shape of Ancient Thought* (New York: Allworth Press, 2002), 550, believes that Plotinus learned about Indian thought in Alexandria (although he does not consider Ammonius as a source).

8. Perhaps the Stoic, mentioned by Longinus ap. Porph. *Plot.* 20.47: he was a teacher, not particularly interested in writing.

9. Like Ammonius, Numenius believed that the teaching of Platonism had been corrupted by Plato's skeptical followers in the Academy (Numenius frag. 24, 70 des Places). He taught that Plato had unified the teaching of Pythagoras and Socrates, building up "a doctrine that was fully consistent with that of all peoples and ancient wise men." (Marco Zambon, "Middle Platonism," in *A Companion to Ancient Philosophy,* ed. Mary Louise Gill and Pierre Pellegrin [Malden, MA: Blackwell, 2006], 568). He strove to develop a systematic philosophy that restored "Plato's doctrine to its original, i.e. Pythagorean, integrity." Plato, thus refined, was heavily dependent on Pythagoras. Moreover, Numenius's belief that ancient Egyptian, Persian, Indian, and Jewish doctrines corroborated Pythagoras (Dominic J. O'Meara, *Pythagoras Revived: Mathematics and Philosophy in Late Antiquity* [Oxford: Clarendon Press, 1989], 12–13) opened up a variety of scriptures to Platonist exegesis. Among such texts were the Hermetic corpus and the *Chaldaean Oracles.* The latter agree so closely with Numenius's doctrines that it is impossible to tell in which direction the influence ran, especially given the murky chronology for both the philosopher and the diviners who produced these texts.

10. Or is he? The Athenian P. Herennius Dexippus, author of a chronicle, extant now only in a handful of fragments, was Plotinus's almost exact contemporary. On Dexippus and his biography, see Fergus Millar, "P. Herennius Dexippus: The Greek World and the Third-Century Invasion," *JRS* 59 (1969): 12–29. No one has ever identified him as Plotinus's colleague. Nevertheless, in writing a chronicle, Dexippus was working within the Ammonian school's exegetical traditions: in order to ascertain the authenticity of texts one had to be intimately familiar with the context in which they

Platonist."[11] This Origen once dropped in on Plotinus's seminar in these early years, provoking his colleague's embarrassment—probably because he was in fact teaching Ammonius's doctrines. (According to Porphyry, Plotinus complained that "it damps one's enthusiasm for speaking when one sees that one's audience knows already what one is going to say" [14.23–25].) Porphyry's story, however, is that Plotinus focused "his lectures on his studies with Ammonius" only after his two colleagues had broken their vow of secrecy (3.33–36). In 253,[12] Plotinus began to write down his teachings, perhaps in response to the treatise *On the King as the Only Creator* (3.35–36), usually attributed to "Origen the Platonist." Origen's title suggests that he and Plotinus disagreed over the supreme hypostasis, with Plotinus having adopted a more Numenian approach, perhaps due to his association with Amelius. Plotinus also differed here with Origen the theologian, if he was, in fact, distinct from "the Platonist."[13] This quarrel occurred against the background of Decius's reign (249–51). Responding to a series of natural disasters (Cyp. *Ad Dem.* 2–3), Decius required all citizens to obtain a *libellus,* a certificate from a priest indicating that the recipient had participated in a temple sacrifice,[14] probably as part of a panprovincial ritual

---

purported to be written. Although the notion that Porphyry wrote a chronicle is now discredited (B. Croke, "Porphyry's Anti-Christian Chronology," *JThS* 34 [1983]: 168–85), such was the detail in his *Philosophical History* that modern scholars assumed he had written one. Christian authors with Ammonian connections also wrote chronicles, including Julius Africanus, friend of Origen and Heraclas, whose historical scholarship, like Porphyry's, led him to question the authenticity of the book of Daniel, and Eusebius, who used Julius's work as the backbone of his *Ecclesiastical History.* According to Millar (22), Dexippus rejected the Roman emphasis of Cassius Dio and Asinius Quadratus and took "the mythical period of Greek history as a starting point," relating "Roman chronology to Greek." Thus he was "almost exactly like" Porphyry in approach. Eusebius (who cites Dexippus *Chron.* F2 Jacoby) was less keen than Porphyry to evaluate the authenticity of individual texts, but, like Porphyry, he used historical research to trace a line of people who preserved divine knowledge intact and conveyed it to their students.

It would not be surprising if, like Longinus, another Athenian, Dexippus, had studied in Alexandria. Inscriptions show his family to have been prominent in Athens: his great-grandfather and his father were "sophists"; he himself was eponymous archon, a priest of Eleusis, and an agonothete of the Great Panathenaia (Proclus would later have similar responsibilities). Eunapius knew Dexippus as a contemporary of Plotinus and Porphyry and drew on him amply for his history. This Dexippus should not be confused with the author whose *Commentary on Aristotle's Categories,* in citing Iamblichus (unless this is a later gloss), proves him to be a fourth-century author: A. Busse, "Der Historiker und der Philosoph Dexippus," *Hermes* 23, no. 3 (1888): 406–7.

11. See chapter 2.

12. The year in which Origen "the theologian" died.

13. See Elizabeth DePalma Digeser, "Origen on the *Limes:* Rhetoric and the Polarization of Identity in the Late Third Century," in *The Rhetoric of Power in Late Antiquity: Religion and Politics in Byzantium, Europe, and the Early Islamic World,* ed. Robert M. Frakes, Elizabeth DePalma Digeser, and Justin Stephens (London: I. B. Tauris, 2010), app. 1.

14. Decius's decree should be seen in the context of Caracalla's 212 Edict of Citizenship. In bestowing citizenship on all of the empire's inhabitants as an act of thanksgiving, Caracalla made it

of *supplicatio,* a formal petition to the gods on behalf of the empire's defense. The resistance of Fabian, Rome's bishop, together with Christians throughout the empire, led to their deaths.[15] Decius died in battle, and Plotinus's circle would have experienced all the tumultuous events in Rome leading up to the accession of Valerian and Gallienus as co-Augusti in 253.[16]

The ten years between Plotinus's founding his school and the death of Origen "the theologian" in 253 were Porphyry's formative period. Born to a distinguished family in 232/3 in or near Tyre,[17] young Malchus was dubbed "Porphyry" by his teacher, Longinus, who said that the shade of imperial purple was a good nickname for a fellow whose name meant "king."[18] Before he studied grammar, rhetoric, and philosophy in Athens with Longinus (Eun. *VS* s.v. "Porphurios"), however, Porphyry spent time with Origen, either in Caesarea or after the elderly theologian had moved to Tyre.[19] Perhaps he was his student: Athanasius Syrus makes this claim in the biographical information preceding his translation of Porphyry's *Isagogē*.[20] Perhaps he was also Christian, as the fifth-century church historian Socrates Scholasticus declares (*HE* 3.23.37–39). Socrates may have assumed Porphyry's religion because of his relationship with Origen. But Socrates' source is Eusebius, which boosts the claim's credibility even though the passage no longer survives.[21] Moreover, Socrates mingled with Platonist scholars in the empress Athenaïs-Eudocia's circle in Constantinople, lending his account further weight. Modern authors have strenuously resisted the notion that Porphyry

---

possible for later emperors to think of the residents of the empire as a large *civitas* whose piety could avert the sort of global catastrophes that were besetting Rome's far-flung domains.

15. How resisters came to the attention of civic authorities is unknown. As with the Severan martyrdoms in Alexandria, one can assume that Christians publicly resisted this edict.

16. 250: the usurpation of Licinianus in the city, his execution several days later, and the appointment of Valerian, from an old Roman senatorial family, to handle civic affairs; 251: the death, deification, and then condemnation of Decius, the usurpation of Priscus, and the arrival of the emperor Gallus; 253: the assassination of Gallus, soon after leaving the city, and the rise of Valerian.

17. Date: Porph. *Plot.* 4 (thirty years old in the tenth year of the reign of Gallienus); family: Eun. *VS* s.v. "Porphurios"; Tyre: Porph. *Plot.* 7.51.

18. Original name and its meaning: Porph. *Plot.* 17.7–11; it was his father's name also; Longinus's nickname for the young Malchus: 17.11–15; 21.13–18.

19. Porph. ap. Eus. *HE* 6.19. See chapter 2.

20. This comes from a tenth-century Syriac manuscript, *Discipulus* (in Asseman's Latin rendition of the Syriac; unfortunately Smith's *Porphyrii philosophi fragmenta* translates Asseman's Latin, not the Syriac afresh). Stephan Evodius Asseman and Joseph Simon Asseman, eds., *Bibliothecae apostolicae Vaticanae codicum manuscriptorum catalogus* (Rome, 1759; reprint, Paris: Maisonneuve frères, 1926), 3: 307 (also frag. 29aT Smith).

21. See also Niceph. *HE* 10.36; *PG* 146, 561A3–11 (who probably uses Socrates as a source) and the ninth- or tenth-century scholiast of Lucian whom Rabe identified as Arethas (Scholia in Luciani Peregrin. 11 p. 216, 8–15 Rabe). Smith, *Porphyrii philosophi fragmenta,* 14–15, includes these two testimonia.

was originally Christian.[22] But no source affirms that Porphyry was *not* Christian when young.[23] Indeed, as chapters 5 and 6 will suggest, he may have been a Christian in the Ammonian tradition. Even if these Byzantine authors assumed he was Christian because of his association with Origen, this still takes seriously the early and deep connection between the two men. According to this tradition, Porphyry was attacked by certain Christians at Caesarea, a mishap that led him to apostatize and write against the faith.[24] Whatever Porphyry's early religious affiliation, his becoming Longinus's student (Eun. *VS* s.v. "Porphurios") is natural, given the Athenian rhetor's own connection with the school of Ammonius (Long. ap. Porph. *Plot.* 20).

Leaving Longinus in 263, Porphyry, aged thirty (Porph. *Plot.* 4.7–9), traveled west to join Plotinus (5.1–5). His arrival in Rome coincided with the Persians' capture of Valerian and thus the first year of Gallienus's sole rule. One of the emperor's first independent acts was to end the hostilities against Christians that his father had initiated in 257. According to Dionysius, bishop of Alexandria (ap. Eus. *HE* 7.10), Valerian's finance minister, Macrianus, "the teacher and chief priest of the *magoi* in Egypt" (ὁ διδάσκαλος καὶ τῶν ἀπ᾽ Αἰγύπτου μάγων ἀρχισυνάγωγος), had convinced the emperor to attack Christians because their activities were interfering with certain rituals.[25] Dionysius brings an Egyptian perspective to hostilities that affected

22. See, e.g., Joseph Bidez, *Vie de Porphyre, le philosophe néo-platonicien avec les fragments des traités "Peri agalmátōn" et "De regressu animae"* (Ghent: E. van Goethem, 1913; repr., Hildesheim: G. Olms, 1964), 6; and Andrew Smith and David Wasserstein, eds., *Porphyrii philosophi fragmenta*, Bibl. Scriptorum Graec. et Roman. Teubneriana (Stuttgart: Teubner, 1993), 16. Adolph von Harnack, "Porphyrius, *Gegen die Christen:* 15 Bücher; Zeugnisse, Fragmente, und Referate," *Abhandlungen der Königlich Preussischen Akademie der Wissenschaften, Philosophisch-historische Klasse* (1916): 4, is an interesting exception.

23. See Harnack, "Porphyrius," 41.

24. Socr. *HE* 3.23.37–39; Niceph. *HE* 10.36; *FrGrTh* 201.1–5. Athanasius Syrus (frag. 25aT Smith; Asseman and Asseman, *Bibliothecae apostolicae Vaticanae codicum manuscriptorum catalogus*, 3: 305) says that Porphyry was "condemned by" (*culpabatur* in Asseman's translation from the Syriac; Smith has "envied") Origen's students because he had dared to attack (*impugnare*) the Gospel in a work that was then opposed by Gregory the Wonderworker. Gregory (if there is a kernel of truth to this account) could not have attacked Porphyry's doctrine as a fellow student of Origen, since he would have preceded him by about twenty years. Accordingly, it is tempting to read this source more loosely: Gregory Thaumaturgos is famous for refuting Paul of Samosata at the first synod of Antioch (263/4). Eusebius equated Paul's doctrine with that of the Theodotans. If Paul was promoting a position to which Porphyry had also adhered, then Porphyry's beliefs would conform to those of Ammonius, namely that Jesus was born man but was able to unite with God through his own moral excellence and the power of the *nous* that he had received upon baptism. Another tantalizing connection is that Lucian of Antioch, whom Eusebius also associated with Paul's teachings, revised the Greek Old Testament and the four Gospels, promoting a system of literal interpretation. Eusebius does not condemn Lucian, who recanted in 289 and was later martyred under Diocletian.

25. Eusebius (*HE* 7.10) cites a letter to a certain Hermammon (otherwise unknown) from Dionysius of Alexandria in which the bishop (247–64) claims that the emperor had first been friendly

Christians elsewhere.[26] Nevertheless, an emperor confronting Germanic invasions, plague, and Persians (Zos. 1.31–37) might have come to think Christian piety was disrupting rituals preserving the *pax deorum*.[27] Annulling his father's policy, Gallienus recognized Christianity as a legitimate association.[28] Accordingly, Porphyry's years in Rome were shaped, not by a context of persecution and martyrdom, but by the relative calm that accompanied the emperor's residence in the city (SHA *Gall.* 7.4–9.8).

Once he gained access to Plotinus's circle, Porphyry discovered that he and the elder philosopher disagreed on several subjects (*Plot.* 13.10–17). For example, the two men wrangled for three days over how the soul and body were joined. Porphyry also wrote, against Plotinus, that the object of thought (*to noēma*) was outside the intellect (*ho nous*), but then says that he converted to his teacher's positions (18.20–24). Ultimately, at least according to Porphyry, the two men became close friends (7.49–50), and Plotinus asked him to edit his writings (7.49–50).[29] Porphyry also became aware of Plotinus's ability to raise "himself in thought, according to the ways Plato teaches in the *Symposium* (210–11), to the First and Transcendent God"; he achieved this union four times while Porphyry was with him (23.7–14).

Porphyry would have found that Plotinus and Origen shared similar approaches to teaching.[30] Before students could hear Plotinus's philosophical reflections, they had to learn geometry, astronomy, arithmetic, and music.[31] In teaching philosophy, Plotinus used to have someone read various Platonist (Cronius and Numenius) and Peripatetic (Aspasius and Alexander) texts aloud.[32] He then shared his thoughts on them with his students. Like

---

toward Christians, but Macrianus convinced him to persecute them as "rivals" (ἀντιπάλους), interfering with his "incantations" (ἐπαοιδῶν).

26. The effects of these hostilities are also attested in Africa (cf. *Acta proconsularia Sancti Cypriani*) and Caesarea (Eus. *HE* 7.12).

27. Christopher Haas, "Imperial Religious Policy and Valerian's Persecution of the Church, AD 257–260," *ChHist* 52, no. 2 (1983): 136: "These difficulties . . . had been fairly common throughout the entire mid third century. In the middle years of Valerian's reign, however, these various problems were multiplied on an unprecedented scale."

28. See the introduction.

29. Plotinus had written twenty-one treatises before Porphyry's arrival (Porph. *Plot.* 4).

30. See also chapter 2 and Elizabeth DePalma Digeser, "Christian or Hellene? The Great Persecution and the Problem of Christian Identity," in *Religious Identity in Late Antiquity,* ed. R. M. Frakes and Elizabeth Digeser (Toronto: Edgar Kent, 2006), 36–57.

31. Elias *In Porph.* 39.8–19 describes Porphyry's recommending such a curriculum for a certain Chrysaorius, a senator who wanted to learn philosophy when Porphyry belonged to Plotinus's circle. See also Ath. Syr. and Ammon. *In Porph.* 22.12–22, all cited in Smith, *Porphyrii philosophi fragmenta,* 23–24 (as frags. 29T, 29aT, 28T).

32. Plotinus's vision was poor, so he needed to employ a reader: Porph. *Plot.* 8; philosophical works: *Plot.* 14.

Origen, Plotinus introduced "a distinctive personal line into his consideration," in this case by bringing "the mind of Ammonius to bear" on the subject at hand (Porph. *Plot.* 14).[33] Like Origen, Plotinus's students came from the Roman elite and included poets (Zoticus; *Plot.* 7), public officials (Zethus, Castricius; *Plot.* 7), and senators (Marcellus Orrontius, Sabinillus, Rogatianus; *Plot.* 7).[34] Like Origen, Plotinus taught female students.[35] Also like Origen, he wrote many treatises that formalized the conversations in his seminars.[36] For both Plotinus and Origen, the philosophical life was an ascetic existence,[37] involving fasting,[38] sleep deprivation,[39] limited possessions,[40] and chastity. Plotinus was also a vegetarian (2.6–10), and Origen may have been as well.[41] It is impossible to know whether these ascetic practices originated with Origen or whether they had their source in Ammonius's teaching. Such a lifestyle, together with his erudition and teaching, enabled Plotinus's students to consider him as a man who exemplified his own interpretation of Plato's guidelines for wisdom,[42] "that he who is to be wise" should draw "his good from the Supreme, fixing his gaze on That, becoming like to That, living by That" (Plot. *Enn.* 1.4),[43] an attitude illustrated by a third-century Ostian bust—perhaps depicting Plotinus—whose upward gaze marks the start of a new style in portraiture.[44]

Beneath the surface of the similarities that Plotinus shares with Origen, however, are important differences. First, in Porphyry's account, Plotinus cares for children and widows, fastidiously seeing—as guardian—that

---

33. ἴδιος ἦν καὶ ἐξηλλαγμένος ἐν τῇ θεωρίᾳ καὶ τὸν Ἀμμωνίου φέρων νοῦν ἐν ταῖς ἐξετάσεσιν.

34. See also Dominic J. O'Meara, *Platonopolis: Platonic Political Philosophy in Late Antiquity* (Oxford: Oxford University Press, 2003), 14–15.

35. Porph. *Plot.* 9. One notable characteristic of the Neoplatonists in general was their willingness to include women among their number. Among them the most famous are Porphyry's wife, Marcella; Sosipatra, leader of the Pergamine school; and Hypatia, leader for a time of the Alexandrian school. O'Meara, *Platonopolis,* 18, 24, 83–86.

36. Eus. *HE* 6.15; Porph. *Plot.* 4–6, 8.

37. Eus. *HE* 6.3.2, 7, 9; Porph. *Plot.* 7.

38. Porph. *Plot.* 2, 8; Eus. *HE* 6.3.9, 12.

39. Porph. *Plot.* 7–8; Eus. *HE* 6.3.9.

40. Eus. *HE* 6.3.11 and the implication of Porph. *Plot.* 11.

41. Eus. *HE* 6.8.2 and the implication of *Plot.* 11, 15. Cf., e.g., Or. *Cels.* 8.27–28. For Origen's vegetarianism, see Mark J. Edwards, "Porphyry's Egyptian 'de Abstinentia' II.47," *Hermes* 123 (1995): 128.

42. Porph. *Plot.* 8, 17, 19.

43. Plotinus, *The Six Enneads,* trans. Stephen Mackenna and B. S. Page (Whitefish, MT: Kessinger Publishing, 2004), 44. See also *Enn.* 1.2; and H. P. L'Orange, *Art Forms and Civic Life in the Later Roman Empire* (Princeton, NJ: Princeton University Press, 1965). In general, I use Armstrong's Loeb translation of the *Enneads,* sometimes with slight modifications.

44. G. Matthew, "The Character of the Gallienic Renaissance," *JRS* 33 (1943): 67.

the law protects their inheritances (*Plot.* 9, 11). Dominic O'Meara describes such activities as "a model of practical virtue, benevolent and selfless stewardship, and fair arbitration," performed in harmony with Plotinus's "contemplation of transcendent principles." Plotinus's responsibilities to his *oikeioi,* those close to him, were those of a philosopher who had contemplated truth outside "the cave," and then returned to enlighten his fellow citizens.[45] Although Plotinus did not share Amelius's enthusiasm for the monthly new moon festival (10), he enthusiastically participated in certain private rituals: he annually celebrated Plato's birthday (2.42), and he allowed an Egyptian priest in Rome's temple of Isis to make manifest his guardian spirit, which turned out to be a higher order of daemon (10.15–28). A. H. Armstrong and other historians of philosophy have downplayed the significance of Plotinus's experience in the Iseum,[46] but the ritual performed there resembles the "theurgic" emanations that Iamblichus would promote in the ensuing generation. Plotinus also knew enough about ritual medicine to ward off a "star-stroke" attack from Olympius, one of his fellow Ammonians (10).

While Porphyry was a member of Plotinus's circle, it interacted with other people interested in theological and philosophical questions. For example, some people accused Plotinus of plagiarizing Numenius (Porph. *Plot.* 17.16–19), a charge that Porphyry wanted vigorously to oppose, not only to set out the master's teaching clearly, but also to increase his reputation (17.25–30). When a certain Diophanes promoted the erotic love between pupil and master that Plato described in the *Symposium,* Porphyry refuted him (15). Plotinus also asked Porphyry to address some questions posed by Eubulus, the Platonist professor in Athens (15). And Porphyry stayed in touch with Longinus, whom he visited in Phoenicia, where the latter had joined Zenobia's court (19). Like Origen, another Ammonian, Longinus rejected some of Plotinus's doctrines, and Porphyry wrote at least one treatise hoping to change the Athenian's position.[47]

At least according to Porphyry's account, however, the school directed its most sustained apologetic effort against the doctrines of certain Gnostics who hovered around the fringes of Plotinus's circle. Porphyry describes a group of philosophically minded Christians who, "abandoning the old philosophy" and arguing on the basis of questionable texts, asserted that Plato "had not

---

45. O'Meara, *Platonopolis,* 15, 73–81, 91–92.

46. A. H. Armstrong, "Was Plotinus a Magician?" *Phronesis* 1 (1955): 76.

47. E.g., Porphyry says that he tried to convince Longinus that Plotinus's doctrine on "the Ideas" was superior to what he held (Porph. *Plot.* 20–21).

penetrated to the depths of intelligible reality" (*Plot.* 16).[48] The school strove
energetically to oppose these people, who would have held a position substantially different from Ammonius's more literalist approach to Christian
and Jewish scripture: Plotinus "often attacked their position in his lectures"
and wrote *Against the Gnostics.* Porphyry's fellow student Amelius wrote
forty volumes against the book of Zostrianus, one of these questionable
apocalyptic texts,[49] and Porphyry wrote "a considerable number" of treatises
against the book of Zoroaster, purportedly the ancient Persian sage. Porphyry says that Zoroaster's text was "entirely spurious and modern, made
up...to convey the impression that it was something older" (*Plot.* 16). This
campaign may have motivated Porphyry to study the book of Daniel, a text,
much like the Gnostic book of Zoroaster, that claimed to be much older
than it was and that, in Porphyry's view at least, had consequently been used
inappropriately. This activity against the Gnostic texts set in full operation
the exegetical approach that both Ammonius and Origen had promoted in
different ways. Before engaging directly with the Gnostics' views, both Amelius and Porphyry looked critically at the texts on which they based their
arguments. In order to determine that they were "spurious," however, both
philosophers would have had to assess whether details in the texts indicated
that they belonged in the historical context they claimed for their own, or
whether anachronistic aspects of the texts revealed a later date of composition.

Plotinus's doctrines and Porphyry's account of his seminars suggest what
"bringing the mind of Ammonius to bear on the investigations at hand"
(*Plot.* 14) might mean. First, the activities of even Plotinus's most advanced
students evince an openness to the possibility that a new text or a new system
of thought might embrace something true. At the same time, they rigorously evaluated the authenticity of such texts and notions before accepting
their doctrinal teachings. Like the Gnostic treatises, many texts failed these

48. See A. H. Armstrong, "Dualism: Platonic, Gnostic, and Christian," in *Plotinus amid Gnostics and Christians,* ed. D. T. Runia (Amsterdam: Free University Press, 1984), 37–41; C. Evangeliou, "Plotinus' Anti-Gnostic Polemic and Porphyry's *Against the Christians,*" in *Neoplatonism and Gnosticism,*
ed. R. T. Wallis and J. Bregman (Albany, NY: State University of New York Press, 1992), 111–28;
J. Igal, "The Gnostics and 'The Ancient Philosophy' in Porphyry and Plotinus," in *Neoplatonism and
Early Christian Thought,* ed. A. H. Armstrong, H. J. Blumenthal and R. A. Markus (London: Variorum Publications, 1981), 138–49. Plotinus's *Enneads* also indicates that certain Christians, trying
to carve out space for human free will, had challenged his teaching on theological grounds. Against
them, he wrote the treatise *On Free Will.* Cf. *Enn.* 6.8, "On Free Will"; and G. Leroux, *Traité sur la
liberté et la volonté de l'Un: Ennéade VI, 8 (39)* (Paris: Vrin, 1990); many thanks to Olivier Dufault for
bringing this to my attention.
49. R. M. Grant, *Paul in the Roman World* (Louisville, KY: Westminster/John Knox Press, 2001),
51.

tests. But others may have passed: one possible such source is the *Chaldaean Oracles*. Although the evidence that Plotinus knew them is equivocal, the texts were known to Porphyry and Amelius.[50] Second, in Plotinus, we get a sense of what "philosophy without conflicts" might mean. Although he seldom alluded to other philosophers in his writings, a modern historian of philosophy describes Plotinus's doctrines as gathering "the legacy of nearly eight centuries of Greek philosophy into a magnificently unified synthesis."[51] He wove Stoic and Peripatetic teachings throughout his writings (14.4–7). The accusation that he had plagiarized Numenius derived from the deeply Pythagorean character of his Platonist metaphysics (21).[52] Finally, Plotinus's philosophy also illustrates the goal of thinking on one's own that Ammonius had advocated: his teachings are not merely a synthesis of the philosophical systems on which he drew, but "in the *Enneads* are to be found basic themes that provide an entirely new inspiration and unity for the ancient doctrines."[53] Evidence for Ammonius's influence here comes from Porphyry's observation that Plotinus was bringing "Ammonius's mind to bear" precisely in those instances where he was not merely commenting on a passage, but infusing it with his own insight.[54]

Eventually Plotinus grew ill in a way that was apparently difficult for his students to witness. In 270, when he died at a friend's estate in Campania,[55] most of his closest followers were absent: Porphyry was in Lilybaeum (having gone to Sicily either to see Etna or as an antidote to depression),[56] Amelius was in Apamea, and Castricius was in Rome (Porph. *Plot.* 2.32–34). Plotinus's sickness coincided with Gallienus's assassination and the rise of Claudius II (268–70) and then Aurelian (270–75). Plotinus's circle may have dispersed because of their teacher's health; but their association with Gallienus may also have made Rome dangerous after the rise of Claudius II, whom Zosimus implicates in the emperor's assassination (1.40). In this case, their plight would

---

50. As well as to Iamblichus; see chapter 4.

51. Maria Louisa Gatti, "Plotinus: The Platonic Tradition and the Foundation of Neoplatonism," in *The Cambridge Companion to Plotinus,* ed. Lloyd Gerson (Cambridge: Cambridge University Press, 1996), 10.

52. Ibid., 10–13.

53. Ibid., 13.

54. Ibid., 13–14.

55. His needs were met through the proceeds of two estates: that of Zethus in Campania (where he died) and Castricius's property in Minturnae (Porph. *Plot.* 2.19–21, 31).

56. Ath. Syr., Bibl. Apost. Vat. Cod. III 305 Asseman says the former; Eun. *VS* s.v. "Porphurios" and Porphyry himself say the latter (*Plot.* 11.12–20). Of course, they are not mutually exclusive reasons. Porphyry, as Plotinus's designated heir and editor, may have felt a need to account for his absence from the master's deathbed. And he may have been depressed about Plotinus's condition.

have resembled that of certain first-century philosophers whom Domitian found insufficiently enthusiastic toward his regime.[57]

At least from Porphyry's account, Plotinus had had a good relationship with Gallienus and his wife, Salonina, and the emperor's last five years in Rome would have seemed a peaceful interlude compared to the city's turbulent political life before his *decennalia*.[58] For Plotinus, this would have been an opportune moment for thinking about how states ought to be governed: Gallienus's willingness to support Plotinus in founding a city in Campania, governed by the *Laws* of Plato, suggests a common interest in the problems of government, even though the emperor's courtiers ensured that Platonopolis never came to fruition.[59] Plotinus published no commentaries on either Plato's *Laws* or the *Republic*—which contributed to an impression that he eschewed political engagement.[60] His treatise *Against the Gnostics,* written during Gallienus's last five years (262–67),[61] however, describes the contemporary Roman state in terms that evoke the regime described in Plato's *Laws*.[62]

Plato's *Republic* argues that rule by philosopher-kings supported by a guardian class is theoretically the best regime; the *Laws* sets out the best possible regime in practical terms.[63] In the latter work, Plato observed that the *Republic*'s polity might never materially exist, but the state described in the *Laws* potentially could, because it did not involve "wives, children, and all property" held in common. In the *Laws,* the Athenian stranger describes this "second-best" polity as suitable for ordinary people, as opposed to the "gods" or "children of gods" who would inhabit the city of the *Republic*.[64]

---

57. Pliny *Ep.* 7.19; Suet. *Dom.* 10.3.

58. This is not to say that affairs were peaceful throughout the empire. Indeed, Gallienus received scathing criticism from the author of the *Historia Augusta* for failing to defend Gaul and Palmyra (SHA *Gall.* 6, 13). Nevertheless, from the perspective of people living in Rome, the years 264–68 would have seemed relatively stable and calm.

59. Lukas de Blois, *The Policy of the Emperor Gallienus* (Leiden: Brill, 1976), 213.

60. See O'Meara, *Platonopolis,* 3; and L. Jerphagnon, "Platonopolis ou Plotin entre le siècle et le rêve," in *Néoplatonisme: Mélanges offerts à Jean Trouillard,* edited by P. M. Schuhl and L. Jerphagnon (Fontenay-aux-Roses: ENS, 1981), 215–16.

61. For the date, see Porph. *Plot.* 5.

62. For Plotinus's favorable impression of Gallienus's regime, see Jerphagnon, "Platonopolis," 216–21.

63. The ensuing discussion draws substantially on Digeser, "Religion, Law, and the Roman Polity," 68–84.

64. Pl. *Leg.* 5.739a–740a. Trans. T. J. Saunders throughout. See also O'Meara, *Platonopolis,* 35–36, 91–93. In the *Republic* (592), Glaucon says that the regime they are discussing exists only "in words" and probably does not occur "anywhere on earth." Socrates notes that such a "pattern" may exist for the one "who wants to see and found a city within himself. . . . It doesn't make any difference whether it is or will be somewhere." Trans. A. Bloom throughout, sometimes with modifications.

Drawing on Plato, Plotinus's *Against the Gnostics* first establishes that the Roman Empire is not governed along the lines of the *Republic* because there is wealth and poverty (*Enn.* 2.9.8–9). Next, he distinguishes the "good and wise" person (*spoudaios*) from "the more human sort" of person (*anthrōpikōteros*). The life of the former should be "directed to the highest point and the upper region." The latter can live in one of two ways: by being virtuous, the *anthrōpikōteros* can "have a share in some sort of good"; or this person can be like the "common crowd," providing "the necessities for the better sort" (2.9.9).[65] Speaking of the imperial government and echoing the polity in the *Laws* (10.904), Plotinus addresses his Gnostic opponents, some of whom, as Christians, might have abstained from the *supplicationes* on Rome's behalf during Valerian's persecution.[66] "How," he asks, "is it possible rightly to disapprove of a polity (*polei*) which gives each man his deserts? In this polity, virtue is honored and vice has its appropriate dishonour, and not merely the images of the gods but gods themselves look down on us from above,... leading all things in order from beginning to end." Whoever "ignores this," he claims, "is one of the rasher sort of humans who deal boorishly with divine things" (*Enn.* 2.9.9.19–27). For Plotinus, because the Gnostics, Christian and otherwise, did not base their system on Plato's teaching, they misunderstood the relationship between the state and the divine. In the present polity, Plotinus concludes, it is never wrong to praise the gods in their "multiplicity," for that is how God is revealed here (2.9.9.36–40). The presence of justice in the Roman system is evidence for Plotinus, not only that the state has a divine foundation, but also that, following Plato, piety is inextricably linked with the empire's pursuit of good government.

Regulating divine worship is very important in both Plato's *Republic* and the *Laws*. The *Republic* focuses more on religious education (especially by

---

65. Trans. A. H. Armstrong here and below, sometimes slightly modified.

66. A. H. Armstrong, "Man in the Cosmos: A Study of Some Differences between Pagan Neoplatonism and Christianity," in *Romanitas et Christianitas: Studia I. H. Waszink a. d. VI Kal. Nov. a MCMLXXIII XIII lustra complenti oblata*, ed. W. den Boer, P. G. van der Nat, C. M. Sicking, and J. C. M. Winden (Amsterdam: North Holland, 1973), 5–14; Chiara Guerra, "Porfirio editore di Plotino e la 'paideia antignostica,'" *Patavium* 8 (2000): 111–37; and Igal, "Gnostics," 138–39, 146 n. 7; contra J. Rist, "Plotinus and Christian Philosophy," in *The Cambridge Companion to Plotinus*, ed. Lloyd P. Gerson (Cambridge: Cambridge University Press, 1996): 394. A. H. Armstrong, "Plotinus and Christianity," in *Platonism in Late Antiquity*, ed. Stephen Gersh and Charles Kannengiesser (Notre Dame: University of Notre Dame Press, 1992), 123, claims that Plotinus speaks "for the whole Hellenic tradition" here against "an alien kind of monotheism" that Gnostics and mainstream Christians share. For T. I. Borodai, "Plotinus's Critique of Gnosticism," *Russian Studies in Philosophy* 42 (2003): 67, identifying which Gnostics Plotinus addressed is unimportant. Rather, the treatise is significant because it argues against positions that several groups, including philosophically minded Christians, shared.

censoring misleading poetry about the gods)[67] and delegates religious legislation to Apollo at Delphi. The religious legislation discussed in the *Laws*,
however, is specific and conservative. According to the Athenian stranger, the
citizens of the colony Megillus is founding at Magnesia must believe that only
a steadfast pursuit of justice will bring happiness. Justice, in turn, involves
piety because it requires taking God, not man, as a model (one thinks again
of the so-called Plotinus portrait bust with its eyes raised to heaven).[68] Piety,
finally, depends on revering "gods, spirits, heroes, and ancestors" according
to the guidance of the oracles at Delphi, Dodona, and Ammon or from
"ancient stories, visions, or divine inspiration." Regardless of the source of
the latter, "the lawgiver should not tamper with these."[69] Piety reinforces the
regime's foundation, whereas impiety undermines it.[70] Book 10 emphasizes
the importance of divine worship and piety by establishing serious punishments for impiety.[71] This "second-best" regime reflects the cosmic order as
much as possible. Thus it embodies justice as much as possible, in seeking
that everyone receives what he or she deserves.[72] The gods may seem indifferent to individuals when there are individual injustices. Such instances can
lead people toward impiety (*Leg.* 10.899–900). Nevertheless, the city's leaders
must convince their citizens to allow the gods to govern. Only then will the
city cultivate virtue (10.906) and reinforce a cosmic system of justice, allowing every soul after death to live in the region appropriate to its character.[73]

For a long time, modern historians of philosophy thought that Porphyry,
like Plotinus, was disinterested in political philosophy.[74] Nevertheless, some
of the texts he wrote against Christianity suggest that he, like Plotinus and
Plato, saw divine worship as having a foundational character in a proper state,
and that, like Plotinus, he saw certain forms of Christianity as undermining
this foundation. (Although my discussion of Porphyry's political philosophy draws primarily on works that he wrote after Plotinus's death, his ideas
accord so closely with his teacher's position that it makes sense to discuss

67. Pl. *Rep.* 427b–c; 376e–398b; see O'Meara, *Platonopolis,* 117.
68. Pl. *Leg.* 4.716a–718a. See O'Meara, *Platonopolis,* 118.
69. O'Meara, *Platonopolis,* 118; Pl. *Leg.* 5.738.
70. Pl. *Leg.* 10.889b–e. See O'Meara, *Platonopolis,* 118.
71. See also O'Meara, *Platonopolis,* 118–19.
72. Pl. *Rep.* 443b–c and 434c; *Leg.* 10.904. See also A. Sodano's (1979) commentary on Porphyry's *Sentences* (*Introduzione agli intelligibili,* 58–59 n. 21, regarding chap. 40).
73. Cf. R. F. F. Stalley, *An Introduction to Plato's Laws* (Indianapolis: Hackett, 1983), 175–77.
74. Although Proclus (*In Remp.* 2.96) refers to Porphyry among those philosophers who have
commented on the role of mythology in Plato's *Republic,* it is uncertain whether Porphyry wrote
a commentary on the entire work. See Smith and Wasserstein, *Porphyrii philosophi fragmenta,* 206
(frag. 181T).

both together.) For example, in his *Philosophy from Oracles,* Porphyry suggests that Christians are "in every way impious and atheist" because they have "apostatized from the ancestral gods through whom each *ethnos* and *polis* has come together (*sunestēten*)."[75] Like the Athenian stranger in the *Laws,* Porphyry here suggests that apostates from traditional rites merit no tolerance for abandoning "those who, for generations, among all Hellenes and *barbaroi,* throughout *poleis* and rural areas, in all holy places, sacred rituals (*teletais*) and mysteries are the subjects of theology for all emperors, lawgivers and philosophers." Porphyry's criticism of the practice of certain Christians here is particularly telling since this passage echoes Origen's *Peri archōn* almost verbatim (4.1.1). In this case, however, Origen argued that various peoples' apostasy from civic law and the teachings of philosophers was evidence for the divinity of Jesus.[76]

For Porphyry in the fragment above, like the Athenian stranger in the *Laws,* the foundational character of divine worship for all political communities, *ethnos* or *polis,* Hellene or barbarian, means that divine worship contributes to a polity's identity. Porphyry links religious law to political identity in the same fragment of the *Philosophy from Oracles.* He asks whether Christians are "Hellenes or *barbaroi,*" or whether there is anything "between these" *ethnoi,* suggesting that Christians have aspects of both groups. Their barbarian quality, their "foreignness (*xenos*)," concerns "the revolutionary character (*neōterismos*)" of their "way of life." Finally, Porphyry accuses Christians of undermining Roman religious communities by abrogating their laws and "hew[ing] out for themselves" a "new and solitary dead end."[77] In opposition to these Christians, Porphyry defines "Hellenes" in political, cultural, and religious terms as respectful of Greco-Roman law, traditional piety, and philosophy. At the same time he directly challenges Origen's boast that Christians have found in Jesus a legislator whose appeal seemed to prove both that traditional law and philosophy were illegitimate and that Mosaic law was only an image of reality (Or. *PA* 4.1.1). Further evidence that Origen's type of Christianity is Porphyry's target comes from the fragment with which chapter 1 started, the passage attributed to *Against the Christians,* written perhaps

75. Porphyry in Eusebius *Preparation for the Gospel* 1.2.1f.; my trans. For attribution to Porphyry as well as a discussion of this passage as first a paraphrase and then a quotation, see U. von Wilamowitz-Möllendorff, "Ein Bruchstück aus der Schrift des Porphyrius gegen die Christen," *ZNTW* 1 (1900): 101. For the argument that this passage introduces Porphyry's *Philosophy from Oracles* and the anti-Christian character of the work, see R. L. Wilken, "Pagan Criticism of Christianity: Greek Religion and Christian Faith," in *Early Christian Literature and the Classical Intellectual Tradition,* ed. W. Schoedel and R. Wilken (Paris: Editions Beauchesne, 1979), 127.

76. See chapter 2.

77. In Eus. *PE* 1.2.1f. See note 75 above.

in the mid-290s.[78] Here Porphyry compares Ammonius's behavior with that of Origen: Ammonius "brought up in Christian ways...turned himself without reserve toward his *politeia* to live according to its laws, when he attached himself to thinking of philosophy. But Origen, a Hellene, educated in the arguments of the Hellenes, drove headlong into shameless barbarian activity...living like a Christian in his manner of life—lawlessly—but Hellenizing in his opinions."[79]

According to Platonist teachings and traditions, a philosopher's activities should be determined by his level of advancement. Would-be philosophers who attended Plotinus's school in Rome were taught that divinization, assimilation to, or union with God should be their overriding goal.[80] Porphyry and Plotinus's many successors also energetically promoted such a goal. For his part, Porphyry devoted at least two major works to philosophers seeking this goal, of which *On Abstinence* and the *Sentences* are still extant (or mostly so).[81] Assimilation to God was a strenuous task, involving not only philosophical study, but a rigorous asceticism and a talent for deep contemplation. The ultimate goal, union with the One, the "First and Transcendent God...throned above intellect," was a rare experience even for the wisest philosopher (according to the *Life,* Plotinus achieved this feat at least four times, and Porphyry, at least once).[82] Plotinus and Porphyry emphasize that for aspiring philosophers, this goal and no other should be the focus of their lives.

Once a philosopher had achieved union with the One, however, he acquired new responsibilities. Plotinus acknowledges that some who have experienced the One choose to remain withdrawn from the distractions of daily life (*Enn.* 6.9.7.26–28). But this experience so moves a few people that they want to become guides for others. Although this motivation could be understood as a person's wanting to establish or continue a philosophical school, Plotinus also suggests that such people could and even should direct their attention more generally. "Having been in [the] company" of the One, the soul "must come and announce, if it could, to another that transcendent union. Perhaps

---

78. See the conclusion to this book.

79. Porph. *Chr.* 39 ap. Eus. *HE* 6.19.2f. In a letter to his wife, Marcella, written perhaps within the decade, Porphyry identifies three types of law: "one, the law of God; second, the law of mortal nature; third, the law established in nations and states (*ethnē kai poleis*)." The latter "strengthens social interaction through mutual agreement about the laws that have been established" and is "written in different ways at different times" (*Marc.* 25; trans. Wicker, slightly modified). For the date, see H. Whittaker, "The Purpose of Porphyry's Letter to Marcella," *SymbOsl* 76 (2001): 150, 156.

80. See, for example, Plot. *Enn.* 1.2.

81. The *Sentences* break off at chap. 43; cf. Sodano, *Introduzione agli intelligibili,* 7–12.

82. Porph. *Plot.* 23.

also it was because Minos attained this kind of union that he was said in the story to be 'the familiar friend of Zeus,'[83] and it was in remembering this [experience] that he laid down laws that were its images, being filled full of lawgiving by the divine touch."[84] "The story," in this case, is the *Odyssey*, and Plotinus's figural use of the poem shows that he is reading Homer through a Platonist lens—similar to Origen's Christian reading of Hebrew scripture. As Dominic O'Meara sees it, Plotinus believed that a person who had achieved transcendent union should become a kind of missionary, working with the centers of power to promote legislation in the divine image. Such a position is implicit in Plato's *Laws:* as they discuss the best type of polity for Megillus's future colony at Magnesia, the Athenian stranger and his companions are on their way to descend into Zeus's cave,[85] which the *Republic*'s readers know as a symbol of the terrestrial, sensible world.[86] Plotinus, however, made explicit for his students the mandate implicit in Plato, both through his conduct and through his teachings. Porphyry presents Plotinus not only as a contemplative, but also as simultaneously and deeply engaged with political life—whether as guardian and advocate for several wards, as mentor for a number of Roman senators, as a member of the emperor Gallienus's circle, or even as the potential founder of Platonopolis, where the philosopher and his followers hoped to live according to the laws of Plato.[87]

Porphyry, too, promoted this mission, not only in highlighting that element of Plotinus's career in his biography, but also in how he portrayed Pythagoras in the *Philosophical History*. Pythagoras, "purified from the pollutions of his past life and taught the things from which a virtuous man ought to be free,"[88] descended into Zeus's cave, like Minos and the Athenian stranger, staying there twenty-seven days.[89] Subsequently, Pythagoras traveled all over Italy, giving laws to the cities of Magna Graecia, some of which constituted communities similar to the polity in Plato's *Republic*.[90] Others—which also established "good government"—were more conservative (like the polity in Plato's *Laws*), working within their current constitution.[91] For

---

83. *Od.* 19.178–79.

84. Plot. *Enn.* 6.9.7.22–26.

85. Plato also notes in this text that Minos, legendary king of Megillus's Crete, was inspired by Zeus (*Leg.* 624a).

86. Pl. *Rep.* 514a–519a.

87. Porph. *Plot.* 9, 12; O'Meara, *Platonopolis,* 13–16.

88. Porph. *VP* 12.

89. Ibid. 17.

90. In that citizens "held all property in common"; *VP* 20 (trans. Guthrie).

91. A good example is Centoripae, where Siricius's legacy clearly keeps private property intact; Porph. *VP* 21.

these efforts, Porphyry notes, the inhabitants of southern Italy "ranked" Pythagoras "among the divinities."[92] If the theme of this *vita* represents Porphyry's own view, it indicates his belief that philosophers who had achieved divine union could be effective political reformers, constituting communities either along the lines of the polity in the *Republic,* where appropriate, or, probably more commonly, reconstituting them along the lines suggested in the *Laws.* Porphyry's own career bears out this idea, as we shall see in the conclusion to this book.

In the *Laws,* Plato sets out one model for the inspired philosopher who seeks to reform a polity's laws according to the image of the Divine. Here the Athenian stranger observes that, to be especially effective, a lawgiver wanting to achieve reform should work closely with a tyrant—an arrangement giving the lawgiver maximum flexibility and efficacy. At the same time, the stranger acknowledges, the lawgiver will be working to reform an existing system.[93] Hence, although guided by the legislative program of the *Laws,* every lawgiver who acted thus would fashion a unique polity, an outcome very different from the single, radical vision promoted in the *Republic.* The third-century Platonists cultivated a relationship with the Roman equivalent of Plato's tyrant, the emperor at the imperial court: so Plotinus and Gallienus, but also Porphyry and Diocletian's Nicomedian court, as I shall argue in the conclusion.[94]

If the Neoplatonists followed the advice of the Athenian stranger in the *Laws,* as Dominic O'Meara suggests,[95] they hoped their legal reforms would promote virtue among Rome's citizens. In the *Laws* (and in the *Republic*), Plato establishes four cardinal virtues: courage, temperance, (practical) wisdom, and justice;[96] the Athenian stranger believed that his legislative program would inculcate these virtues in the Magnesians. Likewise, for Plotinus, the political realm should cultivate these four cardinal virtues (*Enn.* 1.2.123–26). As we shall see, not only does such a polity, in Plotinus's view, benefit all of its citizens by promoting justice as far as possible, but for some citizens it also facilitates their assimilation to God. Since, over time, a proper polity would create the best conditions for each soul to advance as far as it could toward the divine, it provided the foundation on which the progress of all souls depended.

---

92. Porph. *VP* 20.

93. Pl. *Leg.* 4.711.

94. O'Meara, *Platonopolis,* chap. 2.

95. Ibid., 91–93.

96. Pl. *Rep.* 441d1–443b2; *Leg.* 5.733e. In the *Republic* the term for being wise is *sophos,* whereas for Plotinus the goal is the less ambitious *phronēsis.*

One way in which a polity whose laws promoted Plato's four cardinal virtues divinized individual citizens was by inculcating a type of virtue that was the first step in a process that could ultimately bring them closer to the One. Starting with Plotinus and Porphyry, Neoplatonists believed in a hierarchy of virtues, each step of which brought some good to the soul who had mastered them, but which also potentially led to acquiring the virtues at the next level. Plato's *Laws* sought to promote the cardinal virtues of *phronēsis* (practical wisdom), courage, *sōphrosunē* (temperance), and justice through the legislation that the Athenian stranger devised for Magnesia, whereas Plotinus and Porphyry taught that mastery of these virtues improved the human soul. Building on the framework of the virtues that Plato developed in the *Laws*, Plotinus and Porphyry saw the virtue of *phronēsis* as improving the soul's higher rational faculty by developing correct reasoning (*logismos*). The next two virtues brought the soul's lower orders under the rational faculty: courage, restraining anger, worked on the spirited faculty, and *sōphrosunē* likewise operated on the soul's lustful or appetitive faculty. The virtue of justice was achieved when all of the soul's faculties performed their proper function at the same time. When this happened the person's soul also properly governed the body. For Plotinus and Porphyry, these virtues are inherently political (and hence forge a further connection with Plato's *Laws*) because they "look to society (*koinōnian*)," the "security of one's neighbors," and the "coming together of people (*sungelasmou*)." People who act according to such virtues are moral (*spoudaios*) and have achieved a state of excellence in which their human life is lived according to nature (*phusis*),[97] because their passions are limited through activities (*energeias*) that have a relationship with nature. Plotinus would even accord a kind of divinity to such a person,[98] but one who had mastered the political virtues would also potentially be in a position to tackle the "purificatory" virtues, those that the Neoplatonists thought genuinely divinized the soul.[99]

Although the Neoplatonists saw the political virtues inculcated by a good polity's laws as the first stage in a person's deification, they, like Plato, did not view their mastery as an easy accomplishment. For Plato in the *Laws*, because the polity's laws have a divine foundation, the key to achieving these virtues, "to latch onto justice," is to take God as one's model and pursue the

---

97. *Porph. Sent.* 34. This is why this is the realm of necessity or fate, since nature is governed by necessity. See below.

98. *Enn.* 1.2.1.23–26: "It is unreasonable to suppose that we are not made godlike in any way by the civic virtues . . . tradition certainly calls men of civic virtue *godlike* and we must say that somehow or other they were made like by this kind of virtue."

99. Plot. *Enn.* 1.2; Porph. *Sent.* 34.

forms of traditional piety. "A good man must sacrifice to the gods" (including those of the underworld and Olympus, the patron gods of the state,
daemons, heroes, and one's ancestral gods); wicked, polluted people, however,
got no benefit from such rituals (*Leg.* 4.716–17). Pursuing these goals was
difficult. As the Athenian stranger notes, "The road to vice is smooth and
can be traveled without sweating, because it is very short; but 'as the price of
virtue' [Hesiod] says,

> the gods have imposed the sweat of our brows, and long and steep is the
> ascent that you have to make and rough, at first; but when you get to
> the top, then the rugged road is easy to endure.[100]

Porphyry also associated the practice of traditional piety with acquiring
political virtue, an arduous task that allowed the soul to master the body by
taming the passions.[101] He also discussed how people might purge themselves
of physical pollution in order to benefit from the traditional rituals that Plato
associated with pursuing virtue. Quoting an oracle of Apollo that echoes
Plato's reference to Hesiod, Porphyry marvels at "how much effort" it takes
for a person to carry out the sacrifices required to purify the body, "to say
nothing of . . . finding the salvation of the soul."[102]

Because mastering the cardinal virtues in the political realm was so difficult, the Neoplatonists believed that citizens needed a guide to help them.
For Plato, a citizen of the polity described in the *Laws* could pursue virtue
through the guidance of the laws themselves as well as by following the
example of the lawgiver and a properly virtuous political leadership (*Leg.*
12.945–46, 960f.). Plotinus and Pythagoras, at least according to Porphyry's
portraits, also acted as exemplars of virtue within their political communities,
men whose behavior citizens could emulate and thus keep the community
aligned with its divine foundation. In this view, the political virtues that
shape the behavior of a polity's leaders promote justice because they ensure
that the community's rational faculty tames and guides the citizenry's appetitive and choleric elements. The rational soul of the community, you might
say, is properly governing the citizen body.

---

100. Pl. *Leg.* 4.718e–719a; Hes. *Works and Days* 287–92.

101. Porph. *Chr.* frag. 1 Harnack ap. Eus. *PE* 1.2f.

102. Porph. *Phil. or.* frag. 324 Smith ap. Eus. *PE* 14.10. The oracle as Eusebius quotes it: "The
way of the blessed ones is steep and very rough, opening at the beginning to gates adorned with
bronze. But there are infinite pathways that have arisen." Plotinus also thought that the "good" person should acknowledge the existence of good spirits, the gods in this world, and the intelligible gods,
for "it is not contracting the divine into one but showing it in that multiplicity in which God himself
has shown it, which is proper to those who know the power of God, inasmuch as, abiding who he is,
he makes many gods, all depending on himself and existing through him and from him." *Enn.* 2.9.9.

In the Neoplatonists' cosmos, because Soul ruled the sensible world, a citizen who had mastered the political virtues (who had allowed the rational soul to rule the other faculties and hence the body) would have brought the government of her self into alignment with that of the best earthly polity and with that of the sensible world. In other words, the organization of a soul imbued with political virtue is an image of the sensible world, a domain that Plotinus and Porphyry sometimes described, in figural language appropriated from Hesiod's *Theogony,* as the realm of Zeus.[103] Accordingly, each polity structured in such a way that its laws cultivate political virtue is, in turn, a different image of the sensible world. For the Neoplatonists, each polity is a unique reflection of Zeus's kingdom, brought into alignment through the efforts of the Platonist lawgiver, who, like Minos, had listened to the god's counsels. Insofar as they reflect the organization of the cosmos, the best polities, like souls endowed with the political virtues, participate in the divine order. Nevertheless, the bodies in them, because they participate in the material, sensible world, are also subject to the laws of nature, or fate.[104]

Promoting Plato's four cardinal virtues through a polity's legislation or, in the Neoplatonists' terms, using law to promote the "political virtues" created a just and peaceful society, insofar as was humanly possible. This aspect of such legislation is clearly articulated in Plato's *Laws,* and Plotinus believed this as well.[105] For philosophers, people fairly advanced in virtue (by the Neoplatonists' reckoning), the achievement of a well-ordered state created circumstances beneficial for the philosophers' own quest for divinization and perhaps even union with the One. For example, Plotinus believed that within Gallienus's polity, where "virtue is honored and vice has its appropriate dishonor," the moral person's life should be directed beyond the sensible world. This goal was achieved by practicing the "purificatory" virtues, a distinction that distinguishes the Neoplatonists from Plato.[106] The philosopher did not reject the political virtues, for Plotinus believed that whoever had achieved higher-order virtues necessarily possessed the lower-order ones.[107] Porphyry likewise promoted purificatory virtues as those directing the soul upward. He set them out systematically in his *Sentences* as "the virtues of the human soul which is purifying itself" and "withdrawing toward true being." Although these comprise the same four cardinal virtues, because their aim is

103. Porph. *De anima* frag. 438 Smith ap. Aug. *Serm.* 241.7.
104. Plot. *Enn.* 5.8.7.
105. *Enn.* 2.9 ("Against the Gnostics").
106. Armstrong, *Enneads* 2: 135 (a note on Plot. *Enn.* 1.2).
107. *Enn.* 1.2.7.

not merely to moderate but to "eradicate the passions," the way they manifest themselves is different than in the political realm. In this effort, one acts with *phronēsis,* not by "glorifying the body, but in acting by oneself—perfected with pure thought (*noein*)." *Sophrosunē* consists in "not even being involved with the passions," and courage in "no longer fearing separation from the body." If these are accomplished, then "reason (*logos*) and intellect (*nous*) rule" the soul. Because these virtues also detach the soul from bodily concerns and from the natural world, they free souls from the grip of fate.[108] Porphyry came to believe that theurgy might also free the spirited part of the soul from the effects of fate, from its attachment to the body and the material world (see chapter 5 and the conclusion). Theurgy, by Porphyry's definition, was a process of divination by which a god could be coaxed into a material vessel, either a human body or a statue. Presumably because this activity produced visions of the intelligible world, it led a participant to the divine by providing evidence for its existence and the value of pursuing it, strengthening the soul's rational faculty as a result.[109]

The philosopher who has mastered the purificatory virtues has brought herself into alignment with the cosmic relationship between the sensible and intelligible worlds, since Intellect, insofar as is possible in a human body, rules her soul. This is an arrangement that Plotinus likened, reading Hesiod's legends figurally, to Zeus's presence within Kronos before he was born as part of the creation of the sensible world.[110] Using intellect to govern soul and body, the philosopher has made himself an image of Intellect or Kronos, whom Plotinus described as king of the intelligible realm. Plotinus even implied that he was the son of Ouranos, an inexact metaphor for the One. (This systematic mapping of Hesiod's three chief divine progenitors onto the three divine hypostases first appears with Plotinus and again shows that he was not averse to reading the Greek poets figurally from a Platonist perspective.)[111] King of the small realm of his own person, the philosopher

---

108. *Sent.* 34.

109. Porph. *Phil. or.* frags. 316–21, 330–39 Smith; Porph. *Regr.* ap. Aug. *Civ.* 10.

110. Elsewhere, Plotinus uses the analogy of the perceptible house and the intelligible house: "The perceptible house participates in arrangement and order, but there, in its formative principle [i.e., the intelligible house], there is no arrangement or order or proportion" because these appear only when form is extended into matter. *Enn.* 1.2.1.43f., with Armstrong, *Enneads* 1: 130.

111. These metaphors work together with Plotinus's other reference to Hesiod's *Theogony* 453f. in his analysis of Soul as Zeus (see *Enn.* 3.8 [30] 11.35–45; 5.8 [31] 12.3–7; and 5.5 [32] 3.16–24). Plotinus has perhaps drawn this analogy from Plato's own observation in the *Laws* (4.712e–714a): "To name a proper *politeia* after what governs it, it should be a theocracy under the guidance of Kronos, the god who rules over men rational enough to let him. . . . Kronos knew that human nature could not take control of human affairs without arrogance and injustice, so he appointed kings and rulers who were beings of a superior and more divine order. . . . Where rulers are mortal we should

has achieved the "city" of the *Republic* insofar as is possible on earth. The realm of Intellect, Kronos's kingdom, embodiment of the "Golden Age,"[112] is where such a philosopher's true citizenship involves him. Unlike the kingdom of Zeus, the sensible world, full of flux and change, and unlike the individuality of each polity constituted according to the program in the *Laws,* the kingdom of Kronos, of which the philosopher creates an image in his soul, that is, the intelligible world, is a state in which all live in perfect justice and equality.[113] It is eternal, unchanging, and universal, since Intellect governs it, and it embraces the unchanging Forms. It constitutes the "source and nature of justice," Plotinus claims.[114] And like the citizen of its image, the sensible world, the person who seeks this true justice, through the pursuit of the purificatory virtues, must follow the divine law that embraces them. This "divine law," Porphyry explains, is an eternal and unchanging law "for the salvation of rational souls."[115] As this is a difficult process, Porphyry encourages whoever seeks this realm to embrace the form of piety proper to this realm. "God," he says, "being the Father of all, is in need of nothing; but for us it is good to adore Him by means of justice, chastity and other virtues, and thus to make life itself a prayer to Him, by inquiring into and imitating His nature. For inquiry purifies and imitation deifies us, by moving us nearer to Him."[116] By keeping the divine at the forefront of one's mind, these practices encourage the contemplative to follow the precepts of the divine law that can unite the rational soul to Intellect and even bring a vision of the One. Adding that the divine law is "unknown to impure souls," Porphyry argues that it "shines forth in the pure soul" and is the guide to deification.[117]

---

imitate the life people led under Kronos as much as possible" (trans. Saunders, slightly modified). For Plotinus's distinctive use of this passage, see P. Hadot, "Ouranos, Kronos, and Zeus in Plotinus' Treatise against the Gnostics," in *Neoplatonism and Early Christian Thought,* ed. A. H. Armstrong, H. J. Blumenthal, and R. A. Markus (Rugby, UK: Variorum Publications, 1981), 124–37. For most Middle Platonists, Intellect was the first principle (Armstrong, "Plotinus and Christianity," 119).

112. Pl. *Leg.* 4.713 (trans. Saunders), in describing the "wonderfully happy life" over which Kronos presided when there was "peace, respect for others, good laws, justice in full measure, and a state of happiness and harmony among the races of the world," is clearly referring to Hesiod's characterization of Kronos's golden age in *Works and Days* 110. This motif is implicit in Plotinus's notion that when Intellect presides there exists "the true life of Kronos" (*Enn.* 5.1.4.10; trans. Armstrong).

113. Hadot, "Ouranos, Kronos, and Zeus," 43.

114. *Enn.* 5.8.10.

115. See Armstrong, "Plotinus and Christianity," 120–21, for the "essential unity" of the metaphysics of Porphyry and Plotinus, together with K. Corrigan, "Amelius, Plotinus, and Porphyry on Being, Intellect, and the One: A Reappraisal," *ANRW* 2.36.2 (1987): 975–93; contra, e.g., Salvatore Lilla, "Un dubbio di S. Agostino su Porfirio," *NAFM* 5 (1987): 319–29.

116. Porph. *Phil. or.* ap. Aug. *Civ.* 19.23.

117. Porph. *Marc.* 25–26.

One should "fly to our dear country,"[118] Plotinus exhorted his auditors, using the figural Homeric allusion to suggest that from the perspective of his place even in the best earthly realm, the philosopher lived, like Odysseus, as a kind of exile. Because he is both king of the sensible world and always a child of Kronos held within the intelligible, Zeus, Plotinus says, is an infallible guide to the upper realm, a position that reinforces the role that a polity's laws play in the process of divinization.[119] Taking Zeus as a model, the philosopher too lived partly in the sensible world and partly in the intelligible world. In Porphyry's description, in fact, Plotinus is an example of a person living simultaneously in both realms.[120] This existence in two spheres makes the mature philosopher a compelling guide for the polity and its citizens: because the intellectual part of his soul resides in the intelligible world, he can see the ideal form in every material thing. For this reason, the mature philosopher can see what is true within every ritual, image, and mythological legend.[121]

For those who managed to orient themselves successfully to Kronos's kingdom, to the realm of the Intelligible, the rewards were great. Plotinus's soul after his death, at least according to an Apolline oracle reported by Porphyry, had eternally joined the company of heaven.[122] Having purified itself from all traces of the material world, Plotinus's soul, like all other pure souls, had taken up permanent residence in the area around the moon. This is the region, Porphyry says, that the poets called "Elysium," and it was also home to the children of Zeus.[123] Philosophers have access to this realm through contemplation, and pure souls abide in it after the death of the body.[124] Souls still bearing impurities, however, repeatedly return to the terrestrial world in new mortal bodies,[125] until they learn how to purify themselves.[126] A

---

118. *Il.* 2.140.

119. *Enn.* 5.8.10–13.

120. *Plot.* 8.

121. See Plot. *Enn.* 5.8.

122. Porph. *Plot.* 23. We might suspect that Apollo's priest, priestess, or theurge has some connection to Plotinus's school. This is not to say that the oracle was manipulated, but to observe that people in the act of interpreting ambiguous signs, symbols, and impulses might understandably be predisposed to read them in a particular way.

123. In *Sent.* 32 Porphyry suggests that a soul who had mastered the purificatory virtues, the best that a human person could achieve, could become a good daemon, i.e., a soul worthy of living with Zeus's offspring. See also Porph. *Regr.* frag. 298 Smith ap. Aug. *Civ.* 10.30.20f.; Porph. frag. 382 ap. Stob. *Anth.* 1.49.61; Porph. frag. 404 ap. Serv. *Aen.* 5.735.

124. Porph. *Stug.* frag 377 ap. Stob. *Anth.* 1.49.53. Porphyry also taught that Jesus' soul arrived here after his death. Porph. *Phil. or.* frag. 345 Smith ap. Eus. *DE* 3.6.39–3.7.2.

125. Porph. *Stug.* frag. 377 ap. Stob. *Anth.* 1.49.53. See also Pl. *Phaed.* 107d–115a.

126. Porph. *Regr.* ap. Aug. *Civ.* 10; Pl. *Rep.* 618.

properly organized polity, then, was key not only to the philosopher's quest for salvation, but also for everyone else. Only in a community where there was justice, where each met with his due (Porph. *Sent.* 32), could philosophically oriented souls best pursue the paths of virtue leading to Elysium. Only in such a polity could all other souls take the first step in that direction by learning to order themselves under reason through the political virtues. Only in such a polity, too, could some of that latter group make the jump from the political to the purificatory virtues and so begin their ascent to heaven.

Neither Plotinus nor Porphyry understood the path of the purificatory virtue leading to Elysium as a *via universalis,* a route appropriate for all of a polity's citizens.[127] Rather, drawing on Plato's *Laws,* but also his *Gorgias* and *Phaedo,* they thought that the journey to Elysium was a staged journey comprised of several paths: each led upward; for each the soul had a guide. A citizen who had ascended the path of political virtue, however difficult the ascent might have been, might not have a soul well suited for the next stage of the journey (for the path of purificatory virtues). In the *Laws,* the Athenian stranger observes that in a properly constituted polity, one whose order reflects the structure of the cosmos,

> [God] contrived a place for each constituent [of the soul] where it would most easily and effectively ensure the triumph of virtue and the defeat of vice throughout the universe. Small changes in unimportant aspects of character entail small horizontal changes of [a soul's] position in space, while a substantial decline into injustice sets the soul on the path to the depths of the so-called "under" world, which men call "Hades" and similar names. (*Leg.* 10.904)

In this view, because this rough and steep ascent to political virtue did not improve the soul as much as it allowed the soul to tame the body, a successful ascent did not necessarily allow a soul access to the next stage in the journey. For example, Plotinus argues that weak souls, incapable of contemplation, cannot ascend further upward but rather satisfy this restless impulse to "grasp the vision" by devoting themselves to lives of political action (*Enn.* 3.8.4, 6). Likewise, Porphyry states that, while possessing the higher virtues means that a soul has mastered the lower ones, possessing the lower ones is no guarantee that one can master the higher ones (*Sent.* 32). This is also the implication

---

127. See Gillian Clark, "Augustine's Porphyry and the Universal Way of Salvation," in *Studies on Porphyry,* ed. George E. Karamanolis and Anne Sheppard (London: Institute of Classical Studies, 2007), 127–40.

of his overt claim, reported by Augustine, that "no doctrine has yet been established...which offers a universal way for the liberation of the soul."[128]

Although we must always remember that we are seeing him through Porphyry's eyes, Plotinus brings into sharp focus the role that Platonist philosophy played in the third-century public sphere. In Plotinus's hands, it is at once a way of life, an educational method, a discipline leading one to the divine, a system for proper exegesis and hermeneutics, a technique for deriving doctrines without conflicts from a wide range of philosophical sources, and a guide for a person's proper relationship to the state. The shadows of these practices are evident in Ammonius, and the outlines are more clearly apparent in Origen (although his belief that Jesus was the *logos* incarnate led him to apply them in different ways). With Plotinus we see clearly both this system in full operation and the obvious influence it had on his student, Porphyry. Indeed, both men conceived of their political visions in opposition to specific Christian antagonists. After Plotinus's death, Porphyry was left with his mentor's legacy to manage. He seems first to have done so simply through continuing to teach Plotinus's doctrines in Rome (Eun. *VS* s.v. "Porphurios"). In this capacity, he drew the attention of a younger scholar, fresh from Alexandria and eager to learn about Plotinus's teachings. Iamblichus, however, in trying to build a theological system addressing the needs of ordinary people as well as philosophers, would ultimately present a serious challenge to Porphyry, one that led him not only to defend his understanding of Plotinus's system with vigor, but also to do so in a way that strove to undermine the foundation of any universal system. In this way, Origen's brand of Christianity and Iamblichus's form of Platonism together felt the heat of Porphyry's attack.

---

128. Porph. *Regr.* frag. 302 Smith ap. Aug. *Civ.* 10.32.5–16.

✒ CHAPTER 4

Schism in the Ammonian Community

Porphyry v. Iamblichus

The split that developed among third-century Hellenes who could trace their lineage to Ammonius concerned the value of rituals. As far as the sources indicate, this disagreement, centered around Porphyry and Iamblichus, first focused on the role that rituals played for members of the philosophical community. As the schism developed, however, they came to debate also the value of rituals for the souls of ordinary persons. After issues of common ground and terminology among Platonists are addressed, Plotinus's view of rituals will be discussed, since both Iamblichus and Porphyry claimed to draw their positions from his. Amelius, Plotinus's disciple of twenty-four years, is often blamed for first breaking with this circle over the value of rituals for the philosopher. But, I argue, another Plotinian, Castricius, was actually the first to do so. Castricius came to accept Iamblichus's perspective on the merits of blood sacrifice for the philosopher, a position that Porphyry strenuously opposed in his treatise *On Abstinence*. A heated exchange with Iamblichus, preserved in the latter's *On Mysteries*, resulted in Porphyry's further rejection of the Syrian philosopher's claim that material rituals were a path along which the souls of all people must travel to return to their source. I conclude by showing how Porphyry, in several treatises, formulated his own theology for the return of the soul in a system that stipulated different practices for different types of souls.

Although the rift between Porphyrians and Iamblichaeans filtered into priestly and political circles by the end of the third century, these Hellenes broadly agreed about two categories of rituals: the most elevated form, appropriate only for philosophers, and the basest form, or magic. At one extreme was the abstract form of ritual that Plotinus described as a method or exercise, the purpose of which was to facilitate *henosis theoi,* contact with Nous or the One.[1] Iamblichus claimed to differ with Porphyry over how to achieve such contact, but both agreed that it was an important goal for people like them. The Platonist community also agreed that certain practices were "magic."[2] Plotinus used the term to apply to the manipulation of the ties of *sympatheia* for what E. R. Dodds called "mean personal ends."[3] An example of such activity and Plotinus's belief in its potency comes from Porphyry's *Life of Plotinus* (10). Olympius, a fellow Ammonian who "claimed to be a philosopher," apparently saw Plotinus as an undesirable rival—so much so that he attempted "to bring a star-stroke upon him by magic."[4] Plotinus's soul, however, in Porphyry's account, was "able to throw" these attacks back at "those who were seeking to do him harm." Plotinus "said that his limbs on that occasion were squeezed together and his body contracted 'like a money-bag pulled tight.'"[5] Whatever rituals Olympius had performed, thus, were "magic" because they were intended to advance his career and not his soul. Although he acknowledged that ritual use of powers inherent in certain substances, gestures, potions, and incantations might be used to such ends,[6] Plotinus argued that magic cannot harm the good man,

---

1. Gregory Shaw, "Eros and Arithmos: Pythagorean Theurgy in Iamblichus and Plotinus," *AncPhil* 19, no. 1 (1999): 135–37.

2. In order clearly to delineate the tensions in the Platonist community, one must use their terminology. Some scholars (e.g., S. Eitrem, "La théurgie chez les néo-platoniciens et dans les papyrus magiques," *SO* 22 [1942]: 49; E. R. Dodds, "Theurgy and Its Relationship to Neoplatonism," *JRS* 37 [1947]: 57, 58) equate magic and theurgy, a habit that confuses rather than explicates these intra-school tensions.

3. Dodds, "Theurgy," 57. See also A. H. Armstrong, "Was Plotinus a Magician?" *Phronesis* 1 (1955): 73. Plotinus discusses magic throughout *Enn.* 4.4, "On Difficulties about the Soul II." See 4.4.37f., but especially 4.4.35 (in that choices should not be self-directed, but toward the Good) and 4.4.40 (on the magical manipulation of what Plotinus has defined as *sympatheia* in 4.4.26.4). See also Mark J. Edwards, "Two Episodes in Porphyry's *Life of Plotinus,*" *Historia* 40 (1991): 459–60.

4. Porph. *Plot.* 10: ὥστε καὶ ἀστροβολῆσαι αὐτὸν μαγεύσας ἐπεχείρησεν. According to LSJ, the term means to be "sun-scorched." The other reference in the dictionary (besides this passage) is Thphr. *HP* 4.14.2.

5. Armstrong, "Was Plotinus a Magician?" 74 n. 1; and P. Merlan, "Plotinus and Magic," *Isis* 44 (1953): 343 n. 19; both think that this event took place at Alexandria, not Rome.

6. Dodds, "Theurgy," 57; Edwards, "Two Episodes," 459: "The philosophy of Plotinus...admitted the efficacy of magic"; G. Luck, "Theurgy and Forms of Worship in Neoplatonism," in *Religion, Science, and Magic in Concert and in Conflict,* ed. J. Neusner (Oxford: Oxford University Press, 1989), 204–5.

since it affects only his body and irrational parts, not his soul or his rationality (*Enn.* 4.4.43.2–6).[7] Nevertheless, the good man can fight off the harmful powers that would affect his irrational parts through "counter-chants and counter-inclinations" (4.4.43.8–12),[8] as Porphyry described Plotinus doing. Thus defined, "magic" is something over which the Plotinian community agreed.[9] Since I am interested in exploring the social and political implications of the Hellenes' rift over rituals, I will not discuss either spiritual exercises or magic further.

Before analyzing the third-century disagreement over the value of rituals, however, it is important to recognize that certain terms are often applied differently in Platonist and modern parlance and even between different ancient authors. One example is the term "salvation." Our Protestantized society tends to view souls as being either deserving or unworthy of salvation, an all-or-nothing status. Third-century Platonists, however, thought that a range of activities positioned the soul, depending on its condition, at different levels within the celestial spheres, even to union with transcendent divinity, or *henosis theōi*. Philosophers were especially interested in divine union, which, according to Porphyry, might allow their souls to break out of the cycle of metempsychosis. Activities were salvific if they improved the condition of the soul; for ordinary persons certain activities would perhaps allow their souls to achieve *henosis theōi* in a *future* life.

While the concept of "salvation" differs in modern and ancient Platonist usage, the term "theurgy" is also used in different ways, not only by contemporary historians and ancient philosophers, but also by Porphyry and Iamblichus, who defined the concept differently in staking out opposing positions. Modern scholars often distinguish traditional local or imperial cultic rituals (e.g., prayers, processions, offerings, sacrifices, and feasting) from "theurgic" activities, which they usually associate with Iamblichus's circle and link with Chaldaean practice, at least as described in or extrapolated from the

---

7. Luck, "Theurgy," 205. Far less can it harm the visible gods, the higher soul, Nous, or the One (4.4.42.20–30). See Armstrong, "Was Plotinus a Magician?" 77–78.

8. Armstrong, "Was Plotinus a Magician?" 75, argues—rightly I think—contra Merlan, "Plotinus and Magic," 341–48, that Plotinus is not advocating here that philosophers can or ought to practice magic. Rather, as Edwards, "Two Episodes," 459, observes, "Plotinus...is prepared to speak of a sort of *goēteia* as the legitimate and necessary equipment of the sage."

9. Cf. E. R. Dodds, *The Greeks and the Irrational* (Berkeley: University of California Press, 1951), in Armstrong, "Was Plotinus a Magician?" 73, for Plotinus. According to Luck, "Theurgy," 188–89, 204–5, both Porphyry (*Abst.* 2.43) and Iamblichus (*DM* 3.28–29) distinguish *goēteia* from theurgy. It was the Christians, Luck emphasizes, that catalogued both together.

Chaldaean Oracles.[10] The Egyptian frame in which Porphyry sets his letter to Anebo (answered by Iamblichus's *De mysteriis*), together with the questions he asks, however, indicate that this term can also apply to Egyptian rituals connected to Hermetic treatises and other texts.[11] Both Chaldaean and Egyptian rituals included activities believed to produce a divine manifestation for the ritual's participants, an incident similar to what an oracle's prophet experienced, but accessible to other practitioners and witnesses. While Porphyry apparently endorsed the distinction that I have just outlined between theurgy and traditional cultic ritual, however, Iamblichus would not have accepted it. In his view, every ritual act—from the goriest sacrifice to Plotinus's most abstract spiritual exercise—was "theurgy" because it performed "works" (*erga*) required by the gods (*theoi*), who had also established the formulae for performing it. Thus Iamblichus's broad concept of theurgy even included rites that the *Chaldaean Oracles* rejected. The *erga* of the oracles themselves were intellectual, however, and this is how Porphyry understood them. Nevertheless, Iamblichus expanded the term to include material rites and sacrifice.[12] In making this conceptual move, Iamblichus's attitude toward matter is closer to the Hermetic than the Chaldaean or Platonist tradition.[13]

Analyzing the debate between Porphyry and Iamblichus over rituals must start with Plotinus, since both his successors based their own positions on his doctrine. Nevertheless, the dominant modern view is that Plotinus disdained all rituals except his spiritual exercises: although he thought that traditional cults were necessary for ordinary people, he did not see them as useful for the advance of his own or any philosopher's soul.[14] Porphyry provides the evidence usually brought to bear, describing Plotinus's refusal to accompany Amelius when he became fond of sacrifices (*philothutos*) and "took to ... visiting the temples at the New Moon and the [festivals] of the gods."[15] Rejecting Amelius's invitation, Plotinus answered: "They ought to come to me (*erchesthai*), not I to them," a remark that, according to Porphyry, no one

10. Carine Van Liefferinge, *La théurgie des Oracles Chaldaïques à Proclus* (Liège: Centre International d'Etude de la Religion Grecque Antique, 1999), 105.

11. Cf., e.g., Luck, "Theurgy," 207; Sarah Iles Johnston, *Hekate Soteira: A Study of Hekate's Roles in the Chaldean Oracles and Related Literature* (Atlanta: Scholars Press, 1990), 6.

12. Alberto Camplani and Marco Zambon, "Il sacrificio come problema in alcune correnti filosofiche di età imperiale," *AnnSE* 19 (2002): 90–91.

13. Van Liefferinge, *La théurgie,* 91, n. 416.

14. Jay Bregman, "Judaism as Theurgy in the Religious Thought of the Emperor Julian," *AncW* 26, no. 2 (1995): 135.

15. L. Brisson, "Amélius: Sa vie, son oeuvre, sa doctrine, son style," *ANRW* 2.36.2 (1987): 813.

understood or "dared" to question (*Plot.* 10).[16] Philip Merlan thought Plotinus meant that he could "compel the gods to come to him" by theurgy. But most historians see Plotinus as indifferent at best to theurgy as either Porphyry or modern scholars define it.[17]

This portrait of Plotinus, however, is too monochromatic. First, a careful reading of the *Enneads* shows that Plotinus does not condone abolishing ancestral practices. Not only did he uphold traditional beliefs, but Plotinus often used motifs from mythology and religious poetry as metaphors in a positive way.[18] Porphyry's *Life of Plotinus,* read simply as a factual account, also depicts Plotinus's involvement in a range of ritual activities. For example, he annually celebrated Plato's birthday. His ascetic habits, vegetarianism, and sleep deprivation might also count as rituals. Moreover, he willingly accompanied an Egyptian priest to Rome's Iseum,[19] and he accepted as valid the ritual's indication that his guardian spirit was "a god…and not a companion of the subordinate order" (Porph. *Plot.* 10).[20] Not only does Porphyry say that Plotinus "continually kept the divine eye of his soul fixed on this companion," but this experience also motivated him to write the treatise *On Our Guardian Spirit* (*Enn.* 3.4.6), in which he considers the character of this spirit and its utility.[21]

E. R. Dodds warned against accepting Porphyry's account of the Iseum ceremony at face value, since it occurred before Porphyry went to Rome and some thirty-five years before he wrote Plotinus's biography.[22] The incident is, in fact, less important as a historical vignette than as an example of what Porphyry thought was acceptable ritual practice for a philosopher.[23] In interpreting this account, the reader must remember that the preface to the

---

16. Armstrong, "Was Plotinus a Magician?" 77, thinks this remark was meant to put Amelius off: Plotinus did not want to go "church crawling," a comment that says more about Armstrong than Plotinus.

17. Merlan, "Plotinus and Magic," 346 in Armstrong, "Was Plotinus a Magician?" 77. Historians discounting Plotinus's interest in theurgy include Dodds, "Theurgy," 57; John M. Dillon, "Iamblichus on the Personal Daemon," *AncW* 32, no. 1 (2001): 7; see also Armstrong, "Was Plotinus a Magician?" 73, who draws on Dodds, *Greeks and the Irrational;* Johnston, *Hekate Soteira,* 79. Cf. also A. Smith, *Porphyry's Place in the Neoplatonic Tradition: A Study in Post-Plotinian Neoplatonism* (The Hague: Nijhoff, 1974), 128; J. M. Rist, "Mysticism and Transcendence in Later Neoplatonism," *Hermes* 92 (1964): 225; Bregman, "Judaism as Theurgy," 135.

18. Cf. esp. *Enn.* 2.9.9.58; Robbert Maarten Van den Berg, "Plotinus' Attitude to Traditional Cult: A Note on Porphyry VP 10," *AncPhil* 19, no. 2 (1999): 355.

19. Luck, "Theurgy," 207, contra Edwards, "Two Episodes," 456.

20. Luck, "Theurgy," 207; Johnston, *Hekate Soteira,* 79.

21. Edwards, "Two Episodes," 458.

22. Dodds, "Theurgy," 60.

23. Accordingly, Dodds, "Theurgy," 58, rather missed the point, in thinking that this story was merely "school gossip."

Enneads is hagiography, that despite Porphyry's objective stance, meticulous chronology, and eyewitness testimony, the biography presents his image of the ideal philosopher. Written in 300 (*Plot.* 23), this narrative describing Plotinus's relationship to ritual practice, read within the context of Porphyry's split with Iamblichus over what type of rites were proper for whom, implies that the philosopher was open to a variety of ritual forms and practices, including theurgy. Before investigating Porphyry's portrait of his mentor more deeply, however, the evidence for rupture in the Plotinian community needs to be addressed.

Gentilianus Amelius is often portrayed as a student of Plotinus who rejected the master's approach to rituals even during his lifetime.[24] A prolific author, Amelius wrote many treatises while with Plotinus in Rome, including "On the Problem of Justice in Plato" and "Against the Book of Zostrianus" in addition to his *scholia* on the master's seminars and his treatise against Porphyry's *aporiae*. By age fifty or so (ca. 270), however, he had relocated to Apamea in Syria with his adopted son, Hostilianus Hesychius (Porph. *Plot.* 2–3, 7).[25] Continuing to write ("On the Doctrinal differences between Plotinus and Numenius"),[26] Amelius probably lived in Apamea until the end of his life.[27] In his own commentaries, Porphyry refers to Amelius's interpretations of Plato's *Timaeus, Republic, Parmenides,* and *Philebus,* but it is impossible to tell whether these were formal treatises or remarks that Amelius made in the course of discussions at Plotinus's school.

Amelius may have settled in Apamea because of his interest in Numenius, whose writings he knew by heart (Porph. *Plot.* 3),[28] and for whom he is one of the most important extant sources.[29] Numenius was born in Apamea and had taught there. Although a school is unlikely to have survived him, traditions and materials from his teaching probably circulated in the city after his

24. Brisson, "Amélius," 796.

25. G. Fowden, "The Platonist Philosopher and His Circle in Late Antiquity," *Philosophia* 7 (1977): 372, thinks Aemilius went there directly from Rome. Brisson, "Amélius," 800, thinks that Amelius, after Rome, went first to Tyre; see note 44 below; on Amelius's age.

26. Jean C. Balty, "Apamea in Syria in the Second and Third Centuries A.D.," *JRS* 78 (1988): 95, and H. D. Saffrey, "Les néoplatoniciens et les Oracles chaldaïques," *Etudes Augustiniennes* 27 (1981): 225, think that Amelius wrote most of his work in Apamea. But see Brisson, "Amélius," 820–30.

27. The Suda, s.v. "Amelios"; Brisson, "Amélius," 800, 816–17. To my knowledge no one has been able to discern whether Amelius's adoption of Hostilianus motivated his move to Apamea, or whether the adoption occurred after he moved there for other reasons.

28. Balty, "Apamea in Syria," 95;

29. Polymnia Athanassiadi, "The Oecumenism of Iamblichus: Latent Knowledge and Its Awakening," *JRS* 85 (1995): 245.

death.[30] Apamea was home to the oracle of Bel,[31] whose imposing temple was associated with later Neoplatonist and Babylonian/Chaldaean beliefs.[32] Amelius's interest in Numenius seems also to have led him to explore texts closely related to the Apamean philosopher's doctrines.[33] For example, he appropriated the concept of three demiurges[34] from the *Chaldaean Oracles*.[35] Historians speculate that in Apamea, Amelius taught Numenian philosophy,[36]

---

30. Polymnia Athanassiadi, "The Chaldaean Oracles: Theology and Theurgy," in *Pagan Monotheism in Late Antiquity,* ed. Polymnia Athanassiadi and Michael Frede (New York: Oxford University Press, 1999), 153; H. D. Saffrey, "Abamon, pseudonyme de Jamblique," in *Philomathes: Studies and Essays in the Humanities in Memory of Philip Merlan,* ed. R. B. Palmer and R. Hamerton-Kelly (The Hague: Nijhoff, 1971), 231; Brisson, "Amélius," 802. See also J. M. Dillon, *The Middle Platonists* (Ithaca, NY: Cornell University Press, 1996), 361. Such materials may have been housed in the temple of Bel. See Athanassiadi, "Chaldaean Oracles," 156 and n. 33, who thinks that the *Chaldaean Oracles* may have been preserved here. See also Polymnia Athanassiadi, "Apamea and the *Chaldaean Oracles:* A Holy City and a Holy Book," in *The Philosopher and Society in Late Antiquity: Essays in Honour of Peter Brown,* ed. Andrew Smith (Swansea: Classical Press of Wales, 2005), 117–43.

31. Athanassiadi, "Chaldaean Oracles," 153; and Balty, "Apamea in Syria," 94.

32. Neoplatonist: Proclus equated Bel with the Twice-Beyond, the creative principle in the *Chaldaean Oracles;* Athanassiadi, "Chaldaean Oracles," 154. Babylonian/Chaldaean: First, Palmyra and Apamea boasted huge monuments to Bel, which Athanassiadi assumes "perpetuated a venerable tradition firmly rooted in pre-Seleucid Babylon." In this context, she cites an inscription referring to KLDY from Roman Palmyra as referring to "Chaldaeans," and assumes that they are "a local priestly caste involved with the cult of Bel." Second, she claims that in the temple of Bel at Apamea, "a caste of hereditary priests may have continued the Palaeo-Babylonian tradition of enthusiastic divination," to produce the oracles that "enjoyed such high credence in the Roman empire." Third, she speculates that "one priest by the name of Julian seems to have produced a revelation in the theological idiom of the region … and yet firmly rooted in the millennial Babylonian tradition. The heritage of Posidonius and especially that of Numenius are discernible in the theology of the fragments that we possess, so that the hypothesis that the two Julians may have moved in Numenius' circle in Apamea … appears highly attractive." Athanassiadi tries further to link Apamea, Bel, and the *Chaldaean Oracles* through an altar found at Vaison-la-Romaine (Vasio) in southern France and now at the Musée des Antiquités Nationales at Saint-Germain-en-Laye. According to its inscription (*IGRR* 1, 4 = *IG* XIV, 2482 = *CIL* xii, 1277) a certain Sextus dedicated it to Bel, "the ruler of fortune," in "remembrance of the Apamean oracles" (τῶν ἐν Ἀπαμείᾳ μνησάμενος λογίων), which Athanassiadi, "Chaldaean Oracles," 154–55, equates with the "collection of oracles which was to become universally known as 'the Chaldaean Oracles'." On this inscription, see also Balty, "Apamea in Syria," 94–95 incl. n. 37.

33. E. R. Dodds, "New Light on the Chaldaean Oracles," *HThR* 54 (1961): 271. See Elizabeth DePalma Digeser, "The Late Roman Empire from the Antonines to Constantine," in *The Cambridge History of Philosophy in Late Antiquity,* ed. Lloyd Gerson (Cambridge: Cambridge University Press, 2010), 23–24.

34. The first puts his hand to the clay (i.e., is an artisan who works with his hands), the second creates by command (e.g., as an architect), and the third creates by an act of will (e.g., as king). The "artisan who works with his hands," Saffrey, "Les néoplatoniciens," 224, notes, is an expression for the demiurge from the *Chaldaean Oracles*. See Proclus *In Tim.* 1.361.26–362.2; see also Brisson, "Amélius," 811–12, 832; John Dillon, "Iamblichus of Chalcis (c. 240–325 AD)," *ANRW* 2.36.2 (1987): 889; Athanassiadi, "Chaldaean Oracles," 156 n. 31. Ruth Majercik, "The Chaldean Oracles and the School of Plotinus," *AncW* 29, no. 2 (1998): 101–2, is more cautious.

35. Athanassiadi, "Chaldaean Oracles," 153.

36. Brisson, "Amélius," 817–18; Athanassiadi, "Oecumenism of Iamblichus," 245.

and that after Plotinus's death he traveled to a sanctuary of Apollo, Daphne perhaps,[37] to question the oracle about the fate of Plotinus's soul.[38]

Porphyry's sometimes defensive tone toward Amelius in his *Life of Plotinus*, Plotinus's refusal to join him in the new moon rituals, and Amelius's later residence in Apamea led some historians to conjecture that his ritualism estranged him from the Roman school. Porphyry's insistent assertion that *he* was the chosen editor of Plotinus's treatises (despite Amelius's earlier collation and help on the project)[39] and his open criticisms of how Amelius had handled Plotinus's texts seem to convey a negative opinion of Amelius.[40] If Amelius's journey to Apamea and the value he placed on ritual also meant that he was closer to what would become the Iamblichaean faction,[41] then his departure from the Roman Plotinian community would indeed have been threatening. Given Iamblichus's criticisms of Amelius, both in a treatise he wrote against him, linking him to a student of Porphyry,[42] and in remarks in *De anima* (e.g., ap. Stob. 1.372), however, he and the Apamean transplant had no close affinity.[43]

Porphyry's defensive attitude toward Amelius more likely developed as he systematized and published Plotinus's writings as *The Enneads*, although he was in some respects less qualified to do so. Amelius's standing with the master had been very high, and he had been intimately connected with the production of his texts. Amelius was one of Plotinus's oldest and most devoted students, joining him less than three years after he came to Rome (246) and staying twenty-four years (three times as long as Porphyry). He had taken notes at all Plotinus's conferences and wrote them out into approximately one hundred treatises. With Porphyry, he persuaded Plotinus to compose specific studies (e.g., treatises 22 and 23); he also wrote forty volumes against

---

37. Elizabeth DePalma Digeser, "An Oracle of Apollo at Daphne and the Great Persecution," *CPh* 99 (2004): 57–77.

38. Porph. *Plot.* 22. Brisson, "Amélius," 811; R. Goulet, "L'Oracle d'Apollon dans la Vie de Plotin," in *Porphyre: La Vie de Plotin: Travaux préliminaires et index grec complet,* ed. Luc Brisson et al. (Paris: Librarie Philosophique J. Vrin, 1982), 369–412, and J. Igal, "El enigma del oráculo de Apolo sobre Plotino," *Emerita* 52 (1984): 83–115, think that Amelius composed the oracle of Apollo that Porphyry cites; but it is more likely to have come from an oracular site: Aude Busine, *Paroles d'Apollon: Pratiques et traditions oraculaires dans l'Antiquité tardive (IIe-VIe siècles)* (Leiden/Boston: Brill, 2005), 295–315 and especially 309.

39. Smith, *Porphyry's Place*, xv; Brisson, "Amélius," 813–14.

40. Irmgard Männlein-Robert, "Biographie, Hagiographie, Autobiographie—Die *Vita Plotini* des Porphyrios," in *Metaphysik und Religion: Zur Signatur des spätantiken Denkens,* ed. Theo Kobusch and Michael Erler (Munich/Leipzig: K. G. Saur, 2002), 593; Brisson, "Amélius," 795, 813.

41. Saffrey, "Abamon," 231.

42. "Refutations of Amelius and also of Numenius with Theodore of Asine in View"; *Vita Isid.* 166 p. 230.1–2 Zintzen; Brisson, "Amélius," 818–19.

43. Dillon, "Iamblichus of Chalcis," 894.

the rumor that Plotinus had plagiarized Numenius (Porph. *Plot.* 3, 5, 17).[44] Amelius's experience and authority thus forced Porphyry to justify his own standing as Plotinus's heir and the standard-bearer of the Plotinian tradition. Moreover, Porphyry himself was in Sicily at the time of Plotinus's death, so Amelius's departure in itself does not stand as evidence for a rupture in the Plotinian community. Indeed, the Plotinians—who had been closely connected with the court of Gallienus—may have dispersed for political reasons after the emperor's assassination.[45]

One member of the Plotinian community who clearly did set off in a different direction after Plotinus's death was Firmus Castricius. According to Porphyry's *On Abstinence,* Castricius—to whom he dedicated the work—abandoned the vegetarian diet that had been characteristic of Plotinus's inner circle (*Abst.* 1.1.1).[46] Porphyry claims that Castricius was "the greatest lover of beauty (*philokalos*)" of them all and "venerated (*sebomenos*) Plotinus." He was, the *Life of Plotinus* continues, "Amelius's faithful servant and helper in every need" and "devoted" himself to Porphyry "as if" he were "his own brother" (*Plot.* 7.24f.). Castricius had owned property in Campania, specifically at Minturnae, which Zethus, another follower, had purchased and used to support Plotinus once he became ill (2.21–23); Castricius had taken to philosophy after first pursuing a public career (7.24f.).[47]

Porphyry met Castricius only after joining Plotinus's circle.[48] Porphyry then lived in Rome and studied with Plotinus for six years before departing to Sicily (*Plot.* 5.1–10; 6.1; 2.32–34). Porphyry's reference to his friend's whereabouts—with that of other Plotinians—at the time of the master's death (Castricius was in Rome [2.32–34], and Porphyry was in Lilybaeum or Carthage) signals that Castricius was then still in good standing within the circle. In *On Abstinence,* Porphyry says that he "heard from visitors" that Castricius "had condemned fleshless food and reverted to consuming flesh," indicating that the change in his close friend's habits occurred after Plotinus's death. Porphyry thus took responsibility for persuading him back into the fold.

Porphyry knew that Castricius's decision to resume eating meat did not arise from gluttony or, conversely, a concern for his health (*Abst.* 1.1.1–2.2).[49]

---

44. Brisson, "Amélius," 799, 812.

45. Ibid., 799–800. See chapter 3.

46. Gillian Clark, introduction to *Porphyry: On Abstinence from Killing Animals* (Ithaca, NY: Cornell University Press, 2000), 1. I use her trans. throughout.

47. Καὶ οὗτος οὖν ἐσέβετο Πλωτῖνον τὸν πολιτικὸν ᾑρημένος βίον, with the perfect participle (ᾑρημένος) suggesting action before that of the main verb.

48. A. Smith, "Porphyrian Studies since 1913," *ANRW* 2.36.2 (1987): 721; Clark, introduction, 1.

49. Clark, introduction, 3.

Rather, Porphyry's reference to Castricius and others ($\alpha\dot{\upsilon}\tau o\dot{\upsilon}\varsigma$) having been "persuaded by stale and...outdated sophisms" (1.3.1) suggests that *On Abstinence* is directed against a specific philosophical position.[50] This argument gains force from the philosophical character of Porphyry's rebuttal. Porphyry's defense of vegetarianism strangely fails to engage Castricius's arguments directly, instead marshaling all the strongest arguments in favor of consuming meat in order systematically to rebut them (1.3.2).[51] These tactics, however, defuse what might otherwise have been a very personal attack on someone who had been like a brother.

The tight link between meat and sacrifice in antiquity provides one clue to the reason for Castricius's abandoning vegetarianism. In his treatise on abstinence, Porphyry argues that all philosophical aspirants ought to avoid animal food (*Abst.* 2.3.1), implying that Castricius continued to pursue philosophy but was doing so in a context that involved eating sacrificial meat. In setting out arguments against the practice, Porphyry makes explicit a philosophical asceticism that flourished in the school of Plotinus. Not only was meat eating unjust,[52] Porphyry claims, but blood sacrifices were directed only toward evil daemons.[53] Accordingly, civic rites involving animal sacrifice merely appeased these beings—an inappropriate activity for the philosopher, however necessary it might be for the general community (1.27.1; 2.33.1). Moreover, people polluted by contact with either blood or dead bodies could potentially disrupt other sacred rites such as divination.[54]

A likely magnet for Castricius's shift in attention and habits in the 280s is Iamblichus. In his philosophy we find not only a valorization of sacrifice and ritual but also an appropriation and reinterpretation of the Plotinian tradition. Moreover, where Porphyry lambasted meat eaters like Castricius for behaving in a way appropriate only for ordinary people involved in civic rituals, Iamblichus explicitly considered most souls within a philosopher's circle as no better than those of *hoi polloi*. Iamblichus appears to have advocated the daily eating of sacrificial meat by all but those very few philosophers—maybe one or two each generation—who had reached the most sublime heights of knowledge (Iambl. *VPyth.* 1.24.107). He also advocated the performance, for

50. Porphyry of Tyre, *On Abstinence from Killing Animals,* trans. Gillian Clark (London: Duckworth, 2000), 123 n. 10.

51. Clark, introduction, 4.

52. The chief argument of book 1 of *On Abstinence.*

53. *Abst.* 2.26.5; 2.20.2; 2.42.3; 2.58.1.

54. *Abst.* 2.43.1; 2.46.2; 2.47.3; 2.50.1. Elizabeth DePalma Digeser, "Philosophy in a Christian Empire: From the Great Persecution to Theodosius I," in *The Cambridge History of Philosophy in Late Antiquity,* ed. Lloyd Gerson (Cambridge: Cambridge University Press, 2010), 377–81.

all but this same small group (*DM* 5.15, 18), of whatever sacrificial rituals the gods had ordained, whether or not they involved animal flesh and blood.[55] Iamblichus's view that material cultic rituals were necessary for the return of all souls to the One, his theology of the *via universalis,* derived from his belief that the human soul had fully descended from the *nous,* and was the basis for his schism with Porphyry.

Since the accepted date for Iamblichus's birth is ca. 242 or even 240,[56] only some fifteen years separated him and Porphyry. Iamblichus was born in Chalcis, Syria, to a noble family that traced its lineage to the priest-kings of Emesa.[57] The few certain details about Iamblichus's life come from either Eunapius's favorable portrait of him in his *Lives of the Philosophers* or a small corpus of letters, originally attributed to the emperor Julian, preserved in Stobaeus and written to Iamblichus by an adoring student.[58] Eunapius says that Iamblichus "attached himself" (*prostheis*) to Porphyry, after being a pupil (*sungenomenos*) of Anatolius. This statement indicates Eunapius's

---

55. *DM* 5, esp. 5.4, 11–12, 14–15.

56. In saying that he lived in the time of Constantine, the Suda seemed to suggest that Iamblichus was born in 280, but the portrait of him preserved in letters erroneously attributed to Julian led Joseph Bidez, "Le philosophe Jamblique et son école," *REG* 32 (1919): 29–40, to push the date back thirty years. Subsequently Alan Cameron, "The Date of Iamblichus' Birth," *Hermes* 96 (1968): 374–76, noticed that the marriage (before 300 CE) between Iamblichus's son, Ariston, and Amphiclea, a member of Plotinus's circle (Porph. *Plot.* 9.3–5), called for an even earlier date, ca. 242. Cameron's arguments have been widely accepted: see B. Dalsgaard Larsen, *Jamblique de Chalcis, exégète et philosophe: Appendice; Testimonia et fragmenta exegetica* (Aarhus: Aarhus Universitetsforlag, 1972); John Dillon, ed., *Iamblichi Chalcidensis in Platonis Dialogos Commentariorum Fragmenta* (Leiden: Brill, 1973), 6f.; B. Dalsgaard Larsen, "La place de Jamblique dans la philosophie antique tardive," in *De Jamblique à Proclus,* ed. H. Dörrie, Entretiens sur l'Antiquité Classique (Vandoeuvres–Geneva: Fond. Hardt, 1975), 3; T. D. Barnes, "A Correspondent of Iamblichus," *GRBS* 19 (1978): 104; Dillon, "Iamblichus of Chalcis," 865–66; John Vanderspoel, "Iamblichus at Daphne," *GRBS* 29 (1988): 83; and Athanassiadi, "Oecumenism of Iamblichus," 245.

57. According to Photius, Iamblichus descended from Sampsigeramos and Monimos. The former founded the dynasty of priest-kings at Emesa. John Vanderspoel, "Themistios and the Origin of Iamblichos," *Hermes* 116 (1988): 127, with Dillon, *Iamblichi Chalcidensis in Platonis Dialogos Commentaria,* 5, wants to argue, on the grounds that the name "Monimos" appears nowhere else, that Photius's "Monimos" is the "Monikos" whom Stephanos of Byzantium identifies as the founder of Chalkis in Syria. Drawing on A. H. M. Jones, *The Cities of the Eastern Roman Provinces,* 2nd ed. (Oxford: Clarendon Press, 1971), 254, and I. Benziger, *Pauly's Realenzyclopaedie* 3 (1899): s.v. Chalkis (14), (15), Vanderspoel argues further that Monimos's city was actually the Chalkis in Lebanon, not in northern Syria. Yet Jones and Benziger make this identification by associating "Monikos" with yet another name, "Mennaios," the name of the father of a Ptolemaios, who was the earliest known ruler at Chalkis in Lebanon. This identification is hardly watertight. Vanderspoel, "Themistios," 127, thinks he has found corroborating evidence for Iamblichus's Lebanese roots in Themistius *Or.* 24.301b, but Robert J. Penella, *The Private Orations of Themistius* (Berkeley: University of California Press, 2000), 128 n. 1, easily disproves this theory.

58. On the importance and analysis of these letters, *Ep.* 34, 60, 78 [184], 79 [187], see Bidez, "Le philosophe Jamblique," 29, 32; Dillon, "Iamblichus of Chalcis," 874–75; and Barnes, "Correspondent of Iamblichus," 99–106. See also Athanassiadi, "Oecumenism of Iamblichus," 249; Dillon, "Iamblichus of Chalcis," 863.

opinion that Iamblichus absorbed his philosophical training from Anatolius and subsequently, as a philosopher, learned more about Plotinus's system from Porphyry.[59] Given Eunapius's high regard for Anatolius, "who ranks next after Porphyry,"[60] most scholars have identified him as the Alexandrian Aristotelian and Pythagorean scholar who became bishop of Laodicaea (Eus. *HE* 7.32.6–13, 20–21).[61] Anatolius's career provides at least three places where he and Iamblichus might have come into contact: in Alexandria before the 270s,[62] in Caesarea in the 270s,[63] or at Laodicea after 280.[64] Given Iamblichus's birth in the early 240s, he would have been moving into his thirties if their relationship flourished in Caesarea, but in his twenties, a more likely time for an initial training in philosophy (as for Porphyry with Origen and Longinus), if he met Anatolius in Alexandria. The city would have offered him not only rich Pythagorean sources to complement his training with Anatolius, but also unparalleled exposure to the Egyptian religious traditions that became a hallmark of Iamblichus's theology.[65]

Anatolius is known to have participated in a lively defense of the Brucheion quarter (Eus. *HE* 7.32), home to the famous Museon, Alexandria's intellectual center. For supporting Zenobia in 273, queen of the breakaway Palmyrene province, the quarter faced the emperor Aurelian's wrath that same year and then lay in ruins (Amm. Marc. 22.16.15).[66] This tragic disruption

59. Translation and text of Eunapius is from W. C. Wright's Loeb edition.
60. Eun. *VS* s.v. "Iamblichos": Ἀνατολίῳ τῷ μετὰ Πορφύριον τὰ δεύτερα.
61. Athanassiadi, "Oecumenism of Iamblichus," 244, 246; Dillon, "Iamblichus of Chalcis," 866–67; J. A. Philip, "The Biographical Tradition: Pythagoras," *TAPhA* 90 (1959): 190 n. 5; Larsen, "La place de Jamblique," 4. Although Wolff (in Porphyry of Tyre, "De philosophia ex oraculis haurienda: Librorum reliquiae" [Hildesheim: G. Olms, 1962]), and Zeller (in Dillon, "Iamblichus of Chalcis," 867) were unwilling to make this identification, Dillon notes that there is no chronological reason not to link Anatolius and Iamblichus. Moreover, such a relationship goes a long way to explain not only the Aristotelian, but the marked Pythagorean elements in Iamblichus's thought. For the latter point, see Larsen, "La place de Jamblique," 4; Shaw, "Eros and Arithmos," 128; Athanassiadi, "Oecumenism of Iamblichus," 246; and Philip, "Biographical Tradition," 190 n. 5. But cf. Smith, "Porphyrian Studies," 745 n. 157.
62. Larsen, "La place de Jamblique," 4.
63. Dillon, "Iamblichus of Chalcis," 867, thinks this is the likeliest scenario, since it is "quite possible that a boy from Chalcis would study at Caesarea." See also Philip, "Biographical Tradition," 190 n. 5.
64. I. L. Heiberg, *Geschichte der Mathematik und Naturwissenschaften im Altertum* (Munich: C. H. Beck,1925), 40.
65. Cf. Stewart Irvin Oost, "The Alexandrian Seditions under Philip and Gallienus," *CPh* 56, no. 1 (1961): 8, regarding Dionysius of Alexandria's reference to the "synagogue of the Egyptian magicians" (ὁ διδάσκαλος καὶ τῶν ἀπ' Αἰγύπτου μάγων) ap. Eus. *HE* 7.10.4. Under Anatolius, Iamblichus studied Nicomachus of Gerasa's *Theology of Numbers,* and he himself wrote a lengthy (ten-book) treatise, *On Pythagoreanism.* Shaw, "Eros and Arithmos," 128.
66. Christopher Haas, *Alexandria in Late Antiquity* (Baltimore: Johns Hopkins University Press, 1997), 28, 366 n. 18; but see Oost, "Alexandrian Seditions," 15 n. 1.

to their work and living environment likely motivated both Iamblichus and Anatolius to depart, one for Caesarea and the east with his library,[67] and the other, now in his early thirties, for the west.[68] Hoping to learn Plotinus's doctrines, Iamblichus made contact next with Porphyry, now in his middle forties. Iamblichus probably discovered Porphyry through Anatolius, who may have known him as a fellow student of Longinus.[69] To Anatolius, Porphyry had dedicated his *Homerica zētēmata,* a treatise that shows his debt to Longinus.[70] Iamblichus seems to have approached Porphyry as the repository of the texts and doctrines of the venerable Plotinus, clearly the most distinguished Platonist of his age.[71]

After 273, Iamblichus found Porphyry in Rome (Eun. *VS* s.v. "Porphurios").[72] If their connections to Gallienus's court had driven Plotinus's associates from the city after the emperor's murder, the city was safer when the opposing faction fragmented after Aurelian's death in 275. Eunapius says that Porphyry was in his prime between the reigns of Gallienus (253–68) and Probus (276–82), which roughly correspond to the period when he learned Plotinus's philosophy (Gallienus's reign) and then communicated it to Iamblichus (that of Probus). Further evidence for contact between Porphyry and Iamblichus in Rome is that Iamblichus "heard" a certain theory from Porphyry, and Iamblichus's son, Ariston, married Amphiclea, a member of Plotinus's circle (Porph. *Plot.* 9.3–5).[73] Eunapius's reluctance to call Iamblichus Porphyry's student (*VS* s.v. "Iamblichos") probably stems from his tendency to glorify the teachings of the former at the expense of the latter.[74] Nevertheless, the two philosophers had, for a time, a relatively amicable relationship, since

---

67. Where else would an Alexandrian Christian scholar go? The city was home to Origen's library. For Anatolius's bringing his library to the city, see R. M. Grant, "Porphyry among the Early Christians," in *Romanitas et Christianitas,* ed. J. H. Waszink and W. den Boer (Amsterdam: North Holland, 1973), 181–87.

68. Larsen, "La place de Jamblique," 4, assumes that Iamblichus left Anatolius because the latter took up his episcopate after 270.

69. Dillon, "Iamblichus of Chalcis," 867.

70. Dillon, "Iamblichus of Chalcis," 867.

71. Contra Saffrey, "Abamon," 230.

72. Athanassiadi, "Oecumenism of Iamblichus," 245; Barnes, "Correspondent of Iamblichus," 105; E. Zeller, *Die Philosophie der Griechen in ihrer geschichtlichen Entwicklung,* vol. 3.2 of *Die nacharistotelische Philosophie* (Hildesheim: Georg Olms, 1923; repr., 1963), 612 n. 1; Johnston, *Hekate Soteira,* 6.

73. Stob. *Anth.* 1.49.37; cf. *In Tim.* frag. 64.24, in Athanassiadi, "Oecumenism of Iamblichus," 244. For Porphyry as Iamblichus's teacher, see Barnes, "Correspondent of Iamblichus," 105; Saffrey, "Abamon," 230; Johnston, *Hekate Soteira,* 6; Athanassiadi, "Oecumenism of Iamblichus," 245. See note 58 above.

74. Athanassiadi, "Oecumenism of Iamblichus," 244–45. Cf also Smith, *Porphyry's Place,* xvii incl. n. 18.

Porphyry dedicated his treatise *Peri tou gnōthi seauton* (*On Knowing Yourself*) to Iamblichus.[75]

Probably by 282, when Eunapius claims Porphyry's prowess started to wane, Iamblichus returned to the east.[76] At this time, Castricius and other Romans from Porphyry's circle may have gone with him. John Malalas (12312.11–12 Bonn) suggests that Iamblichus was in Daphne during the reigns of Galerius (293–311) and Maximin Daia (305–13).[77] He would thus have been near Antioch during the events that led up to and followed the Great Persecution, not only the failed auspices in 299, and the likely response of Daphne's oracle, but also the affair of the talking Zeus Philios statue during Maximin Daia's reign (Eus. *HE* 9.3, *PE* 4.2). A connection to these instances of religious violence may explain why neither Libanius's orations (especially *Or.* 16, 15, 60) nor Julian's *Misopogon* refer to Iamblichus's residence there.[78] All the same, Malalas's Antiochene sources tend to be good, and neither the letters nor any other evidence prevents Iamblichus from living and teaching near Antioch until the death of Galerius in 311 or Maximin in 313.[79] A likely *terminus ante quem* for his departure to Apamea (Ps.-Jul. *Ep.* 78 [184].418a) is 313, when Licinius punished those involved in Maximin Daia's anti-Christian divinations (Eus. *HE* 9.2–3, 9.11.5–6). By this time, Porphyry was dead.[80]

Eunapius describes Iamblichus as a successor of Plotinus, but his doctrines on the human soul and ritual practice distinguish him dramatically

---

75. *Stob.* 3.21.26 p. 579, 21f. (Hense), in Smith, *Porphyry's Place,* xvii n. 18. Bidez, "Le philosophe Jamblique," 32, is probably incorrect to date the text as late as 290 or 300.

76. Barnes, "Correspondent of Iamblichus," 105; Dillon, *Iamblichi Chalcidensis in Platonis Dialogos Commentariorum,* 9–14; Larsen, "La place de Jamblique," 4; Vanderspoel, "Iamblichus at Daphne," 84. Larsen, "La place de Jamblique," 3–4, and Athanassiadi, "Oecumenism of Iamblichus," 245–46, think that Iamblichus returned to Alexandria after leaving Porphyry. His return is unlikely, however, given the destruction of the Brucheion quarter only a decade before. The quarter remained in ruins even into the late fourth century (Amm. Marc. 22.15).

77. Although Saffrey, "Abamon," 231, read Malalas as saying that Iamblichus was in Daphne at the end of his life, Barnes, "Correspondent of Iamblichus," 105, used the Iamblichaean epistles to demonstrate that Iamblichus was there at the end of these emperors' lives. Malalas actually sets Iamblichus in Daphne during the reigns of Galerius and Maxentius, but per Barnes, Maximin Daia should be read instead. See also Dillon, "Iamblichus of Chalcis," 870; Larsen, "La place de Jamblique," 4; and Vanderspoel, "Iamblichus at Daphne," 83–85.

78. Vanderspoel, "Iamblichus at Daphne," 83–84. This silence leads Vanderspoel to conclude that Iamblichus was not in Daphne near Antioch, but rather in Daphne in Palestine. Malalas, however, is unlikely to have known of Iamblichus's activity in a small Palestinian town, when his own focus was on Antiochene events.

79. Barnes, "Correspondent of Iamblichus," 105; see also Vanderspoel, "Iamblichus at Daphne," 83.

80. The Suda s.v. "Porphurios."

from Porphyry and Plotinus himself.[81] The serious disagreements between Iamblichus and Porphyry are obvious to any reader of Iamblichus's *De mysteriis (On the Mysteries)*,[82] but the significance of their quarrel has never been explored. To some extent this lapse is because historians have only recently seen Iamblichus as a genuine philosopher instead of as a mystic and magician.[83] Iamblichus's pessimistic views regarding the contact of the human soul with the world of the divine led him to argue for what Gregory Shaw calls a *via universalis*, a path involving all types of ritual that all human beings—philosophers as well as ordinary people—had to follow in order for their souls to return to their divine origins. This theology sharply opposed the Plotinian school's creed that philosophers and ordinary persons had such dissimilar souls that no one route could lead both to divine union.[84] The remaining chapters will argue that Iamblichus's *via universalis* prompted a wide-ranging response from Porphyry in which he denied the possibility of any such path. I suggest that Iamblichus's theology, set out in *De mysteriis*, was the stimulus that drove Porphyry to defend the Plotinian and Ammonian tradition from all those, Christian and Hellene, who used it as a basis for any sort of *via universalis*.

The difference between Iamblichus and the Plotinian community over the nature of the soul is profound. Plotinus, Porphyry, and Iamblichus all believed that there were three different types of souls. But Plotinus and Porphyry deemed that part of the human soul remained in contact with the divine, a conviction that sharply separated them from Iamblichus, who believed that all souls were in some respect fully descended. Iamblichus thought that three types of soul existed: material, intermediate, and noetic—the last of which was extraordinarily rare (*DM* 5.15, 21). For Iamblichus,

---

81. C. G. Steel, *The Changing Self: A Study on the Soul in Later Neoplatonism; Iamblichus, Damascius, and Priscianus*, Koninklijke Vlaamse Academie voor Wetenschappen, Letteren en Schone Kunsten van België, Klasse der Letteren, Verhandeligen: jaarg. 40, nr. 85 (Brussels: Paleis der Academiën, 1978), in Shaw, "Eros and Arithmos," 124; see Elizabeth DePalma Digeser, "The Power of Religious Rituals: A Philosophical Quarrel on the Eve of the Great Persecution," in *The Power of Religion in Late Antiquity*, ed. Andrew Cain and Noel Lenski (Aldershot, UK: Ashgate, 2010), 81–92.

82. Emma C. Clarke, John Dillon, and Jackson Hershbell, introduction to *Iamblichus: De mysteriis* (Atlanta: Society of Biblical Literature, 2003), xxii.

83. G. Fowden, *The Egyptian Hermes* (Princeton, NJ: Princeton University Press, 1986), 134–41 and Gregory Shaw, *Theurgy and the Soul: The Neoplatonism of Iamblichus* (University Park: Pennsylvania State University Press, 1995), established that "theurgy was a philosophically sophisticated response to social and philosophical challenges faced by Platonists of the fourth century" (Shaw, "Eros and Arithmos," 124).

84. Gillian Clark, "Augustine's Porphyry and the Universal Way of Salvation," in *Studies on Porphyry*, ed. George E. Karamanolis and Anne Sheppard (London: Institute of Classical Studies, 2007), 127–40.

a completely descended soul housed in a body sent *logoi* into the sensible, material world; thus, to regain its divine nature, it required rituals involving the "natural correspondences" to these *logoi*—their *analogoi* (5.23.233). Iamblichus taught that the gods had established these rituals, the knowledge of which remained among "the sacred races," the Assyrians (Chaldaeans) and the Egyptians—traditions that he linked with the pious communities of Plato's golden age (*Leg.* 716a-b). The authority of these practices, in Iamblichus's eyes, was confirmed by frequent theophanies, or visible manifestations of the gods, among both peoples (*DM* 6.7.249).[85]

Iamblichus achieved a synthesis between these religious rituals and philosophy by linking Egyptian theology to the mathematical connections (Egyptian in origin, according to legend) that Pythagoreans saw between the physical world and the intellectual gods (Iambl. *VPyth.* 151 Dillon and Hershbell 1991; *DM* 1.21.65).[86] Mathematics mediated between the divine and physical worlds by preserving the knowledge of divine forms while providing practical applications to religion, medicine, and political life. It was also a tool that allowed Iamblichus, in a novel move coherent with Hermetic doctrine,[87] to rid matter of its association with evil, which had been a commonplace in Platonist thought. Enabling Iamblichus to view the soul's return to its source as a process accomplished through traditional rites of sacrifice and divination, Pythagoreanism, despite its own vegetarian traditions, allowed him to situate these rituals within a comprehensive framework.[88] It also enabled him to extend to ordinary persons Plotinus's vision of the soul's return, even though it was originally formulated for philosophers. In Iamblichus's view, the embodied life, from its biological drives to the political life, was not merely a necessity to be endured while striving for something better (as Porphyry or Plotinus might have it; e.g., Plot. *Enn.* 4.4.44.7–25). It was instead an opportunity for the soul to experience theophany.[89] Iamblichus could thus construct a *via universalis* that integrated ritual and theology, even

85. Shaw, "Eros and Arithmos," 125, 127–28, 131–32. For the Egyptian aspects of Iamblichus's Neoplatonism, see Fowden, *Egyptian Hermes,* 133.

86. Shaw, "Eros and Arithmos," 128–29 incl. n. 21, and 131, drawing on Peter Kingsley, *Ancient Philosophy, Mystery, and Magic: Empedocles and Pythagorean Tradition* (Oxford: Oxford University Press, 1995), 304–7; for the Egyptian character of the *DM,* see Hervé D. Saffrey, "Relecture de Jamblique, *De mysteriis,* VIII, chap. 1–5," in *Platonism in Late Antiquity,* ed. Stephen Gersh and C. Kannengieser (Notre Dame: University of Notre Dame, 1992), 169–71, who draws attention to Iamblichus's claim that Egyptian metaphysics goes as far as the first cause, i.e., the One.

87. Van Liefferinge, *La théurgie,* 34.

88. Shaw, "Eros and Arithmos," 125, 128–30.

89. Dominic J. O'Meara, *Pythagoras Revived: Mathematics and Philosophy in Late Antiquity* (Oxford: Clarendon Press, 1989), 30.

though he claimed that he was only putting into practice what the gods themselves had revealed.

For Iamblichus, the theophanies that validated the Egyptian and Assyrian systems—and consequently his own—resulted from practices that most scholars label as "theurgy." It is important to note, however, that to Iamblichus *all* rituals identifiable as divinely ordained were theurgic in character. His opinion of Greek thought and practice explains his emphasis on theurgy or god-work as opposed to theology or god-talk. For Iamblichus, Hellenes, specifically his Platonist contemporaries, and Porphyry in particular, had trusted their own logic, rather than the gods' guidance; they preferred to discuss the divine (*theologia*) rather than to venerate or experience it (*DM* 7.5.259).[90] The hieroglyphs of nature (not only the divine numbers, but also minerals, plants, animals, seasonal changes, and traditional songs, prayers, dances, and images), not theology, revealed the path for the soul's return to its divine source. These are the necessary media through which a theurgist, after diagnosing the specific *analogia* that a soul required for its return, restored its resonance with the gods (1.12.42; 5.21, 23). Iamblichus also believed that because every soul desired the good, every person knew the gods innately. Although discursive reasoning distracted people from this knowledge, theurgic ritual could awaken souls to their original *eros* for the divine life.[91]

Iamblichus taught that three types of souls existed, each alienated from its divine source in a different degree, each requiring a different form of theurgic worship (*DM* 5.15.220).[92] Nevertheless, he did not strongly differentiate these types of souls with respect to ritual practice.[93] For example, in Iamblichus's view, material souls, those of the incalculable majority who follow nature and fate, should perform rituals involving matter. Deviating from the theology in the *Chaldaean Oracles* under the influence of Hermetism,[94] Iamblichus believes that these theurgies must use objects corresponding to the form of alienation that these souls suffer. Suitable rituals thus involve material things, such as stones, plants, and eating sacrificial animal victims (5.14, 23).[95] These sacrifices, according to Iamblichus, return the soul to *philia* with

90. Saffrey, "Relecture de Jamblique," 171. See also *DM* 1.1.3.

91. Shaw, "Eros and Arithmos," 125–26, 128. See also Plot. *Enn.* 5.5.12.12–13; and *OC* 43–44 (trans. Majercik), "Chaldaean Oracles."

92. Shaw, "Eros and Arithmos," 131.

93. Moving beyond Smith, *Porphyry's Place,* and its theory of higher and lower theurgy, the scholarship of Van Liefferinge and Shaw on Iamblichus's understanding of theurgy and its implications for all human souls has clarified his differences with Porphyry.

94. Camplani and Zambon, "Il sacrificio," 91.

95. Shaw, "Eros and Arithmos," 132; cf. also Shaw, *Theurgy and the Soul,* 21–57, 162–69; Beate Nasemann, *Theurgie und Philosophie in Jamblichs De mysteriis* (Stuttgart: Teubner, 1991), 231–82; Camplani and Zambon, "Il sacrificio," 90; and Van Liefferinge, *La théurgie,* 208–9.

the gods and daemons present in these substances, who then facilitate the soul's return to the immaterial gods. Intermediate souls, however, should *also* perform material rites, in Iamblichus's system, together with rites involving immaterial elements. Any soul that failed to honor the gods and daemons present in matter would, in Iamblichus's view, remain in thrall to them and unable to return to the divine (5.14.218).[96] In fact, Iamblichus criticizes Porphyry for thinking that philosophers like himself could short-circuit this process and move directly into noetic worship (5.15.220). Doing so would be like a modern Catholic theologian who spent all his time in contemplation without going to Mass. Both immaterial and noetic rituals (probably involving numbers) were appropriate for noetic souls,[97] living according to Nous and not Nature (5.18.225). But these souls, in Iamblichus's view, were extraordinarily rare and were able to worship the One alone only at the end of their lives (15.15, 22). For Iamblichus, Plotinus—but not Porphyry—might have been such a soul. Not only were all three types of souls united by a need to participate in material ritual (for noetic souls, at least in their younger, more embodied lives), but Iamblichus also postulated that a complete return to the divine might be possible even for those who possess the humbler form of soul.[98] In sum, for Iamblichus, material rituals were a path that led all types of souls toward their source, and he considered the possibility that all souls—material, immaterial, and noetic—might be able to achieve divine union.

Iamblichus set out his theology of the soul, theurgy, and theophany in a work now known as *On the Mysteries.* Its ancient title, "The Reply of the Master Abammon to the Letter of Porphyry to Anebo," is significant, indicating not only that Iamblichus wrote the treatise in response to a set of questions Porphyry had sent, perhaps to a former student,[99] but also that he did so in the guise of a high priest, Abammon. Although Plotinus was apparently familiar with the *Chaldaean Oracles,* the source text for Iamblichus's theurgy, Porphyry had become troubled by the increasingly theological and metaphysical claims justifying their use within philosophical circles. The first extant text to use the term "theurge," the late second-century *Chaldaean Oracles,* were an important inspiration for theurgic practice and theory in Iamblichaean circles.[100] Plotinus's ignorance of or disagreement

---

96. Cf. *DM* 228.11–229.13.

97. Shaw, "Eros and Arithmos," 131–33; cf. also Iambl. *On Physical Number* 126; and *VPyth.* 11, 93, and 147.

98. Camplani and Zambon, "Il sacrificio," 91.

99. Saffrey, "Abamon," 232.

100. Johnston, *Hekate Soteira,* 2–3 and chap. 8; John F. Finamore, *Iamblichus and the Theory of the Vehicle of the Soul,* American Class. Stud. 14 (Chicago: Cal. Scholars Pr., 1985), 125f.

with the *Chaldaean Oracles* was once inferred from his failure to mention them in his writings.[101] His failure to mention them by name, however, does not preclude his knowledge, for Plotinus drew on the entire Greek philosophical corpus without referring to many texts verbatim or by title.[102] The Byzantine Platonist Michael Psellus claimed, in fact, that the *Oracles* had inspired the beginning of Plotinus's *Ennead* 1.9,[103] and historians now see that some of Plotinus's terminology derives from these texts.[104] Plotinus's views on the principle of cosmic sympathy were also compatible with the way in which later philosophers understood theurgy to work.[105] Porphyry's *On Abstinence* was one response to this new trend, simply dismissing a philosopher's need to engage in material ritual. The *Letter to Anebo* shows its author probing further in an effort to understand the Hermetic and Chaldaean authority and legitimacy of theurgic practice. Porphyry's quest for information, in turn, motivated Iamblichus's mocking and caustic treatise, *On the Mysteries,* answering Porphyry's questions *seriatim,* often criticizing him for misunderstanding how the divine works through the material world, and for ignorance regarding the subjects about which he asks.[106] The Egyptian and Chaldaean framework shaping Porphyry's questions is evident in Iamblichus's initial assertion, without further justification, that, in answering Porphyry, he will adopt Hermetic and Chaldaean perspectives in a treatise that discusses theurgy, the gods' epiphanies, and the ascent of the soul via Chaldaean rites. Moreover, throughout the work, Iamblichus tries to dismiss Porphyry's doubts by citing the authority of the oracles.[107] While asserting

---

101. Johnston, *Hekate Soteira,* 2–6 incl. n. 20; Dodds, *Greeks and the Irrational,* 285 and n. 26; Dodds, "Theurgy," 57 incl. n. 26a; 58 incl. n. 34; Armstrong, "Was Plotinus a Magician?" 77.

102. Maria Louisa Gatti, "Plotinus: The Platonic Tradition and the Foundation of Neoplatonism," in *The Cambridge Companion to Plotinus,* ed. Lloyd Gerson (Cambridge: Cambridge University Press, 1996), 10.

103. Psellus ap. *PG* 122, 1125d; *OC* frag. 166; Edouard des Places, ed., *Oracles Chaldaïques, avec un choix de commentaires anciens* (Paris: Societé d'édition Les Belles Lettres, 1971), 165 n. 1.

104. John Dillon, "Plotinus and the Chaldean Oracles," in *Platonism in Late Antiquity,* ed. Stephen Gersh and C. Kannengieser (Notre Dame: University of Notre Dame, 1992), 140. Although Eitrem, "La théurgie," 54, was wrong, strictly speaking, to see a link between "theurgy" as practiced in the *Chaldaean Oracles* and Plotinus's interest in contemplating statues (cf. R. Berchman, "Arcana Mundi between Balaam and Hecate: Prophecy, Divination, and Magic in Later Platonism," in *SBL Seminar Papers,* ed. D. Lull [Atlanta: Scholars Press, 1989, 136–47), a practice having its source in certain forms of Egyptian cult, it is possible that the presence of both traditions in Plotinus's thought allowed Iamblichus to connect Chaldaean and Egyptian rituals in his pursuit of theurgy.

105. Johnston, *Hekate Soteira,* 79; Luck, "Theurgy," 190, cites *Enn.* 4.4.32.13 and Porph. *Aneb.* frag. 24 Parthey in this respect. Despite the queasiness of Armstrong, "Was Plotinus a Magician?" 73–79, Merlan, "Plotinus and Magic," 341–48, was not wrong to view Plotinus's ability to fend off Olympius's attacks (see also *Enn.* 4.4.43) in this light.

106. Saffrey, "Relecture de Jamblique," 171.

107. Saffrey, "Les néoplatoniciens," 217.

his confidence in various forms of theophany, Iamblichus affirms their theurgic efficacy in bringing all human souls back to the divine.

As Iamblichus used these theophanies to establish his theology's authority, he also probed the implications of Plotinus's ideas regarding the links between the sensible and intelligible worlds, consequences that the elder philosopher had not analyzed in detail. For example, Plotinus, celebrating Egypt's "wise men," thought that temple hieroglyphics were images directly revealing the intelligible world (*Enn.* 5.8.6). Similarly, he described indications of the gods' existence as "letters" in the heavens and nature (*Enn.* 3.3.6.18–20). Indeed, Plotinus, who saw the cosmos as participating in a dance choreographed by its *erōs* for the One (*Enn.* 3.6.17–18, 25–29; 3.3.7; 4.4.35.13), gave Iamblichus plenty of material for his Pythagorean theology, which infused the material world with divinity. Iamblichus claims that Porphyry simply could not see these aspects of Plotinus's thought (*DM* 1.3).[108]

Just because aspects of Plotinus's philosophy could be used to support a theology of theurgy, however, does not mean that either Plotinus or Porphyry would have favored the project.[109] Instead, Iamblichus's presumption to speak for Plotinus offended Porphyry. He saw Iamblichus as undermining Plotinus's legacy, so he began preserving and defending it in a series of works beyond *On Abstinence*.[110] Neither Porphyry's *Letter to Anebo* nor Iamblichus's *On the Mysteries* have internal evidence for the date of composition. Nevertheless, Porphyry's treatise *On the Return of the Soul* takes firm positions on issues that perplexed him when writing to Anebo.[111] Thus one can deduce that he wrote the *Letter* to gather information and assess the state of the question before setting out his own ideas in *On the Return of the Soul*. Moreover, although few scholars accept John O'Meara's claim that the *Philosophy from*

---

108. Shaw, "Eros and Arithmos," 123, 125–29.

109. A. H. Armstrong, "Tradition, Reason, and Experience in the Thought of Plotinus," in *Plotinian and Christian Studies* (London: Variorum Reprints, 1979), XVII; originally in *Atti del Convegno Internazionale sul tema Plotino e il Neoplatonismo in Oriente e in Occidente* (Rome: Accademia Nazionale dei Lincei, 1974), 187; Shaw, "Eros and Arithmos," 123 n. 8, 128.

110. Saffrey, "Relecture de Jamblique," 171.

111. P. Hadot, "Citations de Porphyre chez Augustin: A propos d'un ouvrage récent," *RE Aug* 6 (1960): 212–13; Saffrey, "Les néoplatoniciens," 217. For example, in *Aneb.* Porphyry asks whether one should have a personal daemon (ap. Iambl. *DE* 1.3.8) and how theurgy and divination work (ap. *DE* 1.9, 11). By the *Regr.* Porphyry had concluded that theurgy might be useful for many, but not for philosophers, and that a personal daemon could help set nonphilosophical types on the path to salvation: *Regr.* frags. 288–90, 292–93 ap. Aug. *Civ.* 10.9.13–45. See also Aug. *Civ.*10.27–32. By the *Phil. or.* Porphyry was quite certain about how divination worked: *Phil. or.* frags. 306 (ap. Firmicus Maternus *De errore profan. relig.* 13.4–5), 308 (ap. Eus. *PE* 5.6.2–7.2), 316 (ap. Eus. *PE* 5.10.13–11.1), 317 (ap. Eus. *PE* 5.12.1–2), 318 (ap. Eus. *PE* 5.13.1–2), 329 (ap. Eus. *PE* 4.19.8–20.1), 339 (ap. Eus. *PE* 6.3.5–4.3), and especially 349 (ap. Eus. *PE* 5.8.11–12).

Oracles and the *Return of the Soul* are one treatise, most historians now see that they share a common theme and perspective and jointly reflect Porphyry's views in the late 290s.[112] Both treatises explicitly reject the claim that there is one path along which all souls must travel in their return to the divine. This aspect of these texts has always been discussed within the context of Porphyry's criticisms of Christianity, admittedly an important theme in the fragments under each title. I think, however, that Porphyry developed arguments against Christianity's being a *via universalis* as part of his campaign against Iamblichus's notion that there *could* be any one path appropriate for all souls.[113] The evidence for this as Porphyry's reaction is plentiful. First, he states plainly in *On the Return of the Soul* that he had searched all known religious practices for a *via universalis*. Next, he delineates the different types of practices that might bring different types of souls closer to the divine. Finally, in the fragments attributed to both titles he uses theophanies in a sophisticated way as the source of what he calls *theosophy* or divine *wisdom* (not philosophy or theology or theurgy). Reading the *Chaldaean Oracles* on their own terms, eschewing Iamblichus's Egyptianizing approach, Porphyry finds that they prescribe intellectual *erga,* not material *erga* involving animal sacrifice.[114] Accordingly, one of these treatises (if they are separate works) is

---

112. Michael Bland Simmons, *Arnobius of Sicca: Religious Conflict and Competition in the Age of Diocletian* (New York: Oxford University Press, 1995), 11, 14, and chap. 8, esp. 222, 319; J. J. O'Meara, *Porphyry's Philosophy from Oracles in Augustine* (Paris: Etudes augustiniennes, 1959), 146. J. Bidez, *Vie de Porphyre* (Ghent: E. van Goethem, 1913; repr., Hildesheim: G. Olms, 1964), 17–28, assumed the *Phil. or.* was a youthful work because it lacked overt references to Plotinus, Porphyry's mentor after age thirty. See also J. Geffcken, *The Last Days of Greco-Roman Paganism,* trans. S. MacCormack (Amsterdam: Holland Pub. Co., 1978); H. Lewy, *Chaldean Oracles and Theurgy: Mysticism, Magic, and Platonism in the Later Roman Empire* (Paris: Etudes augustiniennes, 1978), 449; and T. D. Barnes, *Constantine and Eusebius* (Cambridge, MA: Harvard University Press, 1981), 175. But Simmons, *Arnobius of Sicca,* 26, notes that "the intense research and...philological editorial work that it necessitated presuppose" a "mature scholar" as its author. Those ascribing a later date to the *Phil. or.*: R. L. Wilken, "Pagan Criticism of Christianity: Greek Religion and Christian Faith," in *Early Christian Literature and the Classical Intellectial Tradition,* ed. W. Schoedel and R. L. Wilken (Paris: Editions Beauschesne, 1979), 133–34; P. F. Beatrice, "Un oracle antichrétien chez Arnobe," in *Mémorial Dom Jean Gribomont,* ed. Y. de Andia et. al. (Rome: Institutum Patristicum Augustinianum, 1988), 123–29; Elizabeth DePalma Digeser, "Lactantius, Porphyry, and the Debate over Religious Toleration," *JRS* 88 (1998): 129–46; and J. J. O'Meara, *Porphyry's Philosophy from Oracles in Eusebius' Praeparatio Evangelica and Augustine's Dialogues of Cassiciacum* (Paris: Etudes augustiniennes, 1969). T. D. Barnes, "Monotheists All?" *Phoenix* 55 (2001): 159, acknowledged that the *Philosophy from Oracles* was relevant to the context of the Great Persecution.

113. Hadot, "Citations de Porphyre," 212–13. See also Smith, *Porphyry's Place,* 139, who sees Porphyry as having opened the way to Iamblichus; he doesn't understand Porphyry as reacting *to* Iamblichus.

114. Camplani and Zambon, "Il sacrificio," 91. Contra Smith, *Porphyry's Place,* 139, Porphyry did not "introduc[e] the idea of theurgy into Neoplatonism," because Iamblichus had already been teaching it and had discussed it in the *DM*. Porphyry's *Regr.* is, nevertheless, the first to *discuss* the *OC* publicly in any detail.

probably the work on the *Chaldaean Oracles* that the Suda ascribes to Porphyry. Porphyry's latest known original work, his *Life of Plotinus*, must also
be read in this anti-Iamblichaean context.

Historians of late Platonism all agree with Augustine in the *City of God*
that Porphyry sought but failed to find a "universal way of salvation" (10.32).
Porphyry affirmed that "no doctrine provided a *via universalis animae liberan-
dae*"—neither in the truest philosophy, the moral discipline of the Indians,
nor in the route of the Chaldaeans. Augustine's readers often infer from this
account that Porphyry's search disappointed him, that he expected or wanted
a *via universalis* to exist.[115] In Augustine's view, Porphyry ignored the obvious
solution, Christianity,[116] because it appeared to be weakening under persecution.[117] Augustine's Christianity and Iamblichus's theology were very different: for Christians, the universal way is one, the path revealed by Jesus Christ;
for Iamblichaeans, the universal way was a complex of paths founded by the
gods of traditional religion.[118] Nevertheless, just like Iamblichus, Augustine
thought he held the key to the universal way and that such a path for all was
appropriate and true.[119] Augustine also needed to explain how Porphyry,
such an astute and learned scholar—popular again as Augustine was writing the *City of God*—could have brushed Christianity so easily aside. But
Porphyry was not necessarily disappointed with his fruitless search. In fact,
I suggest that he expected to "find" no *via universalis*.[120]

Porphyry's engagement with the problem of the *via universalis* and his
proposed alternative are most easily seen in the treatise *On the Return of the
Soul*. The theme of this work is "avoid all bodies" (*omne corpus fugiendum
est*),[121] which is consistent with *On Abstinence*. Like that work, *On the Return*

---

115. Hadot, "Citations de Porphyre," 212; P. Courcelle, "Verissima philosophia," in *Epe-
ktasis: Mélanges patristiques offerts à Jean Daniélou,* ed. J. Fontaine and Charles Kannengiesser (Paris:
Beauchesne, 1972), 658–59; Smith, *Porphyry's Place,* 139; Saffrey, "Les néoplatoniciens," 215; Smith,
"Porphyrian Studies," 767; Saffrey, "Relecture de Jamblique," 171.

116. See also Aug. *Iul.* 4.14.72; Courcelle, "Verissima philosophia," 658; and Smith, *Porphyry's
Place,* 136.

117. Shaw, "Eros and Arithmos," 125; Courcelle, "Verissima philosophia," 658.

118. I thank an anonymous reader for this point.

119. Shaw, "Eros and Arithmos," 125.

120. Understanding *On the Return of the Soul* in this way removes an apparent contradiction
between it and the *Philosophy from Oracles*. The latter text (ap. Eus. *PE* 9.10) mentions many paths
within the "road to the gods," whereas Porphyry did not find a *universal* path for the soul's return
in *On the Return of the Soul* (ap. Aug. *Civ.* 10.32). Both O'Meara, *Porphyry's Philosophy,* and Hadot,
"Citations de Porphyre," thought that Porphyry was talking about a *via universalis* in the *Phil. or.*, but
more careful reading indicates that plural paths cannot be a universal way. Accordingly, both texts
deny and reject a *via universalis*.

121. P. Courcelle, "Nouveaux aspects du platonisme chez Saint Ambroise," *REL* 34 (1956):
220–39; id., "Le colle et le clou de l'âme dans la tradition néo-platonicienne et chrétienne (*Phédon*
82e; 83d)," *RBPh* 36 (1958): 72–95.

of the Soul opposes Iamblichus's position in *On the Mysteries* regarding all souls, but especially the philosophical soul. Porphyry's slogan and title reflect his overriding goal of freeing the soul from materiality in order to return to the divine. The only path that truly frees the soul, in Porphyry's view, is the philosophy that he found with Plotinus. Moreover, his description of this path as the *verissma philosophia,* using the superlative, implies that there are different philosophical claims at stake. In Porphyry's view, Plotinus's system offers a return to God, but only to the few with the intellectual capacity and opportunity to follow it (*Regr.* ap. Aug. *Civ.* 10.29.11):[122] few people could escape the fog of human corporeality and regain their vision through philosophy in order to see truth unveiled and bare in its beauty.[123]

Porphyry's assumption that different souls have different abilities to return to the divine is clear in what Augustine preserves of *On the Return of the Soul.* Unlike Iamblichus, Porphyry thinks that only philosophy achieves the soul's return to its source. For those who live according to their intellectual soul (*anima intellectualis*), this philosophical return depends initially on "the practice of virtue," but the soul of a person who attained the higher virtues might return to the divine through the practice of philosophy and the theoretical virtues.[124] For those who live according to their spirited soul (*anima spiritalis*), Porphyry conceded that theurgy and its theophanies might be of some limited use,[125] but, unlike Iamblichus, Porphyry saw no need at all for a philosopher to engage in theurgic rituals on behalf of his spirited soul.[126]

All the same, Porphyry's *On the Return of the Soul* does map out different paths toward the divine for souls not led by their intellectual parts. Both Andrew Smith and Michael Bland Simmons have attempted to articulate Porphyry's soteriology. Smith's work was groundbreaking, but he described Porphyry's theology as embracing multiple paths of salvation, based on the

122. Saffrey, "Les néoplatoniciens," 215. Cf. Courcelle, "Verissima philosophia," 653, 655, 658–59.

123. See also Plat. Rep. 5.473d; Or. *Jo.* 1.8; Meth. *Symp.* 9; Eus. *PE* 7.8.39; and Lact. *Inst.* 3.1.3: Courcelle, "Verissima philosophia," 656.

124. Smith, *Porphyry's Place,* 95, 135, argues that Iamblichus also envisions a dichotomy in souls and a two-staged salvation. This is true in theory, but in practice the difference is really moot—since all souls (except perhaps those of Plotinus, Plato, and Pythagoras) needed to participate in material-oriented rituals. One of Smith's errors is labeling all of Porphyry's paths as "paths to salvation"; what Porphyry is really describing (cf. Eus. *PE* 9.10) are paths that lead to different heavenly spheres. To some extent, Smith mitigates this problem by noting (139) that Porphyry's concern is not with "total salvation," but only that "of the lower self."

125. Saffrey, "Les néoplatoniciens," 215; Smith, *Prophyry's Place,* 215, 135.

126. Smith, *Porphyry's Place,* 136. Porphyry describes (ap. Aug. *Civ.* 10.9) an oracle about a man who wanted to purify his soul with theurgy but was thwarted by another theurge. Such a problem, and its similarity to Plotinus's experience with Olympius, must have convinced Porphyry that theurgy depended on *sympatheia,* nothing more.

part of the soul "saved," a description that deploys inappropriate terminol-ogy.[127] Simmons perpetuates this problem, but he does recognize that Por-phyry advocated three separate paths leading to three separate destinations. His observation, significantly, accords with Arnobius's allusion to the new men (*viri novi*), now identified as Porphyrians, who had been advocating a threefold system.[128] Simmons correctly identifies philosophy as the path along which souls living by their intellectual capacity came to rest with God. And Simmons rightly recognizes theurgy as the path along which souls living by their spirited capacity purified themselves and thus allowed their souls to reach a higher sphere at death than they otherwise would have. Simmons, however, wrongly sees virtue as Porphyry's third path for the soul.[129] He makes this mistake because Augustine chides Porphyry for acknowledging "that the spiritual part of the soul can be purified by the virtue of chastity without the aid of those theurgic arts and mysteries which you wasted your time in learn-ing" (*Civ.* 10.28). But the context shows Porphyry's claim really to be that the virtue of continence purifies the philosopher, negating his need for theurgy. This is the overarching message of *On Abstinence* and *On the Return of the Soul* (ap. *Civ.* 10.23 and 10.9); Porphyry's *Sententiae* reinforce it as well (e.g., 32f.).

Porphyry's first two paths should be summarized before addressing his third. The first path is philosophy: it leads souls, living by their intellectual capacity, to rest with God. Porphyry's second path is theurgy: it allows souls living by their spirited capacity (*anima spiritalis*) to purify themselves and so rise within the celestial spheres. For these people, Porphyry saw theurgy as helpful (though not necessary) because it engendered *phantasiai* that might connect people with the gods and lead their souls to the ethereal sphere after death.[130] Unlike Iamblichus, Porphyry uses the term "theurgy" in the more limited sense of the *Chaldaean Oracles*.[131] For Porphyry, the soul's experience in the ethereal realm might advantage it during its continued quest—in its next life—to return to its source.[132] Porphyry's position on theurgy, however,

---

127. Saffrey, "Les néoplatoniciens," 215, makes a similar mistake.

128. Arn. 2.13; P. Courcelle, "Les sages de Porphyre et les *viri novi* d'Arnobe," *REL* 31 (1953): 257–71; E. L. Fortin, "The *Viri novi* of Arnobius and the Conflict between Faith and Reason in the Early Christian Centuries," in *The Heritage of the Early Church: Essays in Honor of the Very Reverend Georges Vasilievich Florovsky,* ed. David Neiman and Margaret Schatkin (Rome: Pont. Institutum Studiorum Orientalium, 1973), 197–226.

129. Michael Bland Simmons, "The Eschatological Aspects of Porphyry's Anti-Christian Polemics in a Chaldaean-Neoplatonic Context," *C&M* 52, no. 2 (2001): 196.

130. Porph. *Regr.* ap. Aug. *Civ.* 10.9; Saffrey, "Les néoplatoniciens," 215; Smith, *Porphyry's Place,* 135.

131. Camplani and Zambon, "Il sacrificio," 90–91.

132. Elizabeth DePalma Digeser, "Porphyry, Lactantius, and the Paths to God," *Studia Patristica* 38 (2001): 521–28.

dramatically contradicts Iamblichus: First, Iamblichus insists that such rituals produced genuine theophanies and consequently epiphanies. Second, unlike Iamblichus, Porphyry saw no reason why a philosopher should bother with theurgic rites for his or her lower soul, because virtue could be just as useful as theurgy for the spirited soul.[133]

Just as a soul oriented toward intellect might rise to a higher sphere through philosophy, and a soul oriented toward its spirited part might, through theurgy, elevate itself after death, so a soul oriented toward its appetites might at least direct itself toward divinity by participating in the religious practices of its native people. This is Porphyry's third path. Arnobius (2.62) suggests as much in saying that people connected to the *viri novi* are advocating the use of Etruscan rituals:[134] for Romans these would be among the oldest rites associated with their polity.[135] Moreover, both Porphyry and Plotinus thought that something was communicated even to the ordinary soul who gazed upon a beautiful image,[136] a glimmer of insight and a connection that might lead the ordinary soul perhaps to the realm above the moon after death. Abiding in this place might help it climb even higher during its next earthly sojourn.[137]

As Augustine states explicitly, Porphyry's *On the Return of the Soul* derived these insights about the ways in which souls of different propensities might return to different heavenly spheres from a critical analysis of the *Chaldaean Oracles* (*Civ.* 10.32). Given the wide scope of Porphyry's investigation, he probably used other sources of prophecy as well. But his analysis of these texts, as a way of arguing against a *via universalis*, also rebukes his former student, since he is using the sources from which Iamblichus had drawn his own ideas about theurgy and fit them within a Hermetic and Pythagorean framework. Moreover, the theme of Iamblichus's *De mysteriis* is that all forms of divination, properly done, are the gifts of the gods leading all souls heavenward; whereas both *On the Return of the Soul* and *On the Philosophy from Oracles* claim that, if one looks closely at what these same gods say, there is no universal path along which souls might return to the divine. Porphyry has "conceded" that Chaldaean rites can elevate the human soul to the

133. *Sent.* 32f.; Smith, *Porphyry's Place,* 136; Saffrey, "Les néoplatoniciens," 216; Digeser, "Power of Religious Rituals,"

134. See also Garth Fowden, "Late Antique Paganism Reasoned and Revealed," *JRS* 71 (1981): 181.

135. Porphyry's research in this area may have been aided by Cornelius Labeo: Fowden, "Late Antique Paganism," 181. See also P. Mastandrea, *Un neoplatonico Latino, Cornelio Labeone* (Leiden: Brill, 1979); and F. Romano, *Porfirio di Tiro: Filosofia e cultura nel II secolo D.C.,* Univ. di Catania Pubbl. Fac. di Lett. e Filos. 33 (Catania: Università, Facoltà di lettere e filosofia, 1979).

136. Berchman, "Arcana Mundi," 136f.

137. Digeser, "Porphyry, Lactantius, and the Paths to God," 521–28.

ether or the empyrean realm, but will go no further.[138] Indeed, late in his life
Porphyry even warned his wife, Marcella, "against associating with certain
people who can do her harm," those "corrupted by false belief" and "clearly
to be regarded as beyond the reach of true philosophy."[139] This passage is
usually read as Porphyry warning his wife away from Christians,[140] but it is
now evident that there were people wearing the philosopher's pallium whose
influence Porphyry feared just as much.

Augustine presents evidence indicating how Porphyry might have tarred
both the Iamblichaean and the Christian traditions with the same brush
(*Civ.* 10.24). The bishop says that Porphyry refused to understand Christ as
the principle whose incarnation purified us; rather, he hated Christ because
he had assumed the flesh. The argument that Augustine sets out has now
become standard Christian doctrine—that, by assuming the human body,
God expiated human sinfulness through the sacrifice of crucifixion, and
that human beings participate in that sacrifice through the mystery of the
Eucharist. But Augustine's theology has strong Iamblichaean assumptions
undergirding it. Iamblichus, for example, taught that material souls ought
to employ objects that correspond to the suffering of their own alienation,
rites that included eating victims—a description that fits the Eucharistic
sacrament. Iamblichus also claimed that the material world had nothing to
do with evil; rather, matter was the substance through which the divine presence made itself known to the human soul. In arguing that the incarnation
and sacrifice of Christ did not purify the human soul, Porphyry is denying
not only the Christian theophany but also the Iamblichaean understanding
of redemptive sacrifice and the beneficence of matter. Chapter 5 and the
conclusion will further develop the criticisms of Christianity that Porphyry
set out in his campaign against the *via universalis*.

For the philosopher seeking the return of his or her soul to its source, in
place of Christianity and Iamblichaean theurgy, Porphyry maintained that
Plotinian philosophy was the only appropriate path. *On Abstinence* adopts
this perspective, but this is also the message of the *Life of Plotinus*. It is now
time to return to this treatise, written in 300, to see what Porphyry thinks
is the appropriate behavior for heaven-seeking philosophers. Although Porphyry's advocacy of Plotinus's *verissima philosophia* is evident from *On the
Return of the Soul,* and his endorsement of Plotinian asceticism (e.g., vegetarianism, celibacy) is apparent in *On Abstinence,* the *Life of Plotinus* is most

138. Saffrey, "Les néoplatoniciens," 217.
139. H. Whittaker, "The Purpose of Porphyry's Letter to Marcella," *SymbOsl* 76 (2001): 159.
140. Ibid.

informative in showing the proper relationship between the philosopher and material rituals. For example, the "theurgic" character of the ritual in the Iseum indicates not only that Plotinus probably approved of such types of divination, but also a certain limited utility for theurgy in providing evidence for the character of the sage's soul.[141] Where Plotinus's participation in the Iseum rituals suggests a positive, but limited attitude on his (but especially Porphyry's) part to theurgic divination, his reaction to Amelius during the new moon festival (Porph. *Plot.* 10) is also less obviously a rejection of ritual than it initially seems. The first clue that the rituals themselves are significant occurs in Porphyry's *On Abstinence* (2.16).[142] Citing Theopompus, Porphyry describes Klearchos of Arcadian Methydrion, whom the Pythia at Delphi portrayed as the person "who honoured the divine power best and most zealously and who made the most acceptable sacrifices."

> [Klearchos] made offerings and sacrificed with care at the proper times: every month at the new moon he garlanded and polished Hermes and Hekate and the other sacred objects that his ancestors had left, and honoured them with incense and ground grain and cakes. Every year he took part in the public sacrifices, omitting no festival, and in those sacrifices he worshipped the gods not by sacrificing cattle or cutting up victims, but by offering what he had available.[143]

Porphyry uses this passage to make several points. First, the gods value "the quality of the sacrificers," not the "quantity of the sacrifice" (2.15). Second, while it is appropriate to follow traditional religious customs and to sacrifice "in accordance with the law of the city," one should also do this in a "fitting" way, namely by offering the simplest sacrifice possible (2.33); simple ones are better because they most closely resemble sacrifice in its most ancient, most holy, and wisest form (2.5–8). And third, these simple, meatless rites are appropriate for Hermes and Hecate, significantly the two key theurgic divinities in Iamblichus's system, but "different sacrifices" are appropriate for "different powers." When it comes to "the god who rules over all, Porphyry paraphrases Apollonius of Tyana:

> [We] shall offer nothing perceived by the senses, either by burning or in words. For there is nothing material which is not at once impure to the immaterial. So not even *logos* expressed in speech is appropriate

---

141. Johnston, *Hekate Soteira*, 6; Luck, "Theurgy," 207, although Edwards, "Two Episodes," 456, connect the priests' activities more closely to exorcism than to theurgy.

142. Van den Berg, "Plotinus' Attitude," 348.

143. Trans. G. Clark.

for him, nor yet internal *logos* when it has been contaminated by the passion of the soul. But we shall worship him in pure silence and with pure thoughts about him. (Abst. 2.34)

Porphyry, accordingly, used the incident involving the new moon sacrifices to make a complex statement about which rituals are appropriate for which people. Scholars interpreting this passage focus intently on Plotinus's refusal to participate and Porphyry's claim of confusion about what the great sage meant. Nevertheless, Porphyry's failure to criticize Amelius, one of Plotinus's closest followers engaged in this ritual, is significant:[144] he may participate in this kind of pure ritual. The ritual behaviors appropriate for Plotinus, however, are different.[145] Porphyry stresses this distinction by saying that no one knew (or dared ask) what Plotinus meant by remarking that "they" ought to come to him.

The attribute that distinguished Plotinus and Porphyry from Amelius is that they had achieved divine union several times. Plotinus himself discloses not only what sort of ritual practice is appropriate for such a sage, but also that it is something "not to disclose to the uninitiated" (*Enn.* 6.9.11.1–4).

Since then, there were not two, but the seer himself was one with the seen (for it was not really seen, but united to him), if he remembers who he became when he was united with that, he will have an image of that in himself. He was one himself, with no distinction in himself . . . he was as if carried away or possessed by a god, in a quiet solitude and a state of calm. . . . He had no thought of beauties, but had already run up beyond beauty . . . like a man who enters into the sanctuary and leaves behind the statues in the outer shrine; these become again the first things he looks at when he comes out of the sanctuary, after his contemplation within and intercourse there, not with a statue or image but with the Divine itself; they are secondary objects of contemplation. (*Enn.* 6.9.11.5–25)

This, Plotinus concludes, "is the life of gods and of godlike and blessed men, deliverance from the things of this world, a life which takes no delight in the things of this world, escape in solitude to the solitary" (6.9.11.48–51). The

144. Luck, "Theurgy," 208, contra Brisson, "Amélius," 813; and Van den Berg, "Plotinus' Attitude," 355–56.

145. Contra Van den Berg, "Plotinus' Attitude," 345–46, 358, Porphryry's reaction reveals not offense from Plotinus' apparent dismissal of traditional religion. Rather, Porphyry was emphatically (note the term *megalēgoreō*, "to speak loftily, magniloquently") distancing Plotinus's practices from those of Amelius.

uniquely gifted man who had achieved divine union not only ought to concentrate on the One, but also in so doing had the gods themselves—even the
most exalted being aspects of multiplicity, [146] of becoming, not of being—as
companions.

In the end, Porphyry's hagiographical portrait of Plotinus in his introduction to the *Enneads* shows by example, and in opposition to Iamblichus,
the relationship that, at the cusp of the fourth century, he thought philosophers ought to cultivate with material rituals, including theurgy. The philosopher's highest goal ought to be divine union. Indeed, those philosophers
who had achieved this state ought to direct their energies to this "life of the
gods." Theurgy, for philosophers, had a certain utility, in that it could impart
information: it could acquaint you with your companion spirit. According
to Plotinus's treatise, since each human soul was a cosmos in itself, these
spirit companions represented the level of soul immediately above which
a person chose to live and, accordingly, the level to which the soul—if it
lived well—might aspire to live in its next life (*Enn.* 3.4.3, 6). Plotinus's
experience in the Iseum was, then, proof that he ought to aspire only to
live the life of the gods. Philosophers such as Amelius, however, who is not
portrayed—at least in the *Life of Plotinus*—as having achieved divine union,
might participate in those civic cults that involved the simplest forms of
sacrifice: grain, for example, but never blood. And what of ordinary people?
Porphyry gives us a limited but telling view in describing Plotinus's daily
activities. Although Gemina is the owner of the house in which Plotinus
lives, he assumed the role of the *paterfamilias,* serving as guardian for those in
need, ferreting out guilty parties in cases of minor theft (*Plot.* 9). As might
be expected from those who had taken Plato's *Laws* to heart, ordinary
people did best when under the care of the philosopher who had achieved
union with the One.

Porphyry was a polymath and an indefatigable researcher. If he was motivated to write against all universal paths, Hellene and Christian, because he
wanted to protect the legacy of Plotinus's philosophy and its Ammonian
lineage above all, he did not, then, write with the intention to bring physical harm to the communities he addressed. Rather, he was participating in
the long-standing tradition of philosophers asserting and supporting specific
ethical and metaphysical claims. All the same, from the moment that Porphyry's treatises arrived among Iamblichus's circle in Antioch, they began
circulating among an ever-widening circle of readers. It was inevitable, given

---

146. Van den Berg, "Plotinus' Attitude," 346–47, 357, contra P. Henry, "La dernière parole de
Plotin," *SCO* 2 (1953): 115; Armstrong, "Was Plotinus a Magician?" 78–79.

Porphyry's audience and his claims, that his texts reached Christian readers. Some in this group learned for the first time how deeply the Origenists
among them drew on contemporary Hellene philosophy in their theology—
and they did not like it. At the same time, Hellenes within Iamblichus's circle
might conclude, not only that ordinary people at least ought to participate
in traditional cult, but also that they had a responsibility to ensure they did
so. Accordingly, first Origenists and then Christians more generally began to
feel the press of public opinion to conform.

CHAPTER 5

Schism in the Ammonian Community
Porphyry v. Methodius of Olympus

Iamblichus was a revolutionary Hellene. Not only did his theology address the salvific needs of ordinary people by asserting the efficacy of rituals involving matter. But it also insisted that all human souls—even those closest to the divine—ought to participate in them. Porphyry, discovering Iamblichus's theology, concluded that some of Ammonius Saccas's philosophical descendants, in devising their own philosophy without conflicts, had violated fundamental hermeneutical principles. Late in the third century, he decided to explain their errors and set theology back on the right track for everyone. Porphyry's response was typical of many philosophers before him who had taken issue with sectarian peers (*haereticoi*) regarding the right way to live and think (*orthodoxia*). Porphyry's response also resembles that of an earlier author, Irenaeaus of Lyons, the bishop who first took it upon himself to write against Christian Gnostic sectarians (*haereticoi*) and begin to define Christian orthodoxy in the process. The difference between the two traditions is one of effect, not of kind, in that Christian bishops attempted to exclude *haereticoi*—heretics—from their communities, and philosophers apparently did not. Porphyry thus set himself up as the arbiter of orthodoxy for the Ammonian community.

Porphyry's extant works never specifically address Ammonius's Iamblichaean and Origenist descendants together. But they do show that Porphyry had identified a methodological problem, common to these two subgroups, as the root cause for their heresy: in Porphyry's view, both Iamblichaeans and Origenists failed to use appropriately the exegetical tools that were the cornerstone of their shared traditions. Porphyry's exploration of the *Chaldaean Oracles'* philosophical tenets led him to reject how Iamblichus derived from them a theology that envisioned humanity uniting with the divine through matter. Porphyry also denied the theology of Origenist Christians, who applied figural hermeneutics to unsuitable scriptural texts. Chapter 4 explored Porphyry's response to Iamblichus: although he was most concerned to set out the proper way of living for those who aspired to be philosophers, Porphyry also justified the pursuit of traditional ethnic cult rituals for ordinary people.

This chapter considers the implications of Porphyry's response to what he saw as Origenist deviance. Eusebius says that Porphyry directed certain criticisms against Origen himself, but the philosopher's remarks reveal that he was at least as concerned with the activities of Origen's followers, his contemporaries. Historians of theology and philosophy have focused on Porphyry's criticisms of Origen, as Eusebius preserved them in the *Ecclesiastical History*. But no one has identified the Origenist Christian exegetes Porphyry described, who had "boasted that things declared openly by Moses" were "enigmas" (Eus. *HE* 6.19.4–5). This chapter argues that one such exegete was Methodius of Olympus, who, according to Jerome, also wrote against Porphyry at some length.[1] Examined within the context of Porphyry's criticisms of Origen's followers, Methodius's *Symposium, De cibis,* and *Aglaophon* provide extraordinary insight into Roman religious and philosophical tensions at the cusp of the fourth century. More thoroughly than the small fragment of Porphyry's text quoted by Eusebius, they show Porphyry's belief that Origenists were promoting an irrationality that undermined the political order. In so doing, they illustrate how Porphyry's criticisms legitimized a series of complaints against certain types of Christians that culminated in the Great Persecution. Evidence within Methodius's *De cibis* and *Aglaophon* also shows that Methodius was a key player, not only in the dialogue that ensued between Christian exegetes and their Hellene critics, Porphyry especially, but also in the controversy that erupted within the Christian community regarding the value and orthodoxy of Origen's teachings. Methodius's texts, however, have rarely been explored in this context—partly because so few of them have been translated, and partly because Porphyry's complaints about

---

1. Hieron. *Vir. ill.* 83: Methodius…adversum Porphyrium confecit libros; *Ep.* 70: Methodius [contra Porphyrium] usque ad decem millia procedit versuum.

Origenism have not yet been situated in a context beyond Eusebius's *Ecclesiastical History*.

Methodius and Gregory Thaumaturgos are the only third-century Christian teachers working with or after Origen whose extant writings used forms of the word *ainigma* in relation to biblical exegesis.[2] Although both men had connections to Origen,[3] only Methodius used the word in the way that Porphyry had challenged, namely to describe aspects of the Pentateuch (i.e., Exodus and Leviticus).[4] Aspects of Methodius's *Symposium* suggest that he was just the type of Origenist Christian teacher against whom Porphyry directed his criticisms. Porphyry need not have known directly the writing and teaching of Methodius, his contemporary. In order to make his charge regarding Origen's influence (ap. Eus. *HE* 6.19.5), however, Porphyry must have been familiar with the work of at least one of the theologian's students or a student's student.

After setting out the few certain pieces of information concerning Methodius's life, his texts will be addressed. Although it was probably one of Methodius's last works, I will explore the *Aglaophon* first. Among his texts, it is the most strongly critical of Origen (even while still embracing many of Origen's teachings). The *Aglaophon* begins as a dialogue whose characters Aglaophon and Proclus can be shown to articulate Porphyry's views.[5] With this identification established, it is possible to construe how Porphyry used Origen's theology within his critique of the Origenists. Origen's writings, I argue, supported Porphyry's own argument against the popular Christian doctrine of the resurrection of the flesh. This tactic links Porphyry's critiques of Origen to the heated Christian debate about the Alexandrian theologian that erupted at the cusp of the fourth century. One group of Christians learned about Origen's ideas from Porphyry's attacks and vociferously rejected them outright. Anxious about being identified with the Hellene opposition who had criticized but also co-opted Origen, Origenists

---

2. Greg. *In ann. PG* 10.1152.41; *In Orig.* 2.67; 15.5, 13, 37; Meth. *Symp.* 5.7.20; 8.9.24; 9.1.71. Clement of Alexandria and Hippolytus of Rome also did, but, as Origen's elders, they are more apt to have influenced him than to have been influenced by him. Texts of ps.-Justin also use the term, but their content shows them to be fifth-century works. The data come from the *Thesaurus Linguae Graecae*.

3. For Gregory's connections to Origen, see chapter 2.

4. In *The First Homily on the Annunciation to the Holy Virgin Mary*, Gregory uses the word to describe how the prophets, patriarchs, and holy fathers "beheld" Christ. In the panegyric on Origen he (or the author) says that Origen used to interpret *ainigmata* for his students (*Pan. Or.* 15), and uses the expression to describe aspects of the "Divine Word" generally (2).

5. Hendrick S. Benjamins, "Methodius von Olympus, 'Über die Auferstehung': Gegen Origenes und gegen Porphyrius?" in *Origeniana septima*, ed. W. A. Bienert and Uwe Kühneweg (Leuven: Peeters, 1999), 90–100.

like Methodius distanced themselves from Porphyry's criticisms and from some of Origen's teachings, especially as persecution became more likely. In response, Origenists like Pamphilus and Eusebius arose to address Origen's Hellene and Christian critics as well as Origenists whose support had waned. Pamphilus, for example, who had studied with Pierius ("Origen Junior"),[6] wrote a *Defense of Origen* in five books from his prison cell during the persecution.[7] Eusebius, Pamphilus's student, added a sixth book to his mentor's *Defense of Origen* and fingered Methodius as a turncoat (ap. Hieron. *C. Ruf.* 1.11).

Finally, with the help of *De cibis* and the *Symposium*, I use Methodius's work to broaden our understanding of Porphyry's challenge. In *De cibis* (1.1–2), Methodius reveals not only that his earlier work, the *Symposium*, had been sharply attacked, but also that he intended to address his critics in the *Aglaophon*. Thus, because Aglaophon and Proclus voice Porphyry's views, Methodius must have seen Porphyry's attacks on Origenists as relevant to his *Symposium* (whether or not Porphyry knew Methodius's writing directly). And, in fact, the *Symposium*, the treatise that had been criticized, pursued precisely those Origenist exegetical strategies that Porphyry had deplored, according to the fragment of his third treatise "against us" preserved in Eusebius's *Ecclesiastical History*. Methodius had not only deployed these exegetical practices in a text structured as a Platonic dialogue. But the dialogue also portrayed an ascetic philosophical community dedicated to promoting the ascent of the soul. The *Symposium* thus shows that Origen's descendants were pursuing careers, ideas, and projects closely related to those of Porphyry and Iamblichus. Porphyry did not just reject the Origenists as competitors, however. The implication of his criticism is that he thought Origenism eroded the foundations of public law. Independent of Eusebius, then, Methodius's *Symposium, De cibis,* and *Aglaophon* establish a context for Porphyry's anti-Christian criticisms. These works connect Porphyry's criticisms both to his concerns about Iamblichaean theology and to the pressures culminating in the Great Persecution.

Hardly any certain information regarding Methodius survives, a circumstance for which his ambivalent relationship to Origen's theology is to blame. "How could Methodius dare to write now against Origen," Eusebius asks, probably referring to the *Aglaophon,* "after having said *this*...about his

---

6. Phot. *Bibl.* 118; Hieron. *Vir. ill.* 76.
7. Eric Junod and René Amacker, "Avant-Propos," in *Apologie pour Origène,* ed. Pamphile and Eusèbe de Césarée (Paris: Editions du Cerf, 2002), 9.

doctrines?" (ap. Hieron. *C. Ruf.* 1.11).[8] The remark from the *Defense of Origen* in the present tense establishes Methodius as a contemporary of Eusebius and Porphyry, besides supplementing the literary evidence for Methodius's change in attitude toward Origen.[9] Later, after 306,[10] Eusebius recycled his defense of Origen as the sixth book of his *Ecclesiastical History,* completely—and probably deliberately—ignoring Methodius's role in the controversy.[11] Recurrent attacks on Origen's theology, culminating in his sixth-century post–mortem excommunication, discouraged the preservation of texts that defended him, including most of Eusebius's and Pamphilus's *Defense.* Even so, Eusebius has had his revenge: the most basic information about Methodius remains stubbornly elusive. That Methodius flourished in the late third and early fourth centuries, however, is supported by Jerome's *De viris illustribus* (83). According to this short biography, Methodius died at the end of the "most recent persecution."[12] As only one of his writings refers specifically to persecution,[13] the bulk of his work reflects the peaceful period between Valerian's death in 260 and Diocletian's edicts of 303.[14]

---

8. "Quomodo ausus est Methodius nunc contra Origenem scribere, qui haec et haec de Origenis?" The passage survives only as quoted by Jerome.

9. Herbert Musurillo, ed., *St. Methodius, The Symposium: A Treatise on Chastity* (London: Longmans, Green, 1958), 5; T. D. Barnes, "Methodius, Maximus & Valentinus," *JThS* 30 (1979): 51 incl. n. 4.

10. R. W. Burgess, "The Dates and Editions of Eusebius' *Chronici canones* and *Historia ecclesiastica,*" *JThS* n. s. 48 (1997): 471–504.

11. L. G. Patterson, "Notes on *De cibis* and Methodius' View of Origen," in *Origeniana tertia,* ed. Richard Hanson and H. Crouzel (Rome: Ateneo, 1985), 233. For the dependence of book 6 on the *Defense of Origen,* see R. M. Grant, "Early Alexandrian Christianity," *ChHist* 40 (1971): 133–34; L. G. Patterson, "*De libero arbitrio* and Methodius' Attack on Origen," *Studia Patristica* 14.3 (1976): 160. See also note 14 below.

12. Hieron. *Vir. ill.* 83: Methodius, Olympi Lyciae, et postea Tyri eposcopus, nitidi compositique sermonis, adversum Porphyrium confecit libros, et Symposium decem virginum, de resurrectione opus egregium contra Origenem, et adversus eumdem de Pythonissa, et de Autexusio; in Genesim quoque et in Cantica canticorum commentarios; et multa alia, quae vulgo lectitantur. Et ad extremum novissimae persecutionis, sive, ut alii affirmant, sub Decio et Valeriano in Calcide Graeciae, martyrio coronatus est.

13. *De lepra* refers to "green leprosy" or "cowardice in a time of persecution" (6.1). L. G. Patterson, *Methodius of Olympus: Divine Sovereignty, Human Freedom, and Life in Christ* (Washington, DC: Catholic University of America, 1997), 20–21 incl. n. 9; Musurillo, *St. Methodius,* 9.

14. Musurillo, *St. Methodius,* 9. Nevertheless, in referring to the claims of some people that Methodius was martyred in Chalcis (Euboea), Greece, under "Decius and Valerian," Jerome's biography raises the possibility that Methodius died in the mid-third century (see note 12 above). Jerome's second date is clearly wrong, given Eusebius's identification of Methodius as a contemporary (Patterson, "*De libero arbitrio,*" 160; Patterson, *Methodius of Olympus,* 15–17; Barnes, "Methodius, Maximus & Valentinus," 54). Perhaps, however, Jerome's claim should not be read at face value. As continuator of Eusebius's *Chronicle* (in the late 370s), Jerome would have been unlikely in the *De viris illustribus* (written in 393) to place Methodius—Porphyry's opponent and hence, at the earliest, his contemporary—half a century too early. As for Chalcis, the site of Aristotle's suicide after the

Athenians spurned him, at least in Christian tradition (*A Dictionary of Greek and Roman Biography and Mythology*, ed. William Smith, s. v. "Aristoteles"), Jerome might be suggesting—not that Methodius actually died there—but that his "martyrdom" had something to do with his community's rejecting his philosophical views. (Indeed, the author of the passage on Methodius in the Suda clearly puzzled over this locale when translating Jerome's text into Greek, for he substituted "in the east" for "in Greece." Since Jerome himself, however, spent some time in Chalcis in Syria [*OCD* s.v. Jerome], this amendment is wrong). Jerome—who would soon be distancing himself from Origen after Epiphanius revived anti-Origenism—might have felt more than a little sympathy for Methodius as an intellectual in similar straits at an earlier time. See also note 18 below.

Eusebius also discusses Methodius's work within an early third-century context. In his *Preparation for the Gospel* (7.21), Eusebius mentions a treatise on matter by a certain "Maximus," and he quotes a fair portion of it (7.22). This passage cites verbatim chapters 5–12 of *Peri tou autexousiou*, which itself is primarily concerned with God and matter. A. Vaillant, "Le *De autexousio* de Méthode d'Olympe, version slave et texte grec édités et traduits en français," *Patrologia Orientalis* 22 (1930): 641; Patterson, "*De libero arbitrio*," 162. The manuscripts for *Peri tou autexousiou*—Laurent. Plut. IX, 23; Tolstoi. [Petropol.] II.56; No. 110 of the Synodalbibl. in Moscow—clearly credit Methodius as its author; and the latter two MSS are translations of the Greek text in old Slavonic. Cf. D. G. Nathanael Bonwetsch, ed., *Methodius, Die griechischen christlichen Schriftsteller der ersten drei Jahrhunderte* (Leipzig: J. C. Hinrichs, 1917), 144–45; see also V. Buchheit, *Studien zu Methodius von Olympos* (Berlin: Akademie-Verlag, 1958); Vaillant, "Le *De autexousio*," 631. In the earlier *Ecclesiastical History* (5.27.1), however, Eusebius assigns this Maximus, "author of a treatise 'On the Creation of Matter,'" to the era of Septimius Severus. Eusebius, who had mentioned Methodius's rejection of Origen explicitly in the *Defense of Origen*, thus misidentified and misdated Methodius's work both in the *Ecclesiastical History* (ca. 306) (Burgess, "Dates and Editions," 471–504) and in the *Preparation for the Gospel* (ca. 314) (T. D. Barnes, "Eusebius," *Lexicon für Theologie und Kirche* 3 [1995]: 1006–10). Eusebius—who had a strong sense of the power of the written word to create a desired legacy—deliberately condemned Methodius, whom he viewed as a traitor, to a kind of textual oblivion—citing his work, but attributing it to an earlier apocryphal author (contra Patterson, "*De libero arbitrio*," 162 n. 1). If I am correct, then Jerome's reference to an early third-century date for Methodius, "ut alii affirmant," suggests that he is in on the joke. Eusebius was notoriously vindictive, having gotten Eustathius of Antioch (another critic of Origen) deposed and sent into exile (Grant, "Early Alexandrian Christianity," 133). Vaillant, "Le *De autexousio*," 638–39, however, thinks that "Maximus" either was imaginary or was perhaps the name of a character in the dialogue. For the latter view, see also Patterson, "*De libero arbitrio*," 162 incl. n. 2.

T. D. Barnes attempted to reconcile the late third-century date for Methodius with Eusebius's attribution of his texts to "Maximus," writing under the Severans. Barnes claimed that a certain Maximus did write an early third-century treatise on matter, which Eusebius intended to quote in the *Preparation for the Gospel*. (He thinks that Maximus's treatise is identical with *De recta in deum fide*, also known as the *Dialogue of Adamantius*.) But, Barnes speculates, an assistant of Eusebius, charged with copying passages from texts that the bishop cited, mistakenly inserted an appropriate passage from Methodius on the same topic instead of the requisite passage from Maximus (Barnes, "Methodius, Maximus & Valentinus," 53–54). This explanation is not impossible, but it is improbable. First, Barnes relies on an early third-century date for the *Dialogue of Adamantius*, which most scholars have rejected (cf. *Adamantius: Dialogue on the True Faith in God*, trans. Robert A. Pretty [Leuven: Peeters, 1997], 16–17). Contra Barnes, "Methodius, Maximus & Valentinus," 49–51, the *Dialogue*'s remarks (1.21) about the king being in the hand of God and the frequency of persecution do *not* situate the text necessarily in the early third century. Moreover, the *Dialogue*'s concerns—dualism, Marcionites, and Valentinians—remained topics of debate into the early fourth century (cf. Lact. *Inst.* 2.8; 4.30). Second, Barnes's argument rests on an improbable coincidence: Eusebius meant to quote Maximus but instead quoted Methodius—who himself, according to Barnes, is dependent on this very text. For the converse argument, that the *Dialogue* is dependent on Methodius, see Vaillant, "Le *De autexousio*," 637, 648; and Robert Pretty in *Adamantius: Dialogue on the True Faith in God*, 12–13, 17–18.

Very little about Methodius's occupation is certain.[15] The most secure description of Methodius is that he was a Christian intellectual with philosophical pretensions.[16] His writings, especially the *Symposium,* imply that he was a teacher.[17] Starting with Jerome, ancient sources sometimes refer to Methodius as a bishop.[18] Nevertheless, he never described himself as a bishop, the evidence connecting him to various sees is poor,[19] and the earliest extant references do not refer to his office.[20] Moreover, Methodius's *Symposium* advocates a hierarchy of believers independent of episcopal authority.[21] The tradition, beginning with Jerome, that Methodius was a martyr is similarly difficult to substantiate.[22] Methodius's works indicate that he spent enough

---

15. For the "problem of his life," see K. Quensell, "Die wahre kirchliche Stellung und Tätigkeit des fälschlich so gennanten Bischofs Methodius von Olympus" (Diss., Heidelberg, 1952); and Musurillo, *St. Methodius,* 3–5.

16. The Syrian florilegia (Brit. Mus. addit. 17214, 17191, and 14538) identify him as a philosopher. See the incipit to the *Aglaophon/De resurrectione* in Bonwetsch, *Methodius,* 219.

17. Patterson, *Methodius of Olympus,* 18–19. See also Musurillo, *St. Methodius,* 5; and Quensell, "Die wahre kirchliche Stellung." Some scholars have claimed that Methodius was the last "free teacher" of the patristic period. Quensell, in Musurillo, 172 n. 11; and J. Montserrat-Torrents, "Origenismo y gnosis: Los 'perfectos' de Metodio de Olimpo," *Augustinianum* 26 (1986): 101.

18. Hieron. *C. Ruf.* 1.11; *Vir. ill.* 83; John of Damascus *Orat.* 3.138; *Cont. Iac.* 93.1; Phot. *Bibl.* 234.293a; Socr. *HE* 6.13; Niceph. *Eus.* 66.212; and Procopius of Gaza on Gen. 3:21 (*PG* 87a 221c). See also the incipits in the MS copies of the *Symposium* (Ottobon. gr. 59, Mazarin/Paris gr. 946, Patmos gr. 202, Marcian. gr. 451, and Sin. 1139) as well as the old Slavonic translation of *On the Resurrection.* All of these can be found in Bonwetsch, *Methodius;* see also Patterson, *Methodius of Olympus,* 15–16, 17, 18–19 incl. n. 7, 21; Musurillo, *St. Methodius,* 5. Alone in the ancient sources, Jerome reports not only that Methodius was "bishop of Olympus in Lycia," but also that he was later bishop of Tyre (*Vir. ill.* 83; see also the Suda s.v. "Methodius," which depends on Jerome; and Musurillo, 171 n. 11 [c]). Jerome's connection of Methodius to Tyre is a tantalizing claim. This is the only piece of information that potentially links Methodius to a venue close to Origen (since, according to Photius, the theologian died in this city) and to Porphyry as well (Tyre is the city of his birth) (Phot. *Bibl.* 118; Eun. *VS* s.v. "Porphyrius"; Patterson, *Methodius of Olympus,* 15–17; Musurillo, 171 n. 11 [c], suggests that the "tradition" of Tyre may have more to do with Methodius's opposition to Porphyry). Methodius might have moved from Olympus to Tyre, and so have faced martyrdom there (A. von Harnack and Erwin Preuschen, *Geschichte der altchristlichen Literatur bis Eusebius* (Leipzig: J. C. Hinrichs, 1904), 2.2: 147f. incl. n. 3), but he does not appear in the list of Tyrian bishops who served after 310 (F. Diekamp, "Über den Bischofssitz des hl. Methodius," *ThQ* 109 [1928]: 285–308). This problem dissolves, however, if Methodius was not a bishop. Unfortunately, the uniqueness of Jerome's claim, together with the orthographic similarities between "Turos" and "Mura," make it hard to press the point that Methodius spent any time in Tyre (Musurillo, 171 n. 11 [c]; see note 12 above).

19. Barnes, "Methodius, Maximus & Valentinus," 54 incl. n. 4.

20. Musurillo, *St. Methodius,* 172 n. 11. See also Quensell, "Die wahre kirchliche Stellung"; Eustathius of Antioch *De engastrimytho* 22.5.4; Epiphanius *Pan.* 2.420–21, 430, 475, 499–500, 510, 515. Epiphanius calls him a "blessed presbyter" (*Pan.* 2.510.3), and Eusebius is mute on the subject.

21. *Symp.* 3, 8. Cf. Montserrat-Torrents, "Origenismo y gnosis," 93–97, 100–101. See also Musurillo, *St. Methodius,* 172 n. 11.

22. But Jerome's calling him a martyr (see note 12 above) may have more to do with Methodius's condemnation as an Origenist. See also Hieron. *C. Ruf.* 1.11; John of Damascus *Cont. Iac.* 93.1; *Sac. par.* 96.485; Phot. *Bibl.* 162.106a, 235.301b; and the MSS listed in note 14 above. Eustathius's reference to "Methodius of blessed memory" perhaps lends some credibility to Jerome's claim (*De engastrimytho* 22.5.4).

time in Lycia (now southwestern Turkey) to learn its terrain and small cities, including Patara, Olympus, and Termessus.[23] These allusions may have led ancient authors to believe that he either came from or served as bishop of Olympus,[24] Patara,[25] or Myra.[26] Accordingly, it is best to describe Methodius simply as a man who wrote and worked in Asia Minor, especially Lycia.[27]

Methodius was a prolific author.[28] One of his works survives intact in the original Greek (*Symposion ē peri hagneias*),[29] another endures more or less intact

---

For the difficulty in substantiating Methodius's martyrdom, see Patterson, *Methodius of Olympus,* 21. Despite Patterson's hesitancy, Barnes, "Methodius, Maximus & Valentinus," 54 incl. n. 4, claims that Methodius was martyred on 20 June 312 (*Symaxarium Eccl. Cpl.* cols. 757–58; *Propylaeum ad Acta Sanctorum Decembris* [1940], 404) at Patara, "perhaps after a trial by the emperor Maximius who may well have visited Patara during the summer of that year."

23. Musurillo, *St. Methodius,* 5, 11, 170–71 n. 11 (a), (e), 240 n. 1. *Aglaophon* takes place in Patara, whither Methodius says he went with Proclus of Miletus (*Res.* 1.1.1); in this text also Methodius refers to Mount Olympus in Lycia (2.23.1); *Symp.* 11.24 refers to Termessus as the home of one of the dialogue's characters, and the epilogue refers to Telmēsiakē, translated by Musurillo as the "Lady from Termessus," whom he posits as Methodius's benefactor. Musurillo may be incorrect, however, since Telmessus was also a town in Lycia. Cf. J. A. Talbert, ed., *Atlas of Classical History* (London: Routledge, 1985), 160.

24. Hieron. *Vir. ill.* 83; Socr. *HE* 6.13; Zacharias Rhetor's *Syriac Church History,* proem.; the Syriac florilegia that quote *Res.;* a scholion on ps.–Dionysius's *Eccles. Hieron.* 7.7 attributed to Maximus the Confessor; and the old Slavonic translation of *Peri tou autexousiou.* See also Patterson, *Methodius of Olympus,* 17–18 incl. n. 5. Vaillant, "Le *De autexousio,*" 636, showed that references in the old Slavonic MS of the *Autexousio* to Methodius of Philippi were to the result of an early mistranscription of "Olympus." Patterson, *Methodius of Olympus,* 18 n. 5, is persuaded by this; Musurillo, *St. Methodius,* 171 (f), is not.

25. John of Damascus *Orat.* 3.138; *Cont. Iac.* 93.1; *Sac. par.* 96.485; Phot. *Epit.* 9.8, together with the MSS of the *Symposium* mentioned in note 14. See also Barnes, "Methodius, Maximus & Valentinus," 54 incl. n. 4, who thinks this was the site of Methodius's martyrdom (see note 22 above); and Patterson, *Methodius of Olympus,* 17. Might Methodius and Porphyry have crossed paths here? The city was home to an oracle of Apollo that had been refurbished in the late second century by Opramoas of Rhodiapolis (*TAM* ii 905 = *IGR* iii 739; cf. René Lebrun, "Quelques aspects de la divination en Anatolie du Sud-Ouest," *Kernos* 3 [1990]: 185–95; and J. J. Coulton, "Oproamoas and the Anonymous Benefactor," *JHS* 107 [1987]: 171–78).

26. Nicephorus *Antirrhetica; Adv. icon.* 19.1; *Ref. et ev.* 815 57.1; *Eus.* 66.212. According to Musurillo, *St. Methodius* 171 n. 11 (d) (and Diekamp), locating Methodius in Myra might have been due to a misunderstanding of the Greek genitive *marturos* after Methodius's name. Nicephorus's failure to identify Methodius as a martyr gives more weight to this idea. Patterson, *Methodius of Olympus,* 17. The anonymous catena that quotes his commentary on Job gives his see as Side in Pamphylia (Musurillo, 171 n. 11 [b]).

27. Musurillo, *St. Methodius,* 173 n. 11 (f).

28. Bonwetsch, *Methodius,* is the standard edition, "although his Greek text leaves much to be desired from the viewpoint of modern textual criticism, and the Palaeoslavic (or Old Church Slavonic) fragments …are merely presented in German translation." Musurillo, *St. Methodius,* 5. And, as Artemio Vitores, *Identidad entre el cuerpo muerto y resucitado en Orígenes según de 'De Resurrectione' de Metodio de Olimpo* (Jerusalem: Franciscan Printing Press, 1981), 9, observes, the German translations from the Old Slavonic are difficult to read, since Bonwetsch translated them into German "in such a literal way that it is sometimes impossible to understand what the author wanted to say."

29. Bonwetsch, *Methodius,* 3–141, produces a text from six Greek MSS from the eleventh to sixteenth century, supplemented with passages from Photius's *Bibliotheca* and the *Sacra parallela.* See Musurillo, *St. Methodius,* 6–10. For a discussion of the authenticity of these texts, see Buchheit, *Studien zu Methodius.* Jerome mentions these works together with the *Symposium, Autexousio,* and *De resurrectione* in *De viris illustribus* 83. A number of spurious works are also attributed to Methodius; see Musurillo, 10.

in an Old Slavonic translation (*Peri tou autexousiou*),[30] and still others survive in part, in Greek (*Ek tou Xenōnos ē peri tōn genētōn*),[31] in Old Slavonic (*De vita*,[32] *De cibis et de vaca rufa*,[33] *De sanguisuga*[34]), or in both (*Aglaophōn ē peri anastaseōs*,[35] *De lepra*[36]). There are also some fragments of a commentary on a book of Job and a work on the martyrs, and Jerome (*Vir. ill.* 83) refers to several other texts, now lost (*Against Porphyry*,[37] *Commentary on Genesis, Commentary on the Song of Songs, Adversus Origenem De pythonissa*).[38] According to Jerome, *Aglaophon* and *De pythonissa* were written against Origen. In this category he also places *Peri tou autexousiou*, but neither Eusebius, Basil of Caesarea, nor Gregory saw the latter text in this light.[39] Although most of his works are impossible to date,[40] Methodius's remarks in *De cibis* (1.1–2), together with the tone of the *Symposium*, and a comment in *De sanguisuga* (10.1–4),[41] establish the following chronology:[42] (1) the *Symposium* and *De sanguisuga* were completed before any hint of persecution; (2) the *Symposium* circulated and was criticized; (3) Meth-

---

30. The text of Bonwetsch, *Methodius*, 145–206, derives from two copies of the old Slavonic translation, discovered in the nineteenth century, supplemented with passages from a tenth-century MS in Greek, together with passages from the *Dialogue of Adamantius*, Eusebius's *Praeparatio evangelica* 7.22, the *Sacra parallela*, and Photius's *Bibliotheca* 236. See the discussion above and Vaillant, "Le *De autexousio*," for the text.

31. From MSS of Photius's *Bibliotheca* 235; Bonwetsch, *Methodius*, 493–500. According to Socrates *HE* 6.13, Methodius used this text to deflect early criticisms of Origen, but Patterson, *"De libero arbitrio,"* 160–61 n. 4, thinks that Socrates is misled about the text's stance toward Origen by "appreciative remarks made in the course of the dialogue." Buchheit, *Studien zu Methodius*, 129–33, is not certain about its authenticity. See also Musurillo, *St. Methodius*, 9.

32. Two MSS of the Old Slavonic translation; Bonwetsch, *Methodius*, 209–16.

33. Two MSS of the Old Slavonic translation; Bonwetsch, *Methodius*, 427–47.

34. A short treatise interpreting the leech in Prov. 30.15 and a verse of Psalm 18. It survives in two copies of the Old Slavonic translation, Bonwetsch, *Methodius*, 477–89.

35. The text of Bonwetsch, *Methodius*, 219–424, derives from two MSS of the old Slavonic translation, together with supplements in Greek from Epiphanius's *Panarion* 64, the *Sacra parallela*, the Syrian florilegia, Photius's *Bibliotheca* 234, and the *Dialogue of Adamantius*.

36. This is a short dialogue on the meaning of the laws on leprosy in Lev. 13. It is preserved in two MSS of the Old Slavonic translation and one eleventh- to twelfth-century Greek MS; Bonwetsch, *Methodius*, 451–74.

37. The fragments preserved in Bonwetsch are spurious. Cf. Buchheit, *Studien zu Methodius*.

38. Musurillo, *St. Methodius*, 10.

39. Patterson, *"De libero arbitrio,"* 162–65, thinks it confronted Marcionites or Valentinians. The very idea that unsettled *theologoumena* can be debated, however, owes much to Origen.

40. Most scholars assume, however, that later works are increasingly hostile toward Origen (as per Eusebius ap. Hieron. *C. Ruf.* 1.11; see note 8 above) and more reflective of persecution. Accordingly, *De autexousio* is usually listed among the earlier works; *De lepra* and *De creatis* among the later ones. See Vaillant, "Le *De autexousio*," 647–48, 652; Patterson, *"De libero arbitrio,"* 160–61 incl. n. 4, 162; Musurillo, *St. Methodius*, 8–9, 11–12, 173 n. 18; Vitores, *Identidad*, 7; Patterson, *Methodius of Olympus*, 31.

41. Since Methodius says that he has not taken up the significance of Wisdom 7:1–2, it precedes the *Aglaophon*. Patterson, *Methodius of Olympus*, 26–27.

42. Musurillo, *St. Methodius*, 9, 11–12; Patterson, *"De libero arbitrio,"* 160–61; Patterson, *Methodius of Olympus*, 31.

odius began the *Aglaophon* in order to address these criticisms; (4) Methodius wrote *De cibis;* (5) he finished the *Aglaophon,* his sharpest attack on Origen.[43] If the *Aglaophon* was the work that Eusebius cast as Methodius's repudiation of Origen, it should be dated before 306.[44] The sorry state of many of Methodius's texts are one reason that he is sorely understudied.[45]

Writing at the cusp of the Great Persecution, a scholar and theologian who faced trenchant criticisms of his ideas, Methodius not only opens a window onto the tensions brewing between Hellenes and Christians. But his works also show that Hellene criticisms of Origenist theology provoked controversy within the Christian community itself, requiring the Alexandrian theologian's followers to defend themselves on several fronts. The rest of this chapter will explore these developments through a close analysis of Methodius's work. It will start by looking at the *Aglaophon.* Even though Methodius wrote this work late in his career, looking at the work first establishes Porphyry as one person who had attacked Methodius's *Symposium.* It also demonstrates that Porphyry's criticisms were especially corrosive because he had used Origen's opposition to the resurrection of the flesh to argue against the popular Christian theology of bodily resurrection. The chapter turns to *De cibis,* a work written at the same time as the *Aglaophon.* Evidence in this text shows Methodius's awareness of Porphyry's complaint, preserved in Eusebius, that Origenists subject their scripture to inappropriate figural exegesis. Finally, the chapter turns to the *Symposium,* the work by Methodius whose figural exegesis was a target of Porphyry's anger. Evidence in the *Symposium* shows why Porphyry condemned Methodius and Origenists like him: not only does the work deploy a thoroughgoing figural exegesis of Hebrew scripture, but it also shows Methodius as a teacher whose circle closely resembled other Ammonian communities we have seen. Thus Porphyry not only objected to Methodius's theology on logical grounds, but

---

43. Musurillo, *St. Methodius,* 9.

44. Vaillant, "Le *De autexousio,*" 652; Emanuela Prinzivalli, "Aspetti esegetico-dottrinale del dibattito nel IV secolo sulle tesi origeniane in materia escatologica," *AnnSE* 12, no. 2 (1995): 303.

45. V. Buchheit, "Das Symposion des Methodios arianisch interpoliert?" in *Überlieferungsgeschichtliche Untersuchungen,* ed. F. Paschke (Berlin: Akademie Verlag, 1981), 114, argues that Methodius needs "greater consideration" as "a middle link between the great Alexandrians and the Cappadocians," for his "surprisingly direct familiarity with Plato (in which one also must think of Middle and Neoplatonist influences)," and for the strong influence of Clement of Alexandria on his work. The claim in Musurillo, *St. Methodius,* 21, that Methodius's work reflected the "cobwebbed, cluttered mind of the pedant, never profound enough to be satisfying, full of good intentions but deeply illogical and emotional," cannot but have impeded serious scholarship. A more productive tack would have been to ask why such a work was written and why people valued it enough to preserve it—the questions that motivate this chapter.

he also considered him to be a competitor who had corrupted his heritage. Worse still, for Porphyry a Christian like Methodius promoted a mistaken physics and a treacherous politics, attributes that explain the momentum that will begin building in support of persecution.

Written late in Methodius's career, the *Aglaophon* is a complicated and puzzling treatise. For a long time it was viewed as an attack on Origen (Hieron. *Vir. ill.* 83), but the first seventeen chapters do not refer to the elder theologian at all.[46] Moreover, the ideas against the resurrection of the flesh in these initial chapters largely contradict Origen's thinking.[47] Since Origen is not mentioned, and most of the ideas articulated are not his, it is appropriate to ask whose arguments Methodius is so keen to refute.[48] Since Methodius is known to have written a long and serious work against Porphyry (assumed to be lost), it is reasonable to explore whether the views in the beginning of *Aglaophon* agree with those of the Neoplatonist philosopher.[49] And indeed, they do.

---

46. Benjamins, "Methodius von Olympus," 93.

47. H. Crouzel, "Les critiques adressées par Méthode et ses contemporains à la doctrine origénienne du corps ressuscité," *Gregorianum* 53 (1972): 682 n. 14; id., "La doctrine origénienne du corps ressuscité," *BLE* 81 (1980): 175–76 incl. n. 3. As examples of scholars who have wrongly conflated Origen's views with those of Aglaophon and Proclus, see Antonio Orbe, "S. Metodio y la exegesis de Rom. 7,9:'Ego autem vivebam sine lege aliquando'," *Gregorianum* 50 (1969): 93–139; and J. Daniélou, *L'être et le temps chez Grégoire de Nysse* (Leiden: Brill, 1970); Vitores, *Identidad,* 11, 18; L. G. Patterson, "Methodius, Origen, and the Arian Dispute," *Studia Patristica* 17.2 (1982): 915; Calogero Riggi, "La forma del corpo risorto secondo Metodio in Epifanio (Haer. 64)," in *Morte e immortalità nella catechesi dei padri del III-IV secolo,* ed. Sergio Felici (Rome: LAS, 1985), 75–78; Jon F. Dechow, "Origen and Corporeality: The Case of Methodius' *On the Resurrection*," in *Origeniana quinta,* ed. Robert J. Daly (Leuven: Peeters, 1992), 510.

48. Benjamins, "Methodius von Olympus," 94. L. G. Patterson, "Who Are the Opponents in Methodius' *De Resurrectione?*" *Studia Patristica* 19 (1989): 221–22, thinks that Methodius may have had opponents besides Origen in mind, although he does not think they were real people.

49. Surprisingly, given Methodius's known opposition to Porphyry, Benjamins, "Methodius von Olympus," 91, is among the few who have looked for Neoplatonist arguments in Methodius's dialogues. Vaillant, "Le *De autexousio,*" 640–41, had argued that *De autexousio* attacks the Neoplatonist doctrine regarding the origin of evil, but Plotinus does not—as Methodius's opponent does—argue that matter is coexistent with God, who sets it in order. Vaillant's misunderstanding led Musurillo, *St. Methodius,* 21, to infer—wrongly—that Methodius shared the Plotinian view of matter and the material world. And Musurillo, 7, 173 n. 16, 15, 17–18, despite acknowledging Methodius's deep debt to Plato and Aristotle, neither recognizes this inheritance as the hallmark of the Ammonian tradition nor knows quite what to do with the many parallels he notes (but does not identify) between the *Symposium* and Neoplatonist literature, including the *Corpus Hermeticum*, Plotinus, Proclus, and ps.-Dionysius. It is not a "paradox" that Methodius, "one of the first to write against the Neoplatonist Porphyry and the allegorist Origen, should make extensive use of both Platonism and allegory." As this chapter argues, Methodius does so because he is deeply situated within these traditions, which in turn are themselves tightly imbricated. For Methodius's clear familiarity with Plato, see Musurillo, 174 n. 24; and Vitores, *Identidad,* 7.

Aglaophon: On the Resurrection starts out as a dialogue among four men—
Aglaophon, Proclus of Miletus, Eubulius, and Memian (who says very
little)—but it then transforms into an extended critique of Origen's doctrine
of resurrection. At the beginning, the character Aglaophon, a doctor, asks his
companions to consider "this flesh, whether it revives, receiving immortality
with the soul."[50] He argues that the body is the tomb of the soul and serves
its desires (*Res.* 1.4–22). It must disappear after death, he argues, because it
cannot exist in the realm of light.[51] "The body is only a chain and punishment for the soul, which in itself, separated" from the body, "cannot sin."
The body seals off the soul, Aglaophon claims, confusing it and preventing
it from seeing Being clearly. So it is absurd to think that the body would
rise from the dead. According to Aglaophon, God created human beings at
first without bodies, for the "clothes or tunics of skin" from Genesis 3:21
are the bodies that God first made for human beings (i.e., Adam and Eve)
after they disobeyed God by eating from the tree of knowledge.[52] In support
of these views, Aglaophon appeals to a number of biblical texts.[53] In response,
Eubulius says that he and Memian must "prevent their opponents from being
wrecked on the rocks by the song of the Sirens" (1.28.1).[54] These latter two
speakers represent Methodius's views. He responds to Aglaophon's remarks
by asserting that the body cannot be at the same time the cause of sin and a
punishment for sins committed in a disembodied state (1.29–2.18).[55]

---

50. Vitores, *Identidad,* 15.

51. Crouzel, "Les critiques," 682.

52. Methodius's adversary argues that before God's commandment regarding the tree of life,
human beings were pure incorporeal souls, so not subject to any laws regarding carnal functions. In
support of this exegesis, Aglaophon cites Paul's statement in Rom. 7:9 that "once he lived without
the law" (Orbe, "S. Metodio," 138–39). Although, like Aglaophon, Origen also interpreted Paul
as speaking for humanity here, Origen took Paul to be referring to the interval between birth and
the mind's awakening when one is ignorant of natural law (Or. *Comm. in Rom.* 3.6; 6.8; *Philoc.* 9;
Orbe, 94–95, 138). Methodius, in response, claims that Paul was referring to positive law (Orbe,
139). Although Orbe, 93–139 (esp. 114–15), thinks that Aglaophon articulates Methodius's mistaken
understanding of Origen's position, I think that the discrepancies between Origen's views and those
of Aglaophon more likely mean that the latter's views should be attributed to Methodius's Hellene
opponents.

53. E.g., Lam. 3:34f (souls enchained in bodies as punishment for sin); Rom. 7:9–14; Ps. 66:10–
12; and Matt. 22:30. Benjamins, "Methodius von Olympus, 94; *Res.* 1.4–5; Vitores, *Identidad,* 16;
Patterson, "Who Are the Opponents?" 222.

54. Patterson, *Methodius of Olympus,* 156. Plato and the Pythagoreans thought that the Sirens
produced the music of the spheres, and Iamblichus links them to theurgic practice (Iambl. *VPyth.*
82; Pl. *Rep.* 617b). See Sarah Iles Johnston, *Hekate Soteira: A Study of Hekate's Roles in the Chaldean
Oracles and Related Literature* (Atlanta: Scholars Press, 1990), 101–2, 109.

55. Vitores, *Identidad,* 11, 16; Patterson, "Who Are the Opponents?" 223; Patterson, *Methodius
of Olympus,* 158–60.

Aglaophon's arguments have nothing to do with Origen:[56] Origen did not claim that the soul cannot sin on its own,[57] he did not believe that the body was a cause of sin,[58] nor had he ever interpreted Genesis 3:21 in this way.[59] Instead, these arguments draw on a Hellene foundation.[60] In particular, Aglaophon's argument agrees with third-century Platonist views on the soul. For example, Plotinus asserted that the "soul is not in itself evil" (*Enn.* 1.8.4), which suggests that the soul encounters evil when it meets up with matter, through contact with a body, for example.[61] But even more compelling is Aglaophon's claim that the "tunics of skin" in Genesis 3:21 are the bodies that God first made for human beings after they ate from the tree of knowledge. In addition to Philo and a few Gnostics, Porphyry was among the few who used the biblical expression "tunics of skin" to refer to the human body as the covering for the human soul: he does so twice in his treatise *On Abstinence* (1.31.3; 2.46.1).[62] In addition, Aglaophon's use of scripture is compatible with Porphyry's practice. As the extant fragments of his anti-Christian writings make clear, these were techniques—and texts—in which Porphyry was well versed. A comparison between third-century Platonist psychology and that of Aglaophon also shows that Methodius has helped his cause by eliding important nuances in the Hellene's position.[63]

The character Proclus takes up the argument next (*Res.* 1.13) in order to assist Aglaophon.[64] Since the body dissolves into the four elements at death (1.14.4), he argues, how can we think that the same parts of the same flesh reassemble at the resurrection? When the heat of the body, for example, joins with fire in death, how does it come back to one particular body at the resur-

---

56. Benjamins, "Methodius von Olympus," 94–95 incl. n. 26; see also Prinzivalli, "Aspetti esegetico-dottrinale," 308; and Patterson, *Methodius of Olympus,* 143–44, 147, 152 incl. n. 15, 161, 184–85.

57. Cf. *PA* 2.9.2.

58. Cf. *PA* 3.1.4 and 3.2.3.

59. Crouzel, "Les critiques," 708–9; Benjamins, "Methodius von Olympus," 94–95 incl. n. 26.

60. Prinzivalli, "Aspetti esegetico-dottrinale," 303–4, 306. Patterson, *Methodius of Olympus,* 143, 184, thinks that these alternative viewpoints are Gnostic.

61. Benjamins, "Methodius von Olympus," 95; and P. Courcelle, "Le colle et le clou de l'âme dans la tradition néo-platonicienne et chrétienne (*Phédon* 82e; 83d)," *RBPh* 36 (1958): 72–95.

62. P. F. Beatrice, "Le tuniche di pelle: Antiche letture di Gen. 3:21," in *La tradizione dell'Enkrateia: Motivazioni ontologiche e protologiche,* ed. U. Bianchi (Rome: Edizioni dell'Ateneo, 1985), 468, 471–77. See also Porphyry of Tyre, *On Abstinence from Killing Animals,* trans. Gillian Clark (London: Duckworth, 2000), n. 332. Methodius's use of Porphyry suggests that he is familiar with this treatise (see below in this chapter).

63. For example, here Methodius has ignored the role that the quasi-material "vehicle of the soul" played in Origen's psychology and in explaining the soul's gradual fall. Benjamins, "Methodius von Olympus," 95; Patterson, *Methodius of Olympus,* 153; Beatrice, "Le tuniche di pelle," 453.

64. Vitores, *Identidad,* 11; Patterson, *Methodius of Olympus,* 151, 154.

rection (1.15.3–4; 1.16.1)? Moreover, once the body's elements dissolve they mix around into other things, including into other creatures (1.16.2). If any body is revived, it must be a spiritual body (1.17.2). In responding to Proclus, the character Memian denies that the fluidity of the body impedes the resurrection of the flesh. God is capable, he says, of separating out the elements in order to form the same body anew (2.26–30). Memian then disappears from the text, which becomes increasingly focused on Origen.

There is compelling evidence that Porphyry raised Proclus's arguments in his anti-Christian writings.[65] For example, the *Monogenēs* by Macarius Magnes presents a debate between an anonymous Hellene philosopher and the Christian author. Although the Hellene's identity is hotly contested,[66] no one denies that his arguments draw substantially on Porphyry's anti-Christian writings.[67] In particular, the assertion that all things are not possible for God, conveyed in the following passage, is directly associated with Porphyry by Didymus the Blind (*Comm. in Iob* 10.13).[68] "It is ridiculous," the Hellene in the *Monogenēs* asserts,

if, when the whole is destroyed, the resurrection should follow. . . . For many have often perished in the sea, and their bodies have been consumed by fishes, while many have been eaten by wild beasts and birds. How then is it possible for their bodies to rise up? . . . A man was shipwrecked, the mullets devoured his body, next these were caught and eaten by some fishermen, who were killed and devoured by dogs. When the dogs died, ravens and vultures feasted on them and entirely consumed them. How then will the body of the shipwrecked man be brought together, seeing that it was absorbed by so many creatures? Again, suppose another body to have been consumed by fire, and another to have come in the end to the worms, how is it possible for

---

65. Benjamins links Proclus's claims here to Porphyry through a rather circuitous argument, tying them to Neoplatonist views on the vehicle of the soul. Benjamins, "Methodius von Olympus," 96–97. To argue this, Benjamins turns to Proclus's arguments concerning the vehicle of the soul that have their source in Porphyry. But the evidence from Macarius Magnes's *Monogenēs* is much more compelling. Patterson, *Methodius of Olympus,* 144, also recognizes that this argument does not have its source in Origen.

66. Is it the Hierocles whom Lactantius describes in *Inst.* 5.2, and against whom Eusebius wrote? Elizabeth DePalma Digeser, "Porphyry, Julian, or Hierokles? The Anonymous Hellene in Makarios Magnēs' *Apocriticus*," *JThS* 53 (2002): 466–502. Or has the author merely abridged a text by Porphyry? Richard Goulet, *Macarios de Magnésie: Le Monogénès; Edition critique et traduction française* (Paris: Vrin, 2003), introduction.

67. Digeser, "Porphyry, Julian, or Hierokles?" 478–79; Goulet, *Macarios de Magnésie,* introduction; and Guillaume Dye, review of *Macarios de Magnésie,* by Richard Goulet, *BMCR* 2004.07.53 (2004).

68. Didymus in D. R. Hagedorn and R. Merkelbach, "Ein neues Fragment aus Porphyrios' *Gegen die Christen,*" *VChr* 20 (1966): 86–90.

it to return to the essence which was there from the beginning? . . . All things are not possible with [God].[69]

The close parallel between this text, which has its source in Porphyry, and Proclus's arguments indicates that Methodius's opponent is the famous Neoplatonist critic.

In *De cibis* (1.1–2), Methodius disclosed that his *Symposium* had been attacked and that he would address his critics in a work already in progress on the resurrection, that is, in the *Aglaophon*.[70] The arguments of both Aglaophon and Proclus in the later work correspond to points that Porphyry had raised against the resurrection of the flesh, and these characters in the dialogue are clearly presented as Methodius's opponents.[71] Thus it is reasonable to conclude that Methodius saw Porphyry as an important critic of his earlier work, the *Symposium,* and wrote against him in the *Aglaophon*. Indeed it is likely that the *Aglaophon* is the work of several volumes (10,000 lines) that Jerome says Methodius wrote against Porphyry.[72]

Aglaophon raises another argument against the resurrection of the flesh. Although close parallels in the work of Plotinus and Porphyry are lacking, its connection to Origen is evident.[73] The body, according to Aglaophon, is in a state of permanent flux. The substance of the body constantly renews itself with nourishment. Muscles, bones, and blood vessels become hair, nails, and other appurtenances—which we then lose, but which are also renewed by food.[74] What persists is only a certain form of the body. Therefore, which body would revive—old or new?[75] This argument had most recently been set out by Origen in his commentary on the First Psalm, which Proclus—

---

69. Macarius Magnes *Apocriticus* 4.24 (trans. Crafer); Porph. *Chr.* frag. 94 Harnack.

70. Barnes, "Methodius, Maximus & Valentinus," 51 incl. n. 6; Patterson, *Methodius of Olympus,* 27–28, 124; Musurillo, *St. Methodius,* 9; Patterson, "*De libero arbitrio,*" 160–61.

71. Patterson, *Methodius of Olympus,* 150.

72. Hieron. *Vir. ill.* 83; *Ep.* 70.3. As I suggest in the introduction and conclusion to this book, we should expect that works against Porphyry would not have circulated under titles referring to him after Constantine's 325 edict banned his texts. A work of 10,000 lines (*Ep.* 70.3) is a significant project, one roughly equal in length to the original text of the *Aglaophon*. For example, the Moscow MS that conveys the Old Slavonic translation has 22 lines per page and 215 folios. If the MS of Methodius's "Against Porphyry" to which Jerome refers appeared in a similar format, it would take up 454 manuscript pages (10,000/22), or 113 pages per chapter (there were originally four). Three volumes of this work would be roughly 340 pages. Since the Moscow text of the *Aglaophon* is somewhat abbreviated and has combined books 3 and 4 into one, its approximately 328-page *Aglaophon* (calculated by counting pages in the edition and adjusting proportionally) is roughly the same length as the 10,000-line "Against Porphyry" would be if treated similarly.

73. Contra Benjamins, "Methodius von Olympus," 95–96.

74. *Res.* 1.9.2, 14–15; 1.10–11.

75. Crouzel, "Les critiques," 682.

taking up the argument after Aglaophon—cites at length.[76] In doing this, Proclus invokes Origen's authority by name to discourage the hope of those who imagine that the resurrection of the body is like repairing a broken clay pot (Res. 1.18–19). Through Proclus, Methodius then sets out Origen's view on bodily resurrection, as opposed to the resurrection of the flesh (Res. 1.18–26).[77] That this was a key aspect of the debate is clear from Pamphilus's claim that some people had, in fact, accused Origen of affirming the resurrection of the body, not the flesh (ap. Phot. Bibl. 117). Origen's doctrine takes its initiative from Paul's First Letter to the Corinthians (15:35–38) in claiming that the terrestrial body is the seed whence derives the glorious pneumatic body.[78] A spermatic *logos* or seminal reason is present within the terrestrial body, and this develops in order to confer glory. Hence the resurrected body, Origen asserts, is incorruptible and ethereal, like the bodies of angels. All the same, there is a unity between the terrestrial body and the glorious body: they are of the same *ousia,* in that the glorious body can receive all the qualities of the terrestrial body. Alternatively, Origen says, the identity between terrestrial and glorious body is assured by a corporeal form (*eidos*) that ensures that the "body" is preserved, despite its changing materials.[79] Methodius attempts to refute Origen's doctrine throughout book 3, as if Origen himself were involved in the dialogue.[80] He does so by claiming that Origen's *eidos* is simply an external image,[81] a move that renders Origen's doctrine

---

76. Benjamins, "Methodius von Olympus," 95. We are indebted to Methodius for preserving the most significant fragment of Origen's lost dialogue on the resurrection. M. Mees, "Paulus, Origenes und Methodius über die Auferstehung der Toten," *Augustinianum* 26 (1986): 110; Patterson, *Methodius of Olympus,* 151.

77. Crouzel, "Les critiques," 683, 715; id., "La doctrine origénienne," 243 n. 8. See also Vitores, *Identidad,* 15.

78. Origen's aim was to oppose "the simple," millenarians who read *Rev.* 20:5 literally and imagine that the resurrected body is the same as the terrestrial body. Crouzel, "Les critiques," 715; id., "La doctrine origénienne," 178.

79. Origen, Crouzel observes, is battling on two fronts: he wants to accept the resurrection of the human body despite the repugnance of Hellenes and heretics. Yet he is aware that the material elements of the body are constantly renewed. Crouzel, "Les critiques," 680. Crouzel, "La doctrine origénienne," 177 n. 6, also argues that Proclus has tweaked Origen's argument a bit here. For more information on Origen's doctrine of the resurrected body, see Crouzel, "La doctrine origénienne," 175–200, 241–66; Riggi, "La forma del corpo," 79–81.

80. Vitores, *Identidad,* 10.

81. Since Epiphanius's citation of the same passage from Origen on Psalm 1 is more complete, it is possible to see the extent to which Methodius misrepresents Origen's concept of the corporeal *eidos.* "Eubulios" simply does not grapple with the philosophical sense of the term. Crouzel, "La doctrine origénienne," 177 n. 6, 257; see also Patterson, "Who Are the Opponents?" 224. Patterson, *Methodius of Olympus,* 152, thinks—probably correctly—that Methodius's delay in addressing Origen's use of *eidos* "suggests that the direct reference to the views of Origen was only added in a later revision of the work."

absurd—which Methodius easily shows.[82] M. Mees marvels that someone of Methodius's obvious education has not understood Origen's meaning here.[83] But Methodius may have been more interested in defending himself than in representing Origen's views with scrupulous accuracy.

According to Hendrick Benjamins, in the first part of the *Aglaophon*, Methodius presents Porphyry's arguments against the resurrection of the flesh formulated in his anti-Christian writings.[84] This much is correct. Benjamins then argues that because Origen had raised the same objections against the resurrection of the flesh, the refutation of Porphyry's objections necessarily "brings with it the refutation of the Origenist view."[85] This second claim does not go far enough, since it fails to explain why Methodius directed the remaining two and a half books of the *Aglaophon* against problems in Origen's teaching.[86] Methodius, in fact, presents the most extensive extant critique of Origen's doctrine on the resurrection.[87] Origen's doctrines on this topic had become very controversial at the cusp of the fourth century, and Benjamins' solution does not explain why a follower like Methodius came to challenge what he had once accepted.[88] A more reasonable interpretation of this evidence considers the structure of the arguments in Methodius's text as well as the close relationship between Origenist and Plotinian circles: Origen clearly articulated his opposition to the resurrection of the flesh in his commentary on the First Psalm, written while he was in Alexandria and perhaps known to the Ammonian community. Porphyry, I argue, used Origen's theology as ammunition in his own argument against the resurrection of the flesh. Indeed, in Methodius's treatise on the resurrection, Proclus, Porphyry's stand-in, refers to Origen by name as a "well-informed man of the church" (*Res.* 1.19.1) whose "study of the scriptures has led him" to a position that,

---

82. Crouzel, "Les critiques," 715.

83. Mees concludes that Methodius's worldview "constructed an insurmountable barrier." M. Mees, "Paulus, Origenes und Methodius," 111–13. Similarly Patterson, *Methodius of Olympus,* 185, marvels at Methodius's pegging Origen as a dualist. But perhaps Methodius was making a political move more than anything else; if so, it would certainly explain Eusebius' seething anger and the numerous places where modern scholars have found that Methodius "misunderstands" Origen's theology (e.g., Patterson, "*De libero arbitrio,*" 165).

84. Benjamins, "Methodius von Olympus," 97.

85. Ibid.

86. Patterson, *Methodius of Olympus,* 143–45, is aware of this problem. In trying to understand why the *Aglaophon* starts out as a dialogue but then turns into a diatribe directly against Origen, he had wondered why Origen was such a "late-comer to that dialogue as it now stands."

87. Crouzel, "Les critiques," 681.

88. Pamph. *Apol.* 1.7–8 (*PG* 17.593c–601c); Crouzel, "Les critiques," 680. Conversely, Patterson's notion that Methodius gradually came to believe that Origen's teachings entailed a "belief in an evil material substance" does not explain his attention to Neoplatonist positions here and in *De cibis.* Patterson, "*De libero arbitrio,*" 165.

with Aglaophon, all three men share but "the many" reject. Origen accordingly appears as a frontier figure: his exegesis, Porphyry thought, crossed the line into impropriety, but he nevertheless maintained a set of sensible views accepted more by Hellenes than by his Christian successors. Porphyry thus set Origen's texts at variance with themselves, just as the philosopher's future opponents would do to him.

Porphyry's appropriation of the theologian helps to explain why Origen's name was involved in a variety of controversies that spread across the Roman Empire in the late third century.[89] That a Hellene would attack the Christian doctrine of resurrection would not have been surprising—for Celsus had done so a century earlier and had been answered by Origen himself (e.g., *Cels.* 2.5). But if Hellenes had claimed that Origen, the famous and respected Christian theologian, had held opinions that accorded more with their own "correct views" than with popular Christian doctrine, Origenist Christians would have been put in a difficult position. From the perspective of Christians outside their tradition, Origenists would have looked more like Hellenes than Christians.[90] In order to address such criticism from fellow Christians, we would expect Origen's followers either to argue that Origen's views were not as Porphyry claimed (which Eusebius and Pamphilus did),[91] or to distance themselves from Origen's views that Porphyry had accepted.

Methodius's theology in the *Symposium* would easily have exposed him to criticism from Christians and Hellenes. For example, the dialogue of Tusiane illustrates his quandary. Here Methodius applies a figural reading to Leviticus

---

89. According to Prinzivalli, "Aspetti esegetico-dottrinale," 309, both Pamphilus (*Apol.* 2.7 in *PG* 19.598–599) and Methodius seem to be reacting to the circulation of Origen's *Comm. in Psal.* This would certainly have been the case if Porphyry were using this text of Origen as support for his own views against the resurrection of the flesh. Prinzivalli, 281. Note also that the *De res.* attributed to Athenagoras is "probably a response to issues raised on embodiment roughly contemporary with Methodius." Indeed Athenagoras (4.3–4) is concerned with what happens to bodies being eaten by animals. Patterson, *Methodius of Olympus*, 146 n. 7, 158 n. 23. For the late date of ps.-Athenagoras, see Athenagoras, *Athenagoras: 'Legatio' and 'De resurrectione'*, trans. W. R. Schoedel, xxvf., xxviii. Ps.-Justin, too (*De res.* 2, 8), demonstrates that the agenda defined by Aglaophon and Proclus was a matter of contemporary interest, since he "describes as sophistical the notion that a resurrection of bodies is undesirable, and that the body is the cause of sins." Patterson, *Methodius of Olympus*, 151 n. 14. And, of course, there is Macarius Magnes. Patterson, argues that Methodius's criticism of Origen "sheds light on Arius's own critique. Patterson, *Methodius of Olympus*, 4–5; id., "Methodius, Origen, and the Arian Dispute," 912–23. Is it not more likely, however, that Porphyry's critique and co-option of Origen motivated both?

90. This view of Origen is perhaps reflected in Methodius's use of the term "centaur" to describe the Origenist position in the dialogue *De creatis*. See L. G. Patterson, "Methodius on Origen in *De creatis*," in *Origeniana quinta*, ed. Robert J. Daly (Leuven: Peeters, 1992), 497.

91. Crouzel, "Les critiques," 681. Pamphilus claims that Origen maintained the resurrection of the flesh for Christ and others, but Photius notes that Origen denied the resurrection of the flesh.

23:39–43, the procedures for observing the festival of Sukhot, also called the Festival of the Tabernacle or Tents. Methodius claims first that there will be a resurrection of the flesh at the Second Coming of Christ (*Symp.* 9.2). But after that seventh millennium, the true Sabbath, celebrated with Christ, the soul will "arrive in heaven, just as the Jews after the rest of the Tabernacles came to the Promised Land." Speaking for the soul, Tusiane claims that she "will not abide in the Tabernacles, that is, the tabernacle of my body will not remain the same, but after the Millennium it will be changed from its human appearance and corruption to angelic grandeur and beauty.... We shall pass from the wondrous place of the Tabernacle to the larger and better one, going up to the very house of God above the heavens" (9.5).[92] Methodius's text thus indicates that he began the *Aglaophon* simply to respond to Porphyry's critique of the doctrine of the resurrection of the flesh, which the former had embraced in the *Symposium*.[93] This much Methodius probably did before writing *De cibis*. But as time passed, Methodius seems also to have received criticism for his Origenism, including his vision of the soul's ultimate transcendence of the flesh (*Symp.* 9.5).[94] These attacks from Christians led Methodius to adapt the *Aglaophon* into a more sustained critique against Origen in order to clear his name from any association with him or the Hellenes and to assert his conformity to more popular doctrines.[95] In this case, it is significant that the *Aglaophon* directly asserts "the permanence and finality of the restored tabernacle of the body and eschews the millenarian interpretation of the Feast of the Tabernacles."[96]

While the *Aglaophon* establishes Porphyry as a critic of Methodius's doctrine on the resurrection, *De cibis* indicates that the Hellene had targeted the Christian's figural exegesis. Methodius's introductory remarks in *De cibis* (1.1; 4.2–5.6) complain that he and at least two others, Phrenope and Kilonia, have been completely preoccupied with rebutting challenges to his *Symposium*.[97] Clues in the text reveal that in this short treatise, Methodius addressed crit-

---

92. Clementina Mazzucco, "Il millenarismo di Metodio di Olimpo di fronte a Origene: Polemica o continuità?" *Augustinianum* 26 (1986): 75–79.

93. E.g., at 1.10.2–3, the *Aglaophon* deals with the "question of the literal meaning of all scriptural texts" (cf. also 3.1). Patterson, *Methodius of Olympus,* 184.

94. Patterson, *Methodius of Olympus,* 168, 184.

95. We need not think that the shift in structure is necessarily a product of haste. As Erika Hermanowicz suggested to me, Methodius might have shifted form when he shifted audience, directing a dialogue against his Platonist adversaries, and the more Aristotelian-style treatise toward fellow Christians.

96. Patterson, *Methodius of Olympus,* 168, 184.

97. See also Patterson, "Notes on *De cibis,*" 235 incl. nn. 5–6; id., *Methodius of Olympus,* 27–28.

ics of the *Symposium* who had contested its figural exegesis of the Torah.[98] It is logically possible that such critics might have been Judeo-Christians,[99] because they seem to want a more literal reading and practice of the Law in the Torah. But Methodius associates them with ideas and practices that are more clearly Hellene, specifically Porphyrian. Since Porphyry had condemned Origenists who read the Torah figurally, and since he had levied criticisms relevant to the *Symposium,* a text replete with this type of exegesis, *De cibis* illuminates more clearly the character of the Neoplatonist critique.

Methodius had several goals in addressing *De cibis* to Phrenope and Kilonia. Because both women had suffered from the attacks on the *Symposium,* in the first five chapters of *De cibis* Methodius encourages Phrenope and Kilonia to maintain the doctrines that they all share: good things require endurance, he says, and such trials are really God's way of discovering who is truly faithful; moreover, such suffering for the sake of justice is in itself a good.[100] It soon it becomes clear, however, that Methodius wants to bolster the women's resolve because the challenges to his teachings have undermined their conceptions of purity. Specifically, the women want to know whether coming into contact with "someone who has died in a house" has made them unclean (*Cib.* 6.1), given the strictures set out in Numbers 19.[101]

Methodius's answer comprises the rest of the treatise. He begins by paraphrasing Numbers 19. This passage is key to the concerns of Methodius's correspondents because it explains how to create the lustral water necessary to cleanse those who have come into contact with the dead.[102] According to the Law, lustral water is prepared from the ashes of the hide, flesh, blood, and offal of a pure, unblemished red calf, which are to be burnt along with cedar, hyssop, and scarlet wool. Methodius asserts that "our redeemer" deliberately made this text difficult to understand (*Cib.* 6.3).[103] He then uses passages from the New Testament (e.g., John 13:10) to argue that "whoever is once cleansed by rebirth," or baptism, "pollutes himself by not one of the things

---

98. Patterson, *Methodius of Olympus,* 28–30, 142. Since he does not at all consider the relationship between Methodius's work and Porphyry's criticisms, Patterson assumes that either these questions have arisen in the minds of Methodius' correspondents as a result of their reading the *Symposium* or they are questions that "Methodius assumes might be discussed in relation to it." See also Patterson, "*De libero arbitrio,*" 161 n. 1; id., "Notes on *De cibis,*" 235.

99. Here I am using the term as Daniel Boyarin, *Border Lines* (Philadelphia: University of Pennsylvania Press, 2004), does to indicate people who both upheld the Law in some form as well as accepted Jesus as in some way divine.

100. *Cib.* 1–5, especially 2.2, 4; 5.6–6.1.

101. Especially Num. 19:14–21.

102. Patterson, "Notes on *De cibis,*" 238.

103. Trans. from Bonwetsch's German translations of the Old Slavonic throughout are mine unless otherwise noted.

mentioned in the Law—neither by touching a dead person, or by anything else." One's true concern, he claims, should be not external, but internal purity, namely that of the soul (*Cib.* 6.4).[104] For those "already cleansed," neither the dead nor certain foods nor particular groups of people are impure (6.3–6). Even circumcision is no longer necessary so that "God's gentile converts" would not face "any difficulties."[105] In short, Methodius concludes: "The command of the Holy Spirit and of the apostle, that the pagans are not to be forced to uphold the law of Moses, applies to those who are too *carnally particular* about the law" (6.8).[106]

After arguing that the New Testament abrogates the purity laws of the Torah, Methodius addresses himself specifically to dietary law. "Someone seeks to know this, however, now: Why did God not allow <the Jews> to eat the animals that the rest of the people do, instead of ordering them to abstain from some of them by distinguishing between purity and impurity?" (*Cib.* 7.1). Since Phrenope and Kilonia are named in the text, this "someone" may be a third person of concern whose anonymity points to a living opponent. In setting out to address this question, Methodius argues: "If however now, since we are also able to live from the fruits of the earth, we avoid eating meat and try not to live unjustly so that life may become pure and not participate in evil, we then behave in no way according to justice by slaughtering for our benefit those creatures who did no injustice to us" (7.2). Even if we may eat animals, he continues, "since God made them for our benefit," why do we eat those that serve us instead of those that annoy us? The implication of these remarks, set against the initial question, is that Jews have the moral high ground in that the Torah restricts them from eating a wide variety of animals. But, Methodius observes, it is acceptable under the Torah to eat beef and mutton, but not pork (7.3). For Methodius, this *aporia*, this difference between what the Mosaic law sets out and what justice requires, indicates that the law of the Torah should no longer be read literally, and that God has now given "release from the law" (6.4). God, Methodius claims, "commands nothing useless; rather, so that he may show the many the way to piety, he weeded out Egyptian foods and instead led" the Jews under Moses' leadership "to prudence." The Jews "needed such a law at the beginning," he says, "because of the vapor of idolatry, so that they now accept a lot of customs and are proven." People, Methodius observes, "who do not obey God 'in the

---

104. Methodius cites Peter here, but the passage actually comes from John 13:10.
105. *Cib.* 6.7–8, citing Acts 15:13, 19.
106. Emphasis added; see also *Cib.* 6.9. This is a dig at the Hellene side, since they have accused Christians of being too "carnal" in upholding the resurrection of the flesh.

small thing' [Luke 16:10] will not obey him in more important things either"
(7.5). Therefore, Methodius argues, God, "knowing that 'it is not what goes
into a man's mouth' that can 'make him impure' [Matt. 15:11]," gave the law
to Moses simply as a stage in human discipline and enlightenment (*Cib.* 7.6).
The Law "does not have the true image of things"; rather, it is the shadow
of the truth. "Now what the shadow is in relation to the image," Methodius
asserts, drawing on Hebrews 10:1, "the Law is in relation to the Gospel; what
the image is in relation to things themselves, the Gospel is with respect to
something in the future" (*Cib.* 7.7).

   After describing the rules in Leviticus 11 for determining pure and
impure animals (*Cib.* 8.1–4), Methodius notes that a literal reading of the
Torah's dietary laws produces yet another *aporia* in scripture. Although elephants are technically "unclean," Psalm 45:9–10 describes an "ivory palace" as home to the "daughters of the king" (8.4). "Now," Methodius asks,
"does Scripture contradict itself? Do the prophets disagree with the Law?"
(8.5). Rejecting both of these possibilities, Methodius argues that "it means
something else," for "the divinity does not take delight in the dead bones
of human art" (8.6). Therefore, Methodius concludes, the "ivory" in the
text really refers to our "spiritual bodies": bodies that, having become shining like ivory through good works, "will receive the realm of God" (8.7).
Taken together, both *aporiae* indicate that "from now on... the shadow is
brightened" and "the Law is fulfilled" (9.1). Literal purification—including
the steps once required for handling the dead—is no longer necessary, since
Christ is the heifer of Numbers 19 who has been sacrificed for our eternal
purification (*Cib.* 9.2).

   Methodius then devotes the rest of *De cibis* to an exegesis of Numbers 19
understood in this way. In his interpretation, the sacrifice of the calf foreshadows the death of Christ (*Cib.* 10.1–4). Its flesh, blood, and skin are the
"good works, knowledge, and faith given" to people "through Christ" so
that they may overcome sin.[107] Putting these all to the flame refers to the
"spiritual animation of the heart, by which, having been led as from a prison,
we view the light of God above us" (11.7). The cedar, hyssop, and scarlet
wool for Methodius signify the persons of the Trinity, since it is through
"the indestructibility and evergreenness of the Father, the revivifying power
of the Son, and the sealing of the Spirit that our souls come forth from our
bodies (12.2–3).[108] Since the ashes of the calf are to be used for persons who
are unclean, that is, sinners, Methodius reasons that the ashes really refer to

107. Trans. Patterson; Patterson, "Notes on *De cibis*," 238 incl. nn. 14–16.
108. Patterson, "Notes on *De cibis*," 238 incl. nn. 14–16.

the death of Christ, and their use in the lustral water really refers to baptism. For Christ "came in our flesh and died once to sin, in order to lead the flesh into eternal life" (12.6–8).[109] Methodius also links his exegesis with the resurrection of the flesh, since the purpose of Christ's work is not to "release the soul from the body" but to overcome "sin in the body through the illumination of the soul."[110] Accordingly, Methodius concludes that physical association with dead bodies does not make the soul impure, so touching them is not a concern.[111] In the end, he assures Phrenope and Kilonia that they need not worry about following the purification procedures in Numbers 19 after touching the dead (*Cib.* 13.5), for "true purifications are things of which the gods are afraid, and the sprinklings are things, completed by the body of Christ, through which not only bodies, but souls too are cleaned." "The blood of Christ," still paired here with the sacrificial red heifer, "will cleanse your conscience from the dead works to the service of the living God [Heb. 9:14]."

Like the *Aglaophon*, *De cibis* shows Methodius addressing both Hellene and Christian critics. According to Methodius, he wrote the work at a time when evil daemons were trying to push people off the path to God (*Cib.* 1.4). The tactics of these daemons allowed people to mistake daemonic rulings and verdicts as the way to salvation. These daemonic decrees are probably those of the Hellenes and their oracles because of their evil character. Moreover, Methodius says that the daemons, wanting people to be ignorant of the "*logoi* of nature and theology,"[112] stir the souls of those studying scripture into irrational emotions. In short, the Hellenes' critiques have generated an emotional and illogical Christian response—just what we surmised in reading the *Aglaophon*.

Methodius's primary focus in *De cibis*, however, is to answer people demanding that Methodius's group "uphold the Law" (*Cib.* 10.6). This issue motivated the women's inquiry regarding Numbers 19 and consequently the entire treatise. "How do they order us to uphold the Law?" Methodius asks indignantly. "How does the Law itself and the Holy Spirit instruct us? How do they themselves think that the Law is to be upheld?" (10.6). But, he complains, if he and his followers should model themselves after their critics,

---

109. Ibid., 239 incl. n. 18.

110. Ibid.

111. Ibid., 240–41.

112. I have taken a bit of a liberty here with Bonewetsch's translation. His German reads: "Damit wir ohne Erkenntnis seien des natürlichen und theologischen Wortes," which is a bit puzzling: what are words of nature and theology? If, however, the original Greek used the word *logoi*, then the German (and perhaps Old Slavonic) translation could be rendered into something more coherent.

then they too would be breaking the Law; for his critics (who touch corpses and bones), Methodius avers, live according to neither the letter nor the spirit of the Law (10.6–7). Although these critics could be hypocritical Judeo-Christians, who want Methodius's group to observe the purity legislation in Numbers 19 but do not hold themselves to the same standard, Methodius's treatment of the issue indicates that these challengers are Porphyrian Hellenes.

The identity of Methodius's opponents is evident in the way that he uses Porphyry's *On Abstinence from Killing Animals* in arguing that the Torah's purity laws are no longer binding. In the discussion of dietary law above,[113] Methodius betrays a familiarity with Porphyry's text when he equates vegetarianism with justice. Remember that he saw an *aporia* in Leviticus 11, namely that the Torah's food laws defining pure and impure animals are not truly just: the life of justice that leads toward purity, he argues, should deter us from eating meat because we should not slaughter creatures who have benefited us in some way. In this analysis, however, the standard to which the passage in Leviticus is compared is not Christian, but Porphyrian. Porphyry's *On Abstinence* argues that abstinence from meat leads to a pure life, uninvolved in evil, and it claims that killing domestic animals is unjust. Against the Stoic position that justice extended only to rational beings and so not to animals (*Abst.* 1.4.1–4; 3.1.4),[114] Porphyry argued for the limited rationality of animals by drawing on Aristotle (e.g., *Abst.* 3.6.5–3.7.1)[115] and Plutarch (3.18.3–3.24.6).[116] With Plutarch, Porphyry argued that it was unjust to kill tame animals (*Abst.* 3.18, 26).[117] "We are unjust" in two respects, Porphyry claims, "because we kill" animals, "though they are tame" (i.e., they have become our servants [3.13.2]), "and because we feast on them, and their death is solely with reference to food" (which we do not need [3.26.12]).[118] Only Porphyry, not Plutarch, however, linked abstinence from killing harmless animals with the purity of life that brings one closer to God.[119] Clearly, Methodius is familiar with Porphyry's text and has appropriated his standard.

---

113. See below in this chapter.

114. See also Clark in Porphyry of Tyre, *On Abstinence from Killing Animals,* 124 n. 17 and 162 n. 379.

115. E.g., Arist. *HA* 608a17 and 536b171–79. Cf. Clark, *On Abstinence from Killing Animals,* 167 n. 412.

116. From Plutarch's lost work on animals. See Clark, in Porphyry of Tyre, *On Abstinence from Killing Animals,* 172 n. 459.

117. See also *Abst.* 3.1.4; and Clark, in Porphyry of Tyre, *On Abstinence,* 10, 12, 13.

118. *Abst.* 3.26.4.

119. John Passmore, "The Treatment of Animals," *Journal of the History of Ideas* 36, no. 2 (1975): 206–7. See also G. Clark, "Animal Passions (Pathos, passio, Porphyry)," *G&R* 47 (2000): 88–93;

Porphyry's *On Abstinence* also praised the Jews for abstaining from a wide variety of animals (4.11–14). Remember that Methodius originally voiced the question about why Jews abstain from certain foods in a context where the questioner ("someone") applauded Jews for abstaining from some animal foods.[120] From the questioner's perspective, upholding Jewish dietary law would be seen as an improvement on a practice in which people ate animals indiscriminately (which Christians could well do, while avoiding the products of sacrificial rites). Methodius thus casts Porphyry as hypocritically calling on Christians to uphold the Torah while not following it himself.

Methodius, as we saw earlier,[121] also finds a contradiction in the Jewish dietary law that Porphyry has held up as such a standard, namely that it doesn't go far enough to promote purity, since Jews can—under the law—eat beef and mutton. (As in the *Aglaophon,* Methodius is not above eliding significant details. In this case, he has suppressed the information that Porphyry's greatest praise was reserved for the Essenes and others who eliminated meat from their diet entirely.) This contradiction leads Methodius to argue that Jewish dietary laws are merely disciplinary in character, a shadow of the truth, which can be discerned only through figual readings. In claiming that Methodius's followers should follow the Torah's literal meaning, the opponents whom *De cibis* confronts agree with Porphyry's position preserved by Eusebius: that certain Christians, inspired by Origen, read perfectly plain statements of Moses as *ainigmata* full of hidden meanings. This is precisely what Methodius is doing here, and also aptly describes the exegetical practices of his *Symposium* as well. Later, I will consider why Methodius persisted in figural readings, despite the Hellenes' attacks. Here it is sufficient to point out that Porphyry's complaints in Eusebius agree with the point of view expressed by Methodius's opponents in *De cibis:* both reject nonliteral interpretations of the Torah. Because *De cibis* survives only in Old Slavonic, it is impossible to know whether in this text Methodius described Torah passages as *ainigmata,* as he did in the *Symposium.* There are, however, two places where he may have done so. For example, just after paraphrasing the strictures in Numbers 19 concerning how lustral water should be prepared, Methodius remarks: "It is necessary to understand that, with this commandment being laid down, our redeemer also determined that it not be easy to understand" (*Cib.* 6.3). Also, as he launches into his extended figural reading of the same passage,

---

and Daniel A. Dombrowski, "Vegetarianism and the Argument from Marginal Cases in Porphyry," *JHI* 4 (1984): 141–43.

120. See below in this chapter.
121. See below in this chapter.

later in *De cibis,* Methodius says that "the mysterium of the heifer is retained, among us, however, since we do not hold the *nomos* according to the letter, but according to the spirit" (11.1). The connection with Porphyry's anti-Christian texts is reinforced by Methodius's concluding remark. His statement that "true purifications are things of which the gods are afraid" (15.1) resonates with Porphyry's observation that since Jesus has been worshipped, the gods have left their sanctuaries (ap. Eus. *PE* 5.1.9).

Methodius's use of *On Abstinence* thus shows him targeting Porphyry as an opponent whom he deems hypocritical. His allusion to his opponents as people who—far from upholding Jewish purity laws—actually handle corpses, however, points to an even broader circle of Hellene adversaries. Although Porphyry himself eschewed theurgy for himself, his student Iamblichus was a noted adherent. Iamblichus, as observed in chapter 4, advocated material sacrifice for all souls and even advocated eating sacrifical meat. Porphyry also advocated theurgy, which presumably could have involved some sort of material or animal sacrifice, for most Christians. All the evidence taken together, then, indicates that Methodius seeks to address Hellene opponents throughout *De cibis.*

Nevertheless, Methodius never loses sight of his Christian opposition either. This thread is apparent in his treatment of the second *aporia* to which he draws attention, namely the apparent conflict between the dietary laws of Leviticus 11 and Psalm 45. On the one hand, in Leviticus, elephants are defined as half-impure, yet in Psalm 45 (9–10), the king's daughters are housed in an ivory palace. If Jewish dietary law is to be read literally, then scripture is contradictory, specifically in the sense that the prophet here seems to be disagreeing with the Law. Methodius, rejecting the notion that scripture could be contradictory, concludes that the *aporia* is again evidence that the law of the Torah requires a figural reading. In this case, he asserts that the Forty-fifth Psalm is really about how our bodies will "receive the realm of God" (*Cib.* 8.7). This exegetical digression also gives Methodius an opportunity to "correct" the impression he created in the *Symposium,* that souls will shed their corporeal tabernacles when they enter the realm of God.[122]

Analysis of *De cibis* shows that, after writing the *Symposium,* Methodius faced criticism from Porphyrian Hellenes who decried his Origenist heritage and the figural way in which his community read the Torah. One concern was the Methodians' figural reading of Mosaic purity legislation, a practice that illustrates Porphyry's complaint that Origenists treat perfectly

---

122. Patterson, *Methodius of Olympus,* 28–29, 30. See also Patterson, "*De libero arbitrio,*" 161 n. 1.

plain statements of Moses as *ainigmata* full of occult wisdom. Porphyry may not have directed this statement specifically against Methodius's *Symposium*. Nevertheless, the work's heavy reliance on figural exegesis persuaded Methodius that the Hellenes' criticisms applied directly to him.

It is now time to examine Methodius's *Symposium,* the work that provoked so much criticism from both Christians and Hellenes. The *Symposium* was, if not Methodius's first work,[123] an earlier text than those considered up to now. Its peaceful tone and even-tempered character has long suggested that it was written in a "period of comparative peace for the church," before its author felt a need to distance himself from Origen's theology.[124] The *Symposium* appropriates the structure of a Platonic dialogue, but it is actually a handbook of Christian teaching and theology in a Platonist framework.[125] Chastity is its unifying theme and denotes not just sexual continence, but also restrained apparel, self-discipline, and a diet free from alcohol (*Symp.* 4.5).[126] The text is deeply Platonic in its concern with the ascent of the soul from the world of images to the truly real.[127] It is, however, also an instruction manual on a range of topics, from figural exegesis of scripture to Christ's divinity. It proceeds as a series of dialogues, each with one chief female protagonist.[128] These protagonists may represent real women,[129] but they may also simply personify different types of soul.[130] The dramatic date of the text is probably Methodius's own time, since he appears as a character in the dialogue.[131]

One striking element of the *Symposium* is its use of the typology of Plato's *Republic* (514a-c) together with Hebrews 10 to categorize stages in human history.[132] For Methodius, the three levels of reality set out in Plato's cave—

---

123. Musurillo, *St. Methodius,* 8, places it chronologically second, after *De autexousio.*

124. Musurillo, *St. Methodius,* 11–12, 35, 175–76 n. 25.

125. Ibid., 11.

126. Ibid., 20, 177–78 nn. 48–50.

127. Ibid., 35–36.

128. Ibid., 11, 16–17.

129. If so, they show Methodius's rejection of the Origenist view of women as tied to the flesh. Or. *Hom. in Gen.* 4.4; C. Tibiletti, "L'ambiente culturale cristiano riflesso nel Simposio di Metodio," in *Verginità e matrimonio in antichi scrittori cristiani,* ed. C. Tibiletti (Rome: Pubblicazioni della Facoltà di lettere e filosofia [Università di Macerata], 1983), 128.

130. Contra Musurillo, *St. Methodius,* 11. If this is so, then Methodius has appropriated Origen's view of the soul as feminine. Or. *Hom. in Gen.* 5.2.

131. M. D. Gallardo, "Los Simposios de Luciano, Ateneo, Metodio y Juliano," *Cuadernos de Filología Clásica* 4 (1972): 267–68. Musurillo, *St. Methodius,* 12, believed that Methodius's incorporation of the legendary Thecla as one of the characters in the dialogue necessarily called for a first-century CE dramatic date, whereas Patterson, *Methodius of Olympus,* 70, however, had argued, based on the "paradisiacal" setting and the "liturgical... character for the final gathering in the garden facing east," that it was set just before the *apokatastasis.*

132. Patterson, *Methodius of Olympus,* 96.

the shadow, the image, and reality—are, as they will be in *De cibis,* applied to Christian history in the following way:[133] the Law, the most ancient, is the period of the shadow; the period of the church on earth (i.e., Methodius's own day) is the image; and reality or truth, that of the messianic Parousia, known in Methodius's time by a few elect (*Symp.* 4.5), will become known to all the elect as the eternal residence, the heavenly Jerusalem, at the end of the world (9.5).[134] A precursor to Augustine, Methodius envisions his own age as a "mixed" city, in which the heavenly and the earthly cities "encounter one another" on "earthly ground."[135] He lives during a period of spiritual maternity, in which the mother church illuminates those who are baptized (and so the church is also associated with the moon).[136] The church, thus, is comprised of a multitude among whom one can distinguish those who collaborate with Christ and form properly the body of the church from those who do not participate in this spiritual maternity.[137] The former are the illuminating Christians; the latter are those who are illuminated.[138] The illuminating Christians, for their part, are also participating in the light of the intelligible church, which in reality is celestial, noetic, preexisting, and perfect (5.7).[139]

Methodius develops this unique typology across the dialogue and also links it with stages in human development.[140] For example, Marcella claims that the world empty of inhabitants was like a child.[141] This period includes the period of Hebrew and Jewish history up until just before the birth of

---

133. Calogero Riggi, "Teologia della storia nel Simposio di Metodio di Olimpo," *Augustinianum* 16 (1976): 70; Emanuela Prinzivalli, "Il millenarismo in Oriente da Metodio ad Apollinare," *AnnSE* 15, no. 1 (1998): 129.

134. Gallardo, "Los Simposios," 266; Riggi, "Teologia della storia," 65; Clementina Mazzucco, "Tra l'ombra e la realtà: L'Apocalisse nel Simposio di Metodio di Olimpo," *Civiltà Classica e Cristiana* 6 (1985): 421; Montserrat-Torrents, "Origenismo y gnosis," 100.

135. Riggi, "Teologia della storia," 81 incl. n. 16. Here Riggi has appropriated the vision of Augustine's *civitas terrene spritualis* from Paolo Brezzi, *Analisi ed interpretazione del "De civitate dei" di Sant'Agostino* (Tolentino: Edizione Agostiniane, 1960), 91.

136. Montserrat-Torrents, "Origenismo y gnosis," 97. In Thecla's dialogue, the moon is the star of light that prefigures the faith and a watery star that foretells baptism. It is, moreover, the symbol of Mary, who with her virginal and maternal humor of blood and milk nourished Christ at her breast and generated him for Christian life. Finally, the moon is the image of the church in that image of the church that imbues the soul with Christ through its own maternal humors, raising it to eschatological reality without distinguishing between races and customs. Riggi, "Teologia della storia," 75.

137. Montserrat-Torrents, "Origenismo y gnosis," 97.

138. Ibid.

139. Ibid.

140. Riggi, "Teologia della storia," 63.

141. Ibid., 66.

Christ, yet it can be interpreted as a shadow of the image to come.[142] For Agatha, however, the prudent virgins of the text represent the *primum genus* of the new and truer Israel.[143] For those who have kept to the end "their nuptial garb of virginity" there is the heavenly Jerusalem, or Ouranopolis (*Symp.* 4.5),[144] which should be understood in spiritual rather than material terms (9.1).[145]

Methodius's discussion illustrates another noteworthy aspect of his *Symposium*, namely its sustained insistence on reading Jewish scripture—especially the Pentateuch—figurally. For example, as we saw above,[146] the dialogue of Tusiane offers a figural reading for the Feast of the Tabernacle or Tents (Sukhot). Since Methodius presents this feast as an *ainigma* (*Symp.* 9.1), and it was a ritual prescribed by Moses, it is a compelling example of the type of exegesis that so irritated Porphyry. Leviticus 23:29–43 sets out the guidelines for this feast, but Methodius interprets them against the text of Revelation 20:4.[147] The festival law requires Jews to live in tents for seven days in the seventh month and to bring mature fruits, palms, willow, and chaste tree branches.[148] Far from calling for his community to celebrate the festival as Leviticus describes, Methodius conflates the seven days of creation from Genesis with the seven days of the festival to yield the seven millennia of cosmic history.[149] For him, the text promises that, for believers, the seventh millennium will be the true Saturday when the body will resurrect, and everyone will present for judgment the fruit of his faith: love, justice, chastity, and the signs of victory over passions. Like the Hebrews, escaped from Egypt, who arrived in the tents and then later arrive in the promised land, so Christians after death will experience resurrection, judgment, and repose with Christ. They then will depart for the heavens, where—having become like angels—they will live in God's residence (*Symp.* 9.1–5).[150] In Methodius's interpretation the four types of tree symbolize four stages in salvific history.[151] For example, the fig tree represents the era before the flood (10.5), because, like the era it

---

142. For example, for Theopatra, the refusal of the captive Israelites to sing to God in a strange land is a type of the true Israel that keeps secret from the unworthy the evangelical mystery of divine predilection (*Symp.* 4.5). See also the dialogue of Tallusa. Riggi, "Teologia della storia," 70.

143. Riggi, "Teologia della storia," 73.

144. Ibid., 61.

145. Ibid., 75–76.

146. See 145f.

147. This is the first known Christian use of Jewish millenarian readings of Leviticus. Mazzucco, "Tra l'ombra e la realtà," 402; Patterson, *Methodius of Olympus,* 106.

148. Mazzucco, "Il millenarismo," 75.

149. Patterson, *Methodius of Olympus,* 106; Musurillo, *St. Methodius,* 20, 178 n. 54.

150. Mazzucco, "Il millenarismo," 75.

151. Riggi, "Teologia della storia," 76–77.

represents, it has an ambiguous value in scripture: its foliage provided Adam a decent covering for his nudity, but its "tickling leaves" also "stimulated" him to "luxury."[152] The chaste tree, conversely, represents a Christian era liberated from fear of diabolical intervention.[153] Similarly, the tent that Moses ordered to be built for the festival—as well as the very people of Israel themselves— represents the flesh of everyone in whose heart the Holy Spirit lives, that is, the present church of Methodius's day. This in turn prefigures the celestial Jerusalem, and the temple that the blessed expect after resurrection.[154]

Not only does the *Symposium* indulge in precisely the type of exegesis that Porphyry had condemned in the fragment preserved by Eusebius, but this treatise also shows the extent of Methodius's debt to Origen.[155] Although he seems not to have appropriated Origen's doctrine of the preexistence of the soul or the doctrine of the final restoration of all,[156] he rigorously maintains Origen's habits of figural exegesis—especially in his use of the book of Revelation as a touchstone, and his interpretation of sacrificial offerings.[157] In some cases, the figural parallels are particularly close. For example, before Methodius, only Origen is known to have applied a figural reading to Leviticus 24:2–4: he interpreted as the prophetic word the lamp of pure olive oil that God, via Moses, ordered the Israelites to burn continuously outside the veil of the temple.[158] The analysis is, in fact, almost identical.[159] Moreover, both Origen and Methodius develop an "antithesis between the lamp of the Israelites and the sun of justice" from Malachi 4:1–4, which they read as Christ "who diffuses through the world and renders the lamp useless."[160] In this case, the parallels are particularly close.[161] Also like Origen, Metho-

---

152. Ibid., 79.

153. Ibid.

154. *Symp.* 1.1; 9.2, 5; 5.7, 8; 4.4; 6.2. Mazzucco, "Tra l'ombra e la realtà," 422.

155. Contra the claim in Musurillo, *St. Methodius,* 22, that "Methodius' Origenism … is rather an Asiatic form of Alexandrianism."

156. Musurillo, *St. Methodius,* 18.

157. Cf. Or. *PA* 2.11.2 and *Symp.* 9.1–2; Riggi, "Teologia della storia," 75–78; Emanuela Prinzivalli, "Il simbolismo del sangue in Metodio di Olimpo, III," in *Centro Studi Sanguis Christi, III: Atti della Settimana Sangue e Antropologia nella Letteratura Cristiana* (Rome: Ed. Pia Unione del Preziosissimo Sangue, 1983), 1182; Mazzucco, "Tra l'ombra e la realtà," 403, 421; id., "Il millenarismo," 74, 81 incl. n. 39.

158. Or. *Hom. in Lev.* 13; Meth. *Symp.* 6.4; Marcello Marin, "Origene e Metodio su Lev. 24,2–4," *VetChr* 18 (1981): 471. Although 2 Peter 1:19 makes the connection between prophecy and a lamp, the author doesn't connect it to the passage in Leviticus. Marin, 472.

159. Marin, "Origene e Metodio," 471.

160. Ibid., 473; see also Montserrat-Torrents, "Origenismo y gnosis," 95.

161. Marin, "Origene e Metodio," 475; this analysis would seem to negate the claim of Musurillo (28–29) that Methodius was not directly dependent on Origen. Musurillo, in Prinzivalli, "Il simbolismo del sangue," 1181.

dius subscribed to the doctrine of the eternal creation of the word and an active divine pedagogy, progressively actualizing in the fullness of time until the ultimate Parousia.[162] Like that of Origen, too, is Methodius's concept of the true Sabbath as the seventh day of creation and the end of the world,[163] and his notion of an earthly community of the redeemed in which there are both the proficient and the *perfecti,* who have a special intelligence and form part of the spiritual church even while living in this world.[164] Methodius even shares with Origen the notion that the Law as *typos* and shadow of the image anticipates the Gospel, the image of truth, which in turn foreshadows the Parousia.[165] One key difference, however, is that "while Origen had a notion that all this was happening simultaneously (vertically), in Methodius there is a sense of horizontal progress in time."[166]

Within its intellectual milieu, the *Symposium* is significant because it deployed precisely the kind of Origenist exegesis that Porphyry had deplored, treating passages in the Pentateuch as *ainigmata* (5.7; 9.1) and resolving them through figural exegesis. But Methodius's Origenism, together with his adoption of the structure of a Platonic dialogue, embracing a form of ascesis, and envisioning a teaching and learning community dedicated to promoting the ascent of the soul, also gives Methodius the appearance of being a teacher within the Ammonian community. For these reasons alone, it is not surprising that Porphyry reacted with hostility to texts like the *Symposium.* So keenly did Methodius feel the sting of Porphyry's criticisms, as well as the opposition from fellow Christians that the Hellene provoked, that he spent several years responding to his critics through treatises, including *De cibis* and the *Aglaophon.* Two questions, however, arise as the result of his activity. First, given the strident critique of his exegetical strategies, why did Methodius retain his technique of reading the Pentateuch figurally? Second, since Hellenes themselves were willing to read

162. Riggi, "Teologia della storia," 82–83. Patterson, "Methodius, Origen, and the Arian Dispute," 917. Although Methodius was not a "proto-Arian," this aspect of his work sets him "in the immediate background of the early Arians." As Patterson argues, evidence in Methodius suggests that Arians might have been reacting to Origenist thinking (919). Where Musurillo, *St. Methodius,* 25 thought that there were Arian interpolations in the *Symposium,* these have been disproved by Buchheit, "Das Symposion des Methodios," 113.

163. Although Origen does not share his conception of the duration of the blessed rest of 1,000 years. Mazzucco, "Il millenarismo," 79, 84.

164. Montserrat-Torrents, "Origenismo y gnosis," 100, 96, 89 n. 3.

165. Or. *PA.* 3.6.8; 4.1.6; 2.4, 6; 4.13. Patterson, *Methodius of Olympus,* 108. Emanuela Prinzivalli, *L'esegesi biblica di Metodio di Olimpo* (Rome: Inst. Patrist. Augustinianum, 1985), 129.

166. Prinzivalli, *L'esegesi biblica,* 129.

law figurally, why would Porphyry have attacked people for reading the laws of Moses in this way?

Methodius's reasons for refusing to relinquish figural exegesis are, at heart, what separates his school from that of Porphyry—and probably that of Origen—despite their many similarities. Both Hellenes and Christians took it for granted that the way one understood fundamental physical reality would determine how and when one would deploy various exegetical strategies, as well as inevitably dictating the results. On the one hand, Porphyry worked within a framework in which acts of God did not abrogate the fundamental laws of physics. When Methodius, in the *Aglaophon,* used Proclus to voice Porphyry's argument against the resurrection of flesh dissolved into its constituent elements he spotlighted the Hellene's guiding assumption: all things are not possible for God. The Platonists' God was the utterly transcendent source of a cosmos that operates according to the eternal, fundamental laws of physics. Understanding this ultimate reality required understanding the teachings of those who had reached it (e.g., Pythagoras, Plato, Plotinus), which, in turn, required a solid foundation in natural physics.[167] Christians like Methodius—and his Christian critics for that matter—fundamentally rejected this position.[168] Their God was completely unfettered by physical reality, an assumption that derived from their belief in Jesus' resurrection, a core doctrine of the faith.[169]

Porphyry believed that textual hermeneutics was impossible without knowledge of the world and how it works. For example, in the *Cave of the Nymphs,* he had argued that for certain poems a figural hermeneutics was sometimes appropriate and could reveal religious truths. When a passage is so full of obscurities that it cannot be a poetic fiction designed strictly to delight and cannot be an "account of an actual place," then, he explained, the poet has indicated that there is something to be understood figurally (*Antr.* 4).[170]

167. A. H. Armstrong, "Man in the Cosmos: A Study of Some Differences between Pagan Neoplatonism and Christianity," in *Romanitas et Christianitas: Studia I. H. Waszink a. d.VI Kal. Nov. a MCMLXXIII XIII lustra complenti oblata,* ed. W. den Boer et al. (Amsterdam: North Holland, 1973), 5–14.

168. Cf. Macarius Magnes *Apoc.* 4.30.

169. A. H. Armstrong, "Two Views of Freedom: A Christian Objection in Plotinus VI.8 (39) 7.11–15," *Studia Patristica* 17.1 (1982): 397–406.

170. Porphyry, *The Cave of the Nymphs in the Odyssey: A Revised Text with Translation,* SUNY Buffalo Classics Seminar 609 (Buffalo: Arethusa, 1969), 4: τοιούτων ἀσαφειῶν πλήρους ὄντος τοῦ διηγήματος πλάσμα μὲν ὡς ἔτυχεν εἰς ψυχαγωγίαν πεποιημένον μὴ εἶναι, ἀλλ᾽ οὐδ᾽ **ἱστορίας τοπικῆς περιήγησιν** ἔχειν, ἀλληγορεῖν δέ τι δι᾽ αὐτοῦ τὸν ποιητήν, προσθέντα μυστικῶς καὶ ἐλαίας φυτὸν πλησίον (emphasis added).

In this case, Porphyry read the passage about the cave of the nymphs in the *Odyssey* (13) as a metaphor for how souls ascend to heaven and descend to earth. His application of these techniques to Orphic poetry in fragments now attributed to his treatise *On Images* shows that his exegesis is intimately connected to his understanding of the physical world.[171] Porphyry thus endorses the use of figural reading, as does Methodius, but their conceptions of what is possible in the cosmos will lead them to wildly different ends. Whereas in Porphyry's view, however, Origen had apparently understood enough about the laws of nature to reject the resurrection of the flesh, Methodius believed that he was perfectly justified in using a figural exegesis to support his doctrine of the resurrection because it was done on the basis of an "accurate understanding of reality." Accordingly, throughout *De cibis,* even after the exegetical strategies of the *Symposium* have received such trenchant criticism, he takes pains to show both that figural reading is a legitimate way to resolve scriptural *aporiae* and that the correct application of figural reading actually requires understanding what is possible in the natural world.[172] This is why he can maintain this type of exegesis even in the *Aglaophon,* despite its close connection with Origen.[173] Although this was a reality that Porphyry rejected, the view that all things were possible for God was one to which both Methodius and his Christian critics subscribed.

Porphyry's statements in the *Cave of the Nymphs* (4) and his criticisms of how Christians read the book of Daniel also reveal his belief that the genre of a text determines whether it is open to a figural reading. For example, textual passages fundamentally historical in character should not be read allegori-

---

171. The title *Peri agalmatōn* appears in Stobaeus (1.31.7–10 and 1.25.2), but it is not inconceivable that it was part of the *Philosophy from Oracles.* After Constantine's edict banned Porphyry's anti-Christian work, parts of the *Philosophy from Oracles* may have circulated under other names. In the *Praeparatio evangelica,* just before Eusebius criticized Porphyry for his use of oracles, he objected to the way in which he interpreted poetry, either in the *Philosophy from Oracles* itself or in a closely related work. These particular fragments are collected under the title *On Images,* but Eusebius never indicates that they come from a separate source, even though he cites many examples where Porphyry applies this technique to Orphic poetry, interpreting what the poet says about the gods as conveying information about the structure of the cosmos and the powers of the demiurgic *nous. Agal.* frag. 351 (numbers for fragments correspond to those in A Smith and D. Wasserstein, *Porphyrii philosophi fragmenta* [Stuttgart: Teubner, 1993]) (Eus. *PE* 3.6.7–7.1), 352 (*PE* 3.7.2–4), 354 (*PE* 3.8.2–9.9).

172. Patterson, "Notes on *De cibis,*" 236, 238.

173. In recognizing the "difficult path" that Methodius treads in distancing himself from Origen, on the one hand, while maintaining a figural reading of scripture on the other, Patterson, "Notes on *De cibis,*" 241–42, concluded that Methodius may not have seen this type of exegesis as "Origenist." My argument is that figural reading in itself was not a point of disagreement between Hellenes and Origenists or Christians more generally. What was really at issue was the understanding of nature that lay underneath it.

cally.[174] Porphyry's complaints about how Origen's followers were reading the Pentateuch seem to imply that legal treatises, like historical texts, were not open to figural exegesis. The Neoplatonist position, however, was more nuanced. Neoplatonists believed that laws created for a community (i.e., in the sensible world) by a lawgiver who had made contact with the divine were not only fundamentally just, but were also an image or figure of divine law (i.e., the law of the intelligible world). Pure souls would be able to perceive the relationship between the law of the sensible world and that of the divine or intelligible world,[175] but their enhanced perception did not mean that they could abrogate the laws of the community for themselves. Indeed, Plotinus portrayed the philosopher's life even in the best possible earthly realm as a type of exile,[176] and Porphyry emphasizes for the same reason that when Ammonius took up philosophy after having been raised as a Christian, he turned himself toward his *politieia*.[177] Here Porphyry has Christians in a kind of Catch-22: The law may be a figure of the divine if it is just, but no one can abrogate the just laws of the *politeia*. So if Jewish law is a figure of the divine, then it must be just; if it is just, it should be followed. If Jewish law is not just, then it is not a figure of the divine, and it makes no sense to read it figurally. Origen shares the Platonist conception of the law of the *politeia* as the shadow, and that of the community bound by philosophy as the image, of the intelligible word, the world directly ruled by the *logos*. And like the Platonists, Origen sees all these worlds as simultaneous, allowing vertical participation in all three.[178] Insofar as he refused to follow Jewish law, however, Origen would have also been open to these political criticisms (as indeed we saw Porphyry levy them in the fragment quoted by Eusebius). Methodius, however, seems to have tried to finesse this problem with his view that the shadow, the image, and reality are phases in time (although he has maintained a part of the Platonist perspective by allowing his *perfecti* to be inhabitants of the "two cities" at once).[179] To some extent he has this perspective because for most Christians—as for most Jews—God had always been an agent in human history, requiring different types of observances from people at dif-

---

174. In fragments attributed by Jerome to *Against the Christians* (book 12; *Chr.* frag. 43 Harnack = Hieron. *Dan.* pr.) Porphyry condemned how Christians read the book of Daniel. This text, he determined, was actually a veiled history of the Jews, written during the reign of Antiochus IV. Accordingly, it could not be read allegorically as prophesying the coming of Jesus. See, for example, Porph. *Chr.* frag. 43 M Harnack = Hieron. *Dan.* 7.13–14.

175. Porph. *Marc.* 25–26.

176. *Enn.* 2.9.

177. Ap. Eus. *HE* 6.19.

178. Prinzivalli, *L'esegesi biblica,* 129.

179. Ibid.

ferent times. God's interaction with humans had started at the beginning and would continue to the end-time.

More than any other extant author, Methodius allows us to see clearly for the first time the fundamental factors that set Porphyrian Hellenes at odds with Christian communities at the end of the third century. Two profound disagreements separated Christians like Methodius from Hellenes like Porphyry. First, each camp had a profoundly different understanding of how divinity worked through the world around them. For the Hellenes, all things were *not* possible for God; whereas for Christians, God had absolute unbounded freedom, which might allow bodies to be reconstituted after death despite what ordinary physics seemed to dictate. For the Hellenes, the Christian position was fundamentally irrational, an unconscionable lapse into mere faith. This irrationality in turn would have made such Christians—in the eyes of their Hellene neighbors—unfit for positions of leadership within the *politeia*. The attitude of the Hellenes would have been exacerbated by the second deep disagreement between the two camps, namely whether the founding, divinely ordained legislation of a given political community could ever be abrogated. For Hellenes, such law—as a shadow of ultimate truth— was the way by which ordinary souls were not only guaranteed justice, but also brought as close as they could be to the divine. For Christians like Methodius, the law of the Jews—with all its sacrificial rituals—had been abrogated by the advent of Christ. From the perspective of the Hellenes, the Christian position seemed opportunistic and anarchistic, invoking the cachet of Plato's thought simply to mask its true lawlessness.

The role that Origen plays in these controversies is both liminal and critically important. With respect to both disagreements, his position is closer to the camp of the Hellenes than is that of Methodius. Given Origen's position on the spectrum along which the Methodians and Porphyrians were situated, it is not at all surprising that many Christians—unfamiliar with the Alexandrian theology, philosophy, and exegesis that undergirded these disagreements—believed that Origen's teachings were actually outside the boundaries of what they considered to be acceptable. Even more important, however, as we will see in the next chapter, Origen's own Ammonian heritage led him to found a school whose curriculum and practices mirrored and competed with Porphyry's own. If the practical goal of such schools was to produce educated men who might become civic leaders, from Porphyry's perspective Origen's school would have been a direct competitor that threatened to undermine public order. Indeed, it would have sent into the communities of the empire men ignorant of the first principles of nature and scornful of the laws of the *politeia* that they were ostensibly charged with upholding. However, insofar as such schools sought to produce the type of philosopher who, like Plotinus, might have glimpsed the divine and so could potentially serve as pilot of the ship of state, then—at least from Porphyry's view—the project of the Origenists threatened to undermine the very fabric of the Roman state.

Conclusion

The Ammonian Community and the Great Persecution

Although the tensions between Porphyry and Origenists, apparent in Methodius's writings were intramural disagreements, the Hellene's criticisms helped fan the hostility toward Christians that culminated in the emperor Diocletian's persecution of 303. Christians had been tolerated for the last four decades of the third century, and Diocletian himself had appointed Christians to his court (Lact. *Mort.* 10), but imperial officials and oracular priests began lobbying to repress Christian practice at the cusp of the fourth century. Their concern united Porphyry's criticism of Christian doctrines resulting from the rebuttal of Origenist exegesis with the warnings he had voiced to philosophers about the link between evil daemons and blood sacrifice. Although Porphyry had voiced the latter concern as an argument against the Iamblichaean enthusiasm for eating sacrificial meat, his qualms also pertained to the sacrament of the Eucharist. In other words, Porphyry's arguments against the Origenists' reading scripture as a coherent whole led to the conclusion that Jesus was not divine. Porphyry's conclusion that Jesus, however pious and inspired a teacher, was a mere man—a position that harks back to Ammonius's view—allowed his readers to infer that the sacramental transformation of the wine and bread into a dead man's blood and body was a polluting, evil daemon–attracting ceremony carried out by ignorant priests. As a result, certain officials and Apolline prophets not only began to voice concerns that Christians, whom these arguments cast as polluted, were

interfering with the efficacy of traditional civic rites long associated with preserving the community's health and safety, but they also did so in a way that
got imperial attention. The court's interest, in turn, provided a forum for Porphyry himself to advise the emperors, an outcome coherent with the political
role that he and fellow Ammonian Hellenes had espoused, at least since the
time of Plotinus. In the end, the dispute between the different branches of the
Ammonian community, a quarrel whose origins lay in Porphyry's disagreements with Iamblichus, contributed to the efforts of the Roman Empire to
repress Christianity once and for all.[1]

This series of events becomes evident only through a comparison of
accounts by Christian authors defending their doctrines against the criticisms levied during Diocletian's persecution. Although Porphyry's shadow
has loomed over the early fourth-century persecution, the fragmentary character of his anti-Christian writing has made his precise role impossible to
elucidate by using these texts alone as a source. This chapter will first discuss
what little can be gleaned from Porphyry's writings against Christians, and
then will turn to what Ammonian Christian sources themselves say about
the role that Porphyry's ideas played in the onset of the Great Persecution.

Porphyry's fame in late antique Christian sources as the archenemy of
Christianity is unparalleled.[2] This reputation, together with the chronology
of his life—the Suda says that he lived into the reign of Diocletian—suggests,
on its own, that he was an important source of the anti-Christian criticisms
that circulated in the Roman Empire in the late third century, although his
texts are seldom directly connected with this persecution.[3] Moreover, the
work that goes by the title *Against the Christians* is easy to associate with
Porphyry's campaign against Christianity. Fragments attributed to this work
include the criticisms of Origenists and praise of Ammonius motivated, I
argued in chapter 5, by opposition to Iamblichus and all Ammonians whose
mistaken exegesis in constructing a philosophy without conflicts had led them
to advocate a common path to the divine for all people. Indeed, throughout
this book, I have used this fragment of Porphyry's work as a launching point
from which to explore the significance of Ammonius, the problems with

---

1. Accordingly, although Mark Edwards does not think that Porphyry played as prominent a
role in the persecution as I argue here, and he has not developed the implications of the Tyrian philosopher's quarrel with Iamblichus, he is right to think that some Christian rhetoric probably also
targeted Iamblichus's positions. Mark Edwards, "Porphyry and the Christians," in *Studies on Porphyry,*
ed. George E. Karamanolis and Anne Sheppard (London: Institute of Classical Studies, 2007), 122.

2. He is so identified in sources from Eus. *HE* 6.19.9 to the Suda (4.178.14–179.2 Adler).

3. Michael Bland Simmons, *Arnobius of Sicca: Religious Conflict and Competition in the Age of
Diocletian* (New York: Oxford University Press, 1995), and Edwards, "Porphyry and the Christians,"
111–26, are important exceptions.

Origen—including his relationship to Plotinus—and the issues that Porphyry had with contemporary Christian Origenists.

I chose to use Eusebius's quotation of Porphyry thus because the fragmentary character of Porphyry's "anti-Christian writings" precludes any more systematic investigation focused on them alone. Indeed, no intact work by Porphyry entitled *Against the Christians* survives, and the fragment I have relied on is one of the most extensive usually attributed to such a work. Despite Eusebius's claim that Porphyry, in the "third treatise of his writings against Christians," condemned the exegetical sins that led the Origenists to bewitch the soul's critical faculty and violate the laws of the community in which they were educated (*HE* 6.19.1–6, 9), issues readily seen through the work of Methodius, the relationship between these specific concerns, this treatise, and the work that the Suda lists as *Fifteen Arguments (logous) against Christians* is extraordinarily difficult to determine.[4] A number of interrelated problems complicate the analysis. First, although Adolf von Harnack a century ago collected fragments from what he assumed was a systematic fifteen-volume book,[5] scholarship since then has challenged this view. A growing number of scholars now suggest that Porphyry may have written a series of shorter treatises under other titles that were later collected under this overarching title.[6] Since only Eusebius and Jerome (who had visited the bishop's library in Caesarea by 402)[7] quote or paraphrase numbered treatises,[8] the former may have collected those treatises under the broader title and numbered them himself—not necessarily in chronological order.[9] In the *Ecclesiastical History,* Eusebius's description of Porphyry's project can be read in support of this view. Before he sets out his quotation from Porphyry, Eusebius says that after the philosopher had settled in Sicily (i.e., after the onset of Plotinus's

---

4. *Suidae Lexicon,* ed. A. Adler (Stuttgart: Verlag Teubner, 1928–38), s.v. "Porphurios."

5. Adolph von Harnack, "Porphyrius, *Gegen die Christen:* 15 Bücher; Zeugnisse, Fragmente, und Referate," *Abhandlungen der Königlich Preussischen Akademie der Wissenschaften, Philosophisch-historische Klasse* (1916): 1–115.

6. This line of argument began with P. F. Beatrice, "Le traité de Porphyre contre les chrétiens: L'état de la question," *Kernos* 4 (1991): 119–38, and has continued through Robert M. Berchman, *Porphyry against the Christians* (Leiden/Boston: Brill, 2005), and Edwards, "Porphyry and the Christians," 111–16.

7. Hieron. *C. Ruf.* 3.12, in Eric Junod, "L'auteur de l'Apologie pour Origène traduite par Rufin: Les témoignages contradictoires de Rufin et de Jérôme à propos de Pamphile et d'Eusèbe," in *Recherches et tradition: Mélanges patristiques offerts à Henri Crouzel,* ed. A. Dupleix (Paris: Beauchesne, 1992), 174.

8. See Eus. *PE* 1.9.20–21; Eus. *Chron.* pr. ap. Hieron.; Hieron. *Dan.* prol.; and *Matt.* 24:16.

9. The number more likely corresponds to the order in which Eusebius became aware of them or added them to his collection. One need not even assume that Jerome's volume numbers matched those that Eusebius assigned.

terminal illness in 268), "he began treatises against us."[10] Since the possibility that Porphyry gave the title *Against the Christians* to one long work is so contestable, I will refer to fragments conventionally attributed to this work as coming from Porphyry's "anti-Christian texts."

The problem of the title affects the problem of dating Porphyry's "anti-Christian texts." Scholars who had assumed that the title *Against the Christians* referred to a fifteen-volume systematic opus had proposed a range of dates, based on references in specific fragments. Although most fragments reveal no information about the context in which Porphyry wrote them, those preserved by Jerome in his *Commentaries on Daniel* draw in part on Callinicus Sutorius.[11] This dependency yields a *terminus post quem* of 270.[12] But if Porphyry's "anti-Christian texts" are a series of treatises, this *terminus post quem* can apply only to the "twelfth of his books," in which Porphyry addressed the authenticity of the book of Daniel.[13] This result yields little more information than Eusebius's claim that Porphyry starting writing against Christians after he moved to Sicily in 268. A later *terminus post quem* is indicated by Porphyry's references to Britain as a province rife with usurpers, an observation appropriate any time after Allectus's usurpation in 293, which had followed hard upon Carausius's in 286/7.[14] This information comes from a fragment, preserved by Jerome, in which Porphyry contests the Christian claim that no one knew the true law until the coming of Christ.[15]

---

10. *HE* 6.19.2: *[H]o kath' hēmas en Sikeliai katastas Porphurios sungrammata kath' hēmōn enstēsamenos.* (Note the aorist middle *enstēsamenos.*) This statement need not imply that Porphyry actually wrote these treatises in Sicily. Rather, it may simply indicate that Eusebius's knowledge of Porphyry came only through his written work. The only extant text in which Porphyry discusses his own career is the *Vita Plotini.* There, Porphyry mentions his move to Sicily during Plotinus's illness but says nothing more about his own career after Plotinus's death, apart from his decision to edit and publish Plotinus's treatises. According to R. Bodeüs, "Plotin a-t-il empêché Porphyre de mourir de mélancolie," *Hermes* 129 (2001): 569–70, Porphyry probably left Plotinus because of his master's illness; the claim of melancholia masks his absence at his master's death (as Plato was for the death of Socrates).

11. Frag. 43 Harnack = Hieron. *Dan.* prol.

12. B. Croke, "Porphyry's Anti-Christian Chronology," *JThS* 34 (1983): 168–85.

13. *Dan.* prol.; "in the thirteenth volume of his work against him," Jerome adds (*Matt.* 24:16f.), Porphyry addressed the "abomination of desolation" from Dan. 11:31 and 12:11.

14. For the insight that Porphyry is referring to usurpers, cf. T. D. Barnes, "Porphyry *Against the Christians,*" *JThS* 24 (1973): 433–37. Barnes himself dates this to the early fourth century.

15. Frag. 82 Harnack = Hieron. *Ep.* 133.9: "Make your own the favorite cavil of your associate Porphyry, and ask how God can be described as pitiful and of great mercy when from Adam to Moses and from Moses to the coming of Christ He has suffered all nations to die in ignorance of the Law and of His commandments. For Britain, that province so fertile in despots, the Scottish tribes, and all the barbarians round about as far as the ocean were alike without knowledge of Moses and the prophets. Why should Christ's coming have been delayed to the last times? Why should He not have come before so vast a number had perished?" (trans. *NPNF*).

This theme is markedly different from his close textual analysis of the historicity of the book of Daniel, although both are relevant to Porphyry's arguments against the resurrection of the flesh and abrogating Jewish law that Methodius addressed. If Porphyry's "anti-Christian texts" are a series of treatises, however, the reference to Britain can set a *terminus post quem* only for a work concerned, at least in part, with Christian claims to a new universal truth—an issue, I argue, that assumed special relevance for Porphyry in light of Iamblichus's parallel claims to a *via universalis*.

While the context in which Methodius refuted some of Porphyry's criticisms indicates that his "anti-Christian texts" started to circulate in the mid-290s, even if there are no firm indications in the fragments themselves, the *terminus ante quem* is somewhat easier to determine. On the one hand, I have argued that the Roman official Hierocles drew on Porphyry's "anti-Christian texts" for his own treatise *The Lover of Truth,* authored in 302.[16] Another indication for a *terminus ante quem* comes from Eusebius's citation of the attacks against Origen and Christian exegesis in the *Ecclesiastical History.* While Eusebius's reference requires a *terminus ante quem* of 306 for a treatise concerned with these issues, since this is the date after which he published the *Ecclesiastical History,*[17] it yields no new information, for the Suda indicates that Porphyry did not outlive the end of Diocletian's reign in 305. Even if Porphyry's criticisms of Origen that Eusebius locates in "the third treatise of his writings against Christians" are connected with his exegesis of the book of Daniel,[18] which Jerome assigns to "the twelfth of his books," no conclusion can be drawn regarding the structure or date of these texts. Eusebius is clearly counting Porphyry's anti-Christian publications, whereas it is not clear from Jerome's statement whether the criticisms of Daniel might come from the twelfth book of the third anti-Christian treatise described by Eusebius, from a twelfth separate anti-Christian volume, or from a twelfth publication overall. In the end, it is safest to conclude that Porphyry could have begun writing treatises against Christians once he had traveled to Sicily in 268, but that he produced his most influential "anti-Christian texts"—those that provoked Methodius's response and Hierocles' appropriation—between the 290s and 302.

16. Elizabeth DePalma Digeser, "Porphyry, Julian, or Hierokles? The Anonymous Hellene in Makarios Magnēs' *Apocritikos,*" *JThS* 53 (2002): 466–502.

17. R. W. Burgess, "The Dates and Editions of Eusebius' *Chronici canones* and *Historia ecclesiastica,*" *JThS* n. s. 48 (1997): 471–504.

18. R. M. Grant, "The *Stromateis* of Origen," in *Epektasis: Mélanges patristiques offerts à Jean Daniélou,* ed. J. Fontaine and Charles Kannengiesser (Paris: Beauchesne, 1972), 289–90.

The problem of the title also complicates the problem of identifying fragments and associating them with specific works. Harnack and others usually assigned to a work entitled *Against the Christians* quotations or paraphrases of Porphyry's writings that were either generically anti-Christian or attributed to his "writings against us" or to his "writings against Christians."[19] Conversely, Smith's seminal collection of fragments has attributed to other works passages referring to more specific issues—for example, assigning passages interpreting oracles or understanding images to *On Philosophy from Oracles* or *On Images* even though these texts had anti-Christian elements and could thus have ultimately become part of Porphyry's "anti-Christian texts."[20] Indeed, the Suda lists neither *On Philosophy from Oracles* nor *On Images,* as might be expected if they were catalogued under the broader title. The problems with titles and fragments intertwine because a fragment attributed by an ancient Christian author to Porphyry's writings "against us" or "against Christians" could actually have come from a treatise that initially circulated under some other name altogether.

The next problem complicating the analysis of Porphyry's writings against Christians is that by 324 the emperor Constantine had ordered the destruction of Porphyry's anti-Christian work (ap. Socr. *HE* 1.9.30), an edict that would presumably have applied to all of the philosopher's "anti-Christian texts," regardless of their original title. While this decree would not have eliminated every scroll or codex, it has serious implications for the documentary record. At the very least, the edict—where it was known and enforced— would mean that Porphyry's texts circulated less freely and were probably less often copied. Some people may have destroyed their copies. Others, however, surely preserved copies of these texts, either because they strongly endorsed them or because they vehemently opposed them, yet, thinking that they remained popular, persuasive, and in circulation, would have wanted the means to refute them on an ongoing basis (this is probably why copies remained for Jerome to see at the library in Caesarea). It is safe to assume, however, that copies of texts that were preserved for whatever reason may well have circulated with more innocuous titles than *Against the Christians* or their original title. Constantine's edict was reiterated over a century later

---

19. Harnack, "Porphyrius"; A. Benoit, "Le *Contra Christianos* de Porphryre: Où est la collecte des fragments?" in *Paganisme, judaïsme, christianisme: Influences et affrontements dans le monde antique; Mélanges offerts à Marcel Simon* (Paris: E. de Boccard, 1978), 261–75. D. R. Hagedorn and R. Merkelbach, "Ein neues Fragment aus Porphyrios' *Gegen die Christen,*"*VChr* 20 (1966): 86–90.

20. Andrew Smith and David Wasserstein, eds., *Porphyrii philosophi fragmenta,* Bibl. scriptorum Graec. et Roman. Teubneriana (Stuttgart: Teubner, 1993). See now also the Bompiani edition by Giuseppe Muscolino.

(448) by Theodosius II and Valentinian III and preserved in canon law.[21] Together, these edicts would have also discouraged the recopying of Christian texts that had directly addressed Porphyry's criticisms soon after they were levied, leaving only whatever texts referred to him allusively (such as Methodius's *Aglaophon: On the Resurrection*), since the recognition that they referred to Porphyry would have faded over time. The disappearance of Porphyry's texts is compounded by the anathematization of Origen's teaching from the late fourth to sixth century. Since some of those who wrote in response to Porphyry did so in order to defend Origen against his criticisms, later scribes may have destroyed or have been reluctant to copy these texts, thus eliminating another strand of evidence from the documentary record.

Finally, the extant anti-Christian fragments of Porphyry's texts are so few, and most are so spare, that they provide very little insight into the broader rationale of Porphyry's project. Only three known Christian authors deeply engaged with Porphyry by name in their extant apologetical works, Eusebius, Augustine, and Jerome,[22] and only the first had direct and sustained contemporary access to Porphyry's texts in the original language.[23] A survey of passages in which these authors cite Porphyry—and refute him—shows that one of the prominent themes he addressed, in a way that could be considered anti-Christian, was how to read the texts that Christians valued— an issue directly connected to the philosopher's thoroughgoing critique of Origenist exegesis, to which Methodius responded and which I addressed in the previous chapter. Indeed, Eusebius nicely summarizes this theme in the chapter of the *Ecclesiastical History* devoted to Porphyry's comments on Origen. In the treatises that Porphyry began after he left Plotinus, Eusebius says, he tried "to discredit the Holy Scriptures (*theias graphas*) or set them at variance (*diaballein*)."[24] This project must be seen in the context of the

---

21. E. Schwartz, ed., *Acta Conciliorum Oecumenicorum* (Berlin: de Gruyter, 1927–), 1.1.3–4, 2.3.2, 3 (pp. 119.26; 121.22–26).

22. Augustine cites Porphyry sixty-three times, Eusebius sixty-nine, and Jerome forty-five. Only Cyril of Alexandria comes close to these numbers, citing him twenty times in his treatise against Julian. I have not included him here because this work was chiefly concerned with attacking the emperor, not the philosopher. Those Christian authors who cite Porphyry by name more than once include Aeneas Gazaeus, Didymus the Blind, the Greek Theosophy, John Lydus, John Philoponus, Nemesius of Emesa, a scholiast of Basil, and Theodoret.

23. Jerome's knowledge of Porphyry may depend on Eusebius. The source of Augustine's knowledge is more difficult to ascertain; nevertheless, it's important to realize that his early education in Carthage occurred where Porphyry's brand of Platonism had flourished a century before. I am holding Augustine to the side, however, since Porphyry's anti-Christian works had ostensibly been destroyed by the time Augustine wrote (meaning, if anything, that they circulated under different titles), and Augustine probably read his sources in a Latin translation.

24. I've maintained both shades of meaning because it is clear that both apply.

problems Porphyry had raised concerning how Origen and his followers
had been interpreting these texts (Eus. *HE* 6.19.2), for Origen had claimed
that the divine authorship of scripture—from Hebrew Bible to the emerging New Testament canon—meant that they could and should be read as a
"coherent and organic whole" (*PA* pr. 10).[25] And an analysis of passages that
specifically refer to Porphyry in these three authors shows that Porphyry
devoted significant attention to discrediting some texts and pointing out contradictions between the scriptures.[26] For example, Eusebius attests that in the
"fourth part of the case (*hupotheseōs*) against us," Porphyry claimed that Jewish scripture was not an accurate historical record,[27] a criticism that Jerome
indicates extended to the book of Daniel, which the philosopher declared
was a forgery and should not "be thought of as belonging to the Hebrew
Scriptures."[28] Here we can see Porphyry's concern with the rules of exegesis
that had been part of his school's tradition since Ammonius: as we saw in
chapters 2 and 3, once a good edition of a text has been produced, the next
step before interpretation is ascertaining its authenticity. In this case, aspects
of the book of Daniel indicated to Porphyry that it was not the ancient
history of the Jews among the Babylonians (sixth century BCE), but rather
a veiled account of more recent events during the reign of Antiochus IV
(second century BCE). These concerns about the condition of Hebrew
scripture prompted Porphyry to argue, as Augustine indicates, that the "law
composed in the Hebrew language" is "obscure and unknown" and that
there is "need to engage in many inquiries into [the] law and the prophets"
in order to understand it.[29]

The fragments of Porphyry's "anti-Christian texts" also provide numerous examples of his drawing attention to contradictions between Hebrew
and Christian scripture and between different books of Christian scripture.
According to Jerome, Porphyry highlighted passages in Jewish scripture
that contradicted Christian doctrine: for example, that Solomon says that

25. See chapter 3, 60 and Trigg, *Origen,* 23, 262, n.38.

26. For this I have used Berchman, *Porphyry against the Christians;* Harnack, "Porphyrius."

27. Jerome and Syncellus (cited by Harnack) concur on the volume number. See frag. 41
Harnack = Eus. *PE* 1.9.20–21: the most accurate history of the Jews is that of Sanchuniathon of
Berytus; frag. 40 Harnack = Eus. *Chron.* pr. ap. Hieron.: Semiramis lived after Moses but was the wife
of Nimrod, whom Gen. 10:1–8 places in the third generation after the flood; frag. 43a Harnack =
Hieron. *Dan.* prol.: a multifaceted study of history is essential to understand the book of Daniel. Porphyry may also have called attention to passages that were problematic on their own: e.g., that God
forbade the knowledge of good and evil (frag. 42 Harnack = Severianus *De mundi creatione,* oratio 6).

28. Frag. 43b Harnack = Hieron. *Dan.* prol.; see also frag. 47 Harnack = Eus. *DE* 6.18.11; frag.
44 Harnack = Hieron. *Matt.* 24:16f.; and frags. 43a, d, g, l, m–r, u–w Harnack, all from Hieron. *Dan.*

29. Aug. *Civ.* 19.23. Here Augustine seems to be paraphrasing Porphyry; the passage occurs
among fragments usually attributed to Porphyry's *Philosophy from Oracles.*

God has no Son, an argument key to undermining the Origenist position that Jesus was not only divine, but God's *logos* incarnate.[30] With respect to critiques of the New Testament, Jerome is the only reliable witness. His references to Porphyry illustrate the philosopher's dim view of the Gospel writers: they were ignorant, made mistakes in quoting Jewish scripture, invented at least some of Jesus' miracles, and behaved immorally,[31] even acting as magicians who used their arts to seduce women.[32] In following such putative leaders, Christians were simple, ignorant, and stupid.[33] He also seems to have suggested that the Gospel record portrayed Jesus doing things that were unsuitable for God, evidence that would have bolstered Porphyry's case against Jesus' divinity.[34] While this information accords with part of Eusebius's description of Porphyry's project in the *Ecclesiastical History,* not one of these fragments yields any more information than Eusebius's description of the philosopher's complaints regarding Origin, his followers, and scriptural exegesis.[35] There is no information whatsoever regarding Porphyry's motivations for writing these treatises, the conclusions that he drew within them, or the goals that he hoped they would achieve. Moreover, even taking into account the possibility that the surrounding commentary of a source text may embody more information about a fragmentary work than the quoted or paraphrased passage itself,[36] it is important to remember that Augustine and Jerome, both writing a century after Porphyry, are more concerned to

---

30. Eccles. Solom. 4:8; frag. 85 Harnack = Aug. *Ep.* 102.28. See also *Chr.* frag. 12 (ap. Epiphan. *Haer.* 51.8).

31. Ignorant: frag. 5 Harnack = Hieron. *Ioel.* 2:28ff.; mistakes citing scripture: frag. 11 Harnack = Hieron. *Dan.* 1; frag. 10 Harnack = Hieron. *Tractatus de psalmo* 77; frag. 9 Harnack = Hieron. *Matt.* 3:3; inventing miracles: frag. 55b Harnack = Hieron. *Quaest. in Gen.* 1:10; immoral behavior: frag. 25 Harnack = Hieron. *Ep.* 130.

32. Frag. 4 (ap. Hieron. *De psalmo* 81).

33. Frag. 5 (ap. Hieron. *Ioel.* on 2.28ff.); frag. 6 (ap. Hieron. *Matt.* on 9.9).

34. Frag. 70 Harnack = Hieron. *Adv. Pelag.* 2:17. See also frags. 81 (ap. Aug. *Ep.* 102.8); 86 (ap. Theophylact. *Enarr. in Joh.* [*PL* 123:1141]); 70 (ap. Hieron. *Adv. Pelag.* 2.17).

35. A few sketchy hints in other sources do corroborate Eusebius's description of Porphyry's exegetical criticisms. For example, a scholiast commenting on Acts 15:20 seems to suggest that Porphyry criticized how the apostles and later authors interpreted the prophets (frag. 8 Harnack = Codex Lawr. [Athos 184 B 64 saccr. x], reproduced in Goltz, Texte und Untersuchungen, Bd. 17.4, p. 41f., fol. 17; see Berchman, *Porphyry against the Christians*), and Didymus the Blind in conjunction with his own exegesis of Ecclesiastes mentions Porphyry's criticism of how Christians "fabricate spiritual explanations and allegories from the literal sense of the text," implying that Christians instead should "don the historical-literary sense of interpretation" (trans. Berchman, *Porphyry against the Christians;* citations of Didymus are from *Commentarii ad eccles.* 9:8–10:20 in Binder, iii. Papyrologische Texte und Abhandlungen 3 [1968], p. 281, 16ff.; and Gronewald, v. Papyrologische Texte und Abhandlungen 24 [1979], p. 38).

36. The dissertation of Ariane Magny at the University of Bristol is an important contribution in this area.

resolve the exegetical and theological issues of their own day than to report on Porphyry's goals and motivations.

In order to identify and assess Porphyry's overarching concerns about Christianity, and how he addressed them, methods beyond studying fragments matched with putative titles must be used. Accordingly, throughout this book I have adopted a different strategy. For example, I used the passage quoted by Eusebius of Caesarea in which Porphyry compared the political and philosophical behavior of Ammonius and Origen as a launching point from which to assess the connections between these three men and the significance of the earlier authors' work for Porphyry. Exploring Ammonius's political and philosophical positions as Porphyry understood them necessitated in turn a study of Plotinus, the man whom Porphyry credited with "bringing the mind of Ammonius to bear" on all matters discussed within his circle. From Plotinus, I then turned to Porphyry himself to see how his Ammonian and Plotinian heritage shaped his conception of his role as a philosopher teaching within the Roman Empire. From this point forward, a series of events unfolds. Although Porphyry himself had brought the philosopher Iamblichus within the Ammonian community, he soon came to differ sharply with his student's theology and the hermeneutics that had produced it. Eusebius's remarks indicate that Porphyry was at the same time engaged with the work of Origen's heirs, men who, however much he might have criticized their interpretation of "plain statements" of the Pentateuch as *ainigmata,* also shared Ammonius's legacy through their adoption of Origen's techniques. Indeed, their shared Ammonian heritage gave Porphyry leverage and authority to criticize Iamblichaeans and Origenists for very similar sins. As chapters 4 and 5 established, Porphyry articulated his opposition to these sectarians in a variety of texts now known as *On Abstinence,* the *Letter to Anebo, On Philosophy from Oracles, On the Return of the Soul,* and *On Images.* Perhaps, as I suggested above, some of these texts were grouped under the heading "Against the Christians" in Eusebius's library. Perhaps this heading also included other treatises elaborating on the additional problems of Christian exegesis mentioned above.

Whatever their titles, Porphyry's texts would have first circulated within the Ammonian community. For example, Porphyry wrote both *On Abstinence* and the *Letter to Anebo* to people associated with Iamblichus's circle. Iamblichus's detailed response to the latter text, often citing Porphyry verbatim, indicates that it reached him when he resided at Daphne near Antioch.[37]

---

37. Since Iamblichus refers to Porphyry as still living, he must have written *On the Mysteries* before Porphyry's death (*terminus ante quem:* 305). See chapter 5 for Iamblichus's residence at Daphne until the reign of Licinius.

Porphyry's challenges to Origenist Christian exegetes were known to Methodius in southwestern Asia Minor late in the third or perhaps early in the fourth century.[38] Eusebius and Pamphilus in Caesarea, Origen's old home, were aware of Porphyry's criticisms of their hero in the early fourth century, well before Eusebius wrote the *Ecclesiastical History*.[39] The Latin authors Lactantius and Arnobius also show intimate familiarity with Ammonian Platonism,[40] and it is likely that Arnobius, at least, who was Lactantius's instructor, came into contact with Porphyry after 268 when he spent some time in Carthage (Porph. *Abst.* 3.4.7).[41]

Once in circulation, however, texts take on a life of their own. The rest of this chapter will argue, on the basis of three eyewitnesses to Diocletian's persecution—Arnobius, Lactantius, and Eusebius—three men also connected to the Ammonian community, that Porphyry's texts gained a readership well beyond the core groups of his community. The evidence comes from a comparison of Arnobius's *Against the Nations* with Lactantius's *Divine Institutes* and Eusebius's *Preparation for the Gospel,* all of which responded to Diocletian's persecution. The audience for Porphyry's arguments came to include the Roman officials and priests who not only sat among other educated auditors of teachers like Iamblichus and Porphyry for their own edification, but also shared the concerns of the latter that the laws and institutions of the Roman state remain sound, and were instrumental in bringing his views to the attention of the court. Among priests of traditional cults and oracle sites, concerns about ritual pollution would have been immediately relevant to their own activities, and in this context they would have seen Christian

---

38. In this case, the date derives from the increasingly anxious tone of Methodius's texts. See chapter 5.

39. As I argued in chapter 5, Porphyry's co-option of Origen likely motivated the early fourth-century attack on Origen from Christians unfamiliar with or unconvinced by the application of Platonist methods and metaphysics to Christian doctrine. To these, Origen and Pamphilus responded in their *Apology* for Origen, which, in turn, served as a source for book 6 of Eusebius's *Ecclesiastical History*. See chapter 5; and R. M. Grant, "Eusebius and His Lives of Origen," in *Forma futuri: Studi in onore di Michele Pellegrino,* ed. Maria Bellis and Michele Pellegrino (Turin: Bottega d'Erasmo, 1975), 635–49.

40. For Arnobius, see Simmons, *Arnobius of Sicca.* Lactantius's familiarity is evident—albeit regrettably unexplored—in his sophisticated appropriation of oracles and Hermetic texts throughout the *Divine Institutes* in his effort to refute the proponents of persecution, Porphyry among them. For Porphyry as Lactantius's chief interlocutor, see Elizabeth DePalma Digeser, *The Making of a Christian Empire: Lactantius and Rome* (Ithaca, NY: Cornell University Press, 1999).

41. Arnobius hailed from Sicca, a town near Carthage. As a condition of his acceptance into the church upon his conversion, his bishop (who would have been the bishop of Carthage) required him to recant his previous position (Hieron. *Chron.* ad ann. 327 *Vir. ill.* 79). *Against the Nations* is the result, and the position Arnobius refutes is that of Porphyry. See Simmons, *Arnobius of Sicca.*

practice as undermining the efficacy and sanctity of traditional rites.[42] Indeed, although the opening lines of Arnobius's *Against the Nations* (1.1),[43] written at the cusp of the fourth century, echo charges against Christians from earlier persecutions, he indicates that their efficacy in justifying religious repression under Diocletian derived from their oracular source. "I have learned that a few,...raving and gibbering," Arnobius reports, "have spoken, prompted as from an oracle: They say that after the Christian *gens* began to exist on earth, the world went to waste, the human race was attacked by many evils, and even the heavenly beings (*caelites*) have been driven out from the earth—since the religious devotions through which they once used to tend to our affairs are being neglected."[44] The source of these charges, in turn, implicated in the persecution the priests, prophets, and theurgists directly involved with these oracles, as well as the recent philosophical arguments reflected in this divination. Once priests became concerned about the possibility of Christian pollution, Roman officials familiar with the teachings of these circles could not have remained uninvolved: government relied on a proper consultation of the auspices before taking action in affairs of state. If these processes were tainted, Roman security was jeopardized. Given the belief among the Hellene Ammonian community that those philosophers who had attained union with the divine had an obligation to advise the sovereign, Porphyry and his colleagues would have had an interest in presenting their concerns to the court. As the rest of this chapter will show, these are precisely the means by which Porphyry's intramural complaints came to affect the empire at large.

For information on the Great Persecution, historians do not usually consult Arnobius,[45] but rather the historical works of Lactantius and Eusebius,

---

42. In using oracle texts as evidence for the attitudes of the prophets, I am not accusing people of cynically manipulating these rituals for their own ideological ends. I assume that the process is more complicated, namely that a prophet approaches the ambiguous signs and symbols or intuitions from which his oracle is inspired with a set of assumptions and preoccupations. It is only natural to assume that oracles might reflect these concerns.

43. Cf. Hieron. *Chron.* ad ann. 327. Although this entry seems to place Arnobius under Constantine, Jerome's later and better-informed *Vir. ill.* 79–80 sets him under Diocletian (284–305). See Simmons, *Arnobius of Sicca,* 90–93; and Y. M. Duval, "Sur la biographie et les manuscrits d'Arnobe de Sicca," *Latomus* 45 (1986): 70–78.

44. Ed. A. Reifferscheid (Vienna, 1875).

45. O. Gigon, "Arnobio: Cristianesimo e mondo romano," in *Mondo classico e cristianesimo* (Rome: Istituto della Enciclopedia Italiana, 1982), 95; H. Le Bonniec, "Tradition de la culture classique," *BAGB* (1974): 207, 213, 218–19; S. Colombo, "Arnobio Afro e i suoi sette libri Adversus nationes," *Did* (1930): 28, 44; and J. Quasten, *Patrology* (Utrecht: Spectrum, 1953), 2: 383–85, saw Arnobius as having written merely a "bookish" polemic. The following argument draws substantially on Elizabeth DePalma Digeser, "Lactantius, Eusebius, and Arnobius: Evidence for the Causes of the Great Persecution," *Studia Patristica* 39 (2006): 33–46.

On the Deaths of the Persecutors and the *Ecclesiastical History.*[46] Nevertheless, each of these three authors wrote apologetic and theological treatises addressing problems and people connected to Diocletian's persecution. For example, the key opponents whom Arnobius addresses in *Against the Nations,* written during this persecution, were the *viri novi,* Hellenes linked to and including Porphyry, a group that once included Arnobius himself.[47] Arnobius, in turn, gives Porphyry's *Philosophy from Oracles* sustained attention, and he connects it to arguments justifying the forcible coercion of Christians. In chapter 4, I argued that Porphyry's treatise interpreted oracles resulting from Apolline, Hermetic, and Chaldaean divination in a way that opposed Iamblichus's theology of the *via universalis.* Arnobius's treatment of Porphyry's treatise implicates it in the arguments supporting persecution. Porphyry's *Philosophy from Oracles* also sets out the Hellene position that Eusebius addresses in the *Preparation for the Gospel,* written during and shortly after the first decade of the fourth century.[48] Eusebius's theological treatise is thus both germane to the Great Persecution and the most abundant repository of fragments from the *Philosophy from Oracles,* which no longer survives intact.[49] Finally, Lactantius's *Divine Institutes* strove to answer the broad issues that Porphyry and the emperors had used against Christians, addressing them in such a way as also to make a sustained case for religious toleration instead of persecution.[50] Surprisingly, no one has ever used these three apologies together

46. See, e.g., N. H. Baynes, "The Great Persecution," *CAH* 12 (1939): 661–77.

47. Simmons, *Arnobius of Sicca,* 7, 11–13, 90–93, 130, 217–18, 261, 286. See also P. F. Beatrice, "Un oracle antichrétien chez Arnobe," in *Mémorial Dom Jean Gribomont,* ed. Y. de Andia et al. (Rome: Institutum Patristicum Augustinianum, 1988), 120–23; P. Courcelle, "La polemique antichrétienne au debut du IVe siècle," *REL* 31 (1953): 257–71, id., "Anti-Christian Arguments and Christian Platonism from Arnobius to St. Ambrose," in *The Conflict between Paganism and Christianity in the Fourth Century,* ed. A. Momigliano (Oxford: Clarendon Press, 1963), 151–92; and E. L. Fortin, "The *Viri novi* of Arnobius and the Conflict between Faith and Reason in the Early Christian Centuries," in *The Heritage of the Early Church,* ed. D. Neimann and M. Schatkin (Rome: Pont. Institutum Studiorum Orientalium, 1973), 197–226.

48. P. Athanassiadi, "Dreams, Theurgy, and Free-Lance Divination," *JRS* 83 (1993): 115–30, esp. 118 incl. n. 18. See also D. S. Wallace-Hadrill, *Eusebius of Caesarea* (London: Mowbray, 1960), 190.

49. Already recognized by J. Stevenson, *Studies in Eusebius* (Cambridge: Cambridge University Press, 1929), 72; F. J. F. Foakes-Jackson, *Eusebius Pamphili* (Cambridge: Heffer, 1933), 48–49, 118, 120–32; Quasten, *Patrology,* 3: 329–30; E. des Places, "Eusèbe de Césarée juge de Platon dans la *Préparation évangélique,*" in *Mélanges de philosophie grecque* (Paris: J. Vrin, 1956), 70; F. W. Norris, "Eusebius on Jesus as Deceiver and Sorcerer," in *Eusebius, Christianity, and Judaism,* ed. H. W. Attridge and G. Hata (Detroit: Wayne State University Press, 1992), 525; and M. Frede, "Eusebius' Apologetic Writings," in *Apologetics in the Roman Empire,* ed. M. Edwards et al. (Oxford: Oxford University Press, 1999), 225–31, reflect the older view.

50. Digeser, *Making of a Christian Empire,* esp. 91–114; A. Wlosok, "Christliche Apologetik gegenüber kaiserlicher Politik bis zu Konstantin," in *Kirchengeschichte als Missiongeschichte* (Munich: Kaiser, 1974), 1: 160; N. Baynes, "The Great Persecution," in *The Cambridge Ancient History,* ed. S.

for evidence illuminating the arguments and agents who made the case for persecution.

The first theme that results from comparing the three treatises is that people were associating Christian pollution and the abrogation of traditional cult with harms to the Roman polity. Arnobius reports the claim that the world had deviated from its laws, evils had plagued the human race, and divine beings had all fled since Christianity began to flourish (1.1). Enumerating the material harms that the gods' anger at the Christians' "wrongful and offensive acts" had caused, besides the gods' banishment (1.3),[51] Arnobius says that Jesus was, to his opponents, a "destroyer of religion" and "author of impiety" because he had diverted people from the traditional cults and so angered the gods (2.2).[52] Christians, from this perspective, were "profane," "impious," "atheist," "ill-omened," and "irreligious,"[53] and Christianity "an accursed and ill-omened religion, full of sacrilege and impiety, polluting... the sacred ceremonies established long ago" (1.25).[54] These descriptions mirror concerns derived from Porphyry's treatises: worship of the human Jesus through the sacrament of the Eucharist had attracted harmful daemons into the cities; in turn, the pollution of urban space prevented the efficacy of rites directed toward the gods and beneficent daemons.

Eusebius's *Preparation for the Gospel* begins by quoting a "certain Hellene" (1.2), now recognized as Porphyry,[55] voicing the same concerns. Eusebius's source says that Christians are "impious" and "atheists" for apostatizing from the "ancestral gods" (τῶν πατρίων) "by whom every nation and every state is sustained" (δι᾽ ὧν πᾶν ἔθνος καὶ πᾶσα πόλις συνέστηκεν). "Deserting the customs of their forefathers," to what "kind of punishments would they *not* justly be subjected?"[56] This fragment not only summarizes Porphyry's opinion that Christians have wrongly abandoned Jewish and

---

A. Cook et al. (Cambridge: Cambridge University Press, 1981), 650; and Quasten, *Patrology,* 2: 396. But see R. Pichon, *Lactance: Etude sur le mouvement philosophique et religieux sous le règne de Constantin* (Paris, Librairie Hachette, 1901), 55–57.

51. Cf. Arn. 1.4, 13, 16, 17, 24, 26; 3.11, 36; 5.15.

52. Cf. Arn. 1.36; 2.3.

53. Arn. 1.2; 1.26, 29; 4.30.

54. Cf. Arn. 1.29.

55. Harnack, "Porphyrius," 45; and U. von Wilamowitz-Möllendorff, "Ein Bruchstück aus der Schrift des Porphyrius gegen die Christen," *ZNTW* 1 (1900): 101–5. Harnack thought that this passage was a fragment of Porphyry's *Against the Christians,* but since it raises issues that Eusebius discusses when addressing the *Phil. or.,* it should be assigned to the latter work. Cf. R. Wilken, "Pagan Criticism of Christianity: Greek Religion and Christian Faith," in *Early Christian Literature and the Classical Intellectual Tradition,* ed. W. Schoedel and R. Wilken (Paris: Editions Beauchesne, 1979), 127.

56. Ed. K. Mras (Berlin, 1954); trans. E. H. Gifford (Oxford, 1903) with modifications. See also *PE* 4.1.

Roman law;[57] it also directly rebuts Origen by paraphrasing a passage from the theologian's *On First Principles*. In that text, Origen had argued that the divinity and coherence of the scriptures is evident from people's abandoning their native laws for those of Jesus (*PA* 4.1.1).[58] Like Arnobius, Eusebius develops the theme about Christian impiety as he addresses it throughout his apology. He notes two further accusations, that Christians are "profane," and that the gods have vanished and the oracles declined since the teachings of Jesus began to spread.[59] Finally, Lactantius, whose *Divine Institutes* reflects the persecution in progress,[60] says that motivating the violence are charges that Christian practice had forced the gods to abandon the empire (4.27.7) and that Christians had violated divine law, committing sacrilege by avoiding traditional cult (1.21.4–6).

In itself, the association of Christianity with harm to the Roman polity is not new: even Arnobius observes that the attacks were old (3.1). For example, during Decius's reign certain officials blamed Christian apostasy from the gods for causing incessant warfare, plague, famine, and drought.[61] Decius demanded, not persecution per se, but a *supplicatio:* that is, he wanted all Romans to sacrifice, no doubt to seek divine help in overcoming the problems for which some held Christians responsible.[62] Martyrs resulted from Christian defiance of the *supplicatio;* thus Christian sources define it as a "persecution."[63] Not long after, at the start of Valerian's reign, an Egyptian theurgist blamed Christians for the malfunction of his rituals, an event that Dionysius of Alexandria links to subsequent persecution (Eus. *HE* 7.10.4).

A salient difference between the religious violence during the mid-third century and that which erupted under Diocletian, however, is that the gods through oracles appeared to be implicated in the attacks on Christians. The devotion to theurgy and divination among Iamblichaeans makes this feature especially important. In particular, the emperor Constantine, in his 324 Edict to the Provincials (ap. Eus. *VC* 2.49–54), describes a prophecy in 299 from

---

57. See chapter 5.

58. See chapter 3. This paraphrase of Origen makes the attribution of this fragment to Porphyry even more likely. It is unlikely that Eusebius would himself have parodied Origen in this context, and the critique of Origen that the passage contains points directly to Porphyry.

59. Eus. *PE* 4.1; 5.1. At 3.13.3–4 Eusebius admits that Christians are apostates (ἀποστάτας) and deserters (φυγάδας) from paganism and that an oracle has called them profane (βέβηλοι).

60. E.g., Lact. *Inst.* 5.1.6; 5.9.4; 5.11.

61. *Ad Dem.* 2–3; trans. *ANF.*

62. For this insight, I thank Frances Hahn's work. Decius's universal call to sacrifice was made possible by Caracalla's 212 edict that made citizens of virtually all the empire's inhabitants.

63. Cf., e.g., Eus. *HE* 6.39.1.

Daphne near Antioch,[64] where Iamblichus was then resident. It occurred just after Christian ministers in the Antioch palace had crossed themselves during the auspices, and the haruspex was unable to read the signs. According to Constantine, "Apollo, from a dark alcove and a certain inner chamber and not out of a human being, proclaimed that the 'righteous' on earth were an impediment to his being truthful, and on account of this he was composing false oracles from the tripods" (2.50).[65] Both the experience with the auspices and the prophecy instantiate the underlying assumption that Christian ritual can adversely affect human communication with the gods, as Porphyry's *On Abstinence* had claimed. Witnessed by the emperor Galerius, the oracle at Daphne was theurgic and telestic (associated with the god's statue).[66] Once one of the diviners linked the god's "righteous" with Christians, Constantine continues, Diocletian issued "bloody" edicts against them (2.51). The first decree was his decision to flog any Christian courtier who refused to sacrifice (Lact. *Mort.* 10).

The best-known anti-Christian oracle associated with Diocletian's persecution came from Apollo at Didyma in 303. Lactantius says that the emperor, pressured by Galerius, had listened to arguments favoring persecution all winter, but only the god finally persuaded him to legislate against the practice

64. Eus. *VC* 2.49: ὡς πάντων ὁμοῦ τῶν θείων τε καὶ ἀνθρωπίνων πραγμάτων εἰρηνευομένων ed. Ivar Heikel (Leipzig, 1902). This information sets the oracle before 299, when Diocletian punished Christians in the army and court. For the date of the army purge, see T. D. Barnes, *Constantine and Eusebius* (Cambridge, MA: Harvard University Press, 1981), 18–19; P. Davies, "The Origin and Purpose of the Persecution of A.D. 303," *JThS* n. s. 40 (1989): 91–93; and R. W. Burgess, "The Date of the Persecution of Christians in the Army," *JThS* n. s. 48 (1997): 471–504.

65. Eus. *VC* 2.50: τὸν Ἀπόλλω τὸ τηνικαῦτα ἔφασαν ἐξ ἄντρου τινὸς καὶ σκοτίου μυχοῦ οὐχὶ δ' ἐξ ἀνθρώπου χρῆσαι, ὡς ἄρα οἱ ἐπὶ τῆς γῆς δίκαιοι ἐμπόδιον εἶεν τοῦ ἀληθεύειν αὐτόν, καὶ διὰ τοῦτο ψευδεῖς τῶν τριπόδων τὰς μαντείας ποιεῖσθαι. τοῦτο γάρ τοι ἡ ἱερεία αὐτοῦ, κατηφεῖς τοὺς πλοκάμους ἀνεῖσα ὑπὸ μανίας τ' ἐλαυνομένη, τὸ ἐν ἀνθρώποις κακὸν ἀπωδύρετο. ἀλλ' ἰδώμεν ταῦτα εἰς ὁποῖον τέλος ἐξώκειλε.

66. Elizabeth DePalma Digeser, "An Oracle of Apollo at Daphne and the Great Persecution," *CPh* 99 (2004): 57–77. See F. Heim, "L'animation des statues d'aprés les apologistes du IIIe siècle," *REL* 70 (1992): 22–23; and C. van Liefferinge, *La théurgie des Oracles chaldaïques à Proclus* (Liège: Centre International d'Etude de la Religion Grecque Antique, 1999), 12–13, 87–97, 268–74. Arnobius's description of the charges against Christians, described above, may also be a theurgic prophecy: he claims that his opponents *insanire* and *bacchari*—two verbs for speech closely related to prophecy—and then observes that they spoke as prompted from an oracle. Not all theurgic prophecy was telestic or associated with a statue: as Porphyry's *Philosophy from Oracles* demonstrates, an oracle could occur when "an emanation from the heavenly power, having entered into an organized and living body, uses the soul as a basis, and through the body, as its organ, utters speech." Frag. 349 ap. Eus. *PE* 5.8. Cf. frags. 347–48 ap. Eus. *PE* 5.7.6–8.10. Citations of Porphyry's fragments, other than from *Chr.*, follow A. Smith and D. Wasserstein, eds., *Porphyrii philosophi fragmenta* (Stuttgart: Teubner, 1993).

of Christianity that February (*Mort.* 11). Lactantius does not repeat the oracle, however, saying only that Apollo responded as the "Christians' enemy."[67]

Other less famous oracles against Christians also circulated at this time. For example, Zeus at Dodona called Christians *profani* (Arn. 1.26).[68] Porphyry's *Philosophy from Oracles,* cited by both Eusebius and Lactantius, is the best source for these oracles, although their anti-Christian character is more evident from Augustine's ample quotations in the *City of God.*[69] Apollo at Didyma, for instance, called a Christian woman impious and polluted and asserted that Jesus was justly executed.[70] Another oracle, also referenced by Eusebius, calls Jesus pious but rejects Jesus' divinity. It claims that his soul, like the souls of other pious humans, was "endowed after death with the immortality it deserved." Deriving from Hecate, this oracle was probably theurgic.[71] Connecting Christian veneration of a human being with pollution, Hecate asserts that ignorant Christians worship Jesus' soul. Porphyry's introduction to this oracle highlights the problems of Christian worship, saying that while "the gods have pronounced Christ to have been extremely devout... the Christians, by their account, are polluted and contaminated and entangled in error." Before quoting Hecate's oracle, Porphyry then listed some of what Augustine called "slanders of the gods against the Christians" (which the bishop omits). Porphyry also discussed another oracle of Hecate, again likely theurgic: according to the goddess, the gods hated Christians because Jesus' soul entangled them "in error," something that fate imparted to other souls as well.[72]

These prophecies share a number of themes. They accuse Christians of being profane, impious, and polluted. Christians are not only ignorant, but they are entangled in error, prevented by fate from knowing God. Jesus was pious and devout, but the oracles also blame him for Christian error and

---

67. Ed. J. L. Creed (Oxford: Clarendon Press, 1984).

68. See Beatrice, "Un oracle antichrétien," 107–11.

69. Cf. Simmons, *Arnobius of Sicca,* chap. 8.

70. Porph. *Phil. or.* frag. 343 ap. Aug. *Civ.* 19.22.17–23.17 (ed. B. Dombart and A. Kalb [Leipzig, 1928]). Lact. *Inst.* 4.13.11 cites a portion of this in a somewhat altered form, but the texts are assumed to reflect the same oracle. Cf. Porphyry of Tyre, *De philosophia ex oraculis haurienda: Librorum reliquiae,* ed. G. G. Wolff (Hildesheim: G. Olms, 1962), 183–85; and Smith and Wasserstein, *Porphyrii philosophi fragmenta,* 393.

71. R. Berchman, "Arcana Mundi between Balaam and Hecate," in *SBL Seminar Papers,* ed. D. Lull (Atlanta: Scholars Press, 1989), 148. Although this oracle comes from the *DE,* not the *PE,* the former text also addresses concerns that Porphyry raised in the *Phil. or.* Both functioned as a two-volume introduction to Christianity: the *PE* explained why Christians had left the path of the Hellenes, the *DE* why they had abandoned the path of the Jews. Porphyry raised both issues ap. Eus. *PE* 1.2.

72. Porph. *Phil. or.* frag. 345 (ap. Eus. *DE* 3.6.39–7.2) and frag. 345a (ap. Aug. *Civ.* 19.23.43–73); trans. H. Bettenson (London, 1984).

say that he was justly executed. As a human being, they claim, he should not be worshipped. Since worshipping Jesus involves the Eucharistic ritual, these oracles link Christian pollution with blood sacrifice and the presence of harmful daemons. This connection explains the oracles' accusation that the gods hated Jesus' "gift," which was deadly to Christian souls. Finally, the oracles charge Christians with harming the world, its peoples, and the gods, accusations compatible with the belief that Christian rituals brought evil daemons into the cities. Specifically, the oracles blame polluted Christians for the gods' exile from the world and for Apollo's false prophecies. Not only does the connection between pollution and divine desertion appear after the aborted Antiochene auspices in 299 (Lact. *Mort.* 10), but also in Porphyry's statement that "the plague has attacked the city" for so many years because "Asclepius and the other gods" are "no longer resident among us." Ever "since Jesus began to be honoured," Porphyry claims, "no one ever heard of any public assistance from the gods."[73]

Described by Lactantius as devoted to divination,[74] the emperor Diocletian acted quickly, forcefully, and predictably to purge Christians from the army and court when Apollo's oracle blamed them for faulty divination in 299. His decision to issue general edicts of persecution in 303 after discovering the hostility Apollo at Didyma bore toward Christians also makes sense in this context. Just because Diocletian's behavior in these instances is understandable, however, does not mean that persecution was inevitable. If this were the case, the oracles would have simply been a stimulus for a premeditated anti-Christian policy. Although some historians have interpreted tetrarchic ideology as supporting such a strategy,[75] these arguments overlook the significance of the high-ranking Christian ministers present at the aborted auspices in Antioch in 299.[76] These officials were likely to have been Diocletian's appointees. In Nicomedia, Diocletian had invited the Christian Lactantius to teach rhetoric (Hieron. *Vir. ill.* 80). These appointments reveal not the tetrarchy's innate propensity for persecution, but an inclusive policy

73. Porph. ap. Eus. *PE* 5.1.9f.: Νυνὶ δὲ θαυμάζουσιν εἰ τοσοῦτον ἐτῶν κατείληφε τὴν πόλιν, Ἀσκληπιοῦ μὲν ἐπιδημίας καὶ τῶν ἄλλων θεῶν μηκέτ' οὔσης. Ἰησοῦ γὰρ τιμωμένου οὐδεμις τις θεῶν δημοσίας ὠφελείας ᾔσθετο (attributed by Harnack to Porphyry's *Chr.* [frag. 80]).
74. Lact. *Mort.* 10.1; S. Montero, *Política y adivinación en el Bajo Imperio romano* (Brussels: Latomus, 1991), 59.
75. E.g., Frank Kolb, "L'ideologia tetrarchica e la politica religiosa di Diocleziano," in *I cristiani e l'impero nel IV secolo*, ed. G. Bonamente and A. Nestori (Rome: EGLE, 1988), 17–44; K. Stade, "Der Politiker Diokletian und die letze grosse Christenverfogung" (Diss., Frankfurt, 1926).
76. Lact. *Mort.* 10.1–2; *Inst.* 4.27.4.

toward Christians until the events in 299.[77] Diocletian's attitude changed in response to the oracles and the insistence of Galerius, who may have been even more influenced by oracles than his senior partner. Even Galerius, however, was unconcerned with Christians until the problems with the oracle and auspices in 299. Although some historians have seen him as a prime mover in the persecution, gradually pressuring Diocletian as his own power and influence grew stronger,[78] this position ignores the role and attitudes of the people associated with these anti-Christian oracles.[79]

The emperor's attitudes may have been the persecution's immediate cause. The underlying cause, however, was the activity of augurs, prophets, haruspices, priests, priestesses, and theurgists whose prejudices against Christians led them to read ambiguous signs in a certain way when asked to speak with and for the gods.[80] The character of the recorded oracles in the sources thus reveal a strong anti-Christian faction among such personnel in the late third century. Constantine's account of the oracle at Daphne supports this conclusion. He says that the presence in the empire of the "righteous" people—later identified as Christians—was what "Apollo's priesthood . . . were lamenting as the evil within human society" (ap. Eus. VC 2.50). This faction was especially influential because virtually all people, including many Christians, believed that the divine spoke to humanity in such a way.[81]

The oracles for which these Hellene religious professionals were responsible reveal their belief that Christians were polluted, ignorant, estranged from God, and responsible for the world's current problems, because the gods were in exile, forced to flee by evil daemons whom blood sacrifices venerating the human Jesus had attracted. Each of these issues, in turn, had been addressed in Porphyry's "anti-Christian texts" of the late third century. These identified important discrepancies in Christian scripture, discredited the proficiency of the Gospel writers as well as their interpreters, and undermined prophecies that Christians claimed predicted the work and death of Jesus. Reflecting a thoroughgoing critical exegesis of Jewish and Christian scripture, all of these claims related directly to Porphyry's efforts to undermine Origen's reading of scripture as a coherent whole. In addition to Porphyry's "anti-Christian texts," *On Abstinence,* written to dissuade Castricius from adopting a Iamblichaean approach to the philosophical life, also

---

77. Lactantius probably joined the court in 299: Lact. *Inst.* 5.2.2 with 4.27.4–5.

78. Barnes, *Constantine and Eusebius,* 19, 21; Baynes, "Great Persecution," 664–69.

79. Beatrice, "Un oracle antichrétien," esp. 107–9, is a notable exception.

80. Cf. E. R. Dodds, *The Greeks and the Irrational* (Berkeley: University of California Press, 1951), 74.

81. E.g., Lact. *Inst.* 1.7.

shaped late third-century attitudes. In this text, deeply concerned with the effects of pollution on the human soul, Porphyry established a taxonomy of daemons while considering what sacrifices are appropriate for the philosopher. For Porphyry, good daemons included "transmitters" who carried up "our prayers to the gods" and carried "back to us their advice and warnings through oracles" (*Abst.* 2.38.2–3).[82] Good daemons, like Apollo at Daphne, also warned people "so far as they are able" about "dangers impending from the maleficent *daimones*" (2.41.3). Bad daemons, Porphyry cautioned, caused material harm "around the earth" (2.40.1). Magicians, a term that Porphyry had also used for Jesus' apostles, stirred them up "to gratify their lusts," and any interaction with them brought pollution (2.45.1; 2.46.2).[83] Thus, Porphyry reasoned, "priests and diviners" knew that people should avoid "tombs" and "sacrilegious men,... for often something that disturbs the diviner comes from the presence of unclean people"; those polluted by contact with blood or dead bodies could disrupt sacred rites such as divination.[84] This sentence describes precisely the reaction to the Antioch auspices in 299. Porphyry made these arguments against Iamblichaean practice, but they were also relevant to Christians active in the public sphere. Beginning with Justin Martyr, Christians had claimed that the bread and wine consumed as the Eucharist were indeed the flesh and blood of Jesus.[85] Evidence that *On Abstinence* played a role in late third-century anxieties about Christian pollution comes from Methodius's *De cibis*: women in his circle have worried that coming into contact with a dead body made them polluted, and their teacher answered them in a work dependent on this very treatise by Porphyry.

Porphyry's *On Abstinence* and his anti-Christian texts thus created a theological framework that allowed educated people to rationalize and articulate misgivings concerning Christianity. By the late third century, Christians were serving in official positions that involved performing sacrifices and taking auspices. Even if they did not directly participate in them, Christians in local or imperial government would have been expected to attend the rituals

---

82. Trans. Clark; ed. J. Bouffartigue and M. Patillon (Paris, 1979).

83. Cf. Clark, *On Abstinence from Killing Animals,* 157 n. 330: "Sorcerers... were blamed for trying to constrain divine powers, usually for worldly purposes, whereas theurgists claimed to use similar techniques... to purify their souls.

84. *Abst.* 2.43.1; 2.46.2; 2.47.3; 2.50.1.

85. Gospel texts: Matt. 26:26; Mark 14:22; Luke 22:18; John 6:53–56 (see also 1 Cor. 11:24); Justin *1 Apol.* 66. See also Ignatius of Antioch's letter to the Smyrnaeans 7, written in the early second century; Elizabeth DePalma Digeser, "Philosophy in a Christian Empire: From the Great Persecution to Theodosius I," in *The Cambridge History of Philosophy in Late Antiquity,* ed. Lloyd Gerson (Cambridge: Cambridge University Press, 2010), 57–77.

that marked the rhythm of urban life.[86] The situation in Diocletian's palaces offers an excellent window onto this issue. All of the late third-century prophecies against Christians need not have known Porphyry's texts. All the same, some religious professionals shared interests and concerns with Ammonian Hellenes, especially given the Iamblichaeans' interest in theurgy. Accordingly, it is not surprising that the theurgic oracle at Daphne was quick to associate Christians with the emperor's problems taking the auspices, since there is evidence that Porphyry's texts were in circulation there. *On Abstinence* had been directed not only to Porphyry's friend Castricius, who had abandoned vegetarianism for a Iamblichaean way of life, but Iamblichus also seems aware of its arguments in *On the Mysteries* (e.g., 5.1). Moreover, the Roman official Hierocles resided in the city during this period, and, I have argued, drew on Porphyry's "anti-Christian texts" for his *Lover of Truth*.[87] Iamblichus's own work, despite his lack of direct association with the persecution, was hardly Christian-friendly.[88]

Thus when drought struck the Gaetuli or crops failed in Africa (Arn. 1.16), the kind of disasters that *On Abstinence* connected with the activities of evil daemons (2.40), some religious professionals began to participate— with some Ammonian Hellenes—in conversation articulating their anxieties about the growing numbers of Christians at their rituals. Apollo's oracle at Daphne in 299 expressed such anxieties in warning that the god's prophecies were unreliable due to the rising presence of Christians. If Apollo's theurgists hoped that Diocletian would deal forcefully with the problem, they were disappointed in the short term. For after lashing out against Christian soldiers and courtiers in 299, Diocletian refused for three more years to target Christianity further, despite Galerius's pressure (Lact. *Mort.* 10–12). In this policy Diocletian probably had the support of the other members of the tetrarchy, men who were comfortable sharing the political, social, and even religious life of the court with Christians. Constantius and Maximian did not enforce more than the first general edict of persecution, calling for the destruction of Christian buildings and texts. Moreover, their sons, Constantine and Maxentius, rescinded this edict after their usurpations.[89]

---

86. Christian officials "free[d] from agony of mind as regards sacrificing (*to thuein*)": Eus. *HE* 8.1; Christians attending sacrificial and divinatory rites: Lact. *Mort.* 10; E. G. Cuthbert and F. Atchley, *A History of the Use of Incense in Divine Worship* (London: Longman, Green, 1909), 174; the potential involvement of magistrates in sacrificial rites is implicit in Canon 56 of the Council of Elvira. See also Digeser, "Philosophy in a Christian Empire."

87. Digeser, "Porphyry, Julian, or Hierokles?" 466–502.

88. Cf., e.g., *DM* 3.31.

89. Lact. *Mort.* 24.9; Optatus 1.18; Eus. *Mart. Pal.* (S) 12.13f.; Eus. *HE* 8.14; and Barnes, *Constantine and Eusebius,* 38–39.

Acting in the interest of the anti-Christian faction of Hellenes thus required lobbying these ecumenical officials, a group that originally included all of the emperors, to abandon their support for Christians. In this effort, several anti-Christian Hellenes launched an apologetic campaign.[90] The writings of Lactantius, Arnobius, and Eusebius are full of evidence for this interest group. As part of this drive, Lactantius reports that a philosopher and a judge delivered anti-Christian arguments at Diocletian's Nicomedian court shortly before the emperor issued the general edicts of persecution in 303. The judge was Sossianus Hierocles, one of the persecution's chief instigators (Lact. *Mort.* 16.4; *Inst.* 5.2.12). His two-volume *Lover of Truth* derided the inconsistencies in Christian scripture, drawing on Porphyry to do so,[91] and asserted that Christians were wrong to worship the human Jesus (*Inst.* 5.2–3). I have argued elsewhere that the philosopher was Porphyry himself, presenting the *Philosophy from Oracles.*[92] According to Lactantius, he "spewed out (*evomuit*) three books against the Christian religion and name" (*Inst.* 5.2.4). He declared that a philosopher's chief duty "was to undermine people's errors and to call them back to the true path,... to the *cultus* of the gods by whose *numine* and *maiestate* the cosmos is governed, and not to allow ignorant people to be misled by the deceptions of certain others" (5.2.5). Thus he decided "to reveal the light of wisdom to those not seeing it, not only so that they might be healed by resuming the gods' *cultus,*" but also to avert persecution. It was, he claimed, "for the good of human affairs that all people, repressing impious and old-womanish superstition, should be free for legitimate *sacris* and should know by experience that the gods were propitious toward them" (5.2.6–7). It may seem odd that the man who wrote *On Abstinence,* urging Iamblichaeans away from blood sacrifice (e.g., Iambl. *DM*

---

90. Cf. W. H. C. Frend, "Prelude to the Great Persecution: The Propaganda War," *JEH* 38 (1987): 1–18.

91. See Digeser, "Porphyry, Julian, or Hierokles?" 484.

92. Elizabeth DePalma Digeser, "Lactantius, Porphyry, and the Debate over Religious Toleration," *JRS* 88 (1998): 129–46; Wilken, "Pagan Criticism of Christianity," 124. As noted in 5 n. 14 above, T. D. Barnes, "Monotheists All?" *Phoenix* 55 (2001): 158, maintains that Porphyry could not be this philosopher because the one whom Lactantius heard was "blind" (Lact. *Inst.* 5.2.9), and if Porphyry were blind we should certainly have known about his handicap from another source. Leaving aside the very real possibility that Porphyry—who would have been an elderly man of seventy—really was blind from old age (as many elderly Romans must have been before corrective lenses, glaucoma treatments, and cataract surgery), and that Lactantius's passage brilliantly lampoons a pompous old man, Lactantius's description also works as figurative language: for Lactantius, one "who is ignorant of" God, "though he may see, is blind" (*Inst.* 6.9; cf. also *Inst.* 1.1, 5, 8; 2.1, 3, 5; 3.9, 14, 18, 19, 28, 29, 30; 4.16, 19, 20, 26, 27; 5.6, 12, 13, 20, 21, 22; 6.1, 4, 9; 7.3, 13). In a literal reading, pagans (1.8; 2.1, 3; 4.20, 26; 6.1), Jews (4.19), the persecutors (5.13, 20, 21, 22), and Hierocles (5.3) would be blind; indeed, the mental blindness of philosophers (2.5; 3.9, 18, 28, 30), including Plato (3.19) and Cicero (3.14), is a key theme. See also Edwards, "Porphyry and the Christians," 117–18.

5.1–16), endorsed traditional cult practice publicly at court. This work, however, did not address proper worship for ordinary people.[93] Rather, as chapter 4 described, Porphyry's subsequent texts, *On the Return of the Soul, On Images,* and *On Philosophy from Oracles* (or the works now known by these titles), had considered a three-path theology that addressed the needs of ordinary people. Thus, speaking before the emperors, he did not seek "to destroy the customs which prevail among each people" (Porph. *Abst.* 2.33.1). Moreover, as a philosopher who had achieved divine union (*Plot.* 23), Porphyry saw it as his obligation to advise the emperors as they sought to govern justly.[94]

Whether or not Porphyry was the philosopher at Diocletian's court, or simply an acolyte presenting his position, the apologies of Arnobius, Eusebius, and Lactantius testify that the Hellene anti-Christian campaign promoted his texts and Hierocles' positions. The writings of these three apologists mirror those by Porphyry and Hierocles so clearly that the cogency, force, and persuasiveness of the early fourth-century Hellene crusade is manifest. Educated themselves in the Ammonian Hellene tradition, all three Christian authors use the method of "literary retortion" that Porphyry used to such great effect in his "anti-Christian texts."[95] This strategy undermines the opposition's arguments by finding inconsistencies within and between its most important texts. Lactantius, Eusebius, and Arnobius also reveal the importance and novelty of the *Philosophy from Oracles,* which preoccupies each of them in their work. The three apologists are also familiar with Porphyry's ideas from texts that we know under different titles. Chapter 4 discussed *On the Return of the Soul* as a treatise that had challenged and presented an alternative theology to Iamblichus's doctrines, but it was known to these Christian authors together with *On Images.*[96] In fragments attributed to *On Images,* Porphyry claims that perceiving the gods' attributes in their statues could lead the human mind toward genuine insights regarding God's powers,

---

93. *Abst.* 1.27.1; trans. Clark: "My discourse will not offer advice to every human way of life: not to those who engage in banausic crafts, nor to athletes of the body, nor to soldiers, nor sailors, nor orators, nor to those who have chosen the life of public affairs, but to the person who has thought about who he is and whence he has come and where he should try to go."

94. See chapters 4–5.

95. See Simmons, *Arnobius of Sicca,* 14, 226, 244.

96. The traces of Porphyry's "anti-Christian texts," *Philosophy from Oracles,* and *On Images* in Arnobius convinced Beatrice, "Un oracle antichrétien," 114–15, that the *Philosophy from Oracles* actually comprised all of them. He also argued in "Towards a New Edition of Porphyry's Fragments against the Christians," in *Sophiēs maiētores,* ed. M.-O. Goulet-Cazé et al. (Paris: Institut d'études augustiniennes, 1992), 348–49, that these three texts were part of *Against the Christians.* But Hierocles' dependency on *Chr.* and its concern for scriptural exegesis may indicate otherwise. See Digeser, "Porphyry, Julian, or Hierokles?" 478–84.

if not directly to God.[97] In response, the three apologists decry the notion that images could direct anyone to a concept of true divinity. Nothing could be "more violently unreasonable," Eusebius says, "than to assert that lifeless materials... bear representations of the light of the gods and manifestations of their heavenly and ethereal nature." These, Eusebius says, are "modern sophistries" (*PE* 3.7).[98] The Hellenes assert that they "worship and reverence" in images "those whom sacred dedication introduces and causes to inhabit" in them (6.17), according to Arnobius. But how, Arnobius wonders, can they "possibly mean to say that by these images the *praesentiam* of these divinities is represented" (6.8)? "Who... is so *ineptus,*" Lactantius adds, as to think that "there is something of God in *simulacra?*" (*Inst.* 2.2.16).[99] Porphyry's *Philosophy from Oracles* had claimed that not only a statue's symbols, but even the very rites to the gods bore a symbolic meaning.[100] This symbol, properly interpreted, brought divine wisdom.[101] Lactantius appropriates the argument, condemning images of the gods, but asserting that Jewish rituals carry a *figura* or image of such wisdom for Christians who know how to read them.[102] This argument closely resembles Methodius's position in the *Symposium*.

Finally, all three authors know Porphyry's *On the Return of the Soul*. In this text, Porphyry claimed that, despite exhaustive research, he had never found one path by which the souls of all people might return to their source.[103] The one certain path that he had found was, he thought, the property only of philosophers.[104] It was not Christianity, and it was not Iamblichus's *via universalis* with its blood sacrifices.[105] For people unable to pursue philosophy, as most people—including most Christians—were, Porphyry argued that theurgy cleansed the spirited portion of the soul, releasing it from the stain of fate, thus from the pollution that Jesus worship conferred.[106] Responding to this claim, Eusebius asks why Porphyry told us "to practice magic

---

97. Cf. Berchman, "Arcana Mundi," 150; *Agal.* frag. 351 ap. Eus. *PE* 3.7.1f.

98. Note that Eusebius's *PE* is the principal source for the fragments of Porphyry's *Agal.* (including this one), as well as for the *Phil. or.* His description of these arguments as "modern" coheres with Arnobius's label *viri novi* for Porphyrian Hellenes. Indeed, Iamblichus makes a similar criticism at *DM* 7.5, railing against Hellenes who refuse to use the time-honored rituals.

99. Ed. S. Brandt and G. Laubmann (Vienna, 1890–97).

100. Frag. 326 (ap. Eus. *PE* 4.22.15–23)—only one of many similarities in theme between *Agal.* and the *Phil. or.*

101. Cf. *Phil. or.* frag. 303 (ap. Eus. *PE* 4.6.2–7.2).

102. See Lact. *Inst.* 4.26.38–41 for a good example of this type of argument.

103. Frag. 302 (ap. Aug. *Civ.* 10.32.16–21).

104. Frag. 287 (ap. Aug. *Civ.* 10.27.8–25).

105. Aug. *Civ.* 10.32.38.

106. Frags. 288–90, 292–93 (ap. Aug. *Civ.* 10.9.13–45).

[Eusebius's term for theurgy] and pursue forbidden arts"? Why, the bishop wonders, did Porphyry not urge Christians to become philosophers, since the "path of virtue and philosophy is sufficient for a happy and blessed life" (*PE* 5.14). Contrary to Porphyry's claim that he could not find a universal path for liberating the soul, Eusebius avers that "Jesus Christ provided the way of escape for all men, by preaching to all alike, Greeks and Barbarians, a cure for their ancestral malady and deliverance from their bitter and inveterate bondage" (4.21).[107] Describing his adversaries, the *viri novi,* as men who combine Platonist and Chaldaean wisdom, Arnobius points clearly to *Return of the Soul* (Arn. 2.11, 15 62).[108] Finally, Lactantius follows Eusebius: "The one hope for people, the one *salus,* has been laid down in this *doctrina* that we [Christians] maintain.... This, this is that which all philosophers looked for throughout their entire lives but still never discovered, understand, hold, or value, since they either retained *pravam religionem* or did away with it altogether. Therefore let all those depart who do not provide for human life but disturb it" (*Inst.* 3.30.3–5).[109]

"Let their *pontifices* come into the public," says Lactantius, "let them invite us to the assembly. Let them urge the acceptance of the cults of their gods; let them persuade us that there are many by whose *numine* and *providentia* all things are ruled; let them explain the *fons,* what the *ratio* is; let them make known what reward there is in the religion, what penalty awaits for scorning it; why they want people to venerate them; what, if they are [already] blessed, human piety will contribute to them. Let them confirm all these points, not by their own vehement assertion... but by some divine testimonies.... Let them unsheathe the swords of their smartest men.... Let them teach in this way if they have any confidence of the truth. Let them speak, let them open their mouths; let them dare... to discuss with us something of this sort, and... their error and foolishness will be ridiculed" (*Inst.* 5.19.8–14). Such derision was precisely the attitude of Arnobius, Eusebius, and Lactantius himself. These apologists did not set out to assess the causes and motivations of the Great Persecution. Nevertheless, when the texts of all three are read together, they reveal a loose network of Hellenes, intellectuals, and religious professionals working behind the scenes. These Hellenes, having gradually come to fear the growing presence of Christians in the empire, turned to

---

107. The link between this point and the Greek and barbarian theme is, as J. J. O'Meara, *Porphyry's Philosophy from Oracles in Augustine* (Paris: Etudes augustiniennes, 1959), and Beatrice, "Towards a New Edition," 347–55, argued, an example of the similarity between the *Phil. or.* and *Regr.*

108. Simmons, *Arnobius of Sicca,* 286.

109. Here Lact. unites themes from *Agal.* (see frag. 351 ap. Eus. *PE* 3.6–7) and *Regr.*

oracles and apology in their effort to rectify the situation. Ironically, their concerns had been fed by arguments initially crafted to settle an intramural disagreement among several branches of the same philosophical sect, the circle of Hellenes who could all trace their intellectual lineage to Ammonius Saccas.

In the short term, the anti-Christian Hellene campaign succeeded. After the philosopher and Hierocles spoke in Nicomedia, and after the further advice of Didymaean Apollo, Diocletian issued edicts of persecution requiring Christians to put down Christianity and "return to the institutions of their ancestors" (Lact. *Mort.* 11, 34).[110] The traditional rite that these edicts tried to instill in practice was simply the burning of incense as a ritual act, primarily by compelling the Christian leadership to do so. Since Lactantius notes that altars were placed in courts "so that every litigant might offer incense before his cause could be heard" (*Mort.* 15), the emperor's interest in promoting sacrificial rites extended further than the Christian population per se.

By 311, however, the anti-Christian campaign had largely failed. Not only did Diocletian's western colleagues refuse fully to implement his edicts,[111] Maximian and Constantius's pro-Christian sons, Maxentius and Constantine, seized power after Diocletian and his Herculean colleague retired in 305 (Lact. *Mort.* 24, 26).[112] Finally, on his deathbed, Galerius admitted failure in his 311 edict of toleration, allowing Christian worship and replacing sacrifice with prayer as the proof of a citizen's loyalty (Lact. *Mort.* 34). This policy not only recognized the reasons Christians had for abstaining from sacrifice, encouraging them to engage in the prayers for the empire's well-being that, as apologists had always argued, Christians were ready and willing to offer. The policy also achieved a certain consensus, since it was consonant with Porphyrian Platonists' reservations regarding blood sacrifice. This is not to say that the Iamblichaean position was immediately discredited, for Maximin Daia, the tetrarch of the east, continued to pursue an anti-Christian policy supported by Platonist theurgists especially around Antioch (Eus. *HE* 9.2–3).[113]

---

110. Measures designed to repress Christianity included demolishing churches, burning scripture, denying Christians the rights of citizenship, and imprisoning clergy. See Lact. *Mort.* 12–13, 15; and Eus. *HE* 8.2.5.

111. G. E. M. de Sainte-Croix, "Aspects of the 'Great' Persecution," *HThR* 47 (1954): 75–113.

112. Digeser, "Philosophy in a Christian Empire."

113. For the theurgic activities of Maximin Daia's associates, see Digeser, "Oracle of Apollo," 57–77; and O. Nicholson, "The Pagan Churches of Maximinus Daia and Julian the Apostate," *JEH* 45 (1994): 1–10. See also Digeser, "Philosophy in a Christian Empire."

Nevertheless, the ground had eroded from under the anti-Christian position by 313. In 312, conquering under the sign of the Christian god (Lact. *Mort.* 44), Constantine ousted Maxentius from Rome, and within the year he and Licinius, Galerius's replacement in the tetrarchy, had issued a proclamation reiterating Galerius's edict of toleration and allying against Maximin Daia, who was quickly defeated. After sharing power with Licinius for little more than a decade, Constantine moved against the eastern emperor, defeating him and attaining sole power in 324. Although the first Christian emperor's regime is portrayed in brightly Christian colors by Eusebius, that he faced no serious opposition from Licinius's supporters suggests a more nuanced, tolerant approach in practice. For example, although Constantine's legislation brought Christian worshippers and leaders to a position of equality under Roman law, his edicts also carved out a protective space for Platonists who preferred celibacy and venerated the sun.[114] It is also likely that Constantine's much disputed putative edict against sacrifice (*to thuein*), if it was enacted, targeted blood sacrifice only. This is the meaning of *to thuein* as Porphyry defined it (*Abst.* 2.5.3) and would have been a measure that would have garnered the support of Porphyrian Platonists. Being antisacrifice in the aftermath of the arguments culminating in the Great Persecution should not be confused with being "antipagan" or anti-Hellene. Although it might be construed as being anti-Iamblichaean, Constantine's request that Iamblichus's student Sopater become court philosopher after 324—thus formalizing the advisory relationship Platonist philosophers had enjoyed with emperors since Plotinus—was clearly a gesture of conciliation aimed at the Iamblichaean community.[115]

This book has argued that the ideas and networks of a small group of philosophers had a dramatic influence on the religious and political culture of the Roman Empire in the third and early fourth centuries. In the early third century, the remarkably fluid intellectual culture of Alexandria fostered a climate in which Platonists who considered Jesus divine (like the Christians Origen and Anatolius) and Platonists who did not (like the Christian Ammonius and the Hellenes Plotinus and Iamblichus) could study with, learn from, and influence one another. In their efforts to craft a philosophy without conflicts that integrated the diverse traditions of their multiethnic, pan-Mediterranean culture, they developed sophisticated exegetical strategies that they deployed to distinguish sacred texts from profane. By midcentury, Plotinus had taken these techniques and way of life to Rome where he

---

114. Digeser, *Making of a Christian Empire,* chap. 5.
115. Digeser, "Philosophy in a Christian Empire."

cultivated his own circle, developed important connections to the imperial court, and eventually introduced his most famous student, Porphyry of
Tyre, to the doctrines of Ammonius. Porphyry then initiated Iamblichus
within these traditions, but the two men eventually split over the extent to
which philosophers should involve themselves with material sacrifices and
the salvation of ordinary persons. For Porphyry, the similarities between
the positions of Iamblichus and Origen's followers—both endorsing blood
sacrifice, both concerned with the salvation of all, both interested in a wide-
ranging philosophy without conflicts—derived from the same problem, an
inability to apply properly the rules of exegesis and textual criticism that
were the hallmark of the group's progenitor, Ammonius Saccas. The texts
and arguments that Porphyry generated in an effort to return these sectarians to orthodoxy circulated far beyond the walls of their schools to temples
and basilicae where priests and officials heard them and became increasingly
convinced that Christianity was undermining the fabric of the Roman state.
In taking their concerns to Diocletian's court, these men launched the opening salvo of the Great Persecution.

❧ BIBLIOGRAPHY

Ancient Sources

Adamantius: Dialogue on the True Faith in God. Translated by Robert A. Pretty. Leuven: Peeters, 1997.

Ammianus Marcellinus. *Ammianus Marcellinus.* Translated by John C. Rolfe. 3 vols. Cambridge, MA: Harvard University Press, 1939.

Ammonius. *In Porphyrii Isagogen sive quinque voces.* Edited by A. Busse. CAG 4.3. Berlin, 1891.

Arnobius of Sicca. *Adversus nationes libri vii.* Edited by August Reifferscheid. CSEL 4. Vienna: C. Gerold, 1875.

———. *The Case against the Pagans.* Translated by George E. McCracken. 2 vols. New York: Newman Press, 1949.

Athenagoras. *Athenagoras: 'Legatio' and 'De resurrectione'.* Edited and translated by W. R. Schoedel. Oxford: Clarendon Press, 1972.

Augustine. *Contra Iulianum (opus imperfectum).* Edited by Ernst Kalinka and Michela Zelzer. Vienna: Hoelder-Pichler-Tempsky, 1974–2004.

———. *De civitate dei.* Edited by B. Dombart and A. Kalb. Turnholt: Brepols, 1955.

———. *Sermones.* Edited by J. P. Migne. PL 38. Paris, 1685.

Bibliothecae apostolicae Vaticanae codicum manuscriptorum catalogus. Edited by Stephan Evodius Asseman and Joseph Simon Asseman. Rome, 1759. Reprint, Paris: Maisonneuve frères, 1926.

Cassius Dio Cocceianus. *Roman History.* Edited by Herbert Baldwin Foster. Translated by Earnest Cary. Cambridge, MA: Harvard University Press, 1968–80.

The Chaldaean Oracles: Text, Translation, and Commentary. Edited and translated by Ruth Majercik. Leiden: Brill, 1989.

———. As *Oracles chaldaïques.* Edited and translated by Eduard des Places. Paris: Les Belles Lettres, 1971.

Chronica minora. Vol. 1. Monumenta Germaniae Historica: Scriptores. Edited by Theodore Mommsen. Berlin: Weidmann, 1961.

Clement of Alexandria. *Stromateis 1–3.* Translated by J. Ferguson. Fathers of the Church 85. Washington, DC: The Catholic University of America Press, 1991.

———. *Les stromates.* Edited and translated by Claude Mondésert and Marcel Caster. SC 1–2, 4–7. Paris: Editions du Cerf, 1951–.

Collatio legum Mosaicarum et Romanarum. In *Manichaean Texts from the Roman Empire,* edited by Iain Gardner and Samuel N. C. Lieu. Cambridge: Cambridge University Press, 2004.

Cyprian of Carthage. *Correspondance.* Edited and translated by Louis Bayard. Paris: Les Belles Lettres, 1945–61.

——. *The Letters of Saint Cyprian of Carthage.* Translated by G. W. Clarke. New York: Newman Press, 1984–.

Damascius. *Damascii Vitae Isidori reliquae.* Edited by Clemens Zintzen. Hildesheim: G. Olms, 1967.

Dexippus of Athens. *Dexipp von Athen: Edition, Übersetzung und begleitende Studien.* Edited and translated by Gunther Martin. Tübingen: G. Narr, 2006.

Dio Chrysostom. *Works.* Translated by J. W. Cohoon. Cambridge, MA: Harvard University Press, 1962–79.

Diogenes Laertius. *Vitae philosophorum.* Edited by Miroslav Marcovich. Stuttgart: B. G. Teubner, 1999.

Elias. *In Porphyrii Isagogen.* Edited by A. Busse. CAG 18.1. Berlin: de Gruyter, 1900.

Epiphanius of Salamis. *Panarion.* GCS 25, 31, 37. Leipzig: Hinrichs, 1915–33.

——. *The Panarion of Epiphanius of Salamis.* Translated by Frank Williams. 2 vols. Leiden: Brill, 1987–94.

Eunapius of Sardis. *Lives of the Philosophers and Sophists.* In *Philostratus and Eunapius: The Lives of the Sophists.* Translated by W. C. Wright. Cambridge, MA: Harvard University Press, 1968.

Eusebius of Caesarea. *Démonstration de la prédiction apostolique.* Edited and translated by Adelin Rousseau. Paris: Editions du Cerf, 1995.

——. *Ecclesiastical History.* Translated by J. E. L. Oulton. Cambridge, MA: Harvard University Press, 1962.

——. *Histoire ecclésiastique.* Edited and translated by Gustav Bardy. SC 31, 41, 55, 73. Paris: Editions du Cerf, 1958.

——. *Letter to Carpianus.* Translated by Mark DelCogliano. tertullian.org/fathers/eusebius_letter_to_carpianus.htm.

——. *La préparation évangélique.* Translated by Jean Sirinelli, Guy Schroeder, and Eduard des Places. SC 206, 228, 369, 338. Paris: Editions du Cerf, 1974–91.

Firmicus Maternus. *De errore profanarum religionum.* Edited by R. Turcan. Paris: Les Belles Lettres, 1982.

Die Fragmente der griechischen Historiker. Edited by Felix Jacoby. Leiden: E. J. Brill, 1993–.

Gennadius. *Theodoret, Jerome, Gennadius, Rufinus: Historical Writings.* Translated by Philip Schaff et al. Peabody, MA: Hendrickson Publishers, 1994.

Gregory Nazianzen. *Discours 4–5: Contre Julien.* Edited by Jean Bernardi. SC 309. Paris: Editions du Cerf, 1983.

Gregory Thaumaturgus. *Remerciement à Origène, suivi de la lettre d'Origène à Grégoire.* Edited and translated by Henri Crouzel. Paris: Editions du Cerf, 1969.

Hesiod. *Theogony, Works and Days.* Translated by M. L. West. Oxford: Oxford University Press, 1988.

Hippolytus. *Refutatio omnium haeresium.* Edited by Miroslav Marcovich. Berlin: de Gruyter, 1986.

Homer. *The Iliad.* Translated by Robert Fagles. London: Penguin, 1991.

——. *The Odyssey.* Translated by Robert Fitzgerald. New York: Farrar, Straus and Giroux, 1998.

Iamblichus. *Iamblichi Chalcidensis in Platonis Dialogos Commentariorum Fragmenta.* Edited by John Dillon. Leiden: Brill, 1973.

——. *Iamblichi De mysteriis liber.* Edited by G. Parthey. Amsterdam: Adolph M. Hakkert, 1965.

——. *On the Mysteries.* Translated by Emma C. Clarke et al. Atlanta: Society of Biblical Literature, 2003.

——. *On the Pythagorean Life.* Translated by Gillian Clark. Liverpool: Liverpool University Press, 1989.

——. *On the Pythagorean Way of Life: Text, Translation, and Notes.* Translated by John M. Dillon and Jackson P. Hershbell. Atlanta: Scholars Press, 1991.

Irenaeus of Lyons. *Contre les hérésies.* Edited and translated by Adelin Rousseau et al. SC 100, 152, 153, 210, 211, 263, 264, 293, 294. Paris: Editions du Cerf, 1965–.

Jerome. *Apologie contre Rufin.* Edited and translated by Pierre Lardet. Paris: Editions du Cerf, 1983.

——. *Commentarium in Danielem libri III <IV>.* In *S. Hieronymi presbyteri opera.* Edited by F. Glorie. Turnholt: Brepols, 1964.

——. *Commentary on Daniel.* Translated by Gleason L. Archer, Jr. Grand Rapids, MI: Baker Books, 1958.

——. *De viris illustribus liber.* Edited by E. Richardson. Texte & Untersuch. Leipzig, 1896.

——. *Epistulae.* Edited by I. Hilberg. CSEL 54–55. Vienna: F. Tempsky, 1918.

Julianus Imperator. *Epistulae.* Edited by J. Bidez and F. Cumont. Vol. 1.2 of *Oeuvres complètes.* Paris: Les Belles Lettres, 1924.

——. *The Works of the Emperor Julian.* Translated by Wilmer Cave Wright. 3 vols. Cambridge, MA: Harvard University Press, 1990.

Lactantius. *De mortibus persecutorum.* Translated and edited by J. L. Creed. Oxford: Clarendon Press, 1984.

——. *Divinarum institutionum libri septem.* Edited by Eberhard Heck and Antonie Wlosok. Munich: K. G. Saur, 2005–7.

——. *Divine Institutes.* Translated by Anthony Bowen and Peter Garnsey. Liverpool: Liverpool University Press, 2003.

——. *The Divine Institutes.* Translated by M. F. McDonald. The Fathers of the Church 49. Washington, DC: The Catholic University of America Press, 1964.

——. *Institutions divines.* Edited and translated by P. Monat. SC 204/205, 326, 337, 377, 509. Paris: Editions du Cerf, 1973.

Libanius. *Selected Orations.* Translated by A. F. Norman. Vols. 1–2. Cambridge, MA: Harvard University Press, 2003, 2007.

——. *Selected Works.* Translated by A. F. Norman. Vol. 1. Cambridge, MA: Harvard University Press, 1969.

Macrobius, Ambrosius Theodosius. *Commentarii in Somnium Scipionis.* Edited by J. Willis. Leipzig: Teubner, 1963.

——. *Commentary on the Dream of Scipio.* Translated by William Harris Stahl. New York: Columbia University Press, 1952.

Methodius of Olympus. *Opera omnia.* PG 18. Turnholt: Brepols, 1994.

——. *The Symposium: A Treatise on Chastity.* Translated by Herbert Musurillo. ACW 27. Westminster, MD: Newman Press, 1958.

Nemesius of Emesa. *De natura hominis.* Edited by M. Morani. Leipzig: Teubner, 1987.

——. *On the Nature of Man.* In *Cyril of Jerusalem and Nemesius of Emesa,* edited and translated by William Telfer. Philadelphia: Westminster, 1955.

New Revised Standard Version Bible with Apocrypha. New York: Oxford University Press, 1989.

Nicephorus Callistus Xanthopulus. *Historia ecclesiastica.* Edited by J. P. Migne. PG 145–46. Paris, 1630.

Numenius of Apamea. *Fragments.* Edited and translated by E. des Places. Paris: Les Belles Lettres, 1973.

Origen of Alexandria. *Commentaire sur saint Jean.* Edited and translated by Cécile Blanc. Paris: Editions du Cerf, 1996–.

——. *Commentary on Genesis.* Fragments in Joseph W. Trigg, *Origen.* London/New York: Routledge, 1998.

——. *Commentary on Lamentations.* Fragments in Trigg, *Origen.*

——. *Commentary on the Psalms.* Fragments in Trigg, *Origen.*

——. *Contra Celsum.* Edited and translated by Henry Chadwick. Cambridge: Cambridge University Press, 1965.

——. *De principiis.* Translated by Frederick Crombie. ANF 4. 1885–97. Reprint, Grand Rapids, MI: Eerdmans, 1965–70.

——. *On First Principles.* Translated by G. W. Butterworth. New York: Harper, 1966. Reprint, Gloucester: Peter Smith, 1973.

——. *Origenes vier Bücher von dem Prinzipien.* Translated by H. Görgemanns and H. Karpp. Darmstadt: Wissenschaftliche Buchgesellschaft, 1976.

——. *The Philocalia of Origen: A Compilation of Selected Passages from Origen's Works Made by St. Gregory of Nazianzus and St. Basil of Caesarea.* Translated by George Lewis. Edinburgh: T & T Clark, 1911.

——. *Philocalie, 1–20: Sur les écritures.* Edited and translated by Marguerite Harl. SC 302. Paris: Editions du Cerf, 1983.

——. *Prayer; Exhortation to Martyrdom.* Translated by John J. O'Meara. Ancient Christian Writers 19. Westminster, MD: Newman Press, 1954.

——. *The Song of Songs: Commentary and Homilies.* Translated by R. P. Lawson. New York: Newman Press, 1988.

——. *Sur le libre arbitre: Philocalie 21–27.* Edited and translated by Eric Junod. SC 226. Paris: Editions du Cerf, 1976.

Palladius. *The Lausiac History.* Translated by Robert T. Meyer. Westminster, MD: Newman Press, 1965.

The Passion of Perpetua and Felicity. Translated by W. H. Shewing. London: The Fleuron, 1931.

Philo of Alexandria. *Les oeuvres de Philon d'Alexandrie.* Vol. 9, *De agricultura.* Edited and translated by Jean Gorez. Paris: Editions du Cerf, 1961.

——. *Les oeuvres de Philon d'Alexandrie.* Vol. 3, *De cherubim.* Edited and translated by Jean Pouilloux. Paris: Editions du Cerf, 1963.

——. *Les oeuvres de Philon d'Alexandrie.* Vol. 14, *De migratione Abrahami.* Edited and translated by Jacques Cazeaux. Paris: Editions du Cerf, 1965.

——. *Les oeuvres de Philon d'Alexandrie.* Vol. 1, *Introduction générale—De opificio mundi.* Edited and translated by Roger Arnaldez. Paris: Editions du Cerf, 1961.

———. *Les oeuvres de Philon d'Alexandrie.* Vol. 2, *Legum allegoriae.* Edited and translated by Claude Mondésert. Paris: Editions du Cerf, 1962.

———. *Les oeuvres de Philon d'Alexandrie.* Vol. 15, *Quis rerum divinarum heres sit.* Edited and translated by Marguerite Harl. Paris: Editions du Cerf, 1966.

———. *Philo with an English Translation.* Translated by F. H. Colson. Cambridge, MA: Harvard University Press, 1929–62.

———. *The Works of Philo: Complete and Unabridged.* Translated by C. D. Yonge. Peabody, MA: Hendrickson Publishers, 1993.

Philostorgius. *Kirchengeschichte.* Edited by Joseph Bidez and Friedhelm Winkelman. 3rd ed. Berlin: Adademie-Verlag, 1981.

Philostratus. *The Life of Apollonius of Tyana.* Translated by F. C. Conybeare. London: William Heineman, 1912.

Photius. *Bibliotheca.* Edited by R. Henry. Paris, 1959–.

———. *Interrogationes decem cum totidem responsionibus.* Edited by J. P. Migne. PG 104. Turnholt: Brepols, 1975.

Plato. *Apology.* Translated by Harold North Fowler. Cambridge, MA: Harvard University Press, 1977.

———. *Cratylus, Parmenides, Greater Hippias, Lesser Hippias.* Translated by Harold North Fowler. London: Heinemann, 1963.

———. *Euthyphro, Apology, Crito, Phaedo, Phaedrus.* Translated by Harold North Fowler. Cambridge, MA: Harvard University Press, 1977.

———. *Laws.* Translated by R. G. Bury. Cambridge, MA: Harvard University Press, 1967–68.

———. *The Laws.* Translated by Trevor J. Saunders. London: Penguin, 1970.

———. *Letters.* In *Timaeus, Critias, Cleitophon, Menexenus, Epistles.* Translated by R. G. Bury. 1929. Reprint, Cambridge, MA: Harvard University Press, 1966.

———. *Les Lois.* Edited and translated by Luc Brisson and Jean-François Pradeau. Paris: Flammarion, 2006.

———. *Plato's Symposium.* Translated by Seth Benardette. Chicago: University of Chicago Press, 2001.

———. *The Republic.* Translated by Paul Shorey. Cambridge, MA: Harvard University Press, 1982–87.

———. *The Republic of Plato.* Translated by Alan Bloom. New York: Basic, 1968.

———. *Theaetetus.* Translated by Robin Waterfield. London: Penguin, 1987.

Pliny the Younger. *Letters and Panegyricus.* Translated by Betty Radice. Cambridge, MA: Harvard University Press, 1972–75.

Plotinus. *Enneads.* Translated by A. H. Armstrong. 7 vols. Cambridge, MA: Harvard University Press, 1978–88.

———. *Opera.* Edited by Paul Henry and Hans-Rudolf Schwyzer. Oxford: Clarendon Press, 1964–82.

———. *The Six Enneads.* Translated by Stephen Mackenna and B. S. Page. Whitefish, MT: Kessinger Publishing, 2004.

Plutarch. *Plutarch's Lives.* Translated by Bernadotte Perrin. Cambridge, MA: Harvard University Press, 1967–82.

Porphyry of Tyre. *The Cave of the Nymphs in the Odyssey: A Revised Text and Translation.* Buffalo: SUNY Department of Classics, 1969.

——. *Contra christianos.* Fragments collected in "Porphyrius: Gegen die Christen: 15 Bücher; Zeugnisse, Fragmente und Referate," ed. Adolph von Harnack. *Abhandlungen der Königlich Preussischen Akademie der Wissenschaften, Philosophisch-historische Klasse* (1916).

——. *De philosophia ex oraculis haurienda: Librorum reliquiae.* Edited by G. Wolff. Hildesheim: G. Olms, 1962.

——. *De regressu animae.* Fragments collected in *Porphyrii philosophi fragmenta,* ed. Andrew Smith and David Wasserstein. Stuttgart: Teubner, 1993.

——. *Introduzione agli intelligibili.* Edited and translated by Angelo Sodano. Naples: Assoc. di Studi tardo antichi, 1979.

——. *Life of Pythagoras.* Translated by Kenneth Sylvan Guthrie. In *The Pythagorean Sourcebook and Library.* Edited by David Fideler. Grand Rapids, MI: Phanes Press, 1987, 1988.

——. *On Abstinence from Killing Animals.* Translated by Gillian Clark. London: Duckworth, 2000.

——. *Peri agalmatōn.* Fragments collected in Smith and Wasserstein, *Porphyrii philosophi fragmenta.*

——. *Peri Stugos.* Fragments collected in Smith and Wasserstein, *Porphyrii philosophi fragmenta.*

——. *Peri tēs ek logion philosophias.* Fragments collected in Smith and Wasserstein, *Porphyrii philosophi fragmenta.*

——. *Pros Anebō epistolū.* Fragments collected in Smith and Wasserstein, *Porphyrii philosophi fragmenta.*

——. *Sententiae ad intelligibilia ducentes.* Edited by Erich Lamberz. Leipzig: Teubner, 1975.

——. *To Marcella.* Translated by K. O'Brien Wicker. Atlanta: Scholars Press, 1987.

——. *Vie de Pythagore; Lettre à Marcella.* Edited and translated by E. des Places. Paris: Les Belles Lettres, 1982.

——. *Vita Plotini.* In Plotinus, *Enneads,* vol. 1. Translated by A. H. Armstrong. Cambridge, MA: Harvard University Press, 1978–88.

Priscian of Lydia. *Solutiones eorum de quibus dubitavit Chosroes Persarum rex.* Edited by I. Bywater. Supplementum Aristotelicum 1.2. Berlin, 1886.

Proclus. *Commentaire sur la République.* Edited and translated by A. J. Festugière. Paris: Vrin, 1970.

——. *Commentaire sur le Timée.* Translated by A. J. Festugière. Paris: J. Vrin, 1966–.

——. *Procli Diadochi in Platonis Timaeum commentaria.* Edited by Ernest Diehl. Amsterdam: A. M. Hakkert, 1965.

[Sawirus ibn al-Muqaffa]. *History of the Patriarchs of the Coptic Church of Alexandria.* In *Patrologia orientalis,* edited by B. Evetts. Paris: Firmin-Didot et Cie, 1948.

Scriptores Historiae Augustae. Translated by David Magie. Cambridge, MA: Harvard University Press, 1979–82.

Socrates Scholasticus. *Histoire ecclésiastique.* Edited by Günther Christian Hansen. Translated by Pierre Périchon and Pierre Maraval. SC 477, 493, 505, 506. Paris: Editions du Cerf, 2004–.

Stobaeus, Joannes. *Anthologia.* Edited by C. Wachsmuth and O. Hense. Berlin: Weidmann, 1974.

Suidae Lexicon. Edited by A. Adler. Stuttgart: Verlag Teubner, 1928–38.

[Ps.-]Tertullian. *Adversus omnes haereses.* In *Opera.* Corpus Christianorum 2. Turnholt: Brepols, 1953.

Theodoret of Cyrrhus. *Thérapeutique des maladies hélléniques.* Edited and translated by Pierre Canivet. SC 57.2. Paris: Editions du Cerf, 1958.

Zosimus. *Histoire nouvelle.* Edited by F. Paschoud. Paris: Les Belles Lettres, 1971.

Modern Sources

Amacker, René, and Eric Junot. "L'art d'entrer en matière dans une littérature de controverse: Les premières pages de l' «Apologie pour Origène» de Pamphile." In *Entrer en matière: Les prologues,* edited by Jean-Daniel Dubois and Bernard Roussel, 37–51. Paris: Editions du Cerf, 1998.

Armstrong, A. H. "Dualism: Platonic, Gnostic, and Christian." In *Plotinus amid Gnostics and Christians,* edited by D. T. Runia, 37–41. Amsterdam: Free University Press, 1984.

———. "The Hidden and the Open in Hellenic Thought." *Eranos-Jahrbuch* 54 (1985): 81–117.

———. "Man in the Cosmos: A Study of Some Differences between Pagan Neoplatonism and Christianity." In *Romanitas et Christianitas: Studia I. H. Waszink a. d. VI Kal. Nov. a MCMLXXIII XIII lustra complenti oblata,* edited by W. den Boer, P. G. van der Nat, C. M. Sicking, and J. C. M. Winden, 5–14. Amsterdam: North Holland, 1973.

———. "Plotinus and Christianity." In *Platonism in Late Antiquity,* edited by Stephen Gersh and Charles Kannengiesser, 115–30. Notre Dame: University of Notre Dame Press, 1992.

———. "Plotinus and Christianity: With Special Reference to II.9 [33] 9.26–83 and V.8 [31] 4.27–36." *Studia Patristica* 20 (1989): 83–86.

———. "Tradition, Reason, and Experience in the Thought of Plotinus." In *Plotinian and Christian Studies,* XVII. London: Variorum Reprints, 1979. Originally published in *Atti del Convegno Internazionale sul tema Plotino e il Neoplatonismo in Oriente e in Occidente* (Rome: Accademia Nazionale dei Lincei, 1974), 171–94.

———. "Two Views of Freedom: A Christian Objection in Plotinus VI.8 (39) 7.11–15." *Studia Patristica* 17.1 (1982): 397–406.

———. "Was Plotinus a Magician?" *Phronesis* 1 (1955): 73–79.

Atchley, E. G., and F. Cuthbert. *A History of the Use of Incense in Divine Worship.* London: Longman, Green, 1909.

Athanassiadi, Polymnia. "Apamea and the *Chaldaean Oracles:* A Holy City and a Holy Book." In *The Philosopher and Society in Late Antiquity: Essays in Honour of Peter Brown,* edited by Andrew Smith, 117–43. Swansea: Classical Press of Wales, 2005.

———. "The Chaldaean Oracles: Theology and Theurgy." In *Pagan Monotheism in Late Antiquity,* edited by Polymnia Athanassiadi and Michael Frede, 149–83. New York: Oxford University Press, 1999.

———. "Dreams, Theurgy, and Free-Lance Divination." *JRS* 83 (1993): 115–30.

———. "The Oecumenism of Iamblichus: Latent Knowledge and Its Awakening." *JRS* 85 (1995): 244–50.

Atiya, Aziz S. "Sāwīrus ibn al-Muqaffaʾ." In *The Coptic Encyclopedia* (1991): 2100–2102.

Balty, Jean C. "Apamea in Syria in the Second and Third Centuries A.D." *JRS* 78 (1988): 91–104.

Barbanti, Maria Di Pasquale. "Origene di Alessandria e la scuola di Ammonio Sacca." In *HENOSIS KAI PHILIA = Unione e amicizia: Omaggio a Francesco Romano,* edited by Maria Barbanti, Giovanna Rita Giardina, and Paolo Manganaro, 355–73. Catania: CUECM, 2002.

Bardenhewer, Otto, and Thomas J. Shahan. *Patrology: The Lives and Works of the Fathers of the Church.* Berlin/Munich/Strassburg/Vienna: B. Herder, 1908.

Bardy, G. *Recherches sur l'histoire du texte et des versions latines du 'De principiis' d'Origène.* Paris: E. Champion, 1923.

Barnes, T. D. "The Chronology of Plotinus' Life." *GRBS* 17 (1976): 65–70.

———. *Constantine and Eusebius.* Cambridge, MA: Harvard University Press, 1981.

———. "A Correspondent of Iamblichus." *GRBS* 19 (1978): 99–106.

———. "Eusebius." *Lexicon für Theologie und Kirche* 3 (1995): 1006–10.

———. "Imperial Campaigns, A.D. 285–311." *Phoenix* 30 (1976): 174–93.

———. "Methodius, Maximus & Valentinus." *JThS* 30 (1979): 47–55.

———. "Monotheists All?" *Phoenix* 55 (2001): 142–62.

———. *The New Empire of Diocletian and Constantine.* Cambridge, MA: Harvard University Press, 1982.

———. "Origen, Aquila, and Eusebius." *HSPh* 74 (1970): 313–16.

———. "Porphyry *Against the Christian.*" *JThS* 24 (1973): 433–37.

———. "Sossianus Hierocles and the Antecedents of the 'Great Persecution'." *HSPh* 80 (1976): 239–52.

Bauer, Walter. *Rechtglaubigkeit und Ketzerei im altesten Christentum.* Tübingen: Mohr/Siebeck, 1934.

Baynes, N. "The Great Persecution." In *The Cambridge Ancient History,* edited by S. A. Cooke et al., 646–95. Cambridge: Cambridge University Press, 1981.

Beatrice, P. F. "*Antistes Philosophiae:* Ein christenfeindlicher Propogandist am Hofe Diokletians nach dem Zeugnis des Laktanz." *Augustinianum* 33 (1993): 31–47.

———. "Un oracle antichrétien chez Arnobe." In *Mémorial Dom Jean Gribomont,* edited by Y. de Andia et. al., 107–29. Rome: Institutum Patristicum Augustinianum, 1988.

———. "Porphyry's Judgment on Origen." In *Origeniana quinta,* edited by Robert J. Daly, 351–67. Leuven: Peeters, 1992.

———. "Quosdam Platonicorum libros." *VChr* 43 (1989): 248–81.

———. "Towards a New Edition of Porphyry's Fragments against the Christians." In *Sophiēs maiētores / Chercheurs de sagesse: Hommage à Jean Pépin,* edited by Marie-Odile Goulet-Cazé, Goulven Madec, and Denis O'Brien, 347–55. Paris: Institut d'études augustiniennes, 1992.

———. "Le traité de Porphyre contre les chrétiens: L'état de la question." *Kernos* 4 (1991): 119–38.

———. "Le tuniche di pelle: Antiche letture di Gen. 3:21." In *La tradizione dell'Enkrateia: Motivazioni ontologiche e protologiche,* edited by U. Bianchi, 433–84. Rome: Edizioni dell'Ateneo, 1985.

Bell, H. I., and T. C. Skeat, eds. *Fragments of an Unknown Gospel and Other Early Christian Papyri.* London: The Trustees of the British Museum, 1935.

Benjamins, Hendrick S. "Methodius von Olympus, 'Über die Auferstehung': Gegen Origenes und gegen Porphyrius?" In *Origeniana septima,* edited by W. A. Bienert and Uwe Kühneweg, 91–100. Leuven: Peeters, 1999.

Benoit, A. "Le *Contra Christianos* de Porphryre: Où est la collecte des fragments?" In *Paganisme, judaïsme, christianisme: Influences et affrontements dans le monde antique; Mélanges offerts à Marcel Simon,* 261–75. Paris: E. de Boccard, 1978.

Benziger, I. *Pauly's Realenzyclopaedie* 3 (1899): s.v. Chalkis (14), (15).

Berchman, R. "Arcana Mundi between Balaam and Hecate: Prophecy, Divination, and Magic in Later Platonism." In *SBL Seminar Papers,* edited by D. Lull, 107–85. Atlanta: Scholars Press, 1989.

———. *Porphyry against the Christians.* Leiden/Boston: Brill, 2005.

Bidez, Joseph. "Le philosophe Jamblique et son école." *REG* 32 (1919): 29–40.

———. *Vie de Porphyre, le philosophe néo-platonicien avec les fragments des traités "Peri agalmatōn" et "De regressu animae".* Ghent: E. van Goethem, 1913. Reprint, Hildesheim: G. Olms, 1964.

Blois, Lukas de. *The Policy of the Emperor Gallienus.* Leiden: Brill, 1976.

Bodeüs, R. "Plotin a-t-il empêché Porphyre de mourir de mélancolie?" *Hermes* 129 (2001): 567–71.

Böhm, T. "Origenes, Theologe und (Neu-)Platoniker? Oder: wem soll man misstrauen, Eusebius oder Porphyrius?" *Adamantius* 8 (2002): 7–23.

Bonwetsch, D. G. Nathanael, ed. *Methodius, Die griechischen christlichen Schriftsteller der ersten drei Jahrhunderte.* Leipzig: J. C. Hinrichs, 1917.

Borodai, T. I. "Plotinus's Critique of Gnosticism." *Russian Studies in Philosophy* 42 (2003): 66–83.

Boyarin, Daniel. *Border Lines.* Philadelphia: University of Pennsylvania Press, 2004.

Bregman, Jay. "Judaism as Theurgy in the Religious Thought of the Emperor Julian." *AncW* 26, no. 2 (1995): 135–49.

Brent, Allen. "Was Hippolytus a Schismatic?" *VChr* 49, no. 3 (1995): 215–44.

Brezzi, Paolo. *Analisi ed interpretazione del "De civitate dei" di Sant' Agostino.* Tolentino: Edizione Agostiniane, 1960.

Brisson, L. "Amélius: Sa vie, son oeuvre, sa doctrine, son style." *ANRW* 2.36.2 (1987): 793–860.

Brisson, L., and M. Patillon. "Longinus Platonicus Philosophus et Philologus." *ANRW* 2.36.7 (1994): 5214–99.

Bruns, J. E. "The Agreement of Moses and Jesus in the *Demonstratio evangelica* of Eusebius." *VChr* 31 (1977): 117–25.

Buchheit, V. *Studien zu Methodius von Olympos.* Berlin: Akademie-Verlag, 1958.

———. "Das Symposion des Methodios arianisch interpoliert?" In *Überlieferungsgeschichtliche Untersuchungen,* edited by F. Paschke, 109–14. Berlin: Akademie Verlag, 1981.

Burgess, R. W. "The Date of the Persecutions in the Army." *JThS* n.s. 47 (1996): 157–58.

———. "The Dates and Editions of Eusebius' *Chronici canones* and *Historia ecclesiastica.*" *JThS* n. s. 48 (1997): 471–504.

Busine, Aude. *Paroles d'Apollon: Pratiques et traditions oraculaires dans l'Antiquité tardive (IIe-VIe siècles).* Leiden/Boston: Brill, 2005.

Busse, A. "Der Historiker und der Philosoph Dexippus." *Hermes* 23, no. 3 (1888): 402–9.

Cadiou, R. "La jeunesse d'Origène: Histoire de l'école d'Alexandrie au début du IIIe siècle." *Etudes de Théologie Historique* 17 (1935): 184ff.

Cameron, Alan. "The Date of Iamblichus' Birth." *Hermes* 96 (1968): 374–76.

Camplani, Alberto, and Marco Zambon. "Il sacrificio come problema in alcune correnti filosofiche di età imperiale." *AnnS* 19 (2002): 59–99.

Carriker, Andrew J. *The Library of Eusebius of Caesarea.* Leiden: Brill, 2003.

Chadwick, Henry. *Early Christian Thought and the Classical Tradition: Studies in Justin, Clement, and Origen.* Oxford: Oxford University Press, 1966.

Charrue, J.-M. "Ammonius et Plotin." *Revue Philosophique de Louvain* 102 (2004): 72–103.

Chesnut, Glenn F. *The First Christian Historians: Eusebius, Socrates, Sozomen, Theodoret, and Evagius.* Paris: Editions Beauchesne, 1977. Reprint, Macon, GA: Mercer University Press, 1986.

Clark, G. "Animal passions (Pathos, passio, Porphyry)." *G&R* 47 (2000): 88–93.

———. "Augustine's Porphyry and the Universal Way of Salvation." In *Studies on Porphyry,* edited by George E. Karamanolis and Anne Sheppard, 127–40. London: Institute of Classical Studies, 2007.

———. Introduction to *Porphyry: On Abstinence from Killing Animals,* 1–28. Ithaca, NY: Cornell University Press, 2000.

Clarke, Emma C., John Dillon, and Jackson Hershbell. Introduction to *Iamblichus: De mysteriis,* xiii–lii. Atlanta: Society of Biblical Literature, 2003.

Clarke, G. W. "Some Victims of the Persecution of Maximinus Thrax." *Historia* 15, no. 4 (1966): 445–53.

Colombo, S. "Arnobio Afro e i suoi sette libri Adversus nationes." *Didaskaleion* (1930): 1–124.

Consolino, Franca Ela. "Le prefazioni di Girolamo e Rufino alle loro traduzioni di Origene." In *Origeniana quinta: Historica, text and method, philosophica, theologica, Origenism and Later Developments,* edited by Robert J. Daly, 92–96. Leuven: Peeters, 1992.

Corcoran, Simon. "Before Constantine." In *The Cambridge Companion to the Age of Constantine,* edited by Noel Lenski, 35–58. Cambridge: Cambridge University Press, 2006.

———. *The Empire of the Tetrarchs: Imperial Pronouncements and Government, AD 284–324.* Oxford: Clarendon Press, 1996.

Corrigan, K. "Amelius, Plotinus, and Porphyry on Being, Intellect, and the One: A Reappraisal." *ANRW* 2.36.2 (1987): 975–93.

Coulton, J. J. "Opramoas and the Anonymous Benefactor." *JHS* 107 (1987): 171–78.

Courcelle, P. "Anti-Christian Arguments and Christian Platonism from Arnobius to St. Ambrose." In *The Conflict between Paganism and Christianity in the Fourth Century,* edited by A. Momigliano, 151–92. Oxford: Clarendon Press, 1963.

———. "Le colle et le clou de l'âme dans la tradition néo-platonicienne et chrétienne (*Phédon* 82e; 83d)." *RBPh* 36 (1958): 72–95.

———. "Nouveaux aspects du platonisme chez Saint Ambroise." *REL* 34 (1956): 220–39.

———. "Les sages de Porphyre et les *viri novi* d'Arnobe." *REL* 31 (1953): 257–71.

———. "Verissima philosophia." In *Epektasis: Mélanges patristiques offerts à Jean Daniélou,* edited by J. Fontaine and Charles Kannengiesser, 653–59. Paris: Beauchesne, 1972.

Cribiore, Raffaella. *Gymnastics of the Mind: Greek Education in Hellenistic and Roman Egypt.* Princeton, NJ/Oxford: Princeton University Press, 2001.

Croke, B. "Porphyry's Anti-Christian Chronology." *JThS* 34 (1983): 168–85.

Crouzel, H. "Comparaisons précises entre les fragments du *Peri Archōn* selon la *Philocalie* et la traduction de Rufin." In *Origeniana,* edited by H. Crouzel, G. Lomiento, and J. Ruis-Camps, 113–21. Bari: Ist. di lett. crist. ant., 1975.

———. "Les critiques adressées par Méthode et ses contemporains à la doctrine origénienne du corps ressuscité." *Gregorianum* 53 (1972): 679–716.

———. "La doctrine origénienne du corps ressuscité." *BLE* 81 (1980): 41–66, 175–200.

———. "Origène et Plotin, élèves d'Ammonius Saccas." *BLE* 57 (1956): 193–214.

———. "Origène s'est'il retiré en Cappadoce pendant la persécution de Maximin le Thrace?" *BLE* 64 (1963): 195–203.

Daniélou, J. *L'être et le temps chez Grégoire de Nysse.* Leiden: Brill, 1970.

Davies, P. "The Origin and Purpose of the Persecution of A. D. 303." *JThS* n.s. 40 (1989): 66–94.

Dechow, Jon F. "Origen and Corporeality: The Case of Methodius' *On the Resurrection.*" In *Origeniana quinta,* edited by Robert J. Daly, 509–18. Leuven: Peeters, 1992.

Decret, François. "Le manichéisme en Afrique du Nord et ses rapports avec la secte en Orient." *Aram* 16 (2004): 279–83.

Diekamp, F. "Über den Bischofssitz des hl. Methodius." *ThQ* 109 (1928): 285–308.

Digeser, Elizabeth DePalma. "Christian or Hellene? The Great Persecution and the Problem of Christian Identity." In *Religious Identity in Late Antiquity,* edited by R. M. Frakes and Elizabeth Digeser, 36–57. Toronto: Edgar Kent, 2006.

———. "Lactantius, Eusebius, and Arnobius: Evidence for the Causes of the Great Persecution." *Studia Patristica* 39 (2006): 33–46.

———. "Lactantius, Porphyry, and the Debate over Religious Toleration." *JRS* 88 (1998): 129–46.

———. "The Late Roman Empire from the Antonines to Constantine." In Gerson, *Cambridge History of Philosophy in Late Antiquity,* 13–24.

———. *The Making of a Christian Empire: Lactantius and Rome.* Ithaca, NY: Cornell University Press, 1999.

———. "Methodius and Porphyry." *Studia Patristica* 46 (2010): 21–26.

———. "An Oracle of Apollo at Daphne and the Great Persecution." *CPh* 99 (2004): 57–77.

———. "Origen on the *Limes:* Rhetoric and the Polarization of Identity in the Late Third Century." In *The Rhetoric of Power in Late Antiquity: Religion and Politics in Byzantium, Europe, and the Early Islamic World,* edited by Robert M. Frakes, Elizabeth DePalma Digeser, and Justin Stephens. London: I. B. Tauris, 2010.

———. "Philosophy in a Christian Empire: From the Great Persecution to Theodosius I." In *The Cambridge History of Philosophy in Late Antiquity,* edited by Lloyd Gerson, 376–96. Cambridge: Cambridge University Press, 2010.

————."Porphyry, Julian, or Hierokles? The Anonymous Hellene in Makarios Magnēs' *Apocritikos.*" *JThS* 53 (2002): 466–502.

————. "Porphyry, Lactantius, and the Paths to God." *Studia Patristica* 38 (2001): 521–28.

————. "The Power of Religious Rituals: A Philosophical Quarrel on the Eve of the Great Persecution." In *The Power of Religion in Late Antiquity,* edited by Andrew Cain and Noel Lenski, 81–92. Aldershot, UK: Ashgate, 2009.

————. "Religion, Law, and the Roman Polity: The Era of the Great Persecution." In *Law and Religion in Classical and Christian Rome,* edited by Clifford Ando and Jörg Rüpke, 68–84. Stuttgart: Franz Steiner Verlag, 2006.

Dillon, John, ed. *Iamblichi Chalcidensis in Platonis Dialogos Commentariorum Fragmenta.* Leiden: Brill, 1973.

————. "Iamblichus of Chalcis (c. 240–325 AD)." *ANRW* 2.36.2 (1987): 862–909.

————. "Iamblichus on the Personal Daemon." *AncW* 32, no. 1 (2001): 3–9.

————. *The Middle Platonists.* Ithaca, NY: Cornell University Press, 1996.

————. "Plotinus and the Chaldean Oracles." In *Platonism in Late Antiquity,* edited by Stephen Gersh and C. Kannengieser, 131–40. Notre Dame: University of Notre Dame, 1992.

Dodds, E. R. *The Greeks and the Irrational.* Berkeley: University of California Press, 1951.

————. "Numenius and Ammonius." In *Les sources de Plotin,* edited by E. R. Dodds, 1–61. Geneva: Fondation Hardt, 1960.

————. "Theurgy and Its Relationship to Neoplatonism." *JRS* 37 (1947): 55–68.

Dombrowski, Daniel A. "Vegetarianism and the Argument from Marginal Cases in Porphyry." *JHI* 4 (1984): 141–43.

Dörrie, H. "Ammonios, der Lehrer Plotins." *Hermes* 83 (1955): 439–77.

————. "Ammonios Sakkas." *Theologische Realenzyklopädie* 2 (1978): 463–71.

Downey, Glanville. "Caesarea and the Christian Church." *BASO, Supplementary Studies* 19 (1975): 23–42.

Dubois, Jean-Daniel. "Le 'Traité des principes' d'Origène et le 'Traité tripartite' valentinien: Une lecture comparée de leurs prologues." In *Entrer en matière: Les prologues,* edited by Jean-Daniel Dubois and Bernard Roussel, 53–63. Paris: Editions du Cerf, 1998.

Dye, Guillaume. Review of *Macarios de Magnésie,* by Richard Goulet. *BMCR* 2004.07.53 (2004).

Edwards, Mark J. "Ammonius, Teacher of Origen." *JEH* 44 (1993): 169–81.

————. *Culture and Philosophy in the Age of Plotinus.* London: Duckworth, 2006.

————. "Gnostics, Greeks, and Origen: The Interpretation of Interpretation." *JThS* 44 (1993): 70–89.

————. *Origen against Plato.* Aldershot, UK: Ashgate, 2002.

————. "Porphyry and the Christians." In *Studies on Porphyry,* edited by George E. Karamanolis and Anne Sheppard, 111–26. London: Institute of Classical Studies, 2007.

————. "Porphyry's Egyptian 'de Abstinentia' II.47." *Hermes* 123 (1995): 126–28.

————. "Two Episodes in Porphyry's *Life of Plotinus.*" *Historia* 40 (1991): 456–64.

Eitrem, S. "La théurgie chez les néo-platoniciens et dans les papyrus magiques." *SymbOsl* 22 (1942): 49–79.

Elorduy, E. "Ammonio escriturista." *Estudios Bíblicos* 16 (1957): 187–217.

———. *Ammonio Sakkas, I: La doctrina de la creación y del mal en Proclo y el Ps. Areopagita.* Oña (Burgos): Fac. de Teol., 1959.

———. "Ammonio Sakkas, la legenda de su apostasia." *Pensamiento* 3 (1947): 5–27.

Evangeliou, C. "Plotinus' Anti-Gnostic Polemic and Porphyry's *Against the Christians.*" In *Neoplatonism and Gnosticism,* edited by R. T. Wallis and J. Bregman, 111–28. Albany, NY: State University of New York Press, 1992.

Fabricius, J. A. *Bibliotheca graeca.* Vol. 4. Hamburg, 1723.

Farag, F. R. "The Technique of Research of a Tenth-Century Christian Arab Writer: Severus ibn al-Muqaffa." *Le Museon* 86 (1973): 37–66.

Feng, Lide, and Kevin Stuart. "Folklore concerning Tsong-kha-pa." *Asian Folklore Studies* 51, no. 2 (1992): 219–42.

Ferguson, E. Review of *The Muratorian Fragment and the Development of the Canon,* by Geoffrey Mark Hahneman. *JThS* 44 (1993): 691–97.

Finamore, John F. *Iamblichus and the Theory of the Vehicle of the Soul.* American Class. Stud. 14. Chicago: Cal. Scholars Pr., 1985.

Foakes-Jackson, F. J. F. *Eusebius Pamphili: A Study of the Man and His Writings.* Cambridge: Heffer, 1933.

Fortin, E. L. "The *Viri novi* of Arnobius and the Conflict between Faith and Reason in the Early Christian Centuries." In *The Heritage of the Early Church: Essays in Honor of the Very Reverend Georges Vasilievich Florovsky,* edited by David Neiman and Margaret Schatkin, 197–226. Rome: Pont. Institutum Studiorum Orientalium, 1973.

Fowden, G. *The Egyptian Hermes.* Princeton, NJ: Princeton University Press, 1986.

———. "Late Antique Paganism Reasoned and Revealed." *JRS* 71 (1981): 178–82.

———. "The Pagan Holy Man in Late Antique Society." *JHS* 102 (1982): 33–59.

———. "Pagan Philosophers in Late Antique Society: With Special Reference to Iamblichus and His Followers." D. Phil. thesis, Oxford University, 1979.

———. "The Platonist Philosopher and His Circle in Late Antiquity." *Philosophia* 7 (1977): 358–83.

Frede, Michael. "Eusebius' Apologetic Writings." In *Apologetics in the Roman Empire: Pagans, Jews, and Christians,* edited by Mark Edwards, Martin Goodman, and Simon Price, 223–50. Oxford: Oxford University Press, 1999.

Frend, W. H. C. "Prelude to the Great Persecution: The Propaganda War." *JEH* 38 (1987): 1–18.

Gallardo, M. D. "Los Simposios de Luciano, Ateneo, Metodio y Juliano." *Cuadernos de Filología Clásica* 4 (1972): 239–96.

Gatti, Maria Louisa. "Plotinus: The Platonic Tradition and the Foundation of Neoplatonism." In *The Cambridge Companion to Plotinus,* edited by Lloyd Gerson, 10–37. Cambridge: Cambridge University Press, 1996.

Geffcken, J. *The Last Days of Greco-Roman Paganism.* Translated by S. MacCormack. Amsterdam: Holland Pub. Co., 1978.

Gerson, Lloyd P. *Aristotle and Other Platonists.* Ithaca, NY: Cornell University Press, 2005.

Gigon, O. "Arnobio: Cristianesimo e mondo romano." In *Mondo classico e cristianesimo.* Rome: Istituto della Enciclopedia Italiana, 1982.

Goulet, Richard. *Macarios de Magnésie: Le Monogénès; Édition critique et traduction fran-çaise.* 2 vols. Paris: Vrin, 2003.

———. "L'Oracle d'Apollon dans la Vie de Plotin." In *Porphyre: La Vie de Plotin; Travaux préliminaires et index grec complet,* edited by Luc Brisson, Marie-Odile Goulet-Cazé, Richard Goulet, and Denis O'Brien, 369–412. Paris: Librarie Philosophique J. Vrin, 1982.

———. "Porphyre, Ammonius, les deux Origène et les autres." *RHPhR* 57 (1977): 471–96.

Grafton, Anthony, and Megan Williams. *Christianity and the Transformation of the Book: Origen, Eusebius, and the Library of Caesarea.* Cambridge, MA: Harvard University Press, 2006.

Grant, R. M. *Augustus to Constantine: The Thrust of the Christian Movement into the Roman World.* New York: Harper & Row, 1970.

———. "Early Alexandrian Christianity." *Church History* 40 (1971): 133–44.

———. "Eusebius and His Lives of Origen." In *Forma futuri: Studi in onore di Michele Pellegrino,* edited by Maria Bellis and Michele Pellegrino, 635–49. Turin: Bottega d'Erasmo, 1975.

———. "More Fragments of Origen?" *VChr* 2, no. 4 (1948): 243–47.

———. *Paul in the Roman World.* Louisville, KY: Westminster/John Knox Press, 2001.

———. "Porphyry among the Early Christians." In *Romanitas et Christianitas,* edited by J. H. Waszink and W. den Boer, 181–87. Amsterdam: North Holland, 1973.

———. "The *Stromateis* of Origen." In *Epektasis: Mélanges patristiques offerts à Jean Daniélou,* edited by J. Fontaine and Charles Kannengiesser, 285–92. Paris: Beauchesne, 1972.

Gregorios, Paulos Mar. "Does Geography Condition Philosophy? On Going Beyond the Oriental-Occidental Distinction." In *Neoplatonism and Indian Philosophy,* edited by Paulos Mar Gregorios, 13–30. Albany: SUNY Press, 2002.

Guerra, Chiara. "Porfirio editore di Plotino e la 'paideia antignostica.'" *Patavium* 8 (2000): 111–37.

Haas, Christopher. *Alexandria in Late Antiquity.* Baltimore: Johns Hopkins University Press, 1997.

———. "Imperial Religious Policy and Valerian's Persecution of the Church, AD 257–260." *ChHist* 52, no. 2 (1983): 133–44.

Hadot, P. "Citations de Porphyre chez Augustin: A propos d'un ouvrage récent." *REAug* 6 (1960): 205–44.

———. "Ouranos, Kronos, and Zeus in Plotinus' Treatise against the Gnostics." In *Neoplatonism and Early Christian Thought,* edited by A. H. Armstrong, H. J. Blumenthal, and R. A. Markus, 124–37. Rugby, UK: Variorum Publications, 1981.

Hagedorn, D. R., and R. Merkelbach. "Ein neues Fragment aus Porphyrios' *Gegen die Christen.*" *VChr* 20 (1966): 86–90.

Hanson, R. P. C. "A Note on Origen's Self-Mutilation." *VChr* 20, no. 2 (1966): 81–82.

Harnack, A. von. "Porphyrius, *Gegen die Christen:* 15 Bücher; Zeugnisse, Fragmente, und Referate." *Abhandlungen der Königlich Preussischen Akademie der Wissenschaften, Philosophisch-historische Klasse* (1916): 1–115.

Harnack, A. von, and Erwin Preuschen. *Geschichte der altchristlichen Literatur bis Eusebius.* 2 vols. Leipzig: J. C. Hinrichs, 1904.

Heiberg, I. L. *Geschichte der Mathematik und Naturwissenschaften im Altertum.* Munich: C. H. Beck, 1925.

Heijer, Johannes den. "History of the Patriarchs of Alexandria." In *The Coptic Encyclopedia* (1991): 1238–42.

Heim, François. "L'animation des statues d'aprés les apologistes du IIIe siècle: Tertullien, Minucius Félix, Arnobe." *REL* 70 (1992): 22–23.

Henry, P. "La dernière parole de Plotin." *SCO* 2 (1953): 116–20.

Horbury, William. "The Wisdom of Solomon in the Muratorian Fragment." *JThS* 45, no. 1 (1994): 149–59.

Hornschuh, M. "Das Leben des Origenes und die Entstehung der alexandrinischen Schule." *ZKG* 71 (1960): 1–25, 193–214.

Igal, J. "El enigma del oráculo de Apolo sobre Plotino." *Emerita* 52 (1984): 83–115.

———. "The Gnostics and 'The Ancient Philosophy' in Porphyry and Plotinus." In *Neoplatonism and Early Christian Thought,* edited by A. H. Armstrong, H. J. Blumenthal, and R. A. Markus, 138–49. London: Variorum Publications, 1981.

Jerphagnon, L. "Platonopolis ou Plotin entre le siècle et le rêve." In *Néoplatonisme: Mélanges offerts à Jean Trouillard,* edited by P. M. Schuhl and L. Jerphagnon, 215–29. Fontenay-aux-Roses: ENS, 1981.

———. "Les sous-entendus anti-chrétiens de la *Vita Plotini* ou l'évangile de Plotin selon Porphyre." *Museum Helveticum* 47 (1990): 41–52.

Johnson, Aaron. "Identity, Descent, and Polemic: Ethnic Argumentation in Eusebius' 'Praeparatio Evangelica'." *JECS* 12 (2004): 23–56.

Johnston, Sarah Iles. *Hekate Soteira: A Study of Hekate's Roles in the Chaldean Oracles and Related Literature.* Atlanta: Scholars Press, 1990.

Jones, A. H. M. *The Cities of the Eastern Roman Provinces.* 2nd ed. Oxford: Clarendon Press, 1971.

Junod, Eric. "L'auteur de l'Apologie pour Origène traduite par Rufin: Les témoignages contradictoires de Rufin et de Jérôme à propos de Pamphile et d'Eusèbe." In *Recherches et tradition: Mélanges patristiques offerts à Henri Crouzel,* edited by A. Dupleix, 165–79. Paris: Beauchesne, 1992.

Junod, Eric, and René Amacker. "Avant-Propos." In *Apologie pour Origène,* edited by Pamphile and Eusèbe de Césarée, 9–14. Paris: Editions du Cerf, 2002.

Kaldellis, Anthony. *Hellenism in Byzantium: The Transformations of Greek Identity and the Reception of the Classical Tradition.* Cambridge: Cambridge University Press, 2007.

Karamanolis, George. *Plato and Aristotle in Agreement? Platonists on Aristotle from Antiochus to Porphyry.* Oxford: Clarendon Press, 2006.

Keresztes, P. "The Imperial Roman Government and the Christian Church II: From Gallienus to the Great Persecution." *ANRW* 2.23.1 (1979): 375–86.

Kettler, F. H. "Origenes, Ammonius Sakkas und Porphyrius." In *Kerygma und Logos: Beiträge zu den geistesgeschichtlichen Beziehungen zwischen Antike und Christentum; Festschrift für Carl Andresen zum 70. Geburtstag,* edited by A. M. Ritter, 322–28. Göttingen: Vandenhoeck und Ruprecht, 1979.

———. "War Origenes Schüler des Ammonius Sakkas?" In *Epektasis: Mélanges patristiques offerts au Cardinal Jean Daniélou,* edited by J. Fontaine and C. Kannengiesser, 327–34. Paris: Beauchesne, 1972.

Kingsley, Peter. *Ancient Philosophy, Mystery, and Magic: Empedocles and Pythagorean Tradition.* Oxford: Oxford University Press, 1995.

Kolb, Frank. "L'ideologia tetrarchica e la politica religiosa di Diocleziano." In *I cristiani e l'impero nel IV secolo,* edited by G. Bonamente and A. Nestori. Rome: EGLE, 1988.

Langerbeck, H. "The Philosophy of Ammonius Saccas." *JHS* 77 (1957): 67–74.

Larsen, B. Dalsgaard. *Jamblique de Chalcis, exégète et philosophe: Appendice; Testimonia et fragmenta exegetica.* Aarhus: Aarhus Universitetsforlag, 1972.

———. "La place de Jamblique dans la philosophie antique tardive." In *De Jamblique à Proclus,* edited by H. Dörrie, 1–34. Entretiens sur l'Antiquité Classique. Vandoeuvres-Geneva: Fond. Hardt, 1975.

Law, T. M. "Origen's Parallel Bible: Textual Criticism, Apologetics, or Exegesis?" *JThS* 59, no. 1 (2008): 1–21.

Le Bonniec, H. "Tradition de la culture classique: Arnobe témoin et juge des cultes païens." *Bulletin de l'Association Guillaume Budé* (1974): 201–22.

Lebrun, René. "Quelques aspects de la divination en Anatolie du Sud-Ouest." *Kernos* 3 (1990): 185–95.

Leroux, G. *Traité sur la liberté et la volunté de l'Un: Ennéade VI, 8 (39).* Paris: Vrin, 1990.

Lewy, H. *Chaldean Oracles and Theurgy: Mysticism, Magic, and Platonism in the Later Roman Empire.* Paris: Etudes augustiniennes, 1978.

Lieu, Samuel N. C. *Manichaeism in the Later Roman Empire and Medieval China.* Tübingen: J. C. B. Mohr, 1992.

Lilla, Salvatore. "Un dubbio di S. Agostino su Porfirio." *NAFM* 5 (1987): 319–29.

Löhr, Winrich A. "Theodotus der Lederarbeiter und Theodotus der Bankier—ein Beitrag zur römischen Theologiegeschichte des zweiten und drittne Jahrhunderts." *ZNTW* 87, no. 1 (1996): 101–25.

L'Orange, H. P. *Art Forms and Civic Life in the Later Roman Empire.* Princeton, NJ: Princeton University Press, 1965.

Luck, G. "Theurgy and Forms of Worship in Neoplatonism." In *Religion, Science, and Magic in Concert and in Conflict,* edited by J. Neusner, 185–225. Oxford: Oxford University Press, 1989.

Magny, Ariane. "Porphyry in Fragments: Eusebius, Jerome, Augustine, and the Problem of Reconstruction." PhD diss., University of Bristol, UK, 2011.

Majercik, Ruth. "The Chaldean Oracles and the School of Plotinus." *AncW* 29, no. 2 (1998): 91–105.

Männlein-Robert, Irmgard. "Biographie, Hagiographie, Autobiographie—Die *Vita Plotini* des Porphyrios." In *Metaphysik und Religion: Zur Signatur des spätantiken Denkens,* edited by Theo Kobusch and Michael Erler, 581–609. Munich/ Leipzig: K. G. Saur, 2002.

Marin, Marcello. "Origene e Metodio su Lev. 24,2–4." *VetChr* 18 (1981): 470–75.

Mastandrea, P. *Un neoplatonico Latino, Cornelio Labeone.* Leiden: Brill, 1979.

Matthew, G. "The Character of the Gallienic Renaissance." *JRS* 33 (1943): 65–70.

Mayerson, Philip. "A Confusion of Indias: Asian India and African India in the Byzantine Sources." *JAOS* 113, no. 2 (1993): 169–74.

Mazzucco, Clementina. "Il millenarismo di Metodio di Olimpo di fronte a Origene: Polemica o continuità?" *Augustinianum* 26 (1986): 73–87.

———. "Tra l'ombra e la realtà: L'Apocalisse nel Simposio di Metodio di Olimpo." *Civiltà Classica e Cristiana* 6 (1985): 399–423.

McEvilley, Thomas. *The Shape of Ancient Thought.* New York: Allworth Press, 2002.

McGuckin, John A. *The Westminster Handbook to Origen.* Louisville, KY: Westminster/ John Knox Press, 2004.

Mees, M. "2 Co 6,1–10 und die Auferstehung der Toten nach Origenes und Methodius." *Lateranum* 51 (1985): 153–63.

———. "Paulus, Origenes und Methodius über die Auferstehung der Toten." *Augustinianum* 26 (1986): 103–13.

Merlan, P. "Plotinus and Magic." *Isis* 44 (1953): 341–48.

Millar, Fergus. "P. Herennius Dexippus: The Greek World and the Third-Century Invasion." *JRS* 59 (1969): 12–29.

Montero, Santiago. *Política y adivinación en el Bajo Impero romano: Emperadores y harúspices (193 D. C.–408 D. C.).* Coll. Latomus 12. Brussels: Latomus, 1991.

Montserrat-Torrents, J. "Origenismo y gnosis: Los 'perfectos' de Metodio de Olimpo." *Augustinianum* 26 (1986): 89–101.

Mulvany, C. M. "Notes on the Legend of Aristotle." *CQ* 20, no. 3/4 (1926): 155–67.

Musurillo, Herbert, ed. *St. Methodius, The Symposium: A Treatise on Chastity.* London: Longmans, Green, 1958.

Nasemann, Beate. *Theurgie und Philosophie in Jamblichs De mysteriis.* Stuttgart: Teubner, 1991.

Nautin, Pierre. *Origène: Sa vie et son oeuvre.* Paris: Beauchesne, 1977.

Nicholson, O. "The Pagan Churches of Maximinus Daia and Julian the Apostate." *JEH* 45 (1994): 1–10.

Norris, Frederick W. "Eusebius on Jesus as Deceiver and Sorcerer." In *Eusebius, Christianity, and Judaism,* edited by H. Attridge and G. Hata, 523–40. Detroit: Wayne State University Press, 1992.

O'Brien, Denis. "Origène et Plotin sur le roi de l'univers." In *Sophiēs maiētores / Chercheurs de sagesse: Hommage à Jean Pépin,* edited by Marie-Odile Goulet-Cazé, Goulven Madec, and Denis O'Brien, 317–42. Paris: Institut d'études augustiniennes, 1992.

———. "Plotinus and the Secrets of Ammonius." *Hermathena* 157 (1994): 117–53.

Oliver, Harold H. "The Epistle of Eusebius to Carpianus: Textual Tradition and Translation." *Novum Testamentum* 3 (1959): 138–45.

O'Meara, Dominic J. *Platonopolis: Platonic Political Philosophy in Late Antiquity.* Oxford: Oxford University Press, 2003.

———. *Pythagoras Revived: Mathematics and Philosophy in Late Antiquity.* Oxford: Clarendon Press, 1989.

O'Meara, J. J. *Porphyry's Philosophy from Oracles in Augustine.* Paris: Etudes augustiniennes, 1959.

———. *Porphyry's Philosophy from Oracles in Eusebius' Praeparatio Evangelica and Augustine's Dialogues of Cassiciacum.* Paris: Etudes augustiniennes, 1969.

Oost, Stewart Irvin. "The Alexandrian Seditions under Philip and Gallienus." *CPh* 56, no. 1 (1961): 1–20.

Orbe, Antonio. "S. Metodio y la exegesis de Rom. 7,9: 'Ego autem vivebam sine lege aliquando'." *Gregorianum* 50 (1969): 93–139.

Outler, Albert C. "The 'Platonism' of Clement of Alexandria." *JR* 20, no. 3 (1940): 217–40.

Passmore, John. "The Treatment of Animals." *JHI* 36, no. 2 (1975): 195–218.

Patterson, L. G. "*De libero arbitrio* and Methodius' Attack on Origen." *Studia Patristica* 14.3 (1976): 160–66.

———. *Methodius of Olympus: Divine Sovereignty, Human Freedom, and Life in Christ.* Washington, DC: The Catholic University of America Press, 1997.

———. "Methodius on Origen in *De creatis.*" In *Origeniana quinta,* edited by Robert J. Daly, 497–508. Leuven: Peeters, 1992.

———. "Methodius, Origen, and the Arian Dispute." *Studia Patristica* 17.2 (1982): 912–23.

———. "Notes on *De cibis* and Methodius' View of Origen." In *Origeniana tertia,* edited by Richard Hanson and H. Crouzel, 233–42. Rome: Ateneo, 1985.

———. "Who Are the Opponents in Methodius' *De Resurrectione?*" *Studia Patristica* 19 (1989): 221–29.

Pelland, Gilles. "'Ex ipso sponso splendorum decoris accipiens.'" *Gregorianum* 79, no. 1 (1998): 113–27.

Penella, Robert J. *The Private Orations of Themistius.* Berkeley: University of California Press, 2000.

Perelli, Carlo. "Eusebio e la critica di Porfirio a Origene: L'esegesi cristiana dell'Antico Testamento come metaleptikos tropos." *Annali di Scienzi Religiosi* 3 (1998): 233–61.

Philip, J. A. "The Biographical Tradition: Pythagoras." *TAPhA* 90 (1959): 185–94.

Pichon, R. *Lactance: Etude sur le mouvement philosophique et religieux sous le règne de Constantin.* Paris: Librairie Hachette, 1901.

Places, Edouard des. "Eusèbe de Césarée juge de Platon dans la *Préparation évangélique.*" In *Mélanges de philosophie grecque, offerts à Mgr. Diès par ses élèves, ses collègues, ses amis,* 69–77. Paris: J. Vrin, 1956.

———, ed. *Oracles Chaldaïques, avec un choix de commentaires anciens.* Paris: Societé d'édition Les Belles Lettres, 1971.

Ploton-Nicollet, François. "Septime Sévère et le christianisme: Essai d'étude critique des sources." *LittCael* 1 (2005): 179–88.

Prinzivalli, Emanuela. "Aspetti esegetico-dottrinale del dibattito nel IV secolo sulle tesi origeniane in materia escatologica." *AnnSE* 12, no. 2 (1995): 279–325.

———. *L'esegesi biblica di Metodio di Olimpo.* Rome: Inst. Patrist. Augustinianum, 1985.

———. "Il millenarismo in Oriente da Metodio ad Apollinare." *AnnSE* 15, no. 1 (1998): 125–51.

———. "Il simbolismo del sangue in Metodio di Olimpo, III." In *Centro Studi Sanguis Christi, III: Atti della Settimana Sangue e Antropologia nella Letteratura Cristiana,* 1181–92. Rome: Ed. Pia Unione del Preziosissimo Sangue, 1983.

Quasten, J. *Patrology.* Utrecht: Spectrum, 1953.

Quensell, K. "Die wahre kirchliche Stellung und Tätigkeit des fälschlich so genannten Bischofs Methodius von Olympus." Diss., Heidelberg, 1952.

Reinmuth, O. W. "A Working List of the Prefects of Egypt, 30 BC to 299 AD." *BASP* 4 (1967): 106–9.

Riggi, Calogero. "La forma del corpo risorto secondo Metodio in Epifanio (Haer. 64)." In *Morte e immortalità nella catechesi dei padri del III-IV secolo,* edited by Sergio Felici, 75–92. Rome: LAS, 1985.

———. "Teologia della storia nel Simposio di Metodio di Olimpo." *Augustinianum* 16 (1976): 61–84.

Rist, J. M. "Mysticism and Transcendence in Later Neoplatonism." *Hermes* 92 (1964): 213–25.

———. "Plotinus and Christian Philosophy." In *The Cambridge Companion to Plotinus,* edited by Lloyd P. Gerson, 386–413. Cambridge: Cambridge University Press, 1996.

———. "Pseudo-Ammonius and the Soul/Body Problem in Some Platonic Texts of Late Antiquity." *AJPh* 109 (1988): 402–15.

Romano, F. *Porfirio di Tiro: Filosofia e cultura nel II secolo D.C.* Univ. di Catania Pubbl. Fac. di Lett. e Filos. 33. Catania: Università, Facoltà di lettere e filosofia, 1979.

Rowe, Christopher, Malcolm Schofield, Simon Harrison, and Melissa Lane, eds. *The Cambridge History of Greek and Roman Political Thought.* Cambridge: Cambridge University Press, 2000.

Runia, David T. "Festugière Revisited: Aristotle in the Greek Patres." *VChr* 43.1 (1989): 1–34.

———. *Philo in Early Christian Literature: A Survey.* Minneapolis: Fortress Press, 1993.

Russell, J. B. R. *Dissent and Order in the Middle Ages: The Search for Legitimate Authority.* New York: Twayne, 1992.

———. *A History of Medieval Christianity: Prophecy and Order.* Arlington Heights, IL: Harlan Davidson, 1968.

Saffrey, H. D. "Abamon, pseudonyme de Jamblique." In *Philomathes: Studies and Essays in the Humanities in Memory of Philip Merlan,* edited by R. B. Palmer and R. Hamerton-Kelly, 227–39. The Hague: Nijhoff, 1971.

———. "Les néoplatoniciens et les Oracles chaldaïques." *Etudes Augustiniennes* 27 (1981): 209–25.

———. "Relecture de Jamblique, *De mysteriis,* VIII, chap. 1–5." In *Platonism in Late Antiquity,* edited by Stephen Gersh and C. Kannengieser, 157–71. Notre Dame: University of Notre Dame, 1992.

Sainte-Croix, G. E. M. de. "Aspects of the 'Great' Persecution." *HThR* 47 (1954): 75–113.

———. "Why Were the Early Christians Persecuted?" *P&P* 26 (1963): 6–38.

Savon, H. "Le prêtre Eutrope et la "vraie circoncision." *RHR* 199 (1982): 273–302.

Schenk, Kenneth. *A Brief Guide to Philo.* Louisville, KY: Westminster/John Knox Press, 2005.

Schott, J. M. "Founding Platonopolis: The Platonic 'Politeia' in Eusebius, Porphyry, and Iamblichus." *JECS* 11 (2003): 501–31.

———. "Porphyry on Christians and Others: 'Barbarian Wisdom,' Identity Politics, and Anti-Christian Polemics on the Eve of the Great Persecution." *JECS* 13 (2005): 277–314.

Schroeder, Frederic M. "Ammonius Saccas." *ANRW* 2.36.1 (1987): 493–526.

Schwartz, E., ed. *Acta Conciliorum Oecumenicorum.* Berlin: de Gruyter, 1927–.

Schwyzer, H. R. *Ammonios Sakkas, der Lehrer Plotins.* Opladen: Rheinisch-Westfälische Akademie der Wissenschaften, 1983.

Shaw, Gregory. "Eros and Arithmos: Pythagorean Theurgy in Iamblichus and Plotinus." *AncPhil* 19, no. 1 (1999): 121–43.

———. "Neoplatonic Theurgy and Dionysius the Areopagite." *JECS* 7, no. 4 (1999): 573–99.

———. *Theurgy and the Soul: The Neoplatonism of Iamblichus.* University Park: Pennsylvania State University Press, 1995.

Simmons, Michael Bland. *Arnobius of Sicca: Religious Conflict and Competition in the Age of Diocletian.* New York: Oxford University Press, 1995.

———. "The Eschatological Aspects of Porphyry's Anti-Christian Polemics in a Chaldaean-Neoplatonic Context." *C&M* 52, no. 2 (2001): 193–215.

Sivan, Hagith. "Ulfila's Own Conversion." *HThR* 89, no. 4 (1996): 373–86.

Smith, A. "Porphyrian Studies since 1913." *ANRW* 2.36.2 (1987): 717–73.

———. *Porphyry's Place in the Neoplatonic Tradition: A Study in Post-Plotinian Neoplatonism.* The Hague: Nijhoff, 1974.

Smith, A., and David Wasserstein, eds. *Porphyrii philosophi fragmenta.* Bibl. scriptorum Graec. et Roman. Teubneriana. Stuttgart: Teubner, 1993.

Somos, Róbert. "An Aristotelian Science—Methodological Principle in Origen's *Commentary on John.*" In *Origeniana octava,* 547–52. Leuven: Peeters, 2003.

Stade, K. "Der Politiker Diocletian und die letze grosse Christenverfolgung." Diss., Frankfurt, 1926.

Stalley, R. F. F. *An Introduction to Plato's Laws.* Indianapolis: Hackett, 1983.

Steel, C. G. *The Changing Self: A Study on the Soul in Later Neoplatonism; Iamblichus, Damascius, and Priscianus.* Koninklijke Vlaamse Academie voor Wetenschappen, Letteren en Schone Kunsten van België, Klasse der Letteren. Verhandeligen: jaarg. 40, nr. 85. Brussels: Paleis der Academiën, 1978.

Stefaniw, Blossom. *Mind, Text, and Commentary: Noetic Exegesis in Origen of Alexandria, Didymus the Blind, and Evagrius Ponticus.* Frankfurt: Peter Lang, 2010.

Stevenson, James. *Studies in Eusebius.* Cambridge: Cambridge University Press, 1929.

Szlesák, T. A. "Plotin und die geheimen Lehren des Ammonios." In *Esoterik und Exoterik der Philosophie: Beiträge zu Geschichte und Sinn philosophischer Selbstbestimmung; Rudolf W. Meyer zum 60. Geburtstag,* edited by H. Holzhey and W. C. Zimmerli, 52–69. Basel: Schwabe, 1977.

Talbert, J. A., ed. *Atlas of Classical History.* London: Routledge, 1985.

Taormina, Daniela P. "Giamblico contro Plotino e Porfirio: Il dibattito sull'arte e sul movimento (apud Simplicio, *In Categorias* 301.20–308.10)." *SyllClass* 8 (1997): 95–112.

Theiler, W. "Ammonios der Lehrer des Origenes." In *Forschungen zum Neoplatonismus,* edited by W. Theiler, 1–45. Berlin: de Gruyter, 1966.

———. "Ammonios und Porphyrios." In *Porphyre: Huit exposés,* edited by Heinrich Dörrie, 85–123 Geneva: Fondation Hardt, 1966.

Thurman, Robert A. F. "Buddhist Hermeneutics." *JAAR* 46, no. 1 (1978): 19–39.

Tibiletti, C. "L'ambiente culturale cristiano riflesso nel Simposio di Metodio." In *Verginità e matrimonio in antichi scrittori cristiani,* edited by C. Tibiletti, 99–133. Rome: Pubblicazioni della Facoltà di lettere e filosofia (Università di Macerata), 1983.

Trigg, Joseph W. "The Charismatic Intellectual: Origen's Understanding of Religious Leadership." *ChHist* 50, no. 1 (1981): 5–19.

———. "God's Marvelous *Oikonomia:* Reflections of Origen's Understanding of Divine and Human Pedagogy in the *Address* Ascribed to Gregory Thaumaturgus." *JECS* 9, no. 1 (2001): 27–52.

———. *Origen.* London/New York: Routledge, 1998.

Vaillant, A. "Le *De autexousio* de Méthode d'Olympe, version slave et texte grec édités et traduits en français." *Patrologia Orientalis* 22 (1930): 494–833.

Van den Berg, Robbert Maarten. "Plotinus' Attitude to Traditional Cult: A Note on Porphyry VP 10." *AncPhil* 19, no. 2 (1999): 345–60.

Vanderspoel, John. "Iamblichus at Daphne." *GRBS* 29 (1988): 83–86.

———. "Themistios and the Origin of Iamblichos." *Hermes* 116 (1988): 125–28.

Van Liefferinge, Carine. *La théurgie des Oracles Chaldaïques à Proclus.* Liège: Centre International d'Etude de la Religion Grecque Antique, 1999.

Vitores, Artemio. *Identidad entre el cuerpo muerto y resucitado en Origenes según de 'De Resurrectione' de Metodo de Olimpo.* Jerusalem: Franciscan Printing Press, 1981.

Vogt, H.-J. "Origenes." *LThK* 7 (1998): 1135–36.

Wallace-Hadrill, D. S. *Eusebius of Caesarea.* London: Mowbray, 1960.

Watts, Edward J. *City and School in Late Antique Athens and Alexandria.* Berkeley: University of California Press, 2006.

Weber, K. O. *Origenes der Neuplatoniker.* Munich: Beck, 1962.

Wegenast, K. "Zephyrinus, 198–217 Bischof von Rom." *Pauly's Realenzyclopaedie* 19, no. 2 (1972): 225–27.

Whittaker, H. "The Purpose of Porphyry's Letter to Marcella." *SymbOsl* 76 (2001): 150–68.

Wilamowitz-Möllendorff, U. von. "Ein Bruchstück aus der Schrift des Porphyrius gegen die Christen." *Zeitschrift für neutestamentliche Wissenschaft und die Kunde der altem Kirche* 1 (1900): 101–5.

Wilken, R. L. "Pagan Criticism of Christianity: Greek Religion and Christian Faith." In *Early Christian Literature and the Classical Intellectual Tradition,* edited by W. Schoedel and R. L. Wilken, 117–34. Paris: Editions Beauchesne, 1979.

Williams, Rowan. "Damnosa haereditas: Pamphilus' Apology and the Reputation of Origen." In *Logos: Festschrift für Luise Abramowski,* edited by H.C. Brennecke, E. L. Grasmück, and C. Markschies, 151–69. Berlin: de Gruyter, 1993.

Williams, S. *Diocletian and the Roman Recovery.* London: Routledge, 2000.

Wlosok, A. "Christliche Apologetik gegenüber kaiserlichen Politik bis zu Konstantin." In *Kirchengeschichte als Missionsgeschichte,* vol. 1, *Die Alte Kirche,* 147–65. Munich: Kaiser, 1974

Wolfson, H. A. "Clement of Alexandria and the Generation of the Logos." *ChHist* 20, no. 2 (1951): 72–81.

Zambon, Marco. "Middle Platonism." In *A Companion to Ancient Philosophy,* edited by Mary Louise Gill and Pierre Pellegrin, 561–76. Malden, MA: Blackwell, 2006.

Zeller, Eduard. *Die nacharistotelische Philosophie.* Vol. 3.2, *Die Philosophie der Griechen in ihrer geschichtlichen Entwicklung.* 5th ed. Hildesheim: Georg Olms, 1923. Reprint, 1963.

Ziebritzki, Henning. *Heiliger Geist und Weltseele: Das Problem der dritten Hypostase bei Origenes, Plotin und ihren Vorkaufern.* Tübingen: Mohr, 1994.

✒ INDEX

Aelia Capitolina, 63, 66
Alexander Severus, 66, 68
Alexandria, 2 (inc. n. 3), 3, 17–19, 23, 27–28,
    31–34, 41–43, 45, 47–48, 51–52 (inc.
    nn. 7, 8), 53–54, 61, 63 (inc. n. 54), 64
    (inc. n. 61), 66 (inc. n. 77), 67 (inc.
    nn. 80, 82), 68, 71, 73, 74 n. 7, 75
    n. 10, 76 n. 15, 79 n. 35, 97, 81 n. 5,
    109, 111 n. 76, 137, 144, 157 n. 55,
    162, 190
  Brucheion quarter, 2 (inc. n. 4), 39, 109,
    111 n. 76
Allegorism. *See* Figural exegesis
Ammonius Saccas, 2, 3, 5–7, 9–10 (inc. n. 37),
    14, 16–19, 23–48, 49–50 (inc. n. 1),
    51–56, 58, 60–61 (inc. n. 45), 63–64
    (inc. n. 60), 66 (inc. n. 72), 71–74
    (inc. nn. 7, 9), 75, 77 (inc. n. 24), 79,
    81–82, 87, 97–98, 128, 161, 164–165,
    171, 173, 189, 190–191
Anatolius of Laodicaea, 3, 109 (inc. nn. 61,
    65), 110 (inc. nn. 67–68), 190
Antioch, 1–2, 4–5, 8, 20, 22, 46 n. 106, 66
    (inc. n. 77), 67 (inc. n. 78), 74, 77 n. 24,
    111 (inc. n. 78), 127, 133 n. 14, 173,
    179, 181, 183, 189
Apamea, 6, 82, 103 (inc. nn. 26–27), 104
    (inc. n. 32), 105
Arnobius of Sicca, 3 (inc. n. 5), 5, 13 (inc.
    n. 52), 121–122, 174 (inc. nn. 40–41),
    175 (inc. nn. 43, 45), 176–178, 179
    n. 66, 185–186 (inc. n. 96), 187 (inc.
    n. 98), 188
  Against the Nations, 174 (inc. n. 41),
    175–176
Artemon, 45 n. 105, 46 n. 106
Augustine, 12, 97, 119–123, 155 (inc. n. 135),
    170 (inc. nn. 22–23), 171 (inc. n. 29),
    172, 180
  City of God, 119, 180
Aurelian, 2 n. 4, 82, 110
Auspices, 1, 4–5, 22, 111, 175, 179, 181–184

Bel, 104 (inc. nn. 30, 32)
Brucheion. *See* Alexandria

Caesarea, 3, 17, 26–27 (inc. n. 12), 31–32,
    45, 62 n. 46, 63–64 (inc. n. 60), 66–67
    (inc. n. 83), 68, 69 n. 92, 71, 76–77, 78
    n. 26, 109 (inc. n. 63), 110, 136, 166,
    169, 173–174
  Cappadocian, 54 n. 17, 67 n. 83
Carthage, 106, 170 n. 23, 174 (inc. n. 41)
Chalcis, 3, 108, 109 n. 63, 132 n. 14
  Euboaean, 132 n. 14
Chaldaean
  religion, 100–101, 104 (inc. n. 32), 113
  theurgy, 7, 11, 20, 116, 123, 176
  wisdom, 8 n. 28, 20, 188
Chaldaean Oracles, 6–7, 39, 74 n. 9, 82, 101,
    104 (inc. nn. 30, 32, 34), 114, 115, 116
    (inc. n. 104), 118, 119, 122, 129
Christians,
  in the army, 1, 4
  courtiers, 1, 2, 4, 9, 164, 179, 181
  in government, 3, 4, 48, 179, 183, 184
    n. 86
  law, 57, 62, 65, 71
  students and teachers, 2, 14, 24, 28, 41,
    43, 52–53, 70, 130, 154
  theologians and theology, 5–6, 8, 10 n. 37,
    13, 23, 49
Constantine, ix, 2, 108 n. 56, 175 n. 43, 179,
    182, 184, 189, 190
  edicts of, 11, 24, 142 n. 72, 160 n. 71,
    169, 178, 190
Constantius, 1, 184, 189

Daemons and demons, 91, 107, 115, 150,
    164, 177, 181–184
Demetrius of Alexandria, 31, 52 (inc. n. 4),
    62, 63 (inc. n. 54), 64 (inc. n. 59), 67
    (inc. n. 79)
Diocletian, ix, xi, 1–5, 8–9, 12, 22, 77 n. 24,
    89, 132, 164–165, 168, 174–175 (inc.